Milestones

Introductory

HEINLE
CENGAGE Learning

Australia • Brazil • Japan • Korea • Mexico • Singapore • Spain • United Kingdom • United States

Milestones Introductory

Contributing Writer: Christopher Sol Cruz

Editorial Director: Joe Dougherty

Publisher: Sherrise Roehr

Managing Editor: Carmela Fazzino-Farah

Development Editor: Jennifer Meldrum

Editorial Assistant: Jennifer Kuhnberg

Technology Development Editor:
Debie Mirtle

Executive Marketing Manager:
Jim McDonough

Director of Product Marketing:
Amy T. Mabley

Product Marketing Manager: Katie Kelley

Assistant Marketing Manager:
Andrea Bobotas

Director of Content and Media Production:
Michael Burggren

Senior Content Project Manager:
Maryellen Eschmann-Killeen

Manufacturing Manager: Marcia Locke

Composition and Project Management:
InContext Publishing Partners

Illustrations/Photography: see page 523 for
credits

Interior Design: Studio Montage

Cover Design: Page 2, LLC

Cover Image: VisionsofAmerica/Joe Sohm/
Getty Images

Library of Congress Control Number: 2007940550

ISBN-13: 978-1-4240-0895-7

ISBN-10: 1-4240-0895-6

Heinle Cengage Learning
25 Thomson Place
Boston, Massachusetts 02210
USA

Cengage Learning products are represented in Canada by Nelson Education, Ltd.

Visit Heinle online at **elt.heinle.com**
Visit our corporate website at **www.cengage.com**

Printed in the United States of America
1 2 3 4 5 6 7 12 11 10 09 08

Program Authors

NEIL ANDERSON

Dr. Neil J. Anderson received his Ph.D. from the University of Texas at Austin, where he specialized in research in the teaching of reading. He has done significant work in the area of reading comprehension, reading strategies, and fluency. He has published several books in this area and continues to actively research and publish.

Dr. Anderson has been teaching English and teachers of English for over twenty-five years. He is a professor in the Department of Linguistics and English Language at Brigham Young University in Salt Lake City, Utah. He has received many awards for outstanding teaching and believes that everyone can learn to be a good reader.

Dr. Anderson helped to establish the pedagogical framework of the *Milestones* program with a particular focus on reading strategies and reading fluency.

JILL KOREY O'SULLIVAN

Jill Korey O'Sullivan holds a Masters Degree in Education from Harvard University. Her specific area of research and interest is language and literacy. Ms. Korey O'Sullivan is an experienced author and editor of educational materials with a background in curriculum development and teaching. She has taught and developed materials for students of a broad range of levels and in a variety of educational settings, including kindergarten, middle school, and community college programs.

Ms. Korey O'Sullivan has brought her classroom experience and creativity to the writing of several textbooks and has served as editor on many publications in the field of English language learning.

She helped to establish the pedagogical framework of the *Milestones* program, incorporating the latest in research and pedagogy.

The students she has taught and the students who use her materials serve as her inspiration.

JENNIFER TRUJILLO

Jennifer Trujillo received her Ph.D. in Educational Leadership and Change from Fielding Graduate University, Santa Barbara, CA. Dr. Trujillo grew up in a home where another language besides English was spoken. Her family moved back and forth between her mother's homeland and the United States. Her dedication to reading led her to earn degrees and teaching credentials in English and Reading from the University of Northern Colorado.

She is currently a professor in the Teacher Education Department at Fort Lewis College in Durango, Colorado. Her areas of specialization are reading and writing, ESL, home-school partnerships, professional development, cognitive coaching, differentiated instruction, and diversity training.

Dr. Trujillo feels strongly about the importance of culturally responsive and universally relevant readings, with challenging activities, to help all students succeed. To that end, she helped to establish the pedagogical framework of the *Milestones* program and provided valuable feedback on each of the reading selections to ensure culturally responsive instruction for the pre- and post-reading activities.

Program Advisors

ROBERT J. MARZANO, Ph.D., Vocabulary Advisor

Dr. Robert J. Marzano is president and founder of Marzano & Associates, specializing in long term school reform efforts to enhance student academic achievement. His works guiding teachers to assist students in developing academic language can be found in the books *Building Background Knowledge for Academic Achievement* and *Building Academic Vocabulary*.

Over his 35 years in education, the central theme of his work has been translating research and theory into practical programs and tools for teachers and administrators. He is a Senior Scholar at Mid-continent Research for Education and Learning (McREL) and an Associate Professor at Cardinal Stritch University.

Dr. Marzano received his M.Ed. degree in Reading and Language Arts from Seattle University, and his Ph.D. in Curriculum and Instruction from the University of Washington.

He is the author of more than 20 books, 150 articles, and more than 100 curriculum guides and related materials for teachers and students. His most recent publication is *The Art and Science of Teaching: A Comprehensive Framework for Effective Instruction*.

KEITH LENZ, Ph.D., Differentiated Instruction/Universal Access Advisor

Dr. Keith Lenz specializes in adolescents with learning problems, teacher planning, and strategic instruction for teaching diverse groups. He has degrees in Special Education and Secondary Education from Bradley University and a Ph.D. from the University of Kansas. At the University of Kansas, Dr. Lenz is an Associate Professor, Director of the Institute for Effective Instruction, and Senior Research Scientist at the Center for Research on Learning.

Dr. Lenz is the founder and member of the Board of Trustees at the Strategic Learning Center, Inc., Seattle, WA. He is an adjunct professor at Seattle Pacific University, and a National Trainer of The Strategies Intervention Model.

Dr. Lenz's work with guiding teachers on effective differentiated instruction practices can be found in his co-authored book *Teaching Content to All: Inclusive Teaching in Grades 4–12*, amongst others.

Dr. Lenz taught at Florida Atlantic University and serves as a Project Trainer for the Florida Department of Education.

ANNE KATZ, Ph.D., Assessment Advisor

Dr. Anne Katz has worked for 20 years as a researcher and evaluator for projects connected with the education of linguistically and culturally diverse students. As a teacher educator, she has provided and supported professional development in the areas of curriculum, assessment, and evaluation.

Dr. Katz co-directed a national study of successful leadership strategies to create more harmonious racial and ethnic environments in K–12 schools. She is co-author of *Leading for Diversity: How School Leaders Promote Positive Interethnic Relations* and author of numerous publications on diversity and the development of standards-based assessment systems.

Dr. Katz was instrumental in developing standards for English as a second language with the Teachers of English to Speakers of Other Languages organization, and she has assisted many school districts in developing more authentic assessments of student performance. In all her work, she promotes the links between research and the classroom to support meaningful school change.

Anne Katz holds a doctorate in second language education from Stanford University. She is a lecturer at the School for International Training's graduate teacher education program.

Teacher Reviewers

Sonia Abrew
Orange County Public Schools
Orlando, FL

Ruby Ali
H.L. Watkins Middle School
Palm Beach Gardens, FL

Jean Anderson
Broward County Public Schools
Ft. Lauderdale, FL

Teresa Arvizu
McFarland Unified School District
McFarland, CA

Maridell Bagnal
Fletcher Middle School
Jacksonville Beach, FL

Miriam Barrios-Chacon
Chipman Middle School
Alameda, CA

Cathy Bonner
Bowie High School
El Paso, TX

Irene Borrego
CA State University Bakersfield
Bakersfield, CA

Tanya Castro
Pharr-San Juan-Alamo Independent
School District
Alamo, TX

Nicole Chaput
Metro Nashville Public Schools
Nashville, TN

Vikki Chavez
San Bernardino High School
San Bernardino, CA

Anthony Colonna
Ocala Middle School
San Jose, CA

Catherine Cominio
Howell Watkins Middle School
Palm Beach Gardens, FL

Ayanna Cooper
DeKalb County Schools
DeKalb, GA

James Coplan
Oakland Technical High School
Oakland, CA

Alicia Cron
Austin Middle School
San Juan, TX

Libby Taylor Deleon
Plano ISD
Plano, TX

Farida Doherty
Boston Public Schools
Boston, MA

Mercedes A. Egues
Fort Lauderdale High School
Fort Lauderdale, FL

Karen Ernst
Highland High School
Palmdale, CA

Rafael Estrada
Lake Shore Middle School
Belle Glade, FL

Mary Ford
Pahokee Middle High School
Pahokee, FL

Beverly Franke
Palm Beach County Schools
Greenacres, FL

Helena Gandell
Duval County Public Schools
Jacksonville, FL

Linsey Gannon
Lawrence Cook Middle School
Santa Rosa, CA

Renee Gaudet
New River Elementary School
Wesley Chapel, FL

Nathalie Gillis-Rumowicz
Seminole Middle School
Seminole, FL

Evelyn Gomez
The Academy for New Americans
Middle School
Astoria, NY

Rafael Gonzalez
Wasco Union High School District
Wasco, CA

Sarah Harley
ALBA Elementary School
Milwaukee, WI

Renote Jean-Francois
Boston Public Schools
Boston, MA

Vivian Kahn
I.S. 296 Halsey School
Brooklyn, NY

Tony King
Boston Public Schools
Boston, MA

Christa Kirby
Pinellas County School District
Largo, FL

Letitia Laberee
Angelo Patri Middle School
Bronx, NY

Gemma Lacanlale
Houston Independent School District
Houston, TX

Arthur Larievy
Boston Public Schools
Boston, MA

Alisa Leckie
Billy Lane Lauffer Middle School
Tucson, AZ

Chad Leith
Boston Public Schools
Boston, MA

Arnulfo Lopez
Delano High School
Delano, CA

Carmen Lopez
Cesar E. Chavez High School
Delano, CA

Lana Lysen
Multicultural, ESOL Education
Fort Lauderdale, FL

Vanessa MacDonna
Andries Huddle Middle School
Brooklyn, NY

Rita Marsh-Birch
Sandalwood High School
Jacksonville, FL

Lorraine Martini
Nova Middle School
Davie, FL

Jean Melby-Mauer
Valley High School
Las Vegas, NV

Patsy Mills
Houston Independent School District
Houston, TX

Amy Mirco
Charlotte-Mecklenburg Schools
Charlotte, NC

Gloria Pelaez
University of Miami
Miami, FL

Maria Pena
Doral Middle School
Doral, FL

Yvonne Perez
Alief Middle School
Houston, TX

Lunine Pierre-Jerome
Boston Public Schools
Boston, MA

Yolanda Pokaski
Boston Public Schools
Boston, MA

Diana Ramlall
School District of Palm Beach County
West Palm Beach, FL

Marlene Roney
New River Middle School
Fort Lauderdale, FL

Cheryl Serrano
Lynn University
Boca Raton, FL

Raynel Shepard
Boston Public Schools
Boston, MA

Michele Spohn
Fort Caroline Middle School
Jacksonville, FL

Ilza Sterling
Falcon Cove Middle School
Weston, FL

John Sullivan
Clark County School
District, East Region
Las Vegas, NV

Teri Suzuki
Lincoln Middle School
Alameda, CA

Daisy Torres
Marion County Schools
Ocala, FL

Matthew Trillo
Maxwell Middle School
Tucson, AZ

Heather Tugwell
Oakland Unified School District
Oakland, CA

Cassandra Vukcevic
Ridgewood High School
New Port Richey, FL

Sheila Weinstein
Deerfield Beach Middle School
Deerfield Beach, FL

MaryLou Whaley
Immigrant Acculturation Center
Tampa, FL

Jill Wood
Dr. John Long Middle School
Wesley Chapel, FL

Veronica Yepez
Washington Middle School
Pasadena, CA

Welcome Unit

Page 2

About Me

UNIT 1

Page 100

UNIT 2 Relationships
Page 150

Weather and Activities

UNIT 3

Page 202

UNIT 4

At Home
Page 254

Important People

UNIT **6** # Community

Page 362

Shopping
Page 418
UNIT 7

Welcome to *Milestones!*
Your Steps to Success

The title of this book is *Milestones*. Milestones are rocks set on a road to show the distance from one place to another. Like milestones on a road, this book will help guide you from one step in your learning to the next. It will provide the support you need every step of the way.

There are four specific skills you will learn and practice in *Milestones*:

Reading Reading is the foundation of learning. This book will help you become a more effective reader in many ways. For example, you will learn important vocabulary words that come from the readings. You will also learn academic vocabulary. These are the words that are used frequently in all subject areas. Learning academic vocabulary will help you understand academic texts and succeed in subject areas. Reading Fluency activities will help you learn to read more fluently. Reading Strategies will teach you specific methods for comprehending readings more effectively.

Listening Effective listening requires you to be focused and attentive. This book will provide you with opportunities to practice and improve your listening skills.

Speaking You will have many opportunities to practice your speaking skills by discussing the readings, performing role plays, and working on projects with your classmates.

Writing This book will help you understand and practice the writing process. You will plan, draft, revise, and edit each of your writing assignments. You will learn how to evaluate your own writing and how to give feedback to your classmates on their writing.

Your teachers will provide important guidance as you work through this book. The assessment material at the end of each chapter and unit will help you and your teacher identify material you have successfully learned and areas where you may need more practice.

However, the most important ingredient for academic success is…YOU! You are the one holding the book. You are the one reading these words. You have the power and ability to work towards academic success. As you open this book, open your mind by thinking carefully and critically.

With this book, help from your teacher, and your own determination, you will achieve wonderful academic milestones!

Welcome Unit

Talk About the Theme

Look at the photos. What words do you know?

First Day of School

Objectives

Vocabulary
School
Countries and
nationalities

Listening and Speaking
Greetings
Introductions
Saying where you
are from

Letters and Sounds
Initial consonants:
b, c, f, g
Final consonants: b, f, g
Initial consonants:
m, p, s, t
Final consonants:
m, p, s, t

Reading
The alphabet and names

Writing
Writing the alphabet and
names

Project
A class list

Progress Check

school

principal

nurse

PRINCIPAL

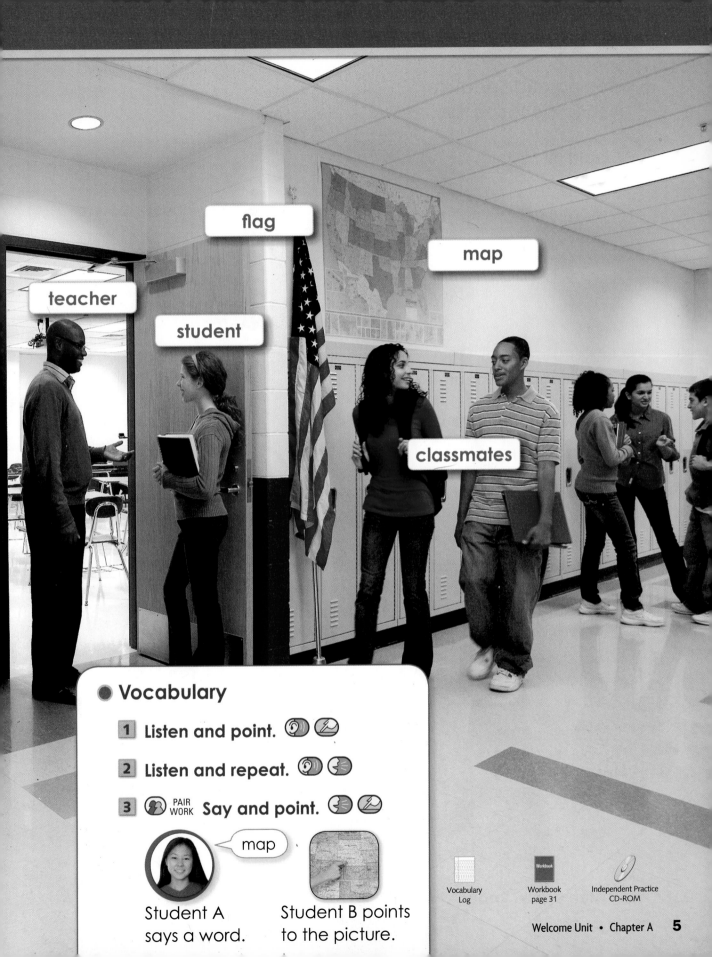

flag

map

teacher

student

classmates

Vocabulary

1 **Listen and point.**

2 **Listen and repeat.**

3 PAIR WORK **Say and point.**

map

Student A
says a word.

Student B points
to the picture.

Vocabulary
Log

Workbook
page 31

Independent Practice
CD-ROM

● Listening and Speaking

Greetings and Introductions

1 **Read and listen.** 📖 🎧

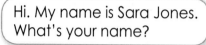

> Hi. My name is Sara Jones. What's your name?

> My name is Pedro Bautista.

2 **Listen again. Repeat.** 🎧 🗣

3 👥 **PAIR WORK** **Introduce yourself.** 🗣

> Hi. My name is ___ . What's your name?

> My name is ___ .

Build Vocabulary

Mr.
Ms.
Miss
Mrs.

4 **Read and listen.** 📖 🎧

> Hi, Pam.

> Hello, Ms. Garcia.

> Good morning.

> Good morning.

> I'm your teacher. My name is Mr. Allen.

Build Vocabulary

Good morning.

Good afternoon.

Good evening.

5 **Listen again. Repeat.** 🎧 🗣

6 GROUP WORK **Greet your classmates.**

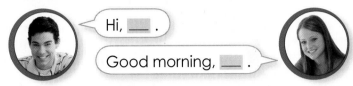

Hi, ____ .

Good morning, ____ .

7 **Read and listen.**

This is your principal. Her name is Ms. Garcia.

Hello, Ms. Garcia. My name is Jade Lee.

Nice to meet you, Jade.

Nice to meet you, too.

8 **Listen again. Repeat.**

9 GROUP WORK **Introduce your classmates.**

____ , this is ____ .

Nice to meet you, ____ .

Nice to meet you, too.

10 **Read and listen.**

Bye.

See you later.

11 **Listen again. Repeat.**

Build Vocabulary

Bye. = Good-bye.
See you later.
See you tomorrow.

Vocabulary Log

Workbook page 32–33

Independent Practice CD-ROM

● Listening and Speaking
Saying Where You Are From

1 Read and listen.

2 Listen again.
Repeat.

3 PAIR WORK **Ask your classmate.**

I'm from Somalia. How about you?

Where are you from?

I'm from Vietnam.

Where are you from?

I'm from ___

I'm from ___. How about you?

Countries and Nationalities

Country	Flag	Nationality	Country	Flag	Nationality
Afghanistan		Afghan	Haiti		Haitian
Brazil		Brazilian	Mexico		Mexican
Cambodia		Cambodian	Russia		Russian
China		Chinese	Somalia		Somali
Cuba		Cuban	United States of America		American
Guatemala		Guatemalan	Vietnam		Vietnamese

4 Listen and repeat.

5 **Read and listen.**

He's from Brazil.
He's Brazilian.

She's from Russia.
She's Russian.

They're from Cuba.
They're Cuban.

6 **Listen again. Repeat.**

7 **Read and listen.**

Where are you from?

I'm Mexican. How about you?

8 **Listen again. Repeat.**

I'm Mexican, too!

9 PAIR WORK **Look at page 8. Where are they from?**

She's from Somalia.

10 GROUP WORK **Ask three classmates. Where are they from? Tell another student.**

Where are you from?

I'm from Guatemala.

This is Mario. He is from Guatemala.

Letters and Sounds

Initial Consonants: b, c, f, g

1 Look at the red letters. Listen to the sounds. 👂

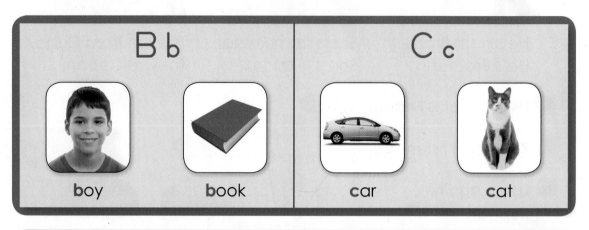

Bb — boy — book
Cc — car — cat

Ff — fan — five
Gg — girl — good-bye

2 Listen again. Repeat. 👂🗣

3 Listen to the words. What is the beginning sound?
Point to the letter. 👂👉

b   c   f   g

4 Listen again. Repeat. 👂🗣

Final Consonants: b, f, g

5 Look at the red letters. Listen to the sounds.

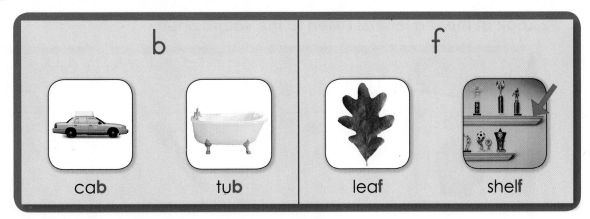

b		f	
cab	tub	leaf	shelf

g	
dog	bag

6 Listen again. Repeat.

7 Listen. Point to the word you hear.

cab   tub   leaf   shelf   dog   bag

Sight Words

8 Look at the words. Listen.

a   the   and   of   to   he   she   for

9 Listen again. Repeat.

10 Listen. Point to the word you hear.

● Letters and Sounds

Initial Consonants: m, p, s, t

1 Look at the red letters. Listen to the sounds.

2 Listen again. Repeat.

3 Listen to the words. What is the beginning sound?
Point to the letter.

m   p   s   t

4 Listen again. Repeat.

Final Consonants: m, p, s, t

5 Look at the red letters. Listen to the sounds. 🔊

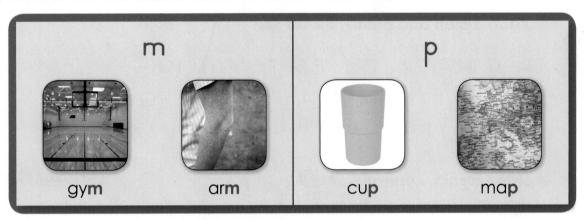

m	p
gy**m** a**r**m	cu**p** ma**p**

s	t
bu**s** dre**ss**	ca**t** ba**t**

6 Listen again. Repeat. 🔊 🗣️

7 Listen. Point to the word you hear. 🔊 ✏️

gym   arm   cup   map   bus   dress   cat   bat

Sight Words

8 Look at the words. Listen. 🔊

with   I   out   go   school   too

9 Listen again. Repeat. 🔊 🗣️

10 Listen. Point to the word you hear. 🔊 ✏️

Workbook
page 37

Independent Practice
CD-ROM

Reading
The Alphabet and Names

1 Read. Listen and point.

A a B b C c D d E e F f G g H h
I i J j K k L l M m N n O o P p Q q
R r S s T t U u V v W w X x Y y Z z

2 Listen again. Repeat.

3 Listen. Point to the letter you hear.

You hear G.

> **Build Vocabulary**
>
> A = *uppercase A or capital A*
> a = *lowercase a or small a*

> Names of people and places always begin with a capital letter.

4 PAIR WORK Spell the names.

Jim

Ana Santos
Puebla, Mexico

REPOSITIA
Tampa

Mr. Bags

5 PAIR WORK Spell your name. Tell your classmate.

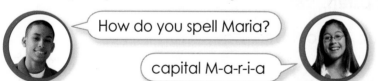

How do you spell Maria?

capital M-a-r-i-a

6 PAIR WORK Spell the words on pages 4, 5, 11, and 13.

● Writing

Writing the Alphabet and Names

1 Write the letters.

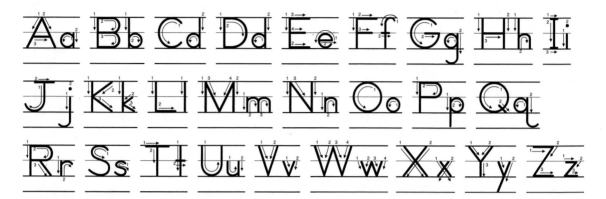

2 Write the missing capital or lowercase letter.

Example: B _b_

1. A ____   3. M ____   5. P ____   7. ____ h   9. ____ j

2. W ____   4. ____ g   6. ____ z   8. L ____   10. T ____

3 Read the words. Look at the first letters.
Write the words in order of the alphabet.

Example: 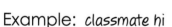 classmate hi

| principal |
| nurse |
| teacher |
| student |
| classmate |
| map |
| hi |

4 GROUP WORK Ask five classmates. Write the
answers in your notebook.

What's your name?	Where are you from?
1.	1.
2.	2.
3.	3.
4.	4.
5.	5.

Workbook
page 38–40

Independent Practice
CD-ROM

● Project

A Class List

1 Write your first and last name on a piece of paper.

2 🔄 **GROUP WORK** Work with your classmates. Stand up. Hold your paper so everyone can see your name.

3 Stand in line <u>in alphabetical order</u>, by last name.

4 Write one list with all the names.

Mr. Allen's Class
Mazen Abdin
Pablo Acosta
Emmanuel Asiwe
Pedro Bautista
Sheena Bhatia
Claudio Brandao
Yuri Bregel
Chi Ying Chan
Yong Chan
Camila Chaves
Lilian Chiang
Alex Chernov
Jin-sung Cho

Look at the spaces between the letters and words.

The Classroom

backpack

dictionary

pencil

● Progress Check
Welcome Unit: Chapter A

1 Complete the sentences. 🗩 🖉

too	are	Haiti	My	I'm	Hi	you	f

Marilyn: Hi. (1) ___ name is Marilyn Etienne. What's you

Ana: Hi. (2) ___ Ana Delarosa. Nice to meet you.

Marilyn: Nice to meet you, (3) ___ . Where (4) ___ you fr

Ana: I'm from (5) ___ . How about (6) ___ ?

Marilyn: I'm from Mexico. This is Li Ying. She's (7) ___ Ch

Ana: Hello, Li Ying.

Li Ying: (8) ___ , Ana.

2 Read the country names. Write the nationalities. 🗩 🖉

1. Brazil ___

2. Guatemala ___

3. Somalia ___

4. United States ___

5. Vietnam ___

3 Write the missing letters. 🖉

A a   B ___   ___ c   D d   E e   F ___   G ___

___ j   K k   L l   M ___   N n   O o   P ___

S ___   ___ t   U u   V v   ___ w   X x   Y y

Ob

Voc
Clas
Num

Liste
Talki
Cou

Lette
Vow

Rea
A sc

Writi
Writi

Proje
A list
clc

Prog

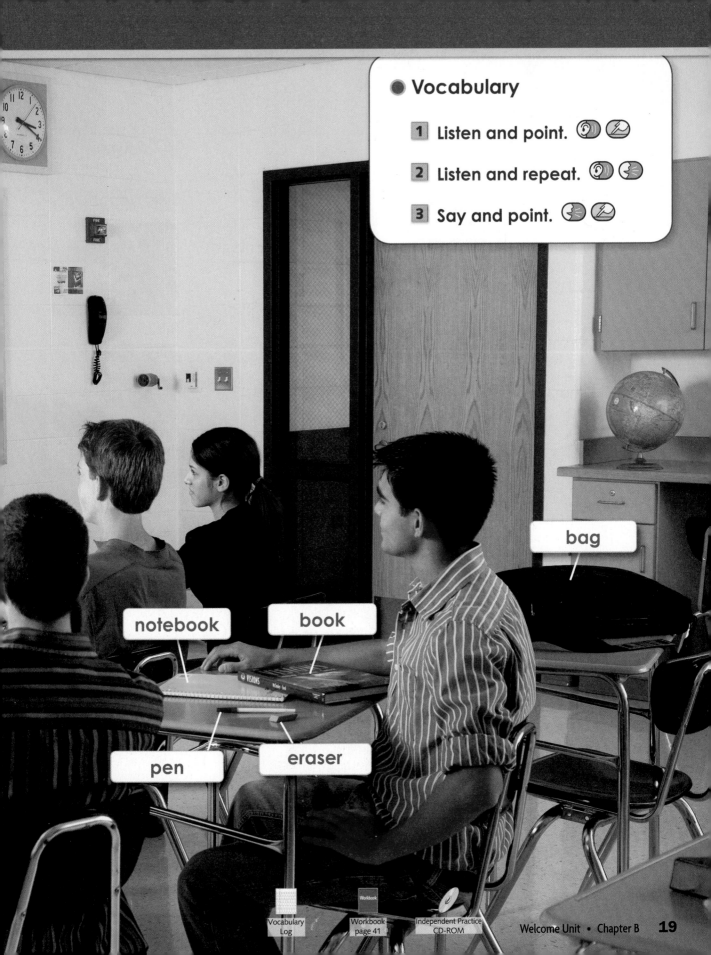

● **Vocabulary**

1 Listen and point.

2 Listen and repeat.

3 Say and point.

bag

notebook

book

pen

eraser

Vocabulary Log

Workbook page 41

Independent Practice CD-ROM

● Listening and Speaking
Talking About Possessions

> your possessions
> = your things

1 Read and listen.

Is this your pen?

Yes, it is. Thanks.

You're welcome.

Is that your bag?

No, it isn't.

Oh, OK.

Build Vocabulary

this book

that book

2 Listen again. Repeat.

3 **PAIR WORK** Say the conversation with your partner.

4 Listen. Are these Mark's things?
Write your answers in your notebook.

	Yes	No
1. pen		
2. notebook		
3. backpack		
4. eraser		
5. marker		
6. book		

5 **PAIR WORK** **Ask your classmate about possessions.**

- Is that your book?
- Yes, it is.

6 **Read and listen.**

- Excuse me. Do you have a dictionary?
- Yes, I do. Here you are.
- Thank you.

Build Vocabulary

a backpack
a dictionary
an eraser

- Excuse me. Do you have an eraser?
- No, I don't. Sorry.
- That's OK. Thanks anyway.

7 **Listen again. Repeat.**

8 **Listen. Write which things are Jade's.**

1. pen   **2.** eraser   **3.** notebook   **4.** dictionary

Vocabulary Log   Workbook page 42–43   Independent Practice CD-ROM

● Listening and Speaking
Counting Objects

1 Read and listen.

I have **one pencil**, **one notebook**, and **one dictionary**.

I have **two pencils**, **two notebooks**, and **two dictionaries**.

2 Listen again. Repeat.

3 Listen and repeat.

_____

Numbers 0 to 10

0	zero	3	three	6	six	9	nine
1	one	4	four	7	seven	10	ten
2	two	5	five	8	eight		

4 Write the missing numbers.

_0_	zero	___	four	8	___
1	___	5	___	___	nine
2	___	___	six	10	___
___	three	7	___		

5 Read and listen.

How many pens do you have?

I have five pens.

6 Listen again. Repeat.

7 **Read and listen.**

> Excuse me. Are these your books?

> Yes, they are. Thanks.

> You're welcome.

> Are those your bags?

> No, they aren't. They're Juan's bags.

> Oh, OK. Thanks.

Build Vocabulary

these books

those books

Build Vocabulary

Juan's bags

Yan's pencils

the teacher's notebooks

8 **Listen again. Repeat.**

9 **Listen. Match the things with the people.**

Example: Trang's bag

1. Jin Lee's
2. Sara's
3. Trang's

a. books
b. bag
c. pencils

10 PAIR WORK **Point to things in the classroom. Ask your classmate.**

> Are these your pencils?

> Yes, they are.

Vocabulary Log

Workbook page 44–45

Independent Practice CD-ROM

Letters and Sounds
Vowel: short a

1 Look at the red letters. Listen to the sound. 🎧

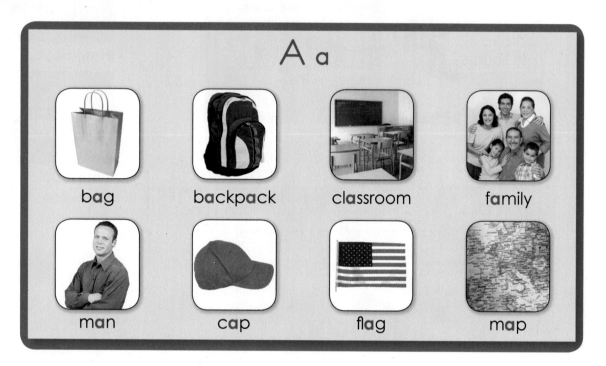

A a

bag   backpack   classroom   family

man   cap   flag   map

2 Listen again. Repeat. 🎧 🗣

3 Listen. Point to the word you hear. 🎧 ✏

bag   backpack   classroom   family   man   cap   flag   map

4 Listen. Do you hear the <u>short a sound</u>?
Choose *yes* or *no*. 🎧 ✏

1. yes   no   4. yes   no
2. yes   no   5. yes   no
3. yes   no   6. yes   no

Decoding

5 Listen and repeat.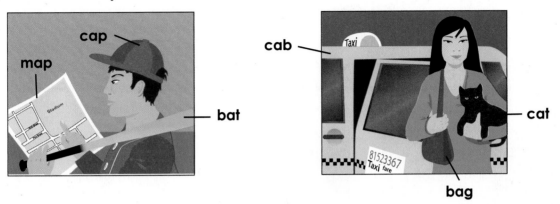

cap

map

bat

cab

cat

bag

6 Read each letter. Say each sound.

1. b a t
2. c a p
3. m a p
4. c a t
5. b a g
6. c a b

> Short a can be a beginning sound.
> at
> Short a can be a middle sound.
> m<u>a</u>p
> Short a can be an ending sound.
> comm<u>a</u>

7 Listen again. Repeat. Put the sounds together.

8 Listen and repeat.

1. a map
2. the fat cat
3. a cap and a bat
4. a bag for Pat

> Short a is different from long a. See pages 262 and 284.

● Reading

A School Newspaper

1 **Read and listen.** 📖 🎧

MEET PEOPLE FROM SCHOOL

What's in your bag?

Shamina Jamal
Los Angeles, California

I have four notebooks
and two dictionaries.

Rosalie Perkins
Hoboken, New Jersey

I have a pen and
an eraser.

Alberto Gomez
Miami, Florida

I have a map,
a notebook, and
ten pencils.

---

2 👥 PAIR WORK **Answer the questions.** 💬

1. What are their names?
   Her name is . . .

2. Where are they from?
   She is from . . .

3. What's in the woman's bag?
   She has . . .

4. What's in the girl's bag?
   She has . . .

5. What's in the boy's bag?
   He has . . .

● Writing
Writing Sentences

1 Read the sentences.

question mark

Questions	Statements
What's in your bag?	I have a pen and an eraser.
Is this your pencil?	Yes, it is.

capital letters

period

Capital Letters

Use a capital letter at the beginning of a sentence.

What's in your bag?

I have a map.

Use a capital letter for names of people.

My name is Marisa Jamal.

> Look at the space between letters and words. Remember, when you write a sentence leave more space between words.

2 Add the punctuation.

1. Is this his bag ___

2. My name is Julie ___

3. Do you have a pencil ___

4. That is Trang's bag ___

3 Write these questions in your notebook. Write the answers.

1. What is your name?
2. What do you have in your bag?

Workbook
page 48

Independent Practice
CD-ROM

Project

A List of Things in Your Classroom

1 GROUP WORK **Make a list of objects in your classroom. Write the number and name of each object.**

door

table

desk

window

bulletin board

globe

1 door
1 globe
24 desks
2 tables
1 bulletin board
4 windows

2 **Rewrite your list. Put the objects in alphabetical order.**

3 **Share your list with the class. Which group has the most objects?**

Progress Check
Welcome Unit: Chapter B

1 Choose the correct word. 🖉

    1. A: Is (1) **this / these** your backpack?
       B: Yes, it (2) **are / is**. Thanks.
       A: You're welcome.

    2. A: Do you have (3) **a / an** eraser?
       B: No, I (4) **not / don't**. Sorry.
       A: No problem.

    3. A: How many (5) **pen / pens** do you have?
       B: I have (6) **one / four** pens.

2 Match the number with the correct word. 🖉

1 ___	6 ___	**a.** eight	**f.** one
2 ___	7 ___	**b.** seven	**g.** ten
3 ___	8 ___	**c.** three	**h.** four
4 ___	9 ___	**d.** nine	**i.** six
5 ___	10 ___	**e.** five	**j.** two

3 Write these sentences. Use capital letters. 🖉

    1. his name is vinh.
    2. my name is luis alvarez.
    3. carrie has two notebooks in her bag.
    4. adela and eric have dictionaries.

4 Say these words. 👄

    1. map   **2.** fat   **3.** tab   **4.** Pam   **5.** nap

CHAPTER C

Objectives

Vocabulary
Addresses and phone numbers
Numbers 11 to 100

Listening and Speaking
Telling your age
Giving phone numbers
Saying addresses

Letters and Sounds
Initial consonants: d, j, l
Final consonants: d, l
Initial consonants: n, r, v
Final consonants: n, r, x

Reading
A Web article

Writing
Introducing yourself

Project
An emergency contact list

Progress Check

● **Vocabulary**

1. **Listen and point.** 🎧 ✏️
2. **Listen and repeat.** 🎧 ✏️
3. **Say and point.** ✏️ ✏️

street

apartment number

zip code

address

city

Name _Jose Delgado_

Address _15 Mission Street, Apt 3B_

Bakersfield, CA 93301

Home _(661) 555 - 3428_

Cell _(661) 555 - 2967_

state

phone number

Vocabulary Log

Workbook page 49

Independent Practice CD-ROM

● Listening and Speaking

Telling Your Age

1 Listen and repeat.

Numbers 11 to 100

11 eleven	18 eighteen	25 twenty-five	50 fifty
12 twelve	19 nineteen	26 twenty-six	60 sixty
13 thirteen	20 twenty	27 twenty-seven	70 seventy
14 fourteen	21 twenty-one	28 twenty-eight	80 eighty
15 fifteen	22 twenty-two	29 twenty-nine	90 ninety
16 sixteen	23 twenty-three	30 thirty	100 one
17 seventeen	24 twenty-four	40 forty	hundred

2 Say and write the missing numbers.

1. 11, ___, 13

2. 96, ___, 98

3. ___, twenty-two, twenty-three

4. 56, 57, ___

5. forty, forty-one, ___

6. sixteen, ___, eighteen

7. ___, 59, 60

8. ninety-eight, ninety-nine, ___

3 Read and listen.

How old are you, Jon?

I'm fourteen.

I'm fifteen. How old are you?

4 Listen again. Repeat.

5  **PAIR WORK Ask your classmate.**

 How old is Jack?

He's thirty-five.

Jack is
35 years old.

May is
62 years old.

Tanya is
16 years old.

Waseem is
20 years old.

Giving Phone Numbers

6 **Read and listen.**

What's your phone number, Henry?

It's (310) 555-2943. What's your phone number, Ana?

It's (562) 555-7786.

Great. Thanks.

Build Vocabulary

(310) 555-2943
area number code

7 **Listen again. Repeat.**

8 **Listen. Write the missing numbers.**

1. (305) ___55-4298   **2.** (83___) 555-1___32   **3.** (41___) 555-109___

(786) 555-___911   (___0) 555-5595   (___0) 555-64___4

9 **PAIR WORK Practice the conversation in activity 6.**
Use the phone numbers from activity 8.

Vocabulary Log

Workbook
page 50–51

Independent Practice
CD-ROM

Listening and Speaking
Saying Addresses

1 Read the numbers. 🔲

	two-two-three-eight
2238 = OR	
	twenty-two thirty-eight

2238 Main Street
649 Main Street

	six-four-nine
649 = OR	
	six forty-nine

2 Read and say these street numbers. 🔲 🗣

1. 1476
2. 3788
3. 345
4. 690
5. 3124
6. 9876

3 Read and say these zip codes. 🔲 🗣

1. 02118
2. 44677
3. 94114
4. 34785
5. 75205

You may hear "oh" for "zero." For example, you can read the zip code **33607** as **three-three-six-oh-seven**.

4 Listen and write the numbers. 🔊 ✏

1. ___ 3. ___ 5. ___
2. ___ 4. ___ 6. ___

5 Say the numbers in activity 4. 🗣

6 Read and listen.

What's your address, Cristina?

It's 2238 Parkview Avenue, Tampa, Florida 33607. What's your address?

It's 649 East Highland Road, Northdale, Florida 33618.

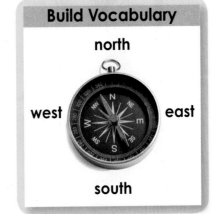

Build Vocabulary

north

west   east

south

7 Listen again. Repeat.

8 Listen. Write the missing numbers.

1. 57___ Prospect Road

   Long Beach, California

   9___80___

2. 70 North Walker Street

   Apartment ___

   Oak Forest, Illinois 604___

3. ___43 East Parkway Drive

   San Antonio, Texas

   ___205

4. 19___ Madison Avenue

   New York , New York 10___

9 PAIR WORK Practice the conversation in activity 6. Use the addresses from activity 8.

● Letters and Sounds

Initial Consonants: d, j, l

1 Look at the red letters. Listen to the sounds. 🎧

D d
desk   door

J j
June   July

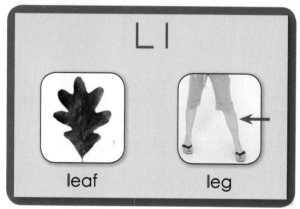

L l
leaf   leg

2 Listen again. Repeat. 🎧 🗣

3 Listen to the words. What is the beginning sound?
Point to the letter. 🎧 ✍

d   j   l

4 Listen again. Repeat. 🎧 🗣

Final Consonants: d, l

5 **Look at the red letters. Listen to the sounds.** 🔊

d		l	
head	board	ball	pencil

6 **Listen again. Repeat.** 🔊 🗣️

7 **Listen. Point to the word you hear.** 🔊 ✍️

head   board   ball   pencil

Decoding

8 **Listen and repeat.** 🔊 🗣️

1. Al is sad.
2. The cap is for Dad.
3. He has a cat.
4. The jam is for Pat.

Sight Words

9 **Look at the words. Listen.** 🔊

they   water   have   eye   you   her   we

Spelling
What letters are in these sight words? Spell the words.

10 **Listen again. Repeat.** 🔊 🗣️

11 **Listen. Point to the word you hear.** 🔊 ✍️

Workbook
Workbook
page 54–55

Independent Practice
CD-ROM

Welcome Unit • Chapter C **37**

Letters and Sounds

Initial Consonants: n, r, v

1 Look at the red letters. Listen to the sounds.

N n
nine   number

R r
run   radio

V v
violin   vacuum

2 Listen again. Repeat.

3 Listen to the words. What is the beginning sound?
Point to the letter.

n   r   v

4 Listen again. Repeat.

Final Consonants: n, r, x

5 Look at the **red** letters. Listen to the sounds. 🎧

n		r	
man	pen	car	teacher

x

six   box

6 Listen again. Repeat. 🎧 🗣️

7 Listen. Point to the word you hear. 🎧 ✍️

man   pen   car   teacher   six   box

Decoding

8 Listen and repeat. 🎧 🗣️

1. The rat ran to the man.
2. Pat has a vat of jam.
3. Jan has a cab.
4. Dan has a map for Nat.

Workbook
page 56–57

Independent Practice
CD-ROM

Reading
A Web Article

1 Read and listen. 📖 🔊

> ## A Famous House
>
>
>
> The White House is the home of the President of the United States of America. There are 132 rooms and 35 bathrooms. There are also 412 doors, 147 windows, 8 staircases, and 3 elevators. More than 1,200,000 (one million two hundred thousand) people visit here each year.
>
> For more information, contact:
>
> **The White House**
> 1600 Pennsylvania Avenue NW
> Washington, DC 20500
>
> (202) 456-1111
>
> **www.whitehouse.gov**

Build Vocabulary

bathroom

staircase

elevator

2 👥 PAIR WORK **Answer the questions. Tell a classmate.** 💬

1. How many rooms are there in the White House?
   There are . . .
2. How many bathrooms are there in the White House?
   There are . . .
3. Who lives in the White House?
4. What is the address of the White House?
5. What is the phone number for information?

● Writing

Introducing Yourself

1 Read the sentences.

My name is Anh Le.

I am from Vietnam.

I am 15 years old.

I go to Washington Middle School.

I live in Clear Lake, Washington.

Ms. Lee is my English teacher.

Capital Letters

Use a capital letter for names of places.

I'm from **M**iami, **F**lorida.

She lives in **G**ary, **I**ndiana.

His address is 28 **C**edar **S**treet, **N**orth **C**onway, **M**aryland.

2 Write five sentences about yourself.

3 Read a classmate's paragraph.

4 Write about a classmate in your notebook.

Claudia Oliveira is my classmate.

She is from Brazil.

She is 13 years old.

She goes to Washington Middle School.

Mr. Lydon is her science teacher.

Ms. Lee is her English teacher.

● Project

An Emergency Contact List

1 Read this list of important places.

- my school
- police station
- fire station
- hospital

Build Vocabulary

police station

fire station

hospital

2 Can you think of others? Make a list. Write the address and phone number of each place.

3 Keep the list in your notebook or in your home.

● Progress Check

1 **Complete the sentences.**

number	zip code	California	old
Street	area code	address	

A: How (1)___ are you, Lara?

B: I'm 14.

A: What's your (2)___, Lara?

B: It's 433 Bayside (3)___, Oakland, (4)___.

A: What's the (5)___?

B: It's 94607.

A: And what is your phone (6)___?

B: It's (7)___ (510) 555-3847.

A: Thanks.

2 **Write the missing numbers from 11–20.**

eleven   ___   ___   seventeen   ___
twelve   fourteen   ___   ___   twenty

3 **Match the number and the word.**

Example: 30 – thirty

30	70	fifty	one hundred
40	80	sixty	seventy
50	90	ninety	thirty
60	100	forty	eighty

4 **Say these words.**

1. Dan is a man.   **2.** tax   **3.** jam   **4.** van   **5.** ram

CHAPTER D

Objectives

Vocabulary
Classroom language
Colors
Shapes
Sizes

Listening and Speaking
Classroom actions
Please for polite requests
Describing and asking
 for objects

Letters and Sounds
Vowel: short o

Reading
The science of colors

Writing
Describing flags

Project
World flags

Progress Check

Classroom Language

classroom

door

piece of paper

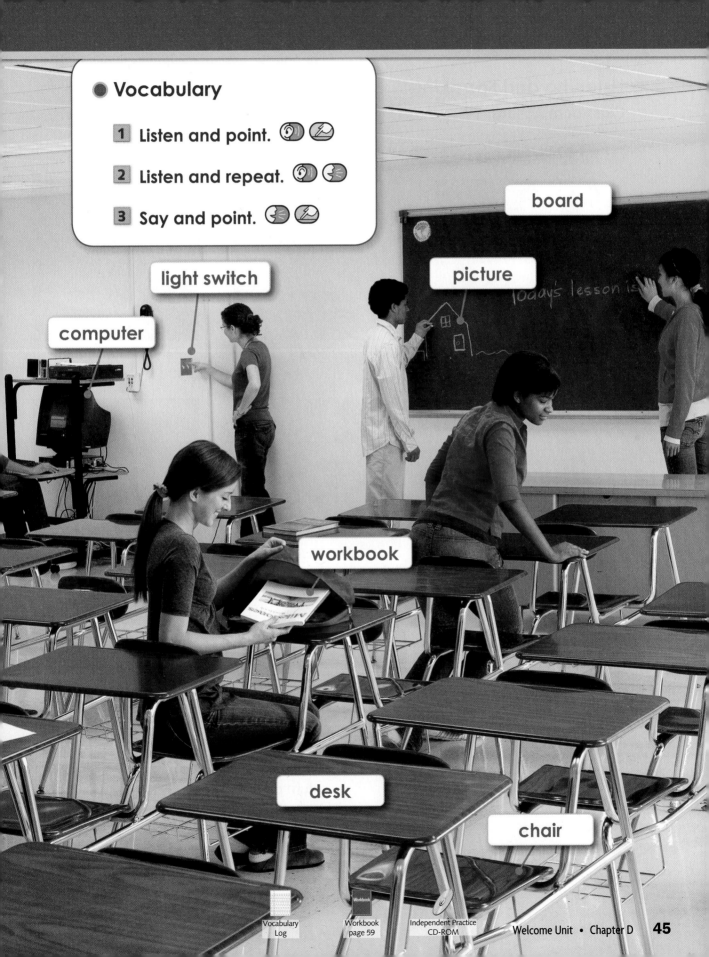

Vocabulary

1 Listen and point.

2 Listen and repeat.

3 Say and point.

board

picture

light switch

computer

Today's lesson is

workbook

desk

chair

Listening and Speaking

Classroom Actions

1 Read and listen. 📖 🔊

Open your book.

Close the door.

Write your name on a piece of paper.

Draw a picture of your house.

Take out your workbook.

Erase the board.

Sit down.

Stand up.

Turn on the computer.

Turn off the lights.

2 Listen again. Repeat. 🔊 🗣

3 PAIR WORK **Make sentences.**

Example: Write your name on a piece of paper.

Open Close	your notebook. your book. the door. your bag.

Write	your name your address your phone number	on a piece of paper. on the board. in your notebook.
Draw	a picture of your house a car a dog	

Take out	your workbook. your dictionary. a pencil.

Erase	the words the picture the sentence	on the board. in your notebook.

Please for Polite Requests

Use **please** before or after requests.

Open your notebook.
Please open your notebook.
Open your notebook, **please**.

4 PAIR WORK **Make polite requests. Your classmate does them.**

Write your name of a piece of paper, please.

Vocabulary Log

Workbook
page 60–61

Independent Practice
CD-ROM

● Listening and Speaking

Describing and Asking for Objects

1 Listen and repeat. 🔊 🗣

Colors

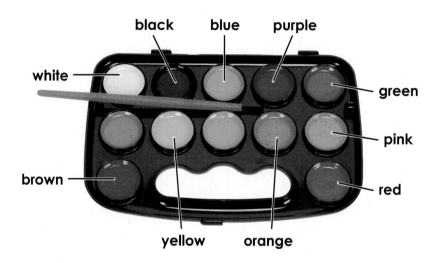

black   blue   purple

white

green

pink

brown

red

yellow   orange

2 👥 PAIR WORK **Point to a color. Your classmate says the color.** ✏️ 🗣

3 👥 PAIR WORK **Listen and repeat.** 🔊 🗣

Shapes

●	■	▲	▬
1. a blue **circle**	**2.** a blue **square**	**3.** a blue **triangle**	**4.** a blue **rectangle**

4 👥 PAIR WORK **Point to the shape. Say the color and the shape.** ✏️ 🗣

1.   **2.**   **3.**   **4.**

5 Listen and repeat.

Sizes

1. a large circle

2. a small circle

3. a large square

4. a small square

6  **PAIR WORK** Read the sentences. Your classmate draws the pictures.

1. Draw a large square.
2. Draw a small triangle.

3. Draw a large circle.
4. Draw a small rectangle.

7 Listen. Choose the correct object.

1. a. **b.**

3. a. **b.**

2. a. **b.**

4. a.  **b.**

8 Read and listen.

Sara: Excuse me. May I have the blue marker, please?

Miguel: Sure. Here it is.

Sara: Thank you.

Miguel: You're welcome.

9 Listen again. Repeat.

10 **PAIR WORK** Practice the conversation. Ask for these objects.

1. the red pencil
2. the small dictionary

3. the brown bag
4. the large box

● Letters and Sounds
Vowel: short o

1 Look at the red letters. Listen to the sound.

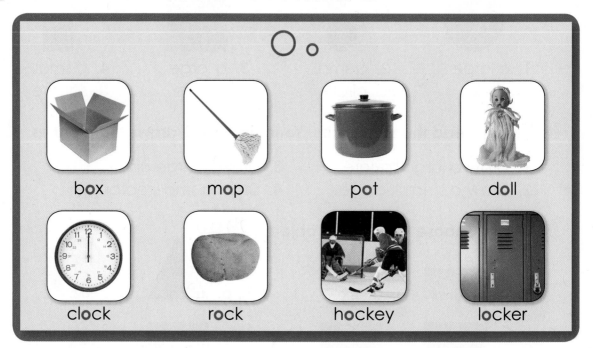

O o

box mop pot doll

clock rock hockey locker

2 Listen again. Repeat.

3 Listen. Point to the word you hear.

box mop pot doll clock rock hockey locker

4 Listen. Do you hear the <u>short o</u> sound? Choose *yes* or *no*.

1. yes   no   3. yes   no   5. yes   no
2. yes   no   4. yes   no   6. yes   no

Decoding

5 Listen and repeat. Read each letter. Say each sound.

1. p o t
2. c o p
3. m o p
4. b o x
5. l o t
6. c o b

> Short o can be a beginning sound.
> **o**x
> Short o can be a middle sound.
> t**o**p

6 Listen again. Repeat. Put the sounds together.

7 Listen. Which word do you hear? Write the word.

1. mop   map
2. pot   pat
3. cob   cab
4. cot   cat
5. cop   cap
6. rot   rat

8 Listen and repeat.

1. The box is for Pat and Don.
2. He has a mop and a pot.
3. The cat is on top of his lap.
4. The man is not Rob.

> Short o is different from long o. See pages 262 and 314.

Workbook
page 64–65

Independent Practice
CD-ROM

● Reading

The Science of Colors

1 Read and listen.

Color Facts

Red, yellow, and blue are primary colors. You mix them to make other colors. Red and yellow make orange. Yellow and blue make green. Blue and red make purple. All colors together make black. Try it!

How many colors can people see? The eye can see seven million (7,000,000) colors! Computers and TVs can make millions of colors from red, green, and blue light.

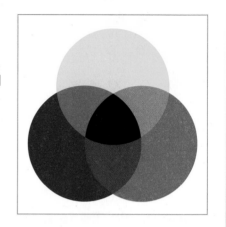

2 PAIR WORK **Read again. Answer the questions. Tell a classmate.**

1. What colors are primary colors?
2. What colors make orange?
3. What colors make green?
4. What colors make purple?
5. What colors make black?

3 PAIR WORK **Look at the pictures. What colors and shapes do you see?**

Woman at Postercolumn
by Kazimir Malevich

The 14th of July
by Roger Andre de La Fresnaye

Writing

Describing Flags

Commas

Use commas (,) for items in a series:

Red, yellow, and blue are primary colors.
Computers make millions of colors from red, green, and blue light.

1 Write these sentences with commas.

1. Red yellow and blue are primary colors.
2. The flag of Ghana is red yellow green and black.
3. Jan has black red green and blue markers.

Ghana

2 Read the sentences.

1. The flag of Chile is red, white, and blue.
2. It has a white stripe and a red stripe.
3. It has one white star.
4. The star is on a blue square.

Chile

3 Now write about the flag of the Philippines.

1. The flag of the Philippines is ____, ____, ____, and ____.
2. It has a ____ stripe and a ____ stripe.
3. It has one ____ sun and ____ ____ stars.
4. The sun and stars are on a ____ ____.

Philippines

4 Write complete sentences about the flag of Togo.

5 PAIR WORK Look at your classmate's sentences. Do you have the same answers?

Togo

● Project

World Flags

1 Draw a flag of a country. Everyone in class draws a different flag.

2 Put your flag on the bulletin board. Tell the class about your flag.

> The flag of the United States is red, white, and blue.
> It has thirteen stripes.
> The stripes are red and white.
> The flag has fifty white stars.
> The stars are on a blue square.

3 **GROUP WORK** **Answer the questions about the class flags.**

1. How many flags are red, white, and blue?
2. How many flags have pictures of stars?
3. How many flags have pictures of the sun?
4. How many flags have a large circle?

4 Share your answers with the class. Does each group have the same answers?

● Progress Check

Welcome Unit: Chapter D

1 Complete each sentence.

write	open	take out	draw

1. _____ the door, please.
2. _____ your phone number.
3. Please _____ your pencils.

2 Draw these pictures.

1. a large square
2. a large circle
3. a small rectangle
4. a small triangle

3 Look at the pictures. Write what you see.

1. ____   2. ____   3. ____   4. ____   5. ____

4 Number the sentences (1–4) in the correct order.

____ **B:** You're welcome.
____ **A:** Excuse me, Pat. May I have the blue notebook, please?
____ **B:** Here it is.
____ **A:** Thank you.

5 Say the words.

1. mop
2. not
3. doll
4. pot

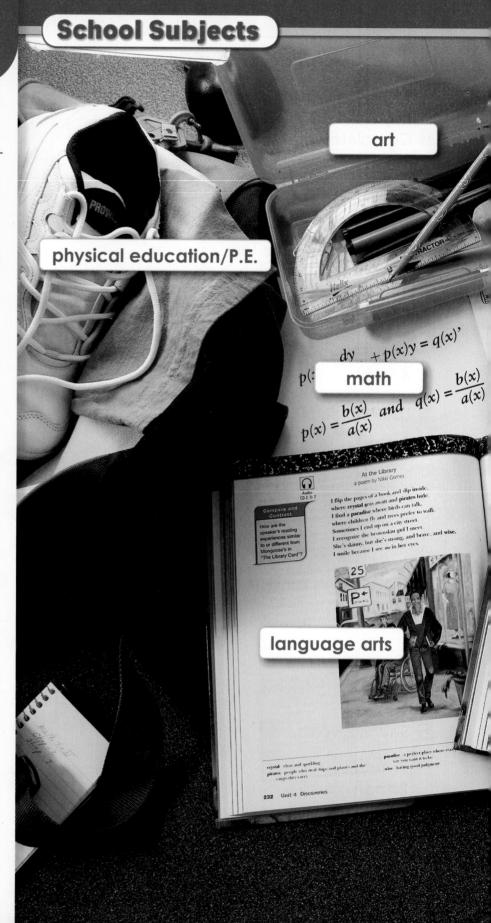

School Subjects

art

physical education/P.E.

math

language arts

Objectives

Vocabulary
School subjects
Days of the week
Months of the year

Listening and Speaking
Talking about classes
Talking about schedules

Letters and Sounds
Vowel: short i
Initial consonants:
h, k, q, w, y, z

Reading
A poem

Writing
Writing your school
schedule

Project
U.S. holidays

Progress Check

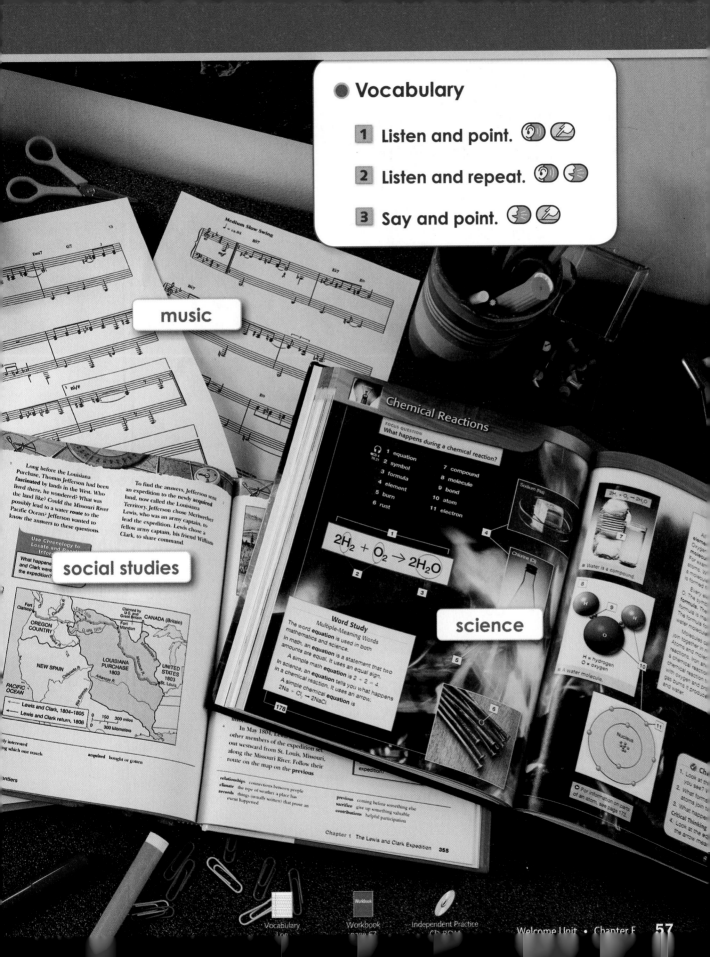

Vocabulary

1. **Listen and point.**

2. **Listen and repeat.**

3. **Say and point.**

music

social studies

science

● Listening and Speaking

Talking About Classes

1 Read and listen.

> What classes do you have?

> I have language arts, math, art, and science.

> I have language arts, social studies, science, and math. What classes do you have?

2 Listen again. Repeat.

3 PAIR WORK Practice with a classmate. What classes do you have?

4 Read and listen.

> Do you have science class?

> Yes, I do.

> No, I don't. Do you have science class?

5 Listen. Which classes does each student have? Write them.

language arts	science	math	art
social studies	P.E.	music	

Marisa has (1) ____, art, and (2) ____ class. She doesn't have (3) ____.

Raj has (1) ____, P.E., and (2) ____. He doesn't have (3) ____.

6 **PAIR WORK Ask about your classmate's classes. Use the subjects on pages 56–57.**

Do you have science class?

Yes, I do.

Use capital letters for the days of the week.
Use periods after the abbreviations.

Days of the Week

7 **Listen and repeat.**

Monday   Tuesday   Wednesday   Thursday

Friday   Saturday   Sunday

8 **PAIR WORK Say a day. Your classmate points to the word.**

9 **PAIR WORK Your classmate says a day. Point to the abbreviation.**

Friday

Build Vocabulary

Abbreviations for days of the week

Monday	=	Mon.
Tuesday	=	Tues.
Wednesday	=	Wed.
Thursday	=	Thurs.
Friday	=	Fri.
Saturday	=	Sat.
Sunday	=	Sun.

10 **Read and listen.**

What day is today?

It's Thursday.

11 **Listen again. Repeat.**

12 **Listen. Write the days you hear.**

Vocabulary Log

Workbook page 68–69

Independent Practice CD-ROM

● Listening and Speaking
Talking About Schedules

1 Read and listen.

> What classes do you have on Monday?

> I have math and science. How about you?

> I have math and art.

2 Listen again. Repeat.

3 **PAIR WORK** What classes do you have on Monday?

4 Read and listen.

> When do you have art?

> I have art on Tuesday and Thursday.

5 Listen again. Repeat.

6 Read the schedule.

Monday	Tuesday	Wednesday	Thursday	Friday
math	science	math	science	P.E.
social studies	art	language arts	art	social studies
lunch	lunch	lunch	lunch	lunch

7 **PAIR WORK** Ask your classmate about the class schedule in activity 6.

> When do you have social studies?

> I have social studies on Monday and Friday.

8 **PAIR WORK** Tell your classmate about your schedule.

Months of the Year

Use a capital letter for the months of the year.

1 Listen and repeat.

January	February	March	April	May	June	July

August	September	October	November	December

2 PAIR WORK **Say a month. Your classmate points to the word.**

3 PAIR WORK **Your classmate says a month. Point to the abbreviation.**

March

= Jan.
= Feb.
= Mar.
= Apr.
= May
= Jun.

Build Vocabulary

Abbreviations for months of the year

January	=	Jan.
February	=	Feb.
March	=	Mar.
April	=	Apr.
May	=	May
June	=	Jun.
July	=	Jul.
August	=	Aug.
September	=	Sep.
October	=	Oct.
November	=	Nov.
December	=	Dec.

4 Read and listen.

When is your birthday?

My birthday is in June.

5 Listen again. Repeat.

Use periods after the abbreviations.

6 PAIR WORK **Practice with a classmate.**

When is your birthday?

My birthday is in September.

● Letters and Sounds
Vowel: short i

1 Look at the red letters. Listen to the sound.

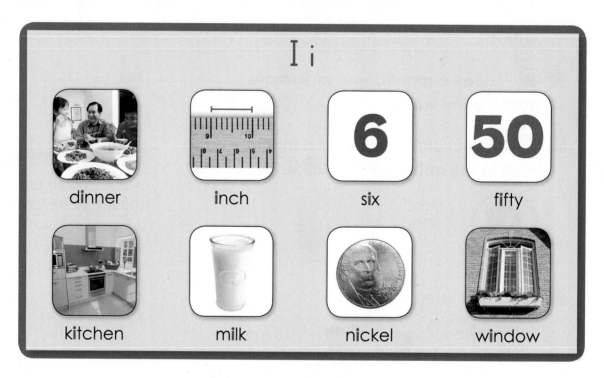

dinner	inch	six	fifty
kitchen	milk	nickel	window

2 Listen again. Repeat.

3 Listen. Point to the word you hear.

dinner   inch   six   fifty   kitchen   milk   nickel   window

4 Listen. Do you hear the <u>short i</u> sound? Choose yes or no.

1. yes   no
2. yes   no
3. yes   no
4. yes   no
5. yes   no
6. yes   no

Decoding

5 **Listen and repeat. Read each letter. Say each sound.**

1. s i x

4. r i d

2. i n

5. s i t

3. l i p

6. f i x

6 **Listen again. Repeat. Put the sounds together.**

7 **Listen. Which sound do you hear? Point to it.**

a   i   o

8 **Listen and repeat.**

1. Pat and Ron sit in the hot cab.

2. Ana has a big bag.

3. He will fix the lid if he can.

4. Rod is not on the mat.

Sight Words

9 **Look at the words. Listen.**

said   says   was   one   are   give

> **Spelling**
> What letters are in these sight words? Spell the words.

10 **Listen again. Repeat.**

11 **Listen. Point to the word you hear.**

> Short i is different from long i. See pages 262 and 315.

● Letters and Sounds

Initial Consonants: h, k, q, w, y, z

1 Look at the red letters. Listen to the sounds. 🎧

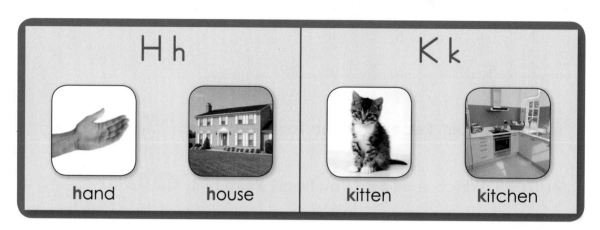

Hh — **h**and — **h**ouse   Kk — **k**itten — **k**itchen

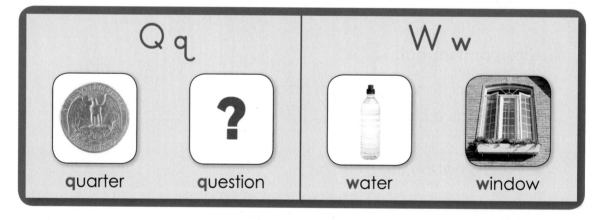

Qq — **q**uarter — **q**uestion   Ww — **w**ater — **w**indow

Yy — **y**ellow — **y**ogurt   Zz — **z**ipper — **z**ero

2 Listen again. Repeat. 🎧 🗣

Decoding

3 Listen. Point to the letter or letters of the beginning sound you hear.

h   k   q   w   y   z

4 Listen again. Repeat.

5 Listen. Write the missing letter or letters.

1. ___ im   5. ___ ot

2. ___ in   6. ___ ip

3. ___ es   7. ___ uiz

4. ___ uit   8. ___ id

> Q or q is usually followed by u and sounds like /k/ /w/.

6 Listen and repeat.

1. The kid bit his lip.
2. Tim has a quiz at six.
3. Sara and Tom win.
4. She got him a mop.

Sight Words

7 Look at the words. Listen.

about   watch   or   words   there   do

> **Spelling**
> What letters are in these sight words? Spell the words.

8 Listen again. Repeat.

9 Listen. Point to the word your hear.

Reading

A Poem

1 Read and listen. 📖 🔊

JANUARY						
Sun	Mon	Tues	Wed	Thurs	Fri	Sat
		1	2	3	4	5
6	7	8	9	10	11	12
13	14	15	16	17	18	19
20	21	22	23	24	25	26
27	28	29	30	31		

FEBRUARY						
Sun	Mon	Tues	Wed	Thurs	Fri	Sat
					1	2
3	4	5	6	7	8	9
10	11	12	13	14	15	16
17	18	19	20	21	22	23
24	25	26	27	28	29	

MARCH						
Sun	Mon	Tues	Wed	Thurs	Fri	Sat
						1
2	3	4	5	6	7	8
9	10	11	12	13	14	15
16	17	18	19	20	21	22
23	24	25	26	27	28	29
30	31					

APRIL						
Sun	Mon	Tues	Wed	Thurs	Fri	Sat
	1	2	3	4	5	6
6	7	8	9	10	11	12
13	14	15	16	17	18	19
20	21	22	23	24	25	26
27	28	29	30			

MAY						
Sun	Mon	Tues	Wed	Thurs	Fri	Sat
			1	2	3	
4	5	6	7	8	9	10
11	12	13	14	15	16	17
18	19	20	21	22	23	24
25	26	27	28	29	30	31

DECEMBER						
Sun	Mon	Tues	Wed	Thurs	Fri	Sat
1	2	3	4	5	6	
7	8	9	10	11	12	13
14	15	16	17	18	19	20
21	22	23	24	25	26	27
28	29	30	31			

30 days has September,
April, June, and November.
All the rest have 31,
except February is great with 28.
And in leap years, February is fine with 29.

JUNE						
Sun	Mon	Tues	Wed	Thurs	Fri	Sat
1	2	3	4	5	6	7
8	9	10	11	12	13	14
15	16	17	18	19	20	21
22	23	24	25	26	27	28
29	30					

NOVEMBER						
Sun	Mon	Tues	Wed	Thurs	Fri	Sat
						1
2	3	4	5	6	7	8
9	10	11	12	13	14	15
16	17	18	19	20	21	22
23	24	25	26	27	28	29
30						

OCTOBER						
Sun	Mon	Tues	Wed	Thurs	Fri	Sat
		1	2	3	4	
5	6	7	8	9	10	11
12	13	14	15	16	17	18
19	20	21	22	23	24	25
26	27	28	29	30	31	

SEPTEMBER						
Sun	Mon	Tues	Wed	Thurs	Fri	Sat
1	2	3	4	5	6	
7	8	9	10	11	12	13
14	15	16	17	18	19	20
21	22	23	24	25	26	27
28	29	30				

AUGUST						
Sun	Mon	Tues	Wed	Thurs	Fri	Sat
					1	2
3	4	5	6	7	8	9
10	11	12	13	14	15	16
17	18	19	20	21	22	23
24	25	26	27	28	29	30
31						

JULY						
Sun	Mon	Tues	Wed	Thurs	Fri	Sat
	1	2	3	4	5	
6	7	8	9	10	11	12
13	14	15	16	17	18	19
20	21	22	23	24	25	26
27	28	29	30	31		

2 👥 PAIR WORK **Read again. Answer questions. Tell your classmate.** 📖 💬

1. How many days does September have?
   September has ____ days.
2. How many days does June have?
   June has ____ days.
3. How many months have 30 days?
   ____ months have 30 days.
4. How many days does January have?
   January has ____ days.

3 Read again. Write a sentence for all 12 months. 📖 ✏️

1. January has 31 days.
2. February has . . .

4 👥 PAIR WORK **Read your sentences to your classmate. Does your classmate have the same sentences?** 📖 💬 🔊

5 Say the poem. 💬

● Writing
Writing Your School Schedule

1 Copy the chart. Write your school schedule.

	Mon.	Tues.	Wed.	Thur.	Fri.
Class 1					
Class 2					
Class 3					
Class 4					
Class 5					
Class 6					
Class 7					

2 Write sentences about your school schedule.

> I have science on Monday, Wednesday, and Friday.
> I have music on Monday.
> I have social studies on Tuesday and Thursday.

3 **PAIR WORK** Read your sentences to a classmate.

Capital Letters

Use a capital letter for the days of the week.

Dan has social studies on **M**onday, **T**uesday, and **T**hursday.

Use a capital letter for months of the year.

It is **J**une.

4 Write these sentences. Use capital letters.

1. pat has social studies, science, and language arts on thursday.
2. nan doesn't have art on tuesday and friday.
3. we don't have school in july and august.
4. september and november have 30 days.

Workbook
page 76

Independent Practice
CD-ROM

● Project

U.S. Holidays

1 Look at the list of U.S. holidays. Do you know them? 📖

New Year's Day	Martin Luther King Jr. Day	Valentine's Day
Flag Day	The Fourth of July	Labor Day
Halloween	Veterans Day	Thanksgiving
Mother's Day		

2 👥 PAIR WORK **Look at the pictures. Write the holiday that matches the picture. Use capital letters for holidays.** ✏️

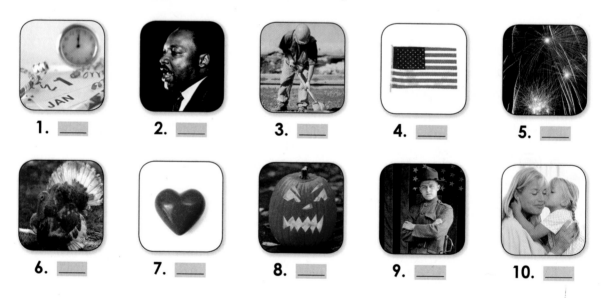

1. _____ 2. _____ 3. _____ 4. _____ 5. _____

6. _____ 7. _____ 8. _____ 9. _____ 10. _____

3 👥 PAIR WORK **What months are the holidays in?** Write complete sentences.

1. New Year's Day is in January.

4 👥 GROUP WORK **Share your list with another pair. What other holidays do you know? Write them.** ✏️

Progress Check

Welcome Unit: Chapter E

1 Write the missing days.

Sunday, _____, Tuesday, _____,

Thursday, _____, _____

2 Write the missing months or abbreviations.

1. Jan. = January   **7.** ____. = July

2. ____. = February   **8.** Aug. = ____

3. Mar. = ____   **9.** ____. = September

4. Apr. = ____   **10.** Oct. = ____

5. May = ____   **11.** Nov. = ____

6. ____. = June   **12.** ____. = December

3 Write the words in the right order. Make sentences.

1. is / What / today? / day
2. Monday, Wednesday, / Ana has / and Friday. / science on
3. today? / social studies / have / Do you
4. I / on Tuesday and Thursday. / science / don't / have
5. do / When / have / P.E.? / you
6. When / birthday? / your / is

4 Say the sentences.

1. The kid bit the tip.
2. Tim has a quiz.
3. Tim will win.
4. She got him a pen.

My Favorite Things

Objectives

Vocabulary
Food and fun

Listening and Speaking
Talking about likes
Talking about favorites

Letters and Sounds
Vowel: short u
Vowel: short e

Reading
A personal Web site

Writing
Writing about your
favorites

Project
Survey: Favorites

Progress Check

sports

basketball player

baseball team

game

food

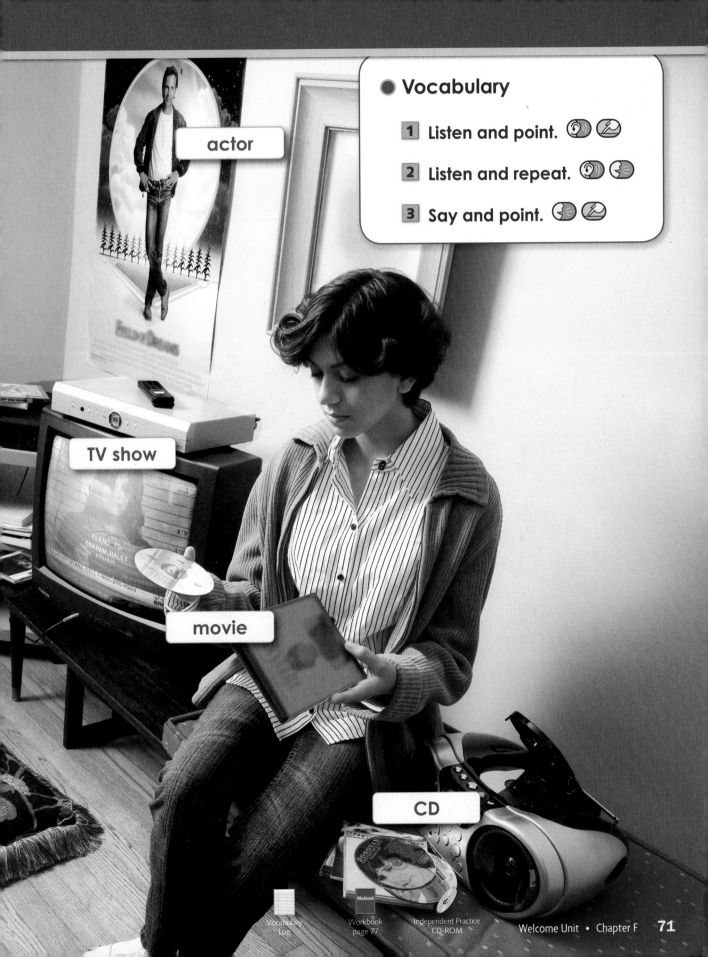

actor

TV show

movie

CD

Vocabulary Log

Workbook page 77

Independent Practice CD-ROM

● Listening and Speaking

Talking About Likes

1 Listen and repeat.

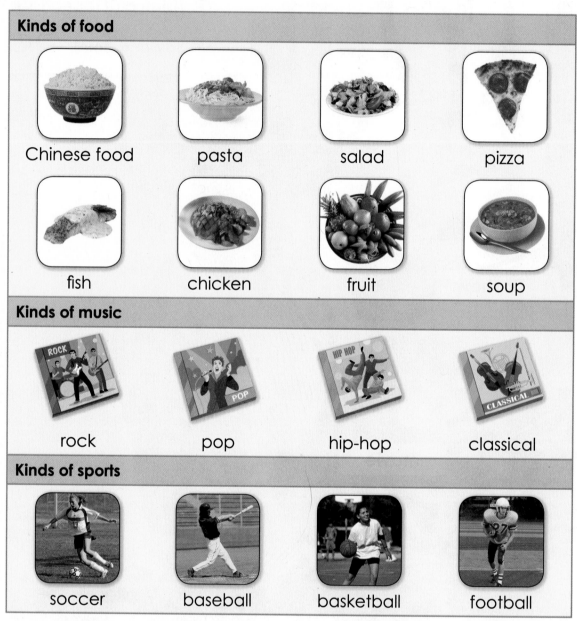

Kinds of food

Chinese food	pasta	salad	pizza
fish	chicken	fruit	soup

Kinds of music

rock	pop	hip-hop	classical

Kinds of sports

soccer	baseball	basketball	football

2 Read and listen.

What kind of music do you like?

I like rock.

I like hip-hop.
How about you?

3 Listen. What food, music, and sports do Luis and Jin-Hee like? Match the person with the right answers.

Luis   Jin-Hee

Food	Music	Sports
Mexican food Korean food pizza soup	classical music rock music pop music hip-hop music	soccer football baseball basketball

4 Listen again. Copy the chart. Write the food, music, and sports that Luis and Jin-Hee like.

	Food	Music	Sports
Luis likes . . .	_____	_____	_____
Jin-Hee likes . . .	_____	_____	_____

5 What do you like? Copy the chart. Write your answers.

	Food	Music	Sports
I like . . .	_____	_____	_____

6  **PAIR WORK** What does your classmate like? Ask questions.

What kind of food do you like?

I like Chinese food.

 Vocabulary Log

 Workbook page 78–79

 Independent Practice CD-ROM

● Listening and Speaking
Talking About Favorites

1 **Read and listen.** 📖 🔊

Do you like Chinese food?

It's OK.

Yes, I like it a lot. How about you?

Build Vocabulary

I like it a lot. ☺

It's OK. 😐

I don't like it very much. ☹

2 **Listen again. Repeat.** 🔊 🗣

3 **Read and listen.** 📖 🔊

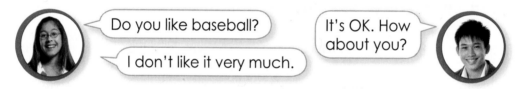

Do you like baseball?

I don't like it very much.

It's OK. How about you?

4 **Listen again. Repeat.** 🔊 🗣

5 **Do you like these things? Write ☺ for "I like it a lot." Write 😐 for "It's OK." Write ☹ for "I don't like it very much."** ✏

_____ **1.** classical music
_____ **2.** Chinese food
_____ **3.** football
_____ **4.** hip-hop music

_____ **5.** soccer
_____ **6.** pasta
_____ **7.** rock music
_____ **8.** ice cream

6 👥 **PAIR WORK** **Ask a classmate about the things in activity 5.** 🗣

Do you like classical music?

It's OK.

7 Read and listen. 📖 🎧

What's your favorite food?

My favorite food is pizza. What's yours?

My favorite food is Mexican food.

8 Listen again. Repeat. 🎧 💨

9 Listen. Whose favorite is it? Write *A* for Ali or *S* for Suzanne. 🎧 ✏️

____ **1.** Italian food	____ **4.** rock music	____ **7.** basketball
____ **2.** fish	____ **5.** pop music	____ **8.** baseball
____ **3.** chicken	____ **6.** hip-hop music	____ **9.** soccer

10 Read and listen. 📖 🎧

What's	your favorite	food? sport? music? song? sports team? movie? TV show? game?

Who's	your favorite	singer? music group? actor? basketball player?

11 Listen again. Repeat. 🎧 💨

12 👥 PAIR WORK Ask a classmate the questions in activity 10. Write your classmate's answers. 🖊️

Who's your favorite singer?

My favorite singer is . . .

Vocabulary Log

Workbook page 80–81

Independent Practice CD-ROM

Letters and Sounds
Vowel: short u

1 Look at the red letters. Listen to the sound. 🔊

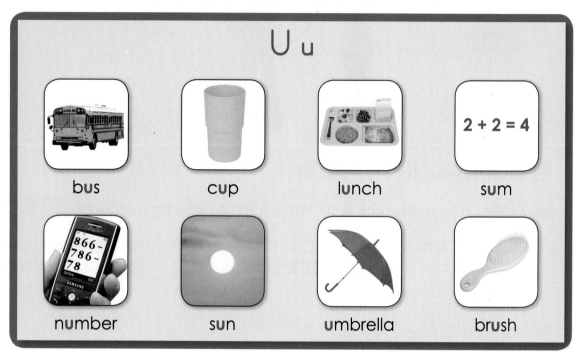

U u

bus cup lunch sum

number sun umbrella brush

2 Listen again. Repeat. 👂 🗣

3 Listen. Point to the word you hear. 👂 ✍

bus cup lunch sum number sun umbrella brush

4 Listen. Do you hear the <u>short u</u> sound? Choose yes or *no*. 🔊 ✍

1. yes   no
2. yes   no
3. yes   no
4. yes   no
5. yes   no
6. yes   no

Decoding

5 Listen and repeat. Read each letter. Say each sound.

1. c u p
2. b u t
3. s u m
4. r u b
5. m u g
6. f u n

6 Listen again. Repeat. Put the sounds together.

7 Listen. Which word do you hear? Write the word.

1. rub   rob
2. but   bat
3. cup   cap
4. cut   cot
5. run   ran
6. bun   bin

8 Listen and repeat.

1. Sam cut his lip.
2. Val got a lot of sun.
3. The cup is in the box.
4. Tom and Liz run to the bus.

Short u is different
from long u. See
pages 262, 426,
and 427.

● Letters and Sounds

Vowel: short e

1 Look at the red letters. Listen to the sounds.

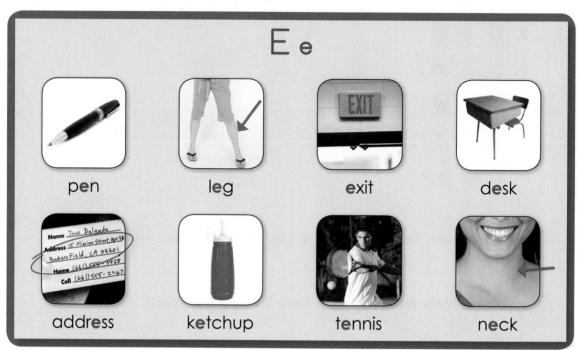

pen	leg	exit	desk
address	ketchup	tennis	neck

E e

2 Listen again. Repeat.

3 Listen. Point to the word you hear.

pen   leg   exit   desk   address   ketchup   tennis   neck

4 Listen. Do you hear the <u>short e</u> sound? Choose yes or no.

1. yes   no
2. yes   no
3. yes   no
4. yes   no
5. yes   no
6. yes   no

Decoding

5 Listen and repeat. Read each letter. Say each sound.

1. s e t
2. b e d
3. p e n
4. f e d
5. d e n
6. l e t

6 Listen again. Repeat. Put the sounds together.

7 Listen. Which word do you hear? Write the word.

1. red   rod
2. met   mat
3. set   sit
4. led   lid
5. bet   but
6. men   man

8 Listen and repeat.

1. Bill fed the cat.
2. Tom put the pen in a cup.
3. Let him set the mat in the den.
4. Dad let the men in.

Short e is different from long e. See page 338.

Decodable
Reader 1

Workbook
page 84–85

Independent Practice
CD-ROM

Welcome Unit • Chapter F   **79**

● Reading

A Personal Web Site

1 Read and listen. 📖 🎧

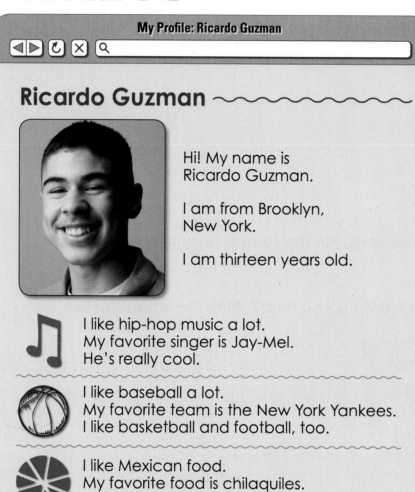

My Profile: Ricardo Guzman

Ricardo Guzman

Hi! My name is Ricardo Guzman.

I am from Brooklyn, New York.

I am thirteen years old.

I like hip-hop music a lot.
My favorite singer is Jay-Mel.
He's really cool.

I like baseball a lot.
My favorite team is the New York Yankees.
I like basketball and football, too.

I like Mexican food.
My favorite food is chilaquiles.
I like pizza, too.

2 👥 PAIR WORK **Read again. Answer the questions. Tell a classmate.** 📖 🗣

1. What is the boy's name?   His name is . . .
2. Where is he from?   He's from . . .
3. Who is his favorite singer?   His favorite singer is . . .
4. What is his favorite team?   His favorite team is . . .
5. What is his favorite food?   His favorite food is . . .

Writing

Writing About Your Favorites

1 Copy the chart. Write your information.

	I like	My favorite
music	_____	_____
singer or group	_____	_____
sports	_____	_____
team or player	_____	_____
food	_____	_____

2 Look at the Web site on page 80 again.
Write a Web site about yourself.

3 Read three classmates' Web sites. Make a chart.
Write their information.

Name	Favorites
_____	_____
_____	_____
_____	_____

4 PAIR WORK Tell a classmate about your other classmates.

> My favorite food is pasta. Adela likes pasta, too.

Project

Survey: Favorites

1 Write a chart like the one here. Ask teachers and students what their favorites are. Write the answers in the chart.

name			
favorite music			
favorite food			
favorite sport			
favorite movie			
favorite book			

Mrs. Mann, what is your favorite music?

My favorite music is classical.

2 GROUP WORK Work in groups. Share your answers. Make a chart with all the answers.

● Progress Check

Welcome Unit: Chapter F

1 Make a chart. Write the words in the correct places.

baseball	chicken	basketball	pizza	hip-hop	pop
soccer	football	ice cream	rock	classical	pasta

Music	Food	Sports

2 Write the missing words.

like	favorite	lot	OK	much	music

A: Do you like Latin (1) _music_ ?
B: Yes, I like it a (2) _a lot_ . How about you?
A: It's my (3) _favorite_ music!
B: Really? My favorite music is hip-hop. Do you (4) _like_ hip-hop?
A: It's (5) _ok_ .
B: How about pop music?
A: I don't like pop music very (6) _much_ .

3 Write the words in the correct order. Make sentences.

1. do you / kind / like? / of food / What
2. favorite / your / What's / sport?
3. very much. / I don't / classical music / like
4. favorite food / Korean / food. / My / is
5. a lot. / baseball / I / like

4 Say the sentences.

1. Bill fed the cat.
2. Tom set the pen on the mat.
3. Let him fix the fan in the den.
4. Don let the men in.

Objectives

Vocabulary
Places in your school
Reading a map

Listening and Speaking
Talking about locations
Giving directions

Letters and Sounds
Digraphs: sh, ch
Trigraphs: tch, dge
Digraphs: th, nk, ng

Reading
A poem, a picture, and
an artist

Writing
Writing directions

Project
A floor plan

Progress Check

● **Vocabulary**

1 Listen and point.

2 Listen and repeat.

3 Say and point.

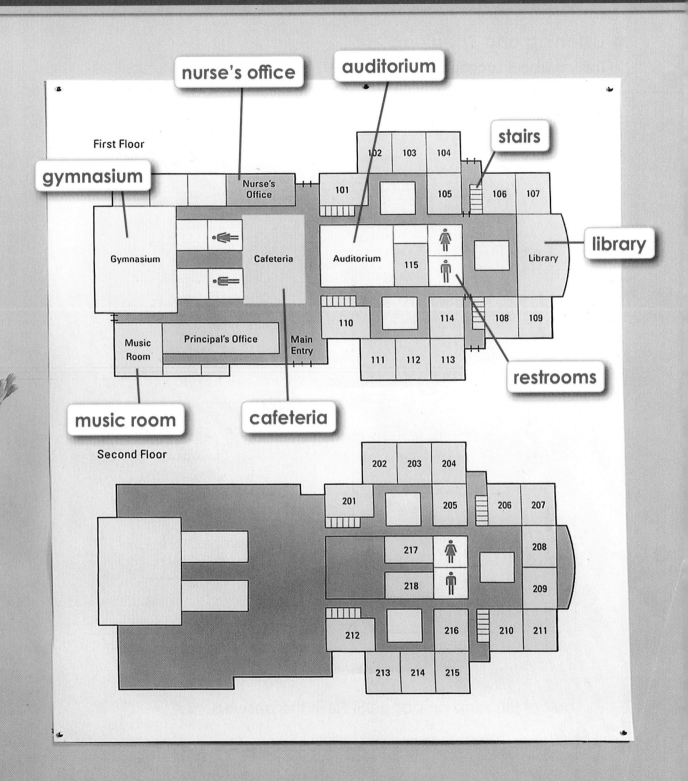

nurse's office

auditorium

stairs

gymnasium

First Floor

library

music room

cafeteria

restrooms

Second Floor

Vocabulary Log

Workbook page 87

Independent Practice CD-ROM

Listening and Speaking
Talking About Locations

1 Listen and repeat.

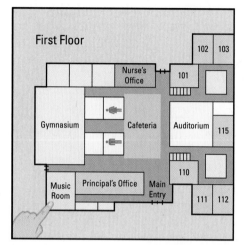

The music room is **on the first floor**.

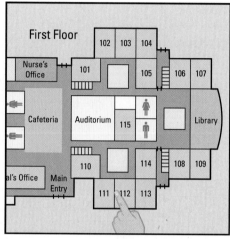

Room 111 is **next to** Room 112.

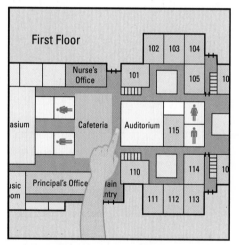

The auditorium is **across from** the cafeteria.

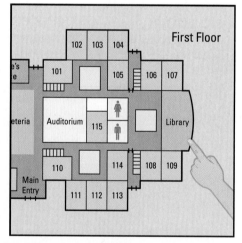

The library is **between** Room 107 and Room 109.

2 Look at the map on page 85. Fill in the answers.

1. Room 202 is on the _____ floor.

2. The nurse's office is _____ the cafeteria.

3. Room 103 is _____ Room 102 and Room 104.

4. The principal's office is _____ the music room.

3 **Read and listen.**

Excuse me. Where's the cafeteria?

The cafeteria is across from the auditorium.

Across from the auditorium?

Yes.

Great. Thanks.

You're welcome.

4 **Listen again. Repeat.**

5 **Listen. Match the words on the left with the locations on the right.**

1. The music room
2. Room 217
3. Room 115
4. Room 109

a. is next to the auditorium.
b. is next to the gymnasium.
c. is between Room 108 and the library.
d. is on the second floor.

6 **PAIR WORK** **Practice with a classmate. Use the map on page 85.**

Where's the gymnasium?

It's across from the music room.

1. the principal's office
2. Room 214
3. the auditorium
4. Room 107

7 **PAIR WORK** **Practice again. Talk about places in your school.**

Where's the nurse's office?

It's next to the principal's office.

Listening and Speaking

Giving Directions

1 Listen and repeat.

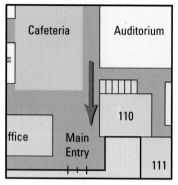

Go straight down this hall.

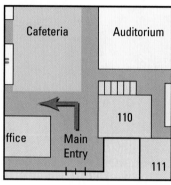

Turn left.

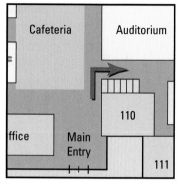

Turn right.

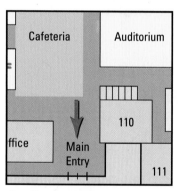

Go through the doors.

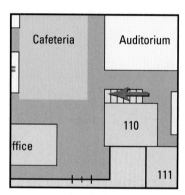

Go up the stairs.

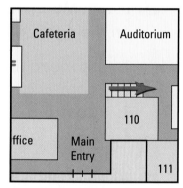

Go down the stairs.

2 Listen. Where do the people want to go? Choose the place.

1. **a.** Room 101   **b.** Room 102
2. **a.** Room 213   **b.** Room 214
3. **a.** nurse's office   **b.** cafeteria
4. **a.** auditorium   **b.** cafeteria

3 Listen again. Which words do you hear? Choose the answer.

1. **a.** before the auditorium   **b.** after the auditorium
2. **a.** go up the stairs   **b.** go down the stairs
3. **a.** on the left   **b.** turn left
4. **a.** after the cafeteria   **b.** across from the cafeteria

4 **Read and listen.**

Excuse me. How do I get to the library?

It's next to Room 112. Thanks.

Go straight down this hallway. Turn left after the girls' restroom. Then turn right. The library is next to Room 112.

You're welcome.

5 **Listen again. Look at the map.**

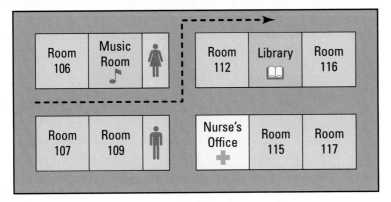

Room 106	Music Room	🚺
Room 112	Library	Room 116
Room 107	Room 109	🚹
Nurse's Office	Room 115	Room 117

6 **Listen again. Repeat.**

7 **PAIR WORK** **Give your classmate directions. Use the map on page 85.**

1. from the music room to the auditorium
2. from the auditorium to room 104
3. from Room 104 to the nurse's office
4. from the nurse's office to Room 208

8 **PAIR WORK** **Ask about places in your school. Repeat your classmate's directions.**

 How do I get to the cafeteria?

Vocabulary Log

Workbook page 90–91

Independent Practice CD-ROM

Letters and Sounds

Digraphs: sh, ch; Trigraphs: tch, dge

1 Look at the red letters. Listen to the sounds. 🔊

sh

| shoes | shirt | fish | cash |

ch

| chair | chin | March | sandwich |

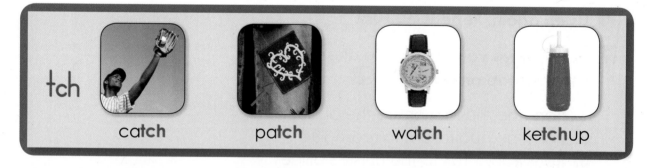

tch

| catch | patch | watch | ketchup |

dge

| bridge | judge | badge | hedge |

2 Listen again. Repeat.

3 Listen. Point to the word you hear.

shoes	shirt	fish	cash	chair	chips
March	sandwich	catch	patch	watch	hedge
ketchup	bridge	judge	badge		

Decoding

4 Listen and repeat. Read each letter. Say each sound.

1. sh o t   **5.** i tch

2. sh i p   **6.** p a tch

3. ch i n   **7.** e dge

4. ch a t   **8.** l o dge

5 Listen again. Repeat. Put the sounds together.

6 Listen. Which word do you hear? Write the word.

1. shop   chop   **4.** cash   catch
2. bash   badge   **5.** etch   edge
3. ship   chip   **6.** bash   batch

7 Listen and repeat.

1. Dan has an itch on his hand.
2. The dish is on the edge of the mat.
3. Ben and Ron catch big fish.
4. She will ship the box for him.

Decodable
Reader 2, 3

Workbook
page 92–93

Independent Practice
CD-ROM

Welcome Unit • Chapter G   **91**

Letters and Sounds

Digraphs: th, ng, nk

1 Look at the red letters. Listen to the sounds. 🔊

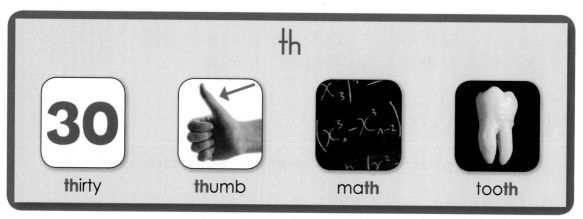

th

thirty   thumb   math   tooth

ng

ring   wing   king   sing

nk

bank   sink   drink   trunk

2 Listen again. Repeat.

3 Listen. Point to the word you hear.

thirty	thumb	math	tooth	ring	wing	king
sing	bank	sink	drink	trunk		

Decoding

4 Listen and repeat. Read each letter. Say each sound.

1. w i th

2. s a nk

3. th i n

4. b a th

5. th a nk

6. th i ng

5 Listen again. Repeat. Put the sounds together.

6 Listen. Which word do you hear? Write the word.

1. sing	sang	**4.** sank	thank		
2. think	sink	**5.** math	bath		
3. bang	bank	**6.** rink	ring		

7 Listen and repeat.

1. Meg and Tim thank the man for the ring.
2. Bob and Jan sing a song for Ken.
3. Ted is with Max in the den.
4. The cup sank in the bath.

Decodable
Reader 4, 5

Workbook
page 94–95

Independent Practice
CD-ROM

Welcome Unit • Chapter G **93**

● Reading

A Poem, a Picture, and an Artist

1 Read and listen.

Lost
by Jennifer Meldrum

Up or down?
Where do we go?

Left or right?
We don't know.

Across or between?
Where are we?

We're looking for an exit
We can't see!

Relativity, 1953, by M.C. Escher

About the artist

Maurits Cornelis Escher (1898–1972) was a famous artist. He was from the Netherlands. He liked to draw "impossible" spaces. Millions of people around the world enjoy Escher's pictures in museums, books, and on the Internet.

2 Answer the questions.

1. What is the title of the poem?
2. Who wrote it?
3. What is the name of the picture?
4. Who drew the picture?
5. Look at the picture. Where is the top of the picture? Point to the top.
6. Where is the bottom? Point to the bottom.
7. Turn the picture around. Point to the people going up.
8. Do you like this picture?

3 Read the poem aloud.

● Writing

Writing Directions

1 Look at the map. Read the directions.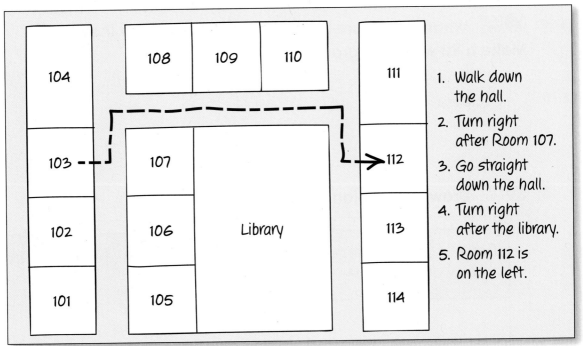

1. Walk down the hall.
2. Turn right after Room 107.
3. Go straight down the hall.
4. Turn right after the library.
5. Room 112 is on the left.

2 Write directions from your classroom to another place in your school. Draw a map.

3 PAIR WORK Read your directions to a classmate. Your classmate listens and points on your map.

4 PAIR WORK Listen again. Write your classmate's directions.

● Project

A Floor Plan

1 GROUP WORK **Work in a group. Look at the floor plan on page 85.**

2 GROUP WORK **What places are in your school? Where are they? Make a list with your group.**

> 1. cafeteria
> 2. principal's office

3 GROUP WORK **Draw a floor plan of your school.**

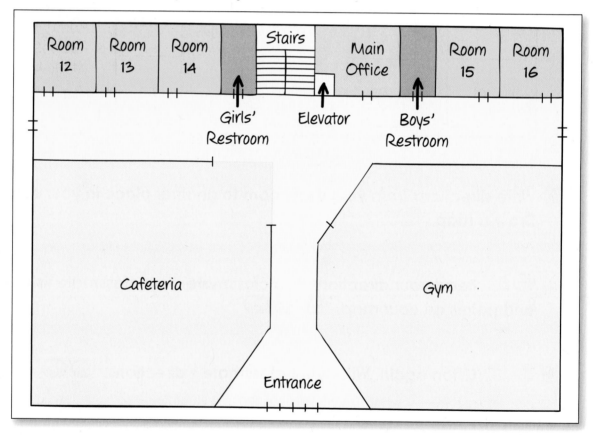

4 GROUP WORK **Share your floor plan with another group.**
How are your pictures the same?
How are they different?

Progress Check
Welcome Unit: Chapter G

1 Look at the map. Write the missing words.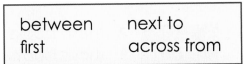

between	next to
first	across from

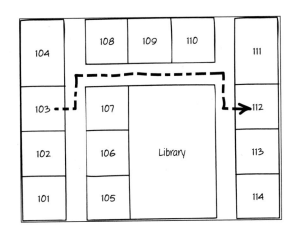

1. Room 108 is ▢ Room 109.
2. Room 112 is ▢ Room 111 and Room 113.
3. Room 107 is ▢ Room 103.
4. The library is on the ▢ floor.

2 Fill in the words.

stairs	this	after	next	up	straight	right	second

A: Excuse me. Is the art room on (1) ▢ floor?
B: No, it's on the (2) ▢ floor.
A: Oh. How do I get there?
B: Go (3) ▢ those (4) ▢ . Turn left.
A: Okay.
B: Then go (5) ▢ down the hall. Turn right (6) ▢ the girls' restroom.
A: Okay.
B: The art room is on your (7) ▢ . It's (8) ▢ to the music room.
A: Thanks a lot.
B: You're welcome.

3 Say the sentences.

1. Dad has an itch on his hand.
2. The dish is on the edge of the sink.
3. Rob and Dan catch fish.
4. Tim put a patch on the mat.
5. Meg and Tim thank the man for the ring.

Milestones to Achievement

● Vocabulary

Choose the correct answer.

1.
   A yellow triangle
   B green square
   C purple square
   D blue rectangle

2.
   A soccer
   B baseball
   C basketball
   D football

3. **33**
   A thirteen
   B thirty
   C thirty-three
   D three-thirty

4.
   A 3 pens
   B 4 bags
   C 4 books
   D 3 pencils

5.
   A these books
   B those books
   C this book
   D that book

6. **555-2943**
   A address
   B phone number
   C street
   D zip code

7.
   A pasta
   B salad
   C fruit
   D soup

8.
   A stairs
   B hallway
   C auditorium
   D library

● Writing

Put the words in the correct order to make sentences and questions. Use correct capitalization and punctuation.

Example: name / my / Jim / is   My name is Jim.

1. address / what's / your
2. take out / notebooks / please / your
3. you / do / have / class / math / on / Wednesday
4. nurse's / room / the / is / office / next to / the art
5. favorite / my / music / hip-hop / is
6. the library / do / how / get / I / to

Reading

Read. Answer the questions about the reading.

This is Anna. Anna is my classmate. She is from Mexico. My name is Marta. I'm from Colombia. Our English teacher is Mr. Thompson. Anna likes pizza in the cafeteria. She likes to listen to classical music in Mrs. Trang's music class. We have music class on Tuesday and Thursday. We have P.E. class on Monday and Wednesday. Anna doesn't like playing basketball in the gym. She likes soccer. I like basketball and soccer. She has a blue bag and I have a red bag.

1 **Anna is ____.**
- A Mexico
- B Mexican
- C Colombia
- D Colombian

2 **What doesn't Anna like?**
- A pizza
- B classical music
- C basketball
- D soccer

3 **When does Anna have music class?**
- A Monday
- B Tuesday
- C Wednesday
- D Friday

4 **What color is Marta's bag?**
- A red
- B blue
- C green
- D yellow

Letters and Sounds

Look. Say the word. What is the beginning sound?

1
- A b
- B f
- C g
- D m

2
- A v
- B n
- C r
- D d

3
- A q
- B z
- C y
- D h

4
- A sh
- B ch
- C th
- D c

Look. Say the word. What is the middle sound?

1
- A short a
- B short i
- C short o
- D short e

2
- A short a
- B short i
- C short u
- D short o

3
- A short i
- B short e
- C short u
- D short a

Look. Say the word. What is the ending sound?

1
- A b
- B f
- C g
- D m

2
- A th
- B nk
- C ng
- D dge

3
- A tch
- B ch
- C sh
- D h

4
- A x
- B r
- C v
- D b

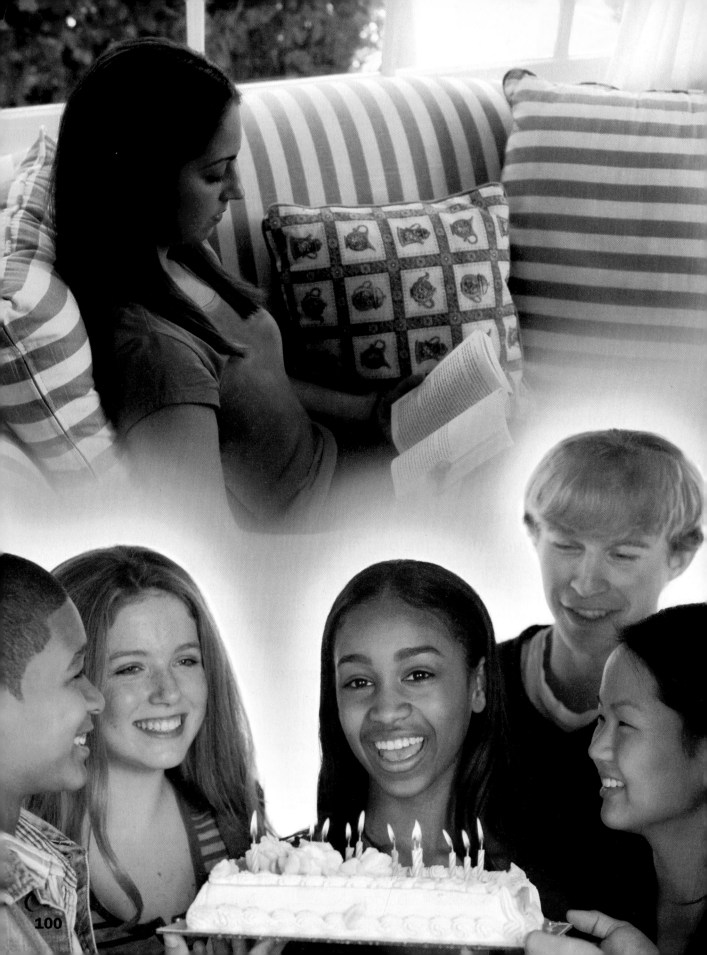

About Me

Talk About the Theme

1. Look at the photos. What are the people doing?
2. Do you do these things? Where? When?

Theme Activity

Write three questions it is OK for your partner to ask you. Your partner asks your questions. You answer. Ask your partner the questions your partner gives you.

CHAPTER 1

Part A

Objectives

Vocabulary
Classroom objects
Forms

Listening and Speaking
Welcoming a new student
Asking to borrow things

Grammar
Nouns and subject pronouns
The verb be
Possessive adjectives
Subjects and verbs

Writing Conventions
Capital letters and end
  punctuation
Declarative, exclamatory,
  and interrogative
  sentences

Word Study
Final blends: nd, nt, st, sk;
  mp, ct, ft
Final blends: lt, lp, lk, lf, ld
Syllabication

Writing
Emergency information form

● Vocabulary
Classroom Objects

schedule

calculator

ruler

computer and printer

workbook

cabinet

textbook

● Listening and Speaking

Welcoming a New Student

1 Listen and repeat the words on page 102.

2 **PAIR WORK** Read the vocabulary words on page 102. Your partner points to those objects in your classroom.

3 Read and listen.

> **Compound Words**
> Compound words are words made from other words. For example, **textbook** is a <u>book</u> with <u>text</u> (or information) but a **workbook** is a <u>book</u> to <u>work</u> in.

Ms. Miller: Welcome to the class. My name is Ms. Miller. I'm your teacher. What's your name?

Alex: Hello. My name is Alex Garcia.

Ms. Miller: Nice to meet you. Here is your textbook and workbook. There are rulers and calculators in the cabinet.

Alex: Thank you.

Ms. Miller: You're welcome.

4 Listen again. Repeat.

5 **PAIR WORK** Say the conversation again. Use new words for the blue words. You can use vocabulary from page 102.

> **✓ Checkpoint**
> 1. Do you have a calculator?
> 2. Does your classroom have a cabinet?

Vocabulary Log

Workbook page 97

Independent Practice CD-ROM

● Listening and Speaking
Asking to Borrow Things

1 **Read and listen.**

Nadia: Excuse me. Do you have a ruler?

Amy: Sorry. No, I don't.

Nadia: That's okay. Do you have a calculator?

Amy: Yes, I have a calculator.

Nadia: May I borrow it?

Amy: Sure. Here you are.

Nadia: Thanks.

Amy: You're welcome.

I have a calculator.   I don't have a calculator.

don't = do not

2 **Listen and repeat.**

3 **PAIR WORK** **Say the conversation again. Use new words for the blue words. You can use vocabulary from page 102.**

4 **Listen. Who has a pencil? Choose yes or no for each person.**

1. Tina	yes	no		4. Olivia	yes	no
2. Pablo	yes	no		5. Sam	yes	no
3. Jordan	yes	no				

5 **PAIR WORK** **Borrow things from your classmates.**

May I borrow a pencil?

Sure. Here you are.

● Vocabulary

Forms

1 Read the form. Look at the blue words.

Student Emergency Information Form

Date: _September 16, 2009_ Grade: _8_ Teacher: _Ms. Miller_

Name: _Garcia_   _Alex_   _Jorge_
       Last name   First name   Middle name

Parent or Guardian: _Ramona Garcia_

Phone Numbers:
     Home: _(512) 555-7689_
      Cell: _(512) 555-3462_

Address: _141 Oakland Avenue_   _#56_
           Street   Apt.
       Austin   _TX_   _78703_
        City   State   Zip Code

Parent or Guardian's Employer: _Woodland Offices_

Work Phone: _(512) 555-2974_

E-mail: _RGarcia@woodlandoffices.com_

2 Answer questions about the form.

1. What is the student's name?
2. Who is Alex's guardian?
3. Where does Alex live?
4. Who works for Woodland Offices?
5. What is Alex's home phone number?

> Alex**'s** address = the address of Alex
> student**'s** name = the name of the student

✓Checkpoint

1. What is Alex's address?
2. What is Alex's cell phone number?

Vocabulary Log   Workbook page 98   Independent Practice CD-ROM

● Grammar

Subjects and Verbs

A complete **sentence** has a **subject** and a **verb**.	
A **subject** tells who or what the sentence is about. A subject can be a **noun** or a **pronoun**.	A **verb** tells what the subject is or does. The verb changes form to match the subject.

	A **noun** is a person, place, or thing.	A **pronoun** takes the place of a noun.
person	**Mr. Jones** likes his job.	**He** is a teacher.
	The girl is a student.	**She** is in fourth grade.
place	**Oakland** is in California.	**It** is a large city.
	The library has many books.	**It** is a good place to study.
thing	**The book** is on the desk.	**It** is my textbook.
things	**The pens** are on the desk.	**They** are blue.

Say the subject pronoun for each noun.

 the students

they

1. Maria
2. Three books
3. Mr. Kim
4. The chair
5. Mr. and Mrs. Song

The Verb be

The verb **be** changes with the subject.

Remember: the subject pronoun **I** is always a capital letter.

The Verb be			
I	**am** a teacher.	We	**are** at school.
You	**are** a student.	You	**are** students.
He	**is** Toni.	They	**are** in the library.
She	**is** Maya.	They	**are** desks.
It	**is** a pen.		

Write the sentences with the correct verb be.

1. Martha ____ a nurse.
2. I ____ Pat.
3. The computer ____ off.
4. They ____ in class.

Workbook
page 99

Independent Practice
CD-ROM

Possessive Adjectives

Possessive adjectives tell who or what something belongs to.

Possessive Adjective	Sentence
my	I am a teacher. **My** name is Mr. Miller.
your	You are a student. **Your** teacher is Ms. Lopez.
his	He is from Colombia. **His** name is Pedro.
her	She is a nurse. **Her** office is in the school.
its	The cat is under the table. **Its** name is Bella.
our	We are in class. **Our** teacher is Mr. Miller.
their	They are from Russia. **Their** names are Ivan and Anna.

Write the sentences with the possessive adjective.

1. They are in class. _____ teacher is Ms. Garcia.
2. Michael is a nurse. _____ office is in a school.
3. She is from Haiti. _____ name is Marie.
4. We are students. _____ school is in Los Angeles.

Writing Conventions

Capitalization and Punctuation *Beginning and Ending Sentences*

Sentences begin with a **capital letter**. They end with a **punctuation mark**.

My name is Berta**.**

> **Declarative** sentences end with a **period (.)**.

Are you the teacher**?**

> **Interrogative** sentences, or questions, end with a **question mark (?)**.

Pat has a pencil**!**

> **Exclamatory** sentences end with an **exclamation point (!)**.

Apply Find examples of a declarative, interrogative, and exclamatory sentence in Unit 1 (pages 100–149).

✓Checkpoint

1. Write a sentence with the **verb be** and each subject pronoun.
2. Write sentences with the **possessive adjectives**.

GRAMMAR EXPANSION

Possessive Pronouns, Workbook page 101

Workbook page 100

Independent Practice CD-ROM

● Word Study

Final Blends: nd, nt, st, sk; mp, ct, ft

Phonemic Awareness

1 **Listen and repeat.**

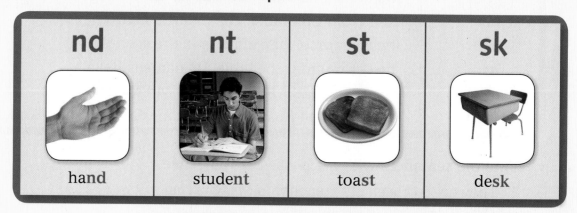

nd	nt	st	sk
hand	student	toast	desk

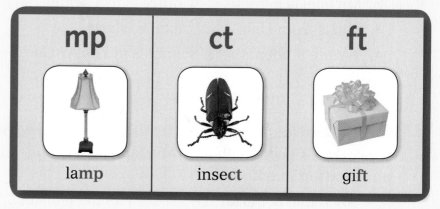

mp	ct	ft
lamp	insect	gift

Decoding

2 **Listen. Write the missing letters.**

1. pa ___   3. a ___   5. be ___   7. e ___
2. ca ___   4. le ___   6. ca ___   8. pe ___

3 **Listen again and repeat.**

Decodable
Reader 13–14

● Word Study

Final Blends: lt, lp, lk, lf, ld

___

Phonemic Awareness

1 Listen and repeat.

lt	lp	lk
salt	help	milk

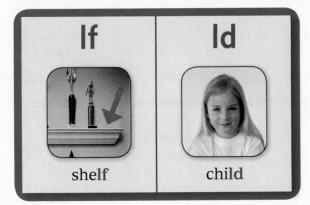

lf	ld
shelf	child

___

Decoding

2 Listen. Choose the word you hear.

1. help   held   4. gulf   gulp
2. welt   weld   5. silk   silt
3. elk   elf   6. melt   meld

3 Listen again and repeat.

✓Checkpoint

Read the words.
> silk
> land
> malt
> pact
> left

Decodable Reader 18

Workbook page 102

Independent Practice CD-ROM

● Word Study

Syllabication

Words are made of **syllables**. A **syllable** is a small group of sounds. Every syllable has one vowel sound and might have one or more consonant sound.

Word	Syllables	Number of Syllables
desk	desk	1
student	stu / dent	2
capital	cap / i / tal	3
dictionary	dic / tion / ar / y	4
interrogative	in / ter / rog / a / tive	5

1 **Listen. How many syllables does each word have?**

1. teacher 3. pencil 5. pen

2. adjective 4. syllabication 6. computer

Here are some rules for dividing words into syllables.

vowel – consonant – consonant – vowel V C C V	Divide between the two consonants. pen / cil let / ter
vowel – consonant – vowel V C V	If the vowel is short, divide after the *consonant*. cab / in If the vowel is long, divide after the *vowel*. ho / tel

2 **Copy the words. Draw lines between the syllables.**

1. textbook 3. borrow 5. pencil

2. adjective 4. schedule 6. printer

Divide these words into syllables.

letter

consonant

Workbook
page 103

Independent Practice
CD-ROM

● Writing Assignment
Emergency Information Form

> **Writing Prompt**
>
> Look at the form. Then fill in your own information form. Use the correct punctuation.

1. Read the student model.

School Emergency Information Form

Date: _September 6, 2009_ Grade: _9_ Teacher: _Ms. Jones_

Name: _____Fernandes_____Manuel_____Jose_____
            Last   **First**   **Middle**

Address: _____2395 La Brea St., #12_____
                              Street

_____Los Angeles_____CA_____90028_____
        City   **State**   **Zip Code**

Parent or Guardian:
Name: _Paulo Fernandes_

Phone: _(213) 555-2343_   Cell: _(213) 555-1013_

2. Copy the form. Fill in your own information.

Writing Checklist
1. I filled in all the spaces on the form.
2. I used capital letters and commas correctly.
3. I wrote the information neatly and clearly.

Part B

Objectives

Reading Strategy
Scan for information

Text Genre
An informal letter

Listening and Speaking
Retell the story

Literary Element
Imagery

Writing Conventions
Spelling irregular sight
words

Writing
Informal letter

Academic Vocabulary

scan | information

Academic Content

letter writing

● About the Reading

You are going to read a letter from a girl. Her name is Luisa. The letter is to her friend Maggie.

● Use Prior Knowledge

Talk About Keeping in Touch

When we talk, write, or call friends, we are "keeping in touch." How do you keep in touch with friends?

1. Copy the chart. Write ways you keep in touch.

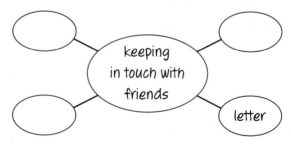

keeping in touch with friends

letter

2. **PAIR WORK** Name some friends or family who do not live with you. How do you keep in touch with them? Use information from your chart.

Vocabulary From the Reading
Learn, Practice, and Use Independently

Key Vocabulary

different

friendly

interesting

miss

nice

Learn Vocabulary Read the sentences. Use the context (the words around the highlighted words) to find the meaning of the **highlighted** words.

1. I am in Mr. Miller's class, but Sara is in a **different** class. She is in Ms. Lopez's class.

2. My new classmates are very **friendly**. Everyone said "hi" to me on my first day.

3. Science class is **interesting**. I learn something new every day.

4. I'm happy in my new school, but I want to see my old friends. I **miss** everybody in my old school.

5. This restaurant is **nice**. The food is good, and the food is served quickly!

Synonyms and Antonyms
 Synonyms are words that have the same meaning.
 Antonyms are words that have the opposite meaning.

Practice Vocabulary Look at the pictures. Match the Key Vocabulary words to their antonyms. The two answers in C are synonyms.

A.

same ____

B.

boring ____

C.

mean

1. ____
2. ____

Use Vocabulary Independently Write one sentence for each Key Vocabulary word. Read your sentences to a partner.

✓**Checkpoint**

1. Name three **friendly** people.
2. Name two **interesting** classes.
3. Name a person you **miss**.

● Academic Vocabulary

Vocabulary for the Reading Strategy

Word	Explanation	Sample Sentence	Visual Cue
scan *verb*	look quickly to find something	Joe **scans** the newspaper every day. He looks for the soccer scores.	
information *noun*	facts or things you can learn about someone or something	Students write personal **information** on the form.	Emergency Contact Form Name: _Joe Smith_ Phone number: _____ (213) 555-1011

Draw a picture or write a sentence for each word.

● Reading Strategy

Scan **for** Information

If you **scan** something, you don't read every word. You look quickly for the **information** you want. For example, you can **scan** a form to find a person's phone number.

● Text Genre

An Informal Letter

A **letter** is a message that you write on paper. An informal letter is to a friend or family member.

Here are parts of an informal letter. Closings and greetings begin with capital letters and have commas.

Informal Letter		
greeting	Dear *name*,	← commas
closing	Your friend,	
signature	*Luisa*	

✓Checkpoint

1. Look at the **information** on page 111. **Scan** to find the teacher's name.
2. Look at the letter on page 115. What is the **greeting**? What is the **closing**?

Vocabulary Log

Workbook
pages 106, 107

Independent Practice
CD-ROM

● Reading

Reading Focus Questions

As you read, think about these questions.

1. Who is Maggie?
2. What is **nice** about Luisa's school?

A Letter to a Friend

1 October 23, 2009

2 Dear Maggie,

3 How are you? I'm fine. San Rafael is a **nice** place.

4 My new school is very **nice**. It's very **different** from our school in Arizona, but the people are **friendly**. My sister likes it, too.

5 I have a lot of new friends. My classmates come from Mexico, Peru, China, Russia, and the United States. The class is very **interesting**.

6 My teacher's name is Ms. Douglas. She is a good teacher. We play a lot of games in her class. I like that! We have a lot of homework, too. Ms. Douglas makes it fun and **interesting**.

7 Write me a letter soon. Here's my new address:

8 Luisa Zarco
   1228 Novato Road
   San Rafael, CA 94903

9 Tell your family "hi" for me. Can you visit me sometime in San Rafael? I **miss** everybody there!

10 Your friend,
   Luisa

> **Reading Strategy**
>
> **Scan for information** Where does Luisa live now?

> ✔ **Reading Check**
>
> 1. **Recall facts** Where is Luisa's old school?
> 2. **Understand author's motivation** Why is Luisa writing to Maggie?

Reading Comprehension Questions

Think and Discuss

1. **Recall facts** What is Luisa's new address?

2. **Explain** What does Luisa like about her teacher?

3. **Make inferences** Why do you think Luisa wrote this letter to Maggie?

4. **Relate to your own experiences** Have you ever started classes at a new school? Did you **miss** your old school? Do you write letters to your friends from the other class?

5. **Revisit the Reading Focus Questions** Go back to page 115 and discuss the questions.

Listening and Speaking

Retell the Story

 **PAIR WORK** Imagine you are Luisa. Instead of writing a letter, you call your friend on the telephone to tell her the **nice** things about your new school.

1. Make a list of the things Luisa wants to tell Maggie.

> 1. San Rafael is **nice**.
> 2. My sister likes it.

2. Look at your notes. Think about the topic. Think about the questions: who, what, when, and where.

3. Tell Maggie about your school. Your notes are to help you stay on topic and be organized. Do NOT read them to your partner.

4. Use complete sentences with a subject and a verb when you speak.

5. As you listen, show your partner that you think he or she is **interesting**. Think about your gestures and expressions. Use the **Phrases for Conversation**.

Phrases for Conversation

Responding to People

Really?
That's **interesting**.
What else?

Workbook
page 108

Independent Practice
CD-ROM

● Literary Element

Imagery

When a writer uses a lot of adjectives to describe a place, we can see that place in our mind. This is called **imagery**.

Look at the adjectives in Luisa's letter: **nice**, good, **friendly**, **interesting**, **different**. These adjectives help you imagine Luisa's new school.

Describe your favorite place to a partner. Use different adjectives to create imagery.

> **Synonyms**
> Use a **thesaurus** to find synonyms. For example, what synonyms can you find for "nice" to describe a place?

Writing Conventions

Spelling *Irregular Sight Words*

Sight words are words you hear and read often.

PAIR WORK Say the words. Spell the words. Say the words.

were, w-e-r-e, were

| were | says | why | what | was | said | who |

Apply Write the sentences with the correct word.

1. W h o is your new teacher?
2. W h a t is her name?
3. W h y isn't Omar here yet?
4. I w a s born in Dallas.
5. The books w e r e already on the desk.
6. Mario s a y s the new teacher is **nice**.
7. Ms. Douglas s a i d our test is Tuesday.

PAIR WORK Say one of the words above. Your partner spells it.

> **✓ Checkpoint**
> 1. What kind of words can you use to describe a place or a person?
> 2. Spell **were** aloud.

● Writing Assignment

Informal Letter

Writing Prompt

Write an informal letter to a friend. Tell your friend about your school, your teacher, and your friends. Use the verb *be*, subject pronouns, and possessive adjectives correctly. Use adjectives to describe people and things.

Write Your Informal Letter

1. Read the student model.

date

Student Model

greeting

November 3, 2009

Dear Raj,

How are you? I'm fine. I am happy here in New York. My new school is very nice. The people are friendly and the classes are interesting. I am on the basketball team. It's really fun! We practice every day after school. I have a lot of new friends here. My classmates are from many different places. They are from the United States, Guatemala, the Philippines, Haiti, Albania, and Ethiopia.

Here's my new address:

Soo Hee Kim

3228 Broome St.

New York, NY 10003

Write me a letter soon!

Take care, ← closing

Soo Hee

signature

body

Writing Cues

Notice the commas.
1. in the date
2. in the greeting
3. in the address
4. in the closing

Notice the capital letters.
1. in the greeting
2. in the names
3. in the address
4. in the closing

2. **Brainstorm.** Write notes for your letter.

    a. Who is the letter to?

    b. What place or people are you describing?

    c. What words can you use to describe them?

3. **Write your letter.**

    a. Use the correct parts of the letter, shown on page 118.

    b. Use correct punctuation.

4. **Revise.** Reread your letter. Add, delete, or rearrange words or sentences to make your letter clearer. Use the editing and proofreading symbols on page 493 to help you mark the changes you need to make.

5. **Edit.** Use the **Writing Checklist** to help you find problems and errors.

Writing Checklist
1. I have all the parts of an informal letter.
2. I used the verb *be,* subject pronouns, and possessive adjectives correctly.
3. I capitalized the first word of each sentence.
4. I used capital letters and end punctuation correctly.
5. I wrote neatly and clearly.
6. I used descriptive adjectives to help the reader imagine my school.

Progress Check

How well did you understand this chapter? Try to answer the questions. If necessary, go back to the pages listed for a review.

Skills	Skills Assessment Questions	Pages to Review
Vocabulary	What classroom objects can you list? What personal **information** can you give?	102–105
Grammar	What is a subject? What is a verb? What are nouns? What are pronouns? What are the forms of the verb **be**? What are possessive adjectives?	106 106 106 107
Writing Conventions	**Capitalization and Punctuation:** What kinds of sentences did you learn about? What is at the beginning of all sentences? What kind of punctuation is at the end of each kind of sentence? **Spelling:** What irregular sight words did you learn to spell?	107 117
Word Study	What rules do you know for dividing words into syllables?	110
Vocabulary From the Reading	What do these words mean? • **different**, **friendly**, **interesting**, **miss**, **nice**	113
Academic Vocabulary	What does **scan** mean? What does **information** mean?	114
Reading Strategy	When do you **scan** for **information**?	114
Text Genre	What is the text genre of "A Letter to a Friend"?	114
Reading Comprehension	What was "A Letter to a Friend" about?	116
Listening and Speaking	**Phrases for Conversation:** What phrases can you use to respond to people and show interest?	116
Literary Element	What does **imagery** mean?	117

Assessment Practice

Read this informal letter. Then answer Questions 1 through 4.

1   January 6, 2009

2   Dear Robert,

3   How are you? I am fine. I have a new friend. His name is Min.
He's in my social studies and science classes. He is very nice and we
have fun. His desk is next to my desk in social studies class. He is in a
different math class.

4   I like my math class, too. It is interesting. We have a new textbook.
We don't have a calculator in class. The teacher says this will make
us good in math. Call me at (123) 555-6789 and tell me how you are.
I miss you!

5   Your friend,

    Miguel

---

1 Find the word that has been divided into syllables correctly.

   A cal-cul-ator

   B cal-cu-la-tor

   C ca-lcu-lat-or

   D calc-u-lator

2 Scan the letter to find Miguel's phone number. What is it?

   A (321) 555-6789

   B (123) 555-9876

   C (123) 555-6789

   D (321) 555-9876

3 What adjective does Miguel use to describe his math class?

   A good   C different

   B interesting   D nice

4 What part of this letter tells you that Robert and Miguel are friends?

   A closing   C date

   B greeting   D signature

Writing on Demand: Informal Letter

Write an informal letter to a family member. Tell your
family member about one class at school. Make sure you
use the verb be, subject pronouns, and possessive adjectives
correctly. **(20 minutes)**

> **Writing Tip**
> Before you
> write, think about
> adjectives that
> describe your class
> at school.

CHAPTER 2

Part A

Objectives

Vocabulary
School events
Ordinal numbers

Listening and Speaking
Talking about school events
Talking about dates

Grammar
Simple present tense

Writing Conventions
Capitalization and
   punctuation: Capital
   letters and commas
   in dates

Word Study
/aw/ sound in all, alk

Writing
Invitation

● Vocabulary
School Events

field trip

school concert

art show

graduation

football game

basketball game

pep rally

school dance

a play

Part A

● Listening and Speaking
Talking About School Events

1 Listen and repeat the words on page 122.

2 **PAIR WORK Do you have these events at your school?**

We have a school dance.

We don't have a play.

Ordinal Numbers

3 Listen and repeat the ordinal numbers.

Ordinal Numbers 1–12

1st	first	5th	fifth	9th	ninth
2nd	second	6th	sixth	10th	tenth
3rd	third	7th	seventh	11th	eleventh
4th	fourth	8th	eighth	12th	twelfth

4 Say and write the correct ordinal number.

Example: 5th _fifth_

1. 3rd ____
2. ____ seventh
3. 2nd ____
4. 10th ____
5. ____ first
6. ____ twelfth
7. ____ eight
8. 6th ____

5 **PAIR WORK Talk about the months of the year.**

What is the fourth month of the year?

April is the fourth month of the year.

Multiple-meaning Words

Multiple-meaning **words** are words that have more than one meaning. For example, **play** in *play basketball* means to take part in a game but *a play* is a show.

Look **dance** up in a dictionary to find the different meanings.

Build Vocabulary

Months of the Year and Their Abbreviations

January (Jan.)
February (Feb.)
March (Mar.)
April (Apr.)
May (May)
June (Jun.)
July (Jul.)
August (Aug.)
September (Sep.)
October (Oct.)
November (Nov.)
December (Dec.)

Vocabulary Log   Workbook page 111   Independent Practice CD-ROM

● Vocabulary

Ordinal Numbers

Ordinal Numbers 13–30

1 Listen and say these words.

Ordinal Numbers 13–30		
13th thirteenth	19th nineteenth	25th twenty-fifth
14th fourteenth	20th twentieth	26th twenty-sixth
15th fifteenth	21st twenty-first	27th twenty-seventh
16th sixteenth	22nd twenty-second	28th twenty-eighth
17th seventeenth	23rd twenty-third	29th twenty-ninth
18th eighteenth	24th twenty-fourth	30th thirtieth

2 **PAIR WORK** Say an ordinal number. Your partner writes it.

Saying Dates

Write dates like this: January 22
Read dates like this: January twenty-second

3 **PAIR WORK** Say the month. Use an ordinal number for the date.

 What's the date today?

It's **October thirteenth**.

1. January 7   3. May 10   5. October 2
2. March 15   4. August 24   6. November 27

4 Read and listen.

 When is **your birthday**?

My birthday is December nineteenth.

5 **GROUP WORK** Ask your classmates when are their birthdays.

● Listening and Speaking

Talking About Dates

1 Listen and repeat.

When is **our science test?**

It's on **February sixth**.

2 **PAIR WORK** Say the conversation again. Use new words for the blue words. Talk about these events.

1. our math test   November 15
2. our field trip   May 21
3. the pep rally   September 19
4. the school concert   April 29
5. the play   January 31

3 Listen. Match the event with the correct date.

1. science test   a. May 3rd
2. school concert   b. May 4th
3. basketball game   c. May 7th
4. Carlos's birthday   d. May 13th

Talking About Days, Dates, and Months

Read the sentences. Look at the bold words. These are called **prepositions**. Look at what follows the prepositions.

> I have a concert **on** Monday.
> I have a field trip **on** February sixteenth.
> I have a school dance **in** April.

What rules can you make?

1. Use ▩▩▩ before days of the week.
2. Use ▩▩▩ before a date.
3. Use ▩▩▩ before a month of the year.

> **✓Checkpoint**
> 1. When is your next English test?
> 2. When is your birthday?

Vocabulary Log

Workbook page 112

Independent Practice CD-ROM

● Grammar

Simple Present: have

The verb **have** changes with some subjects.

Subject	Verb *have*	Subject	Negative of *have*
I You We They	**have** a class today.	I You We They	**do not have** a class today. **don't have** a class today.
He She It	**has** a class today.	He She It	**does not have** a class today. **doesn't have** a class today.

1 Ask three classmates about their school schedules. Write notes.

 When do you have science?

I have science on Friday.

Checkpoint

Write sentences with dates. Use the verb **have**.

2 Tell a partner about your classmates' schedules.

 Lucia has science on Friday. Bryan and Eddie have science on Tuesday.

Writing Conventions

Punctuation *Capitalization and Commas in Dates*

Use capital letters for days of the week and months of the year. Use commas when you write dates.

I was born on Wednesday, January 7th, 1998.

Apply Write these sentences. Put in the commas.

1. We have a math test on Tuesday April 5th.

2. George Washington was born on February 22 1732.

Workbook
page 113

Independent Practice
CD-ROM

● Grammar

Simple Present Tense

Use the **simple present tense** to talk about things that happen regularly.

> I **go** to school five days a week.

Use the **simple present tense** to talk about things that are true.

> Ricardo **speaks** Spanish and English.

Simple Present Tense			
subject	simple present	subject	negative of simple present
I You We They	**read** every day.	I You We They	**do not read** every day. **don't read** every day.
He She It	**reads** every day.	He She It	**does not read** every day. **doesn't read** every day.

Note: Add **s** to the verb if it follows he, she, or it.

1 **PAIR WORK** **Make sentences about yourself.**

 I speak Spanish. I don't play baseball.

I don't speak Spanish. I play baseball.

1. speak Spanish
2. play baseball
3. read books
4. listen to music
5. make breakfast
6. write e-mail

2 **PAIR WORK** **Tell another classmate about your partner.**

 Min-ho doesn't speak Spanish. He plays baseball.

✓ **Checkpoint**

Make these sentences negative.
a. I play football.
b. She reads Chinese.

● Word Study
/aw/ Sound in all, alk

Phonemic Awareness

1 Listen and repeat.

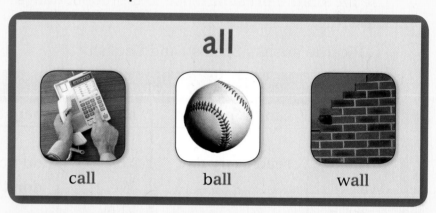

all

call   ball   wall

> You don't say the "l" sound in these words. Be careful!

alk

walk   talk   chalk

Decoding

2 Listen. Write the missing letter or letters.

1. t _____   3. t _____   5. _____ all
2. f _____   4. _____ alk   6. _____ all

3 Listen again and repeat.

Decodable
Reader 9

Workbook
page 116

Independent Practice
CD-ROM

Writing Assignment

Invitation

> **Writing Prompt**
>
> Write an invitation.

1. Read the student model.

You're invited!

What: It's Katie's birthday.
Where: The party is at
28 Cedar Lane
Tallahassee.
When: Sunday, May 17
2:00 – 4:00 p.m.

R.S.V.P.
(850) 555-3459

> **Writing Cues**
> R.S.V.P. is the abbreviation for the French phrase *répondez s'il vous plait*. It means "respond please."

2. Write your own invitation.

    a. What kind of party will you have?

    b. When and where will it be?

Writing Checklist

1. I told people what kind of party it is.

2. I told people where and when the party is.

3. I used capital letters and commas correctly.

4. I used the simple present tense correctly.

Objectives

Reading Strategy
Set a purpose for reading

Text Genre
Textbook

Listening and Speaking
Create and solve a math equation

Text Elements
Graphs and charts

Reading Fluency
Rapid word recognition: multisyllable math words

Writing
Word problems

Academic Vocabulary

set | purpose

Academic Content

math equations

● About the Reading

You are going to read an excerpt from a math textbook.

● Use Prior Knowledge

Solve Math Problems

Look at these math problems. Read and say the sentences.

2	+	3	=	5
two	**plus** three	**equals**	five	

10	−	6	=	4
ten	**minus** six	**equals** four		

> **Synonyms**
> In math problems, **equals** is the same as **is**. You can also say **two plus three is five**.

7	×	2	=	14
seven	**times**	two	**equals**	fourteen

50	÷		5	=	10
fifty	**divided**	**by**	five	**equals**	ten

PAIR WORK Say these math problems with a partner.

1. 5 + 7 = 12
2. 23 − 9 = 14
3. 5 × 6 = 30
4. 100 ÷ 5 = 20
5. 98 + 3 = 101
6. 442 − 137 = 305
7. 17 × 8 = 136
8. 176 ÷ 16 = 11

Vocabulary From the Reading
Learn, Practice, and Use Independently

Key Vocabulary

add

diagram

divide

equation

multiply

operation

solve

subtract

Learn Vocabulary Look at the pictures. What do the **highlighted** words mean?

add

subtract

multiply

divide

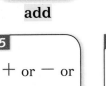
operation

equation

solve

diagram

Practice Vocabulary Write the correct Key Vocabulary word in the sentences.

1. There are 5 people. When you ____ 2, there are 3 left.
2. A ____ is a picture to help you understand an **equation**.
3. If you ____ 5 by 2, the answer is 10.
4. When you ____ $20 between four people, each gets $5.
5. Write this ____ on the board: 2 plus 2 equals 4.
6. This problem is easy to ____ . I can answer it.
7. I have 2 boxes. If you ____ 2 more boxes, I have 4 boxes.
8. There are 3 ____ in the **equation** $(2 + 3) \times (10 \div 2) = 25$.

Multiple-meaning Words

left can mean "remaining"
or
left can mean to the left ←

Use Vocabulary Independently Write an **equation**. Don't write the answer. Your partner **solves** it.

✓**Checkpoint**

Say and **solve** this **equation** in English:

$14 \div 7 = $ ____

Vocabulary Log

Workbook page 118

Independent Practice CD-ROM

● Academic Vocabulary

Vocabulary for the Reading Strategy

Word	Explanation	Sample Sentence	Visual Cue
set *verb*	to decide or plan	Teachers **set** the class rules. They tell students what they need to do.	CLASS RULES
purpose *noun*	a reason for doing something	The **purpose** of a dictionary is to help you understand words you don't know.	Guardian? "Person who takes care of a child."

Draw a picture or write a sentence for each word.

● Reading Strategy

Set a Purpose for Reading

When you **set** a **purpose** for reading something, you decide *why* you read it. For example, you want to **solve** an **equation**. You look closely at the examples in a math textbook.

● Text Genre

Textbook

Look at the features of a math textbook. Find these elements in the reading on pages 133–135.

Textbook	
explanations	tell you how to do something
examples	show you how to do something, and give you the answers
diagrams	pictures and charts that can help you understand something
exercises	math problems for you to **solve**

✓ Checkpoint

1. **Set** a plan for today. Make a list of what you need to do.
2. What is the **purpose** of writing down new vocabulary in a notebook?

Vocabulary Log

Workbook pages 119, 120

Independent Practice CD-ROM

Reading

Reading Focus Questions

As you read, think about these questions.

1. What is a word problem?

2. What can I use to help me understand word problems?

Chapter 2

How to Solve a Word Problem

You know 2 + 2 = 4. You also know how to say "two plus two equals four." Now read this word problem:

> Michael has two books. Lisa gives him two
> more books. How many books does he have?

This is the same as 2 + 2 = 4. A word problem is the same as a math problem. It uses words to tell you the problem.

Explanation

Word problems are not hard to **solve**. Just follow these steps:

1. Read the word problem. Do you understand all the words?	Michael has two books. Lisa gives him two more books. How many books does he have?
2. What is the question? What do you need to find?	How many books does he have? *You need to find the number of books.*
3. What information can you find in the word problem?	Michael has 2 books. Lisa gives Michael 2 more books.
4. What do you need to do to this information? **Add? Subtract? Multiply? Divide?**	Add (+)
5. Write the problem as an **equation**.	2 + 2 = ?
6. **Solve** the **equation**.	2 + 2 = 4

Reading Strategy

Set a purpose for reading What is the purpose of an explanation?

✔ **Reading Check**

1. **Recall facts** Which math **operation** is used in the explanation?

2. **Understand purpose** Why does the author say word problems are not hard to **solve**?

Using Diagrams

Sometimes you can draw a **diagram**. This is a picture that can help you understand the word problem. Look at these examples.

Reading Strategy

Set a purpose for reading How can examples help you in reading?

Example 1

Ms. Walker has 18 pencils to give to her students. There are 6 students in her class. How many pencils does each student get?

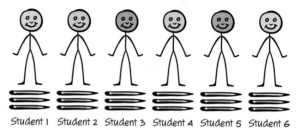

Student 1 Student 2 Student 3 Student 4 Student 5 Student 6

What is the math **equation** for this word problem?
18 (pencils) ÷ 6 (students) = 3 (pencils for each student)

Example 2

Sandra **solved** 25 problems in math class. Vinh **solved** 5 more problems than Sandra. How many math problems did Vinh **solve**?

What is the math **equation** for this word problem?
25 (problems) + 5 (problems) = 30 (problems)

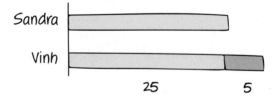

Exercises

Reading Strategy

Set a purpose for reading What do you need to do after reading each word problem?

1. All the students in sixth grade like pizza. Forty-eight students like cheese pizza. Thirty-one students like pepperoni pizza, and twenty-one students like mushroom pizza. How many students are in sixth grade?

Kind of Pizza Students Like

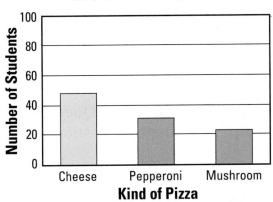

2. Jennifer is reading an interesting book. The book has 324 pages. She can read 36 pages a day. How many days does she need to finish the book?

3. Tom had 24 markers. He gives 5 to his younger brother. How many markers does Tom have now?

4. Dawn likes to run. She runs 5 miles every day. If she runs every day, how many miles can she run in one week?

Reading Check

1. **Recall facts** What is the title of this section?

2. **Identify processes** What is the math **operation** used in each exercise above?

3. **Identify key words** Read a problem from this page. Use your knowledge of vocabulary to guess how to **solve** the problem.

Reading Comprehension Questions

Think and Discuss

1. **Recall facts** How many steps are given to **solve** a word problem?

2. **Identify steps in a process** What is the second step in **solving** a word problem?

3. **Draw conclusions** Why is it important to understand all the words in the word problem before you **solve** it?

4. **Understand genre features** Did you draw any **diagrams** to help you **solve** the problems on page 135? Why or why not?

5. **Revisit the Reading Focus Questions** Go back to page 133 and discuss the questions.

Listening and Speaking

Create and Solve a Math Equation

1. Read these **equations** aloud.

   a. 20 + 38 = 58   **e.** 12 × 13 = 156

   b. 17 × 2 = 34   **f.** 98 – 89 = 9

   c. 48 ÷ 3 = 16   **g.** 184 ÷ 23 = 8

   d. 34 – 21 = 13   **h.** 37 + 36 = 73

2. **PAIR WORK** Present one of the exercises from page 135 to the class. Explain each step, using the steps for **solving** a word problem on page 133.

3. Think about the steps to **solve** the problem. Organize the steps in a logical order.

4. Listen to your classmates' presentations. Take notes. Follow the directions. **Solve** the word problems. As you listen, think about the **purpose** of the presentation.

5. As you **solve** the problem, say the steps again.

Phrases for Conversation

Presenting Steps in a Process

First, I read the problem.
Second, I look for the question.
Third, . . .
Fourth, . . .
Fifth, . . .
Sixth, . . .

Workbook
page 121

Independent Practice
CD-ROM

● Text Elements

Graphs and Charts

Graphs and **charts** can give different information about the same numbers.

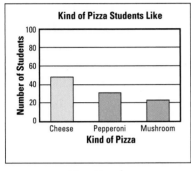

Bar Graph

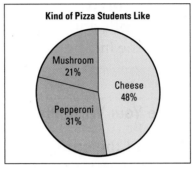

Pie Chart

The **bar graph** shows how many students like each kind of pizza. The **pie chart** shows the percentage of students who like the pizza.

Look at the graph and chart above.

1. How many students like pepperoni pizza?

2. In which **diagram** is it easy to see that almost half (50%) the students like cheese pizza?

> **Build Vocabulary**
>
> A **percentage** (%) is a number from 100.

● Reading Fluency

Rapid Word Recognition: Multisyllable Math Words

In Chapter 1, you learned about syllables. Look at the chart. How many syllables does each word have?

1. Listen and repeat.

mul/ti/ply	sub/tract	di/vide	ad/di/tion	e/qua/tion
mul/ti/pli/ca/tion	sub/trac/tion	di/vi/sion	di/a/gram	e/quals

2. Read the words aloud three times. Have your partner time you.

3. How many words can you say in 30 seconds?

> **✓Checkpoint**
>
> 1. What does a **bar graph** show?
> 2. What does a **pie chart** show?

Workbook
page 122

Independent Practice
CD-ROM

Writing Assignment

Word Problems

Writing Suggestion

Set a **purpose** for each word problem. In a word problem, the question you ask is the main **purpose**.

Writing Prompt

Write a word problem for each: **add**, **subtract**, **multiply**, and **divide**. Use your own information, or use the information in the chart below to help you.

Write Your Word Problems

1. Read the student model.

Student Model

Word Problems

1. Mr. Lydon's class has 24 students. Each student has 2 red pens. How many red pens do Mr. Lydon's students have?

2.

margins

Mr. Lydon's class has:
24 students
13 girls
11 boys
48 red pens
16 dictionaries
4 computers
72 pencils
30 math books
27 desks
2 whiteboards
12 markers

2. **Brainstorm.** For each word problem, first write the question you want to answer. Then choose information you want to use in the problem.

3. **Write your word problems.** As you write, print neatly. Watch your spacing between words and sentences. Leave space for the left and right margins.

4. **Revise.** Read your word problems. Try **solving** each one. **Add**, delete, or rearrange words or sentences to make your paragraph clearer. Use the editing and proofreading symbols on page 493 to help you mark the changes you need to make.

5. **Edit.** Use the **Writing Checklist** to help you find problems and errors.

Writing Checklist
1. I wrote a word problem for each: **add**, **subtract**, **multiply**, **divide**.
2. I **set** a **purpose** for each problem.
3. I numbered my word problems.
4. I wrote neatly and clearly.
5. I used the present tense correctly.

6. **Publish.** Read a word problem aloud to the class. Think about when to pause and when to read without stopping. Try to speak naturally.

7. **Listen.** Listen to your classmates' word problems. Take notes. Follow the directions. Solve the **equations**.

Progress Check

MILESTONESTRACKER

How well did you understand this chapter? Try to answer the questions. If necessary, go back to the pages listed for a review.

Skills	Skills Assessment Questions	Pages to Review
Vocabulary	What events does your school have? What are the months of the year? What are the ordinal numbers from first through thirty-first?	**122–124**
Grammar	When do you use the simple present tense? Make this sentence negative: I have a concert.	**126** **127**
Writing Conventions	**Punctuation and Capitalization:** Write this date correctly: Monday June 14 2010	**126**
Vocabulary From the Reading	What do these words mean? • **add, diagram, divide, equation, multiply, operation, solve, subtract**	**131**
Academic Vocabulary	What does **set** mean? What does **purpose** mean?	**132**
Reading Strategy	How can **setting** a **purpose** for reading help you understand a reading better?	**132**
Text Genre	What is the text genre of "How to **Solve** a Word Problem"?	**132**
Reading Comprehension	What is "How to **Solve** a Word Problem" about?	**136**
Listening and Speaking	**Phrases for Conversation:** What phrases can you use to present the steps in a process for **solving** a word problem?	**136**
Text Elements	What can you tell from reading **graphs** and **charts**?	**137**
Reading Fluency	Why is it helpful to **read numbers aloud**?	**137**

Assessment Practice

Read these paragraphs. Then answer Questions 1 through 4.

How to Use a Bar Graph

1   Kim-Li asks the people in her class what they want to do. Seven people want to play a football game. Three people want to act in a play. Nine people want to go on a field trip.

2   She makes a bar graph to compare these numbers. The title of her bar graph tells you what it is about. The bars show how many students want to do each activity. To read the graph, look at the first bar. You can see that it reaches to the number 7. This means seven people want to play football. Do the same for the second and third bars.

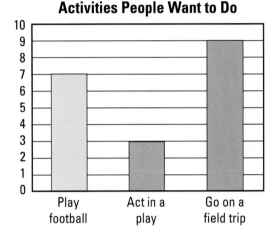

Activities People Want to Do

---

1 Read this sentence from paragraph 1.

> Three people want to act in a play.

What does a play mean in this sentence?

A a show   C a trip

B a game   D a test

2 Why would you read this selection?

A to learn about football

B to learn about field trips

C to learn about bar graphs

D to learn about acting in a play

3 What does the title of a bar graph tell you?

A how many people play football

B how many students want to do each activity

C what Kim-Li likes to do

D what the bar graph is about

4 What is the text genre of this selection?

A form

B informal letter

C short story

D textbook

Writing on Demand: Word Problems

Write a math word problem for adding or subtracting. Use the information in the bar graph. **(20 minutes)**

> **Writing Tip**
> Make sure you ask a question in your word problem. After you write it, try to solve the problem.

Objectives

Listening and Speaking
Describe an event

Writing
Thank-you note

Word Study
Word families

● Listening and Speaking Workshop
Describe an Event

> **Topic**
>
> Describe an activity you do often. Describe a hobby, a sporting event, or something you do. Describe the activity in order. Tell what happens first, second, third, etc.

1. **Choose an Event or Activity to Describe**
   Think about an activity you like and do often.

2. **Brainstorm**
   Think about these focus questions and take notes. Answer these questions in your presentation.
   a. What is the event or activity?
   b. Why do I like it?
   c. What do I do for the activity? In what order do I do these things?
   d. What words can I use to help my listeners imagine the event?

3. **Plan**
   Create a visual to show a part of the event. It can be a poster with pictures. It can be an object you use for the activity. It can be a computer presentation.

4. **Organize Your Presentation**
   Write your ideas on note cards. Use one note card for each focus question. Make a note card to explain the visual. Also, write a note card with the questions you want to ask the class. Use your note cards when you give your presentation.

5. Practice

Practice your presentation several times. You can make an audio recording. Then play the recording to hear how you sound. When you are ready, ask a partner to listen to your presentation. Ask your partner how you can make your presentation better. Then help your partner with his or her presentation.

6. Present

Give your presentation to the class. Think about your listeners as you speak. Look at your listeners. Speak slowly and clearly.

7. Evaluate

Ask the class for feedback. Use the **Speaking Self-Evaluation** to evaluate your presentation. Use the **Active Listening Evaluation** to evaluate and discuss your classmates' presentations.

Speaking Self-Evaluation
1. My presentation answers the focus questions.
2. I have a visual.
3. I speak slowly and clearly enough for people to hear me.
4. I look at the listeners when I speak.

Active Listening Evaluation
1. You speak at the right speed—not too slowly and not too quickly.
2. I learned about your activity or event.
3. You explain the activity in order.
4. I think _____ is the most interesting part of your presentation.
5. I think your presentation needs more information about _____ .

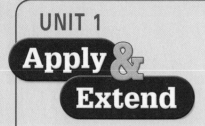
Writing Workshop

Thank-You Note

In a **thank-you note**, you thank someone for a gift or for doing something for you.

> **Writing Prompt**
>
> Write a thank-you note from a party. You can thank someone for a gift they gave you, or you can thank someone for coming to your party.

PREWRITE

1. Look at the student model thank-you note.
2. Brainstorm. Whom do you want to thank? What do you want to thank them for?

Writing Suggestion

Try to include pronouns and possessive adjectives in your writing.

Student Model

Tell why you are writing.

Date

October 22, 2009

Dear Ria,

How are you? I am fine. Thank you for coming to my birthday party. I love to play soccer with you and our friends! Thank you for the great gift. I really like the new soccer shirt. It is nice! This shirt is perfect for me.

Body

Your friend, ← Closing

Avi Gopal ← Signature

Tell why you are thankful / why you like the gift.

WRITE A DRAFT

1. Write the **date** at the top of your thank-you note. Choose an appropriate **greeting** (Dear ____ ; Hello ____ ,).
2. Write the **body** of your note. The body is the main part of the letter. Tell the person why you are writing. Tell them why you are thankful.
3. Write an appropriate **closing** (Your friend, ____ ; Love, ____). Write your **signature**.

REVISE

1. Review your thank-you note. Do you have all the necessary information?

2. Exchange drafts with a partner. Ask your partner to use the **Peer Review Checklist** to review your draft. Your partner will make suggestions.

3. Revise your draft. Look at the editing and proofreading symbols on page 493. Use the symbols to mark the changes you need to make.

EDIT

1. Look at the **Revising and Editing Checklist**. Do the statements on the checklist describe your thank-you note? Make any changes you need to.

2. Fix any errors in grammar, spelling, and punctuation.

Peer Review Checklist
1. You told what you are thankful for and why in the thank-you note. Yes/No
2. Your thank-you note would be better if ____ .

Revising and Editing Checklist
1. I used capital letters and punctuation correctly.
2. I used the verb **be** correctly.
3. I used the simple present tense correctly.
4. I used nouns and subject pronouns correctly.
5. I used possessive adjectives correctly.

PUBLISH

1. Write your thank-you note in your best handwriting. You may want to use stationery, special paper for writing letters, or a computer. If you use a computer, use a spell check and a grammar check.

2. Give your thank-you note to your teacher.

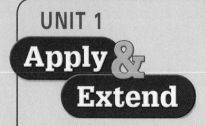

Apply & Extend

● Word Study Workshop

Word Families

Word families are words that sound and are spelled alike but have a different beginning sound and spelling. For example, *might, right,* and *tight* are in the same family because they sound alike and all end in -ight.

Make your own word families. With two classmates, copy and complete the chart.

-oat	-ate	-ay	-ing	-eat
boat	late	play	bring	meat

● Projects

Choose one or more of the following projects to explore the theme of About Me further.

PROJECT 1
Write a Letter to a Pen Pal

1. Choose a student in another class to be your pen pal.

2. Write an informal letter. Write about your interests, activities, likes, and dislikes. Ask your pen pal questions. Ask your pen pal to write you back.

3. Give the letter to your pen pal.

PROJECT 2
Write Directions and Make a Map

1. Write simple directions for getting from school to a familiar place.

2. Draw a map of the directions. Put street names and landmarks on the map.

3. Have a partner check your map and directions.

PROJECT 3
Act Out a Dialogue

1. Imagine a new student comes to your school. Answer these questions:
   - How do you welcome a new student?
   - How do you help him or her?

2. With a partner, plan a dialogue or conversation between you and a new student.

3. Practice the dialogue. One of you be the new student.

4. Perform the dialogue for the class.

PROJECT 4
Your Favorite Food

1. Draw a picture of your favorite food. Use colored markers, crayons, or pencils.

2. Write some sentences about why this is your favorite food. Write what you like about the food. Describe how it smells, tastes, and looks.

3. Display the picture and sentences in the room.

● Independent Reading

Explore the theme of About Me further by reading one or more of these books.

My Brother's Keeper, Virginia's Civil War Diary: **Book One, Gettysburg, Pennsylvania 1863** by Mary Pope Osborne, Scholastic, 2002.

Virginia Dickens promises to keep a journal for her older brother. Ginny finds plenty to write about. She lives through times that lead up to the Battle of Gettysburg.

Dear Juno by Soyung Pak, Viking, 1999.

Juno is a Korean American boy. His grandmother sends him a letter that he cannot read. However, he understands what it means from the photograph and dried flower his grandmother sent with the letter. He decides to send a similar letter in return.

Dear Rebecca, Winter Is Here by Jean Craighead George, Harper Trophy, 1993.

A grandmother describes the sights and sounds of winter in a letter to her granddaughter. She tells her granddaughter about the changes that come with winter.

The Cage by Ruth Minsky Sender, Simon Pulse, 1997.

This is the story of a teenage Jewish girl. She lived through the Holocaust during World War II.

> **Milestones Intro Reading Library**
>
> *The Cave* by Rob Waring and Maurice Jamall, Heinle, 2006.
>
> *Goodbye, Hello!* by Rob Waring and Maurice Jamall, Heinle, 2006.
>
> *Where's Lorena?* by Rob Waring and Maurice Jamall, Heinle, 2006.

Milestones to Achievement

● Reading

Read this informal letter. Then answer Questions 1 through 8.

1   October 24, 2010

2   Dear Jess,

3   How are you? I am fine, but I miss you. I miss Oregon, our old house, and all my friends. I don't like my new school. It is different from my old school. It is very big. The students seem friendly but they know each other. I don't know them.

4   My teachers are very nice. My science class is fun. It is the first class of the day. This school also has a great basketball team. I love to go to basketball games.

5   The marching band is the great thing about my new school. I play the drums. I like it. I walk in the back. It is interesting to watch the people in front of me. It is hard to stay in a straight line. I have to march and play music at the same time.

6   Maybe my new school isn't bad! Please write to me soon. I want to know about your classes. I want to know about your new kitten! Is he much bigger now? Kittens are so cute when they are small.

7   Please write a letter to my new address. I want to hear from you.

Cecelia Kemper
234 Morning Moon Road
Tucson, Arizona 12345

8   Take care,

Cecelia

1 Read this sentence from paragraph 3.

I am fine, but I miss you.

What does <u>miss</u> mean?

A write a letter

B feel bad that someone is not with you

C think something is exciting

D visit

2 What does Cecelia say is the great thing about her new school?

A the marching band

B basketball games

C friendly students

D nice teachers

3 What is one thing Cecelia says she likes to do?

A play drums

B play basketball

C miss her friends

D play with kittens

4 Where does Cecelia live now?

A Oregon

B Arkansas

C Arizona

D October

5 Which part of the letter tells you the name of Cecelia's friend?

A signature

B closing

C greeting

D date

6 In paragraph 3, how does Cecelia describe her new school?

A It is nice.

B It is friendly.

C It is very big.

D It is fun.

7 Read this sentence from paragraph 6.

Kittens are so cute when they are small.

What is the subject of this sentence?

A Kittens

B cute

C are

D small

8 Which paragraph contains an ordinal number?

A 1   C 4

B 3   D 5

Writing on Demand: Invitation

Write an invitation to a party. Tell what kind of party it is. Include the date, time, and place of your party. **(20 minutes)**

Writing Tip

If you want people to tell you if they are coming, include "R.S.V.P." and a phone number.

Relationships

Talk About the Theme

1. Look at the photos. Who are these people?
2. How many people are in your family?

Theme Activity

Who are your friends? Who are the people in your family? Who are the people you know in school? Brainstorm names and put them in a chart.

Friends	Family	People from School

CHAPTER 1

Part A

Objectives

Vocabulary
People's appearance

Listening and Speaking
Describing people's appearance
Identifying people by their appearance

Grammar
Simple past tense

Writing Conventions
Spelling: Consonant doubling for past simple tense

Word Study
Initial blends: br, cr, fr, gr, pr, dr, tr, tw, sw
Common irregular past tense verbs

Writing
Narrative paragraph

● Vocabulary
People's Appearance

brown hair · blond hair · red hair · black hair

dark brown hair · light brown hair

bald

long hair · short hair · shoulder-length hair

curly hair · straight hair

gray hair

● **Listening and Speaking**

Describing People's Appearance

1 Listen and repeat the words on page 152.

2 **PAIR WORK** Look at the words on page 152. Describe your hair.

> I have long hair.

> I have curly hair.

> **Talking About Hair**
> Kate **has** blond hair.
> I **have** short hair.
> Joe **is** bald.

3 Listen and repeat.

1. Lydia has long, straight hair.

2. Mike has short, blond hair.

3. Karl has curly, black hair.

4. Sue has long, curly, red hair.

Talking About People's Hair

He She	has	long short	straight curly	black brown blond red gray white	hair.

4 Make sentences about your classmates. Use the chart to help you.

Example: *Aisha has long, straight, black hair.*

5 **PAIR WORK** Read your sentences to a partner.

> ✓**Checkpoint**
> What kind of hair do you have?

● Vocabulary

More Ways to Describe People's Appearance

1 Listen and repeat.

1. He has brown eyes.   **2.** She has blue eyes.   **3.** She has green eyes.

4. He has a moustache.   **5.** He has a beard.   **6.** She wears glasses.

2 PAIR WORK **Describe a person above. Your partner points to the person.**

He has brown eyes.
He has a beard.

3 Are these hair colors or eye colors, or both? Write **H** for hair. Write **E** for eyes. Write **B** for both.

____ **1.** black   ____ **5.** gray

____ **2.** blond   ____ **6.** green

____ **3.** blue   ____ **7.** red

____ **4.** brown

4 PAIR WORK **Describe your partner.**

You have long, black hair.
You wear glasses.

Multiple-meaning Word

Glasses can be something you wear or something you drink from!

● **Listening and Speaking**

Identifying People by Their Appearance

1 **Read and listen.**

Jasmine: Do you know Antonio?

Ken: I'm not sure. What does he look like?

Jasmine: He has dark brown, curly hair and brown eyes.

Ken: Does he wear glasses?

Jasmine: No, he doesn't.

2 **Listen again. Repeat.**

3 **Say the conversation again. Use new words for the blue words. Use vocabulary from pages 152, 153, and 154.**

4 **Listen. Write J for Jose or C for Cindy.**

_____ **1.** has long, blond hair

_____ **2.** has short, curly black hair

_____ **3.** has brown eyes

_____ **4.** has blue eyes

_____ **5.** wears glasses

5 **PAIR WORK Describe people you know. They can be friends, classmates, or famous people.**

Do you know Yang?

I'm not sure. What does he look like?

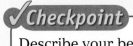
✓ Checkpoint
Describe your best friend.

● Grammar

Simple Past Tense: Regular Verbs

Use the simple past tense to talk about actions that happened in the past. To make the simple past tense of *regular* verbs, add **–ed** to the verb. If the verb ends in **–e**, just add **–d**.

Regular Verb	Simple Past Tense	Affirmative Statement
want	want**ed**	They **wanted** pizza on Saturday.
dance	danc**ed**	Maria **danced** to music last night.
play	play**ed**	We **played** baseball yesterday.

> Verbs in the simple past tense are the same for all subjects.
> I danced.
> She danced.
> They danced.

PAIR WORK **Say three things you did last weekend.**

I watched TV last weekend.

Simple Past Tense: Irregular Verbs

Many verbs are *irregular*. They do not add **–ed** in the simple past tense.

Irregular Verb	Simple Past Tense	Affirmative Statement
have	**had**	He **had** his keys in his pocket.
go	**went**	We **went** to a movie yesterday.
do	**did**	They **did** their homework before class.
make	**made**	I **made** breakfast at 7:00.

> See page 479 for a list of irregular verbs.

Write the sentences with irregular past tense verbs.

1. Hari ____ lunch for us.
2. They ____ to the game.
3. I ____ my homework already.
4. Ben ____ a cold last week.

Workbook
page 125

Independent Practice
CD-ROM

Simple Past Tense: Negative Statements

Make negative simple past tense statements with **didn't** before the verb.

| didn't = did not |

Affirmative Statement	Negative Statement
Celia **listened** to music.	Celia **didn't listen** to music.
We **went** to the concert.	We **didn't go** to the concert.

 PAIR WORK **Say three things you didn't do** last night.

> I didn't watch TV last night.

Simple Past Tense: Be

The simple past tense of **be** is irregular in both affirmative and negative statements.

| wasn't = was not |
| weren't = were not |

Affirmative Statement	Negative Statement
I **was** here.	I **wasn't** here.
You **were** right.	You **weren't** right.
He / She / It **was** late.	He / She / It **wasn't** late.
We **were** happy.	We **weren't** happy.
They **were** on time.	They **weren't** on time.

Choose the correct verb.

1. Pat and Mel **was / were** in class.
2. The test **was / were** on Friday.
3. Yan **wasn't / weren't** at home.
4. I **was / were** sick last week.

Writing Conventions

Spelling *Consonant Doubling for Simple Past Tense*

Some one-syllable, regular verbs that end in a consonant + vowel + consonant have a **double** consonant in the simple past tense.

    stop ➔ sto**pped**   sip ➔ si**pped**

Apply Write the past tense of these verbs.

1. hug   2. drop   3. grab   4. shop

✓Checkpoint

Make three sentences in the **simple past tense**.

GRAMMAR EXPANSION

Wh- Questions in Simple Past Tense, Workbook page 127   Workbook page 126   Independent Practice CD-ROM   Unit 2 • Chapter 1   **157**

● Word Study

Initial Blends: br, cr, fr, gr, pr, dr, tr

Phonemic Awareness

1 **Listen and repeat.**

br	cr	fr	gr
bread	crab	fruit	gray

pr	dr	tr
printer	dress	truck

Decoding

2 **Listen. Write the missing letters.**

1. ___ esh   5. ___ ip

2. ___ ag   6. ___ ap

3. ___ ab   7. ___ op

4. ___ am   8. ___ ib

3 **Listen again and repeat.**

Decodable
Reader 19, 20

✓ Checkpoint

1. Read these words.

    grab

    drab

    crab

    trip

    drip

    grip

2. Which of the words above rhyme?

● Word Study

Initial Blends: tw, sw

Phonemic Awareness

1 Listen and repeat.

SW

sweater   swim

tw

twenty   twins

Decoding

2 Listen. Choose the word you hear.

1. wing   swing   4. wig   swig
2. win   twin   5. will   twill
3. well   swell   6. wig   twig

3 Listen again and repeat.

✓ **Checkpoint**

Read these words.

drink

brand

trim

twin

swim

Decodable
Reader 21

Workbook
page 128

Independent Practice
CD-ROM

● Word Study

Common Irregular Past Tense Verbs

There are many irregular verbs in the simple past tense.

Rule	Simple Present	Simple Past
1. Some verbs do not change in the simple past tense.	cut	Tony **cut** the paper with scissors.
	hit	The boy **hit** the ball with a bat.
	let	My mother **let** us eat pizza.
	put	Jodi **put** her book on the desk.
2. Some verbs only change their vowel in the simple past tense.	write	I **wrote** an e-mail to my sister.
	sit	The teacher **sat** down.
	get	I **got** a book from the nurse.
	come	Lucy **came** to class.
3. Some verbs change both the vowel and the last consonant.	leave	Joe **left** his book at home.
	keep	Barb **kept** her notes in her book.
	tell	John **told** Jessica the answer.
	feel	Nancy **felt** happy yesterday.
4. Some verbs with a **vowel + y** change the **y** to **id**.	say	The principal **said** yes.
	pay	I **paid** for my backpack.
5. Some verbs change the vowel and the last consonant, and add **ght**.	buy	I **bought** a pencil.
	think	Jason **thought** of an answer.

Multiple-meaning Words

For verbs that don't change spelling in the present and past tense, look at the sentence or paragraph the word is in to decide if the action is in the present or past.

 PAIR WORK **Say a present tense verb. Your partner says and spells the past tense.**

think

thought t-h-o-u-g-h-t thought

Workbook
page 129

Independent Practice
CD-ROM

● Writing Assignment

Narrative Paragraph

> **Writing Prompt**
>
> Write a paragraph about what you did last weekend.

A **paragraph** is a group of sentences about one main idea. The first sentence is the **topic sentence**. The topic sentence tells what the paragraph is about. **Indent** this sentence. This means leave a space at the beginning.

The other sentences are **supporting sentences**. They give more information (facts and details) about the topic.

1. Read the student model.

Student Model

indent   topic sentence

Last weekend was fun. On Saturday, I met my friends at the park. My friend Sam brought a ball. We played soccer until it got dark. After the game, Sam and I ate ice cream. We talked. I had a good time! On Sunday, I did my homework and helped my family.

supporting sentences

2. What did you do last weekend? Tell a partner.
3. Write a paragraph. Use the model.

Writing Checklist
1. I indented the first sentence in my paragraph.
2. I used the simple past tense correctly.
3. I have a topic sentence.
4. I have supporting sentences with facts and details.
5. My supporting sentences are on the main topic.
6. I wrote events in the order they happened.

Objectives

Reading Strategy
Understand the author's message

Text Genre
Poetry

Listening and Speaking
Speak with rhythm

Literary Element
Repetition and alliteration

Writing Conventions
Spelling commonly confused homophones

Writing
Descriptive paragraph

Academic Vocabulary

author | message

Academic Content

poetry

● About the Reading

You are going to read two poems about family.

grandmother · grandfather · brother · mother · father · sister · me

● Use Prior Knowledge

Use Family Vocabulary

1. Look at the family photo. Do you know the words? What other family words do you know?

2. Remember that **synonyms** are words that have the same meaning, and **antonyms** are words that have the opposite meaning. Copy the chart. Write synonyms and antonyms for these family words.

Word	Synonyms	Antonyms
1. mother	mom, mama, ma	father
2. brother		
3. grandmother		

3. "Grandmother" is a compound word made up of "grand" that means "big" and "mother." What other compound words do you know with "grand"?

Vocabulary From the Reading
Learn, Practice, and Use Independently

Key Vocabulary

aunt
cousin
daughter
son
uncle

Learn Vocabulary Read the sentences. Use the family tree to find the meaning of the **highlighted** words.

1. Saul is Susana's **uncle**.
2. Sandra is Susana's **aunt**.
3. Alicia and Paul are Susana's **cousins**.
4. Paul is Sandra and Saul's **son**.
5. Alicia is Sandra and Saul's **daughter**.

Practice Vocabulary Look at the family tree. Write the correct word for each sentence.

1. Pablo is Alicia's ____.
2. Alicia and Paul are Maria's ____.
3. Paul is Saul's ____.
4. Sandra is Manuela's ____.
5. Luisa is Alicia's ____.

Manuela and Jorge

Luisa and Pablo

Sandra and Saul

Susana   Maria

Alicia   Paul

Use Vocabulary Independently
 PAIR WORK Describe your family or a famous family.

The Queen of England has four children. She has one daughter, Anne, and three sons: Charles, Andrew, and Edward. She has a husband, Philip, and seven grandchildren.

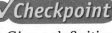 **Checkpoint**

Give a definition for each Key Vocabulary word. Use your own words.

● Academic Vocabulary

Vocabulary for the Reading Strategy

Word	Explanation	Sample Sentence	Visual Cue
author *noun*	someone who writes something, like a story or a poem	The **author** wrote three books.	
message *noun*	piece of information someone is trying to give or communicate to someone else	There was a **message** in the bottle.	

Draw a picture or write a sentence for each word.

● Reading Strategy

Understand the Author's Message

Usually an **author** sends a **message**. This **message** is the real meaning of the story. For example, the **message** in the story "Cinderella" is good things come to good people. Good readers look for the **author's message**.

● Text Genre

Poetry

You are going to read two poems. A poem is a piece of **poetry**. There are different kinds of poems. Some use words that **rhyme** at the end of each line, like **cat/mat**, **like/bike**, and **bun/one**. **Free verse** poems do not rhyme.

Poetry	
rhyme	words that sound alike at the end
free verse	poems that don't rhyme
stanza	a group of lines in a poem

✓ Checkpoint

1. What is the **author's message** in your favorite story?
2. Which word rhymes with *son*?
   on   bun   from

Vocabulary Log

Workbook pages 132, 133

Independent Practice CD-ROM

● **Reading**

Reading Focus Questions

As you read, think about these questions.

1. How do the poems relate to the theme of *relationships*?

2. What is the **author's message** in each poem?

Families

1   Paintings are images or pictures. Artists send messages through pictures. Look at the families in the paintings. Do you think there is a **message** about these families?

Front Porch Conversations by Xaview Cortada

Reading
Strategy

Understand the artist's message Look at the picture. What is the artist's message about family?

Portrait of the Van Cortland Family
by John Wesley Jarvis

Reading
Strategy

Understand the artist's message Who is the artist? What is his message about this family?

2   Now read two poems about family. Poems are another way to create an image in the reader's mind. Poems express **messages** or feelings. Look for the **author's message**. Who is the **author**? How does the poem make you feel?

3   This poem is an example of a **rhyming poem**. Find the rhyming words.

4   The title of this poem is a question. Read the poem to find the answer.

What Is a Family?

by Christopher Sol Cruz

Stanza

1   Some people have a father and mother,
    A **daughter**, a **son**, a sister, a brother.

2   Some people have a lot of **cousins**,
    And **uncles** and **aunts by the dozens**.

3   Some people's grandparents watch with great joy,
    Their grandchildren grow up, each girl and boy.

4   Some people's families live far away,
    Some people see their whole family each day.

5   It's not important how many there are,
    Or if they live near or far.

6   In all of the families that I can think of,
    Just one thing's the same—that one thing is love.

_____

by the dozens many

Reading Strategy

Understand the author's message What does this poem tell us about families?

This poem is a free verse poem. It is also a visual poem. It uses a shape or a picture to help you understand the **author's message**.

Our Grandmother

1 She's our   grandma.

2 She tells us   funny jokes.

3 She takes us to watch movies.

4 She wears warm fuzzy sweaters.

5 She talks about the old days.

6 She brings us delicious food.

7 She lives in a big blue house.

8 She wears a lot of perfume.

9 She wears funny glasses.

10 She has a big heart.

11 She has gray hair.

12 She loves us.

13 She smiles.

14 We love

15 her.

> **Reading Strategy**
>
> **Understand the author's message**
> What does the poem tell us about grandmothers?

> **Reading Check**
>
> 1. **Recall facts**
>   What synonym does the author use for "grandmother"?
> 2. **Make inferences**
>   Why did the author choose a heart shape for this poem?

Reading Comprehension Questions

Think and Discuss

1. **Recall facts** How many stanzas are in the first poem?

2. **Summarize** What are the two poems about?

3. **Compare and contrast** What is the one theme that ties the two poems together?

4. **Describe genre features** What are the similarities and differences between the two poems?

5. Revisit the Reading Focus Questions Go back to page 165 and discuss the questions.

Listening and Speaking

Speak with Rhythm

1. Listen to the poem "What Is a Family?" Listen to how the syllables with dots are stressed, or stronger than the syllables without dots. This pattern of stressed and not stressed sounds is an example of **rhythm**.

> •   •   •   •
> Some people have a father and mother,
> •   •   •   •
> A **daughter**, a **son**, a sister, a brother.
> •   •   •   •
> Some people have a lot of **cousins**,
>   •   •   •   •
> And **uncles** and **aunts** by the dozens.

2. Listen again and repeat the poem.

3. **PAIR WORK** Read the poem aloud. This is called **reciting**. Stress the correct syllables.

4. **PAIR WORK** Did you like the poems? How did the poems make you feel? Tell a partner.

Phrases for Conversation

Reacting to Poetry

I liked the first/ second one better.

The first/second poem made me feel happy/sad/ good.

It makes me think about my family/ my grandmother.

The imagery of the poem is of a loving family.

Workbook
page 134

Independent Practice
CD-ROM

● Literary Elements

Repetition and Alliteration

Poems often use **repetition**. **Repetition** is saying or repeating the same word, or words, again and again. Look at the poem on page 167. Thirteen of the sentences start with "She." The **repetition** shows the poem is about one grandmother.

Alliteration is repeating the same beginning sound. An example of **alliteration** is "Grandmothers grow green grapes." In this sentence, "gr" is repeated as the first sound.

Writing Conventions

Spelling *Commonly Confused Homophones*

You learned these words in Unit 1. Read them aloud. They are homophones. They sound the same but have different spellings.

Homophones	Sentence
you're = you are	**You're** a teacher.
your = possessive adjective	**Your** bag is blue.
it's = it is	**It's** two o'clock.
its = possessive adjective	The desk is broken. **Its** leg is broken.
they're = they are	**They're** students.
their = possessive adjective	**Their** parents are happy.
there = place	Put your bag over **there**.

Apply Write the sentences with the correct word. Check your spelling.

1. ____ name is Paula.
2. ____ are thirty students in class.
3. ____ eight o'clock.
4. ____ doctors at a hospital.

✓Checkpoint

1. What **repetition** can you find in the poem on page 166?
2. Write a sentence with **alliteration**.

Workbook
pages 135, 136

Independent Practice
CD-ROM

● Writing Assignment
Descriptive Paragraph

Writing Prompt

Write a paragraph to describe your best friend when you were a young child.

Write Your Descriptive Paragraph

1. Read the student model.

Student Model

Jose Antonio Herrera

My Best Friend

When I was 6 years old, my best friend was Kevin. He lived next door to me. He lived with his grandmother. He had short brown hair. He had brown eyes. We played together. We both liked to run. He had a bike. I didn't have a bike. I rode his bike. His grandmother and my mother were friends, too.

2. **Brainstorm.** Choose a person to write about. What does he/she look like? Why is this person important to you? Use a graphic organizer to help you get ready.

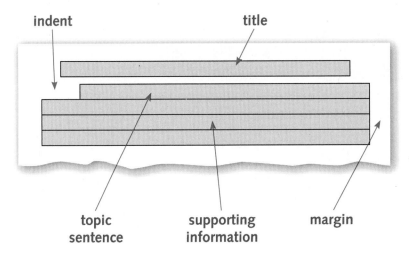

indent   title

topic sentence   supporting information   margin

3. **Write your paragraph.** Write a topic sentence. Write supporting sentences on the same topic. Add a title.

4. **Revise.** Read your paragraph. Add, delete, or rearrange words or sentences to make your paragraph clearer. Use the editing and proofreading symbols on page 493 to help you mark the changes you need to make.

5. **Edit.** Use the **Writing Checklist** to help you find problems and errors.

Writing Checklist
1. I indented my paragraph.
2. I capitalized the first word of each sentence.
3. My paragraph has a topic sentence.
4. My paragraph has supporting sentences.
5. My paragraph is about one main idea.
6. I used past tense correctly.
7. I used descriptive language.

Progress Check

How well did you understand this chapter? Try to answer the questions. If necessary, go back to the pages listed for a review.

Skills	Skills Assessment Questions	Pages to Review
Vocabulary	What words and expressions can you use to describe people's appearance?	**152–155**
Grammar	Give examples of **simple past tense** statements (affirmative and negative).	**156–157**
Writing Conventions	**Spelling:** What spelling rule did you learn about for past tense verbs? Give examples.	**157**
	What is the difference between their/they're/there? its/it's? your/you're?	**169**
Word Study	What are the past tense forms of these words? • let, sit, leave, say, buy	**160**
Vocabulary From the Reading	What do these words mean? • aunt, cousin, daughter, son, uncle	**163**
Academic Vocabulary	What do **author** and **message** mean?	**164**
Reading Strategy	What is the **author's message** in "What Is a Family?"	**166**
Text Genre	What text genre is "Our Grandmother"?	**164**
Reading Comprehension	Say what you thought about the poems you read in this chapter.	**165–167**
Listening and Speaking	**Phrases for Conversation:** What phrases can you use to react to poetry? What is **rhythm**?	**168**
Literary Elements	What are **repetition** and **alliteration**?	**169**

Assessment Practice

Read this poem. Then answer Questions 1 through 4.

My Sister's Wedding

1 It was early June, on a nice spring day,
   We all sat down. The music started to play.

2 My sister wore a dress. It was a long white gown.
   She walked to her husband. We heard a sound.

3 It was my aunt and mother. These sisters started to cry,
   They were so happy as my sister walked by.

4 My sister's dark brown hair was braided tight.
   She looked very beautiful in the light.

5 There were candles lit along the wall.
   Flowers and ribbons filled the large hall.

6 Weddings are times with family and friends.
   They come together and each one sends

7 a card that says, "Through the smiles and tears,
   I hope you are happy for many years!"

1 **Read this line from the poem.**

> It was my aunt and mother.

What does <u>aunt</u> mean?

A your mother's or father's friend
B your mother's or father's sister
C your brother's wife
D your brother's daughter

2 **What is the poem's message?**

A Weddings are boring.
B Weddings are special times.
C Weddings happen in spring.
D Weddings have lots of candles.

3 **Which is an example of alliteration?**

A long white gown
B flowers and ribbons
C along the wall
D family and friends

4 **What kind of poem is this?**

A rhyming
B visual
C free verse
D stanza

> **Writing Tip**
>
> You can describe the way the person looks. You can also describe how the person acts, what the person likes, and what makes the person special.

Writing on Demand: Descriptive Paragraph

Write a descriptive paragraph about your best friend.
(20 minutes)

CHAPTER 2

Part A

Objectives

Vocabulary
Everyday activities
Home activities

Listening and Speaking
Asking about daily routines
Asking about tasks

Grammar
Questions and short
 answers: simple present,
 simple past

Writing Conventions
Spelling: Past tense of verbs
 ending in consonant + y

Word Study
Blends: st, sn, sp, sc, sl,
 sm, sk

Writing
Diary entry

● Vocabulary
Everyday Activities

get up

eat breakfast

get dressed

get ready for school

leave for school

get home

do your
homework

go to bed

● **Listening and Speaking**

Asking About Daily Routines

1 Listen and repeat the words on page 174.

2 **PAIR WORK** What things do you do before school?
What things do you do after school?

―――――――

Telling Time

3 Listen and repeat.

 What time is it?

It's. . .

2:00
two o'clock

2:05
two-oh-five

2:10
two ten
ten past two

2:15
two fifteen
quarter past two

2:30
two thirty
half past two

2:35
two thirty-five

2:45
two forty-five
quarter of three

12:00 am
midnight

12:00 pm
noon

4 **PAIR WORK** Ask and tell time.

1. 1:30   **2.** 4:20   **3.** 10:50   **4.** 6:15

5 Read and listen.

Jared: What time do you usually **get up**?

Katia: I **get up** at **seven o'clock**. What about you?

Jared: I **get up** at **six thirty**.

6 **PAIR WORK** Say the conversation again. Use new words
for the blue words.

✓ *Checkpoint*
1. What time is it?
2. What time does
class begin?

Vocabulary
Log

Workbook
page 137

Independent Practice
CD-ROM

● Vocabulary

Home Activities

1 Listen and say these phrases.

|  |  |  |

wash the dishes

practice
your music

study for
your test

write
your report

2 Complete the sentences with the verb.

| studied   wrote   washed   practiced |

1. He ____ the piano for three hours.
2. I ____ my book report already.
3. They ____ for their math quiz together.
4. He ____ the dishes after dinner.

3 **PAIR WORK** Ask what your partner did yesterday. Use the activities on pages 174 and 176.

> What did you do yesterday?

> Yesterday I got up, ate breakfast, and got ready for school.

4 **PAIR WORK** What other things do you wash? Make a list.

1. wash the dishes
2. wash my hair

Listening and Speaking

Asking About Tasks

1 Listen. Choose **yes** for the things that Brian <u>did</u>.
Choose **no** for the things he <u>didn't do</u>.

1. washed the car   yes   no
2. washed the dishes   yes   no
3. wrote his science report   yes   no
4. practiced for the school concert   yes   no
5. studied for his spelling test   yes   no

2 Read and listen.

Jenna: Can I meet my friends?

Mother: Did you **clean your room**?

Jenna: Yes, I did.

Mother: Did you **write your report**?

Jenna: No, I didn't.

Mother: **Write your report** before you
meet your friends.

Jenna: OK.

3 Listen and repeat.

4 **PAIR WORK** Say the conversation again. Use the phrases
below for the blue words in the conversation.

1. practice your music / study for your math test
2. do your science homework / practice the piano
3. write your social studies report / wash the dishes
4. study spelling words / do your English homework

√ Checkpoint

1. Did you do your homework last night?
2. Do you do your homework before or after school?

Vocabulary Log   Workbook page 138   Independent Practice CD-ROM

● Grammar

Yes/No Questions and Short Answers: be

To make yes/no questions with **be**, put the verb before the subject.

Yes/No Questions and Short Answers: be			
statements	***yes/no* questions**	**short answers**	
He **is** late.	**Is** he late?	Yes, he **is**.	No, he **isn't**.
They **are** here.	**Are** they here?	Yes, they **are**.	No, they **aren't**.
He **was** late.	**Was** he late?	Yes, he **was**.	No, he **wasn't**.
They **were** here.	**Were** they here?	Yes, they **were**.	No, they **weren't**.

isn't = is not
aren't = are not
wasn't = was not
weren't = were not

Write the sentences with the correct verb.

1. (is / were) _____ your sister ready for school?
2. (am / was) _____ Paul in Ms. Green's class today?
3. (are / was) _____ that your bicycle over there?
4. (is / were) _____ those your friends from school?

Yes/No Questions and Short Answers: Simple Present

To make yes/no questions with verbs except *be*, put **do** or **does** before the subject. After the subject, use the simple form of the verb.

Yes/No Questions and Short Answers: Simple Present			
statements	***yes/no* questions**	**short answers**	
He **eats** lunch.	**Does** he **eat** lunch?	Yes, he **does**.	No, he **doesn't**.
They **study** hard.	**Do** they **study** hard?	Yes, they **do**.	No, they **don't**.

don't = do not
doesn't = does not

Change the statements into questions.

Example: I wash the dishes. *Do you wash the dishes?*

1. He washes the dishes.
2. Jo gets up at 8:00.
3. We eat lunch at 1:00.
4. I go to the library.

Workbook
page 139

Independent Practice
CD-ROM

Yes/No Questions and Short Answers: Simple Past

In the simple past tense, to make yes/no questions, put **did** before the subject. After the subject, use the simple form of the verb.

didn't = did not

Yes/No **Questions and Short Answers: Simple Past**			
statements	*yes/no* **questions**	**short answers**	
He **ate** lunch.	**Did** he **eat** lunch?	Yes, he **did.**	No, he **didn't.**
They **studied.**	**Did** they **study**?	Yes, they **did.**	No, they **didn't.**

PAIR WORK Ask your partner questions using simple present and simple past tense.

Do you clean your room every day?

Did you clean your room yesterday?

No, I don't.

Yes, I did.

Writing Conventions

Spelling *Past Tense of Verbs Ending in Consonant + y*

To make the simple past tense of verbs ending in **consonant + y**, change the **y** to **i** and add **ed**.

study → stud**ied**   try → tr**ied**   marry → marr**ied**

Apply Write the sentences with the past tense form of the verb.

1. Carla ____ (cry) when she saw her sister at the airport.
2. They ____ (hurry) to the station to catch their bus.
3. I ____ (carry) these heavy boxes upstairs by myself!
4. We ____ (try) to change the date of the test.

✓ Checkpoint

1. How do you make yes/no questions in the simple present tense?
2. How do you make yes/no questions in the simple past tense?

● Word Study

Blends: st, sn, sp, sc, sl, sm, sk

Phonemic Awareness

1 **Listen and repeat.**

st	sn	sp	sc
star	snow	spoon	scarf

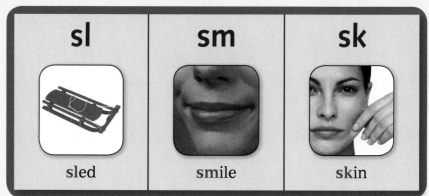

sl	sm	sk
sled	smile	skin

Decoding

2 **Listen. Write the missing letter or letters.**

1. ___ ot   3. ___ im   5. ___ im   7. ___ ap
2. ___ an   4. ___ op   6. ___ irt   8. ___ art

3 **Listen again and repeat.**

✓ **Checkpoint**

1. Read these words.
   - scan
   - span
   - stand
   - slim
   - skim
2. Which words above rhyme?

Decodable
Reader 22

Workbook
page 142

Independent Practice
CD-ROM

● Writing Assignment

Diary Entry

> **Writing Prompt**
>
> Write a diary entry about what you did today, or this week. Use the past tense.

1. Read the student model.

_____
Student Model

> Tues., Oct. 2nd
>
>   School was great today! I got 100% on my math test.
> I'm happy. I thought I got two wrong. I was really worried
> about it. My teacher said she was happy too.
>   I came home after school. I listened to Rap Zone's
> Greatest Hits for about an hour. Then I cleaned my room.
>   Now it's 10:00. I'm tired!

2. Write a diary entry. Talk about things you did yesterday.

Writing Checklist
1. I wrote the date. I used abbreviations correctly.
2. I used proper spacing between my letters and words.
3. I used the simple present and simple past tense correctly.
4. I indented my paragraph.
5. I wrote neatly and clearly.

Objectives

Reading Strategy
Use context to find meaning

Text Genre
Informational text:
   Magazine article

Listening and Speaking
Explaining a diagram

Text Element
Glossary

Reading Fluency
Read aloud with expression
   and intonation

Writing
Informational paragraph

Academic Vocabulary

context | meaning

Academic Content

plants
animals

● About the Reading

You are going to read an article from a science magazine. It is about how energy moves from one living thing to another.

● Use Prior Knowledge

Talk About Living Things

Look at the pictures.

plastic bag

fruit

rock

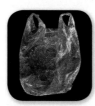
eagle

snake

vegetables

flowers

paper

frog

grasshopper

can

grass

Decide if the items are plants, animals, or nonliving things. Copy the chart. Write the words under the correct category.

Plants	Animals	Nonliving things

● Vocabulary From the Reading
Learn, Practice, and Use Independently

Learn Vocabulary Read the sentences. Use the context (the words around the **highlighted** words) to find the meaning of the highlighted words.

1. Cats, dogs, and fish are all **animals**.
2. **Energy** is the power that comes from things that provide **heat**.
3. **Heat** is warmth, or the quality of being hot.
4. An **organism** is a name for anything that is an **animal** or a **plant**.
5. **Plants** are living things that usually make their own food from sunlight, soil, and water.
6. If you **transfer** something, you move it from one place to another.

Practice Vocabulary Complete each sentence with the correct Key Vocabulary word.

1. Some people do not eat meat. They only eat food that comes from ____ .
2. The sign says that you cannot bring ____ inside the store.
3. After I exercise, I always feel like I have more ____ .
4. The sun gives us ____ and warmth.
5. After I take bus number 49 downtown, I have to ____ to bus 128.
6. Some ____ are so small that you cannot see them with your eyes.

Use Vocabulary Independently 👥 PAIR WORK How many **plants** and **animals** can you name? Make a list.

Key Vocabulary

animal

energy

heat

organism

plant

transfer

Multiple-meaning Words

Heat can be a noun or a verb. What is it in sentence 3?

Transfer can be a noun or a verb. What is it in sentence 6?

✓ **Checkpoint**

Give a definition for each Key Vocabulary word. Use your own words.

Vocabulary Log

Workbook page 144

Independent Practice CD-ROM

● Academic Vocabulary

Vocabulary for the Reading Strategy

Word	Explanation	Sample Sentence	Visual Cue
context *noun*	the information around a word or phrase	You can understand a word by seeing it in context.	**Cats**, dogs, and fish are all **animals**.
meaning *noun*	a definition or an explanation	Dictionaries can help you find the meaning of a word you don't know.	**mean·ing** [mee-ning] 1. what is intended to be, or actually is, expressed or indicated; signification; import: *the three **meanings** of a word.*

Draw a picture or write a sentence for each word.

● Reading Strategy

Use Context to Find Meaning

When you don't know the meaning of a new word or sentence, look at the words around it. These words are the context of the new word, and they may give you some information to help you understand the word or sentence.

nonfiction *(n.)* stories, books, and articles about real people and events.

Dictionary Entry

✓ Checkpoint

1. Which page in Unit 2 of *Milestones* asks you to use **context** to guess the **meaning** of new words?
2. List some **magazines** you know.

● Text Genre

Informational Text: Magazine Article

A **magazine article** is a short work of **nonfiction**. People usually read magazine articles for information and enjoyment.

Magazine Article	
diagrams or illustrations	pictures and charts that can help you understand
captions	explanations of the illustrations
headings	what each section is about

Vocabulary Log

Workbook pages 145, 146

Independent Practice CD-ROM

● Reading

Reading Focus Questions

As you read, think about these questions.

1. How does this reading relate to the theme of *relationships*?

2. How do **plants** and **animals** get their **energy**?

3. How can diagrams help me understand the text?

What Is a Food Chain?

1   **Energy** moves from one **organism** to another in a **food chain**. Look at the diagram. In this diagram, a grasshopper eats grass. A frog eats a grasshopper. A snake eats a frog. The **energy** moves along the food chain.

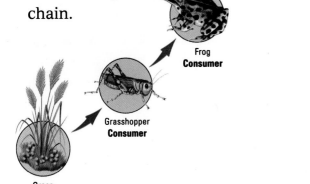

Snake
Consumer

Frog
Consumer

Grasshopper
Consumer

Grass
Producer

> **Reading Strategy**
>
> **Use** context **to find** meaning What is a **food chain**? Which words or expressions helped you find the meaning?

✔
Reading Check

1. **Recall facts** What does a grasshopper eat?

2. **Summarize** What is a food chain?

3. **Inference** Why do **animals** need to eat?

Parts of a Food Chain

rabbit · plant

bobcat · fish

fungi

Reading Strategy

Use context to find meaning Which words helped you find the meaning of **producer** and **consumer**?

2   Green **plants** make, or produce, their own food. **Plants** are **producers**. During **photosynthesis**, **plants** change the **energy** in sunlight to **energy** in food.

3   **Animals** are **consumers**. They eat **plants** and other **animals** to get **energy**. **Animals** that eat **plants** are called herbivores. **Animals** that eat other **animals** are called carnivores.

4   Bacteria and fungi are **decomposers**. They break down waste and dead **plants** and **animals** to get the **energy** they use.

_____

photosynthesis the way that green **plants** make their own food using sunlight

An Energy Pyramid

5   **Energy** moves through a food chain as one **organism** eats another. But not all the **energy** moves to the next level in the chain. An **energy pyramid** shows how much **energy transfers** to the next level in a food chain.

6   Each level gives off some **energy** as **heat**. Therefore, **organisms** transfer less **energy** than they receive. That is why each level is smaller than the one below it. (See diagram below.)

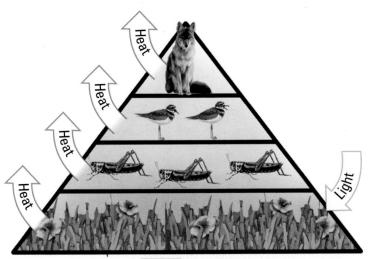

Energy Pyramid

◄ **Reading Strategy**

Use context to find meaning Which word helped you find the **meaning** of **transfer**?

✓ **Reading Check**

1. **Recall facts** What is the name of this section?
2. **Identify processes** What happens at each level in the **energy** pyramid?
3. **Paraphrase** What does an **energy** pyramid show?

● Reading Comprehension Questions

Think and Discuss

1. **Recall facts** Which are the three types of organisms in a food chain?

2. **Identify roles** What do decomposers do?

3. **Describe** How are plants different from animals in the food chain?

4. **Understand genre features** Did you draw any diagrams to help you understand what a food chain and an energy pyramid are? Why or why not?

5. **Revisit the Reading Focus Questions** Go back to page 185 and discuss the questions.

● Listening and Speaking

Explaining a Diagram

1. Look at the energy pyramid diagram from page 187.

2. With a partner, create a short presentation to explain how energy moves through the pyramid and how it is lost. Look at page 187 to help you.

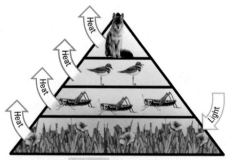

Energy Pyramid

3. Make your own diagram.

4. Write notes on what you want to say. Make it interesting for your classmates.

5. Present your diagram to the class. Look at your classmates, or audience, as you speak.

Phrases for Conversation

Explaining a Diagram

This diagram shows . . . (how energy moves through a food chain)

At each level . . .

Therefore . . .

That is why . . .

Workbook
page 147

Independent Practice
CD-ROM

● Text Element

Glossary

Magazine articles often have specialized vocabulary. If you don't know what a word means, you can guess the meaning from the context. Don't forget to look at the diagrams, too. If you can't guess the meaning, you look up the word in a dictionary.

When textbooks have specialized vocabulary, you can also look in the **glossary** at the back of the book. A **glossary** is a list of words with definitions. Words are listed in alphabetical order. Look at the back of this book. What pages is the **glossary** on?

See page 485 on how to use a dictionary.

● Reading Fluency

Read Aloud with Expression and Intonation

1. Listen to the readings. Listen again and repeat. Try to read aloud with expression.

2. Look at the arrows (⌐‾‾‾↓). Listen. Can you hear how the reader's voice goes up or down? Read it aloud again to your partner. Make your voice go up and down.

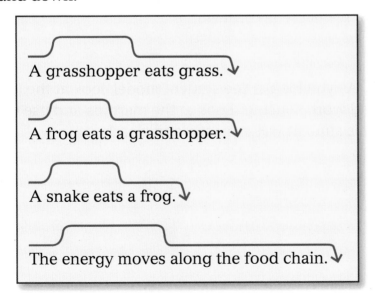

A grasshopper eats grass. ↓

A frog eats a grasshopper. ↓

A snake eats a frog. ↓

The energy moves along the food chain. ↓

✓**Checkpoint**

1. Which word comes first in a **glossary**, *diagram* or *glossary*?

2. Look up the word *imagery* in the glossary. What page is it on? What does *imagery* mean?

● Writing Assignment

Informational Paragraph

Writing Suggestion

Write a topic sentence. Give supporting information.

Writing Prompt

Write an informational paragraph about food chains. Say what a food chain is. Say what the main parts of a food chain are.

Write Your Informational Paragraph

1. Read the student model.

Student Model

Madu Singh

Food Chains

A food chain shows how energy moves from one organism to another. Plants are producers. They get energy from sunlight. Animals are consumers. Some animals eat plants. Some animals eat those animals. Then, decomposers, such as bacteria or fungi, break down the energy in those animals. This is how energy moves along the food chain.

As you look at the student model, look at the letter and word spacing. Look at the margins and use of lines. This student writes neatly and clearly.

2. **Brainstorm.** Use a chart to organize the information you want to write about.

Topic Sentence:
What is a food chain?
Supporting Sentences:
What are the parts of a food chain? 1. 2. 3.

3. **Write your informational paragraph.**

4. **Revise.** Read your paragraph. Add, delete, or rearrange words or sentences to make your paragraph clearer. Use the editing and proofreading symbols on page 493 to help you mark the changes you need to make.

5. **Edit.** Use the **Writing Checklist** to help you find problems and errors.

Writing Checklist

1. I wrote a paragraph with a topic sentence.

2. I used details and examples to support my topic sentence.

3. I gave information from the reading.

4. I used the past and present tenses correctly.

5. I wrote neatly and clearly.

Progress Check

MILESTONESTRACKER

How well did you understand this chapter? Try to answer the questions. If necessary, go back to the pages listed for a review.

Skills	Skills Assessment Questions	Pages to Review
Vocabulary	What activities do you do before and after school? What time do you do these things?	174–176
Grammar	How do you form *yes/no* questions and give short answers in the simple present and simple past?	178–179
Writing Conventions	**Spelling:** What spelling rule did you learn about for past tense verbs? Give examples.	179
Vocabulary From the Reading	Make a sentence with each of these words. • **animal**, **energy**, **heat**, **organism**, **plant**, **transfer**	183
Academic Vocabulary	What do **context** and **meaning** mean?	184
Reading Strategy	How can using **context** help you understand the **meaning** of words?	184
Text Genre	What is the text genre in this chapter?	184
Reading Comprehension	How does **energy transfer** from one **animal** to another?	185–187
Listening and Speaking	**Phrases for Conversation:** Can you **explain a diagram**? What phrases can help you?	188
Text Element	What does a **glossary** tell you?	189
Reading Fluency	How do we show **expression** with our voice?	189

Assessment Practice

Read this selection. Then answer Questions 1 through 4.

A Deep Sleep

1   When you go to bed at night, you wake up the next morning. Imagine you went to bed and woke up weeks or months later. That is what ground squirrels do. When the weather gets cold, they eat extra food. They get very fat. Then they go into a deep sleep. Their heart beats slower. They hibernate, or sleep, this way until they wake up in the spring.

2   Why does a ground squirrel sleep for so long? An animal needs food to have energy. It needs energy to live. But in cold weather, the squirrel can't find food to eat. It goes to sleep to save energy until there is enough food again.

---

1   Read this line from paragraph 2.

> An animal needs food to have energy.

What does <u>energy</u> mean?

A   power from heat or food

B   a kind of animal

C   a squirrel

D   a kind of food

2   **What does the context tell you *hibernate* means?**

A   cold weather

B   eat extra food

C   go into a deep sleep

D   wake up in the morning

3   **What would you find if you looked up *hibernate* in a glossary?**

A   a story about a ground squirrel

B   an article about animals that hibernate

C   a list of animals that hibernate

D   a definition of the word *hibernate*

4   **What kind of selection is this?**

A   informal letter

B   informational text

C   poem

D   short story

Writing on Demand: Diary Entry

Write a diary entry about what you did today at school and at home. Use the past tense. Don't forget to include the date!
(20 minutes)

> **Writing Tip**
> Before you write, make a list of what you did at school and at home. Then use your list to write your diary entry.

Objectives

Listening and Speaking
Make an informational presentation

Writing
A descriptive paragraph

Word Study
Rhyming words

● Listening and Speaking Workshop

Make an Informational Presentation

An **informational presentation** gives facts and details about a topic.

Topic

Make an informational presentation about a topic that interests you.

---

1. **Choose a topic**
   Visit the library or look online for science and nature magazines for kids. Find an article on a topic that interests you. Some good magazines are *Time for Kids*, *National Geographic Kids*, and *Ranger Rick*.

2. **Brainstorm**
   Make a T-chart. Label one side of the chart "Questions." Label the other side of the chart "Information." Write questions that you have about your topic on the "Questions" side of the chart. List the information you learned from your article on the "Information" side of the chart.

3. **Research**
   Find more information about your topic on the Internet. You can also find information from science books or encyclopedias. Record answers to your questions and other facts you find on the "Information" side of the T-chart.

   Encyclopedias arrange topics alphabetically. Look in the "V" volume for volcanoes. Look in the "R" volume for raccoons. Use the index to find the page numbers of your topic.

   Find a diagram or map for your presentation. You can show a magazine's diagram or map, or you can draw one.

4. **Organize**

   Plan what you want to say in your presentation. Write each fact or detail on a note card. Make a card about your diagram or map. Put your note cards in order. What do you want to say first? What do you want to say next? When will you show your diagram or map? What is the last thing you want to tell about your topic?

5. **Prepare**

   Practice your presentation. Use your note cards. Show and explain your diagram or map. When you are ready, ask a partner to watch your presentation.

6. **Present**

   Present your oral report to the class. Speak clearly and loudly. Speak in complete sentences. Make eye contact with your audience. Ask if the audience has any questions. Answer the questions.

7. **Evaluate**

   Think about your presentation. What parts went well? What parts did you want to do better? Use the **Speaking Self-Evaluation** to evaluate your presentation. Use the **Active Listening Evaluation** to evaluate your classmates' presentations.

Speaking Self-Evaluation
1. I practiced the presentation, and I was prepared.
2. I spoke loudly and clearly.
3. All of my information was about my topic.
4. I used a diagram or map.
5. I looked at my audience when I spoke.

Active Listening Evaluation
1. The presentation was interesting. I learned more about ____ .
2. You spoke with confidence.
3. You looked at the audience.
4. Your diagram or map helped me understand ____ .
5. You could improve your presentation by ____ .

● Writing Workshop
A Descriptive Paragraph

> **Writing Prompt**
>
> Write a descriptive paragraph about a special gift you received. It could be a thing or something nice someone did for you.

PREWRITE

1. Read the writing prompt carefully.
2. Read the student model.
3. Think about the best gift you ever received. Make a word web. Write the gift in the center of the web. Write words to describe the gift.
4. Use a dictionary or thesaurus to look up words to describe your gift. Add the new words to your web.

WRITE A DRAFT

1. Write your paragraph. Start with the main idea.
2. Use words in your web to describe the gift.
3. Think about how you felt. Write sentences to say what you did or felt.
4. Write a closing sentence that tells the reader why the gift was special.

Student Model

Elena Flores

My Best Gift

My favorite gift was a picture of my grandfather. My uncle gave the picture to me after my grandfather died. The picture is black and white. It shows my grandfather sitting on a horse. I love horses. My grandfather loved horses, too. The picture was old and the corner was torn. I could still see my grandfather's smile. I cried when I opened the gift. I miss my grandfather. But the picture made me feel happy inside.

REVISE

1. Read your paragraph. Make sure your paragraph starts with a main idea and your writing is clear.

2. Exchange your paragraph with a partner. Use the **Peer Review Checklist** to review. Your partner will give you ideas to improve your paragraph.

3. Revise your draft. Delete sentences that are not about the main idea. Add any important information that is missing from your paragraph.

4. Use the editing and proofreading symbols on page 493 to help you mark the changes you need to make.

EDIT

1. Use the **Revising and Editing Checklist.**

2. Correct your grammar, spelling, and punctuation.

Peer Review Checklist
1. Your paragraph has a main idea.
2. The details help describe the gift.
3. You used past tense to tell what you did or how you felt.
4. You could improve your writing by _____ .

Revising and Editing Checklist
1. I told why my gift is special.
2. I included details about my gift.
3. I used past tense to tell what I did or how I felt.
4. I used the simple past tense correctly.
5. I indented the first sentence of my paragraph.

PUBLISH

1. Write your paragraph in your best handwriting or use a computer. If you use a computer, use a spell check and a grammar check.

2. Be sure your writing is easy to read and the letters and words are spaced correctly.

3. Read your paragraph to the class. Read clearly and slowly. Use your voice to express the important ideas.

Word Study Workshop

Rhyming Words

In Unit 1 you learned word families are spelled and sound alike. All the words in a word family rhyme. But not all words that rhyme are spelled alike. For example *fly* and *tie* rhyme, but *how* and *know* do not rhyme.

Copy and complete the chart with words that rhyme. Don't forget to use some consonant blends from the Word Studies in Unit 2.

love	mother	son	great
above	other	one	straight

Projects

Choose one or more of the following projects to explore the theme of People Around Us further.

PROJECT 1
Make a Relationship Chain

1. Work with a partner. Start with a noun. For example: frog.
2. Write a relationship chain for the word. Go from small to big. For example: frog → amphibian → animal → living thing.
3. Write 5 relationship chains.
4. Use an encyclopedia or the Internet to find relationships. Look up your first noun.

PROJECT 2
Write an Alphabet Poem

1. Work in a small group. Choose a descriptive word as the title and theme of the poem, for example, *Friends*.
2. Write the alphabet down the side of the paper.
3. Each line of the poem should have a word that begins with the letter on that line.
4. Use alliteration to make it interesting.
5. Brainstorm a list of descriptive words. Use a dictionary to find words related to the theme.
6. Revise the poem as a group.
7. Write your initials next to the lines you wrote.

initials *(n.)* the first letters of one's name: John Smith's initials are J.S.

Dictionary Entry

Always capitalize initials.

PROJECT 3

Write a Rhyming Song About a Friend

1. Think of a friend to write a song about.

2. Write down some words to describe your friend. Try to think of rhyming words.

3. Write the song. Use the rhyming words.

4. Give your song a title.

5. Sing your song aloud. Use your voice to show feelings.

Independent Reading

Explore the theme of People Around Us by reading one or more of these books.

Resistance by Ann Jungman, Barrington Stoke, 2002.

Jan lives in Holland during World War II. His father sides with the Germans who invaded his country. Jan wants to help the people in Holland.

The Boxcar Children by Gertrude Chandler Warner, Albert Whitman & Company, 1989.

Four orphans find ways to stay together through all kinds of adventures.

The Table Where Rich People Sit by Byrd Baylor, Simon & Schuster, 1994.

A girl is sure that her family does not know how poor they are. She calls a family meeting. Find out how she finally decides her family really is rich.

Things Not Seen by Andrew Clements, Philomel, 2002.

Bobby wakes up one morning to find that no one can see him. Then Bobby meets a blind girl who doesn't care that he is invisible.

> ### Milestones Intro Reading Library
>
> ***Think Daniela!*** by Rob Waring and Maurice Jamall, Heinle, 2006.
>
> ***The Tickets*** by Rob Waring and Maurice Jamall, Heinle, 2006.
>
> ***Sk8 for Jake*** by Rob Waring and Maurice Jamall, Heinle, 2006.

Milestones to Achievement

● Reading

Read this poem. Then answer Questions 1 through 8.

Family Pictures

1   We visited Grandma last week.
    She went to her bedroom.
    She brought down old books of pictures.
    We looked at the old pictures.

2   We sat at the kitchen table.
    A mother, a grandmother, and a daughter
    looked at photos of mothers,
    grandmothers, and daughters.

3   We turned the yellow pages of the books.
    The pictures were old.
    They had men, women,
    and children I don't remember.

4   We listened to Grandma talk. "There's
    little Bonita," she said. "She had long,
    curly, brown hair and big, brown eyes."
    Grandma touched the page.

5   We listened to stories about aunts,
    uncles, cousins, mothers, fathers, sons, and
    daughters. I don't remember them.
    But from the stories I know them.

1 Find the word that has been divided into syllables correctly.

A gr-and-mo-ther

B grand-mo-ther

C grand-moth-er

D gra-nd-moth-er

2 Where does Grandma keep her books of photographs?

A in the kitchen

B in a closet

C on the table

D in her bedroom

3 Where does this poem take place?

A at the author's home

B at a school

C at Grandma's home

D at a library

4 What is the author's message in this poem?

A Visiting Grandma is boring.

B Stories help you know people.

C Bonita is Grandma's daughter.

D Grandmothers don't like to tell stories.

5 Which is an example of alliteration?

A photos of mothers

B big, brown eyes

C a mother, a grandmother, and a daughter

D yellow pages

6 What word is repeated at the beginning of each stanza?

A Grandma

B Remember

C Books

D We

7 Read this sentence from the poem.

> The pictures were old.

How do you ask a yes/no question from this sentence?

A Was the pictures old?

B Is the pictures old?

C Were the pictures old?

D Are the pictures old?

8 In which stanza does Grandma describe Bonita?

A stanza 2

B stanza 3

C stanza 4

D stanza 5

Writing on Demand: Write a Paragraph

Write a paragraph about a time you and your family did something together. **(20 minutes)**

Writing Tip

Remember that the first sentence of your paragraph is the topic sentence. The other sentences give more information about the topic.

Weather and Activities

Talk About the Theme

1. Look at the photos. What do you see?
2. Do you do these activities?

Theme Activity

Draw pictures of the things you like to do. Share your pictures with your classmates. What activities do many people like to do?

Objectives

Vocabulary
After-school activities
Weather

Listening and Speaking
Talking about after-school activities
Talking about the weather

Grammar
Present continuous tense

Writing Conventions
Spelling: -ing spelling rules

Word Study
Initial blends: bl, cl, fl, sl, pl, gl
Consonant clusters: squ, spr, str, scr, spl
Prefixes: un, dis, non, im

Writing Assignment
Descriptive paragraph

● Vocabulary
After-school Activities

check my e-mail

meet my friends

listen to music

ride my bike

watch TV

play basketball

clean my room

do my homework

● Listening and Speaking

Talking About After-school Activities

1 Listen and repeat the words on page 204.

2 Tell your partner what activities you like to do.

> I like to meet my friends.

3 Read and say these words.

> **Frequency Adverbs**
>
> always   usually   often   sometimes   never
>
> 100% ◄————————————————► 0%

4 What do you do after school? Make sentences.

1. I always . . .
2. I usually . . .
3. I often . . .
4. I sometimes . . .
5. I never . . .

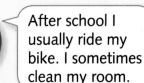

> After school I usually ride my bike. I sometimes clean my room.

5 Read and listen.

Karen: What do you do after school?

Max: I usually listen to music. What about you?

Karen: I usually do my homework.

Max: Do you watch TV?

Karen: I sometimes watch TV.

Max: Really? I never watch TV.

6 Listen again. Repeat.

7 PAIR WORK Say the conversation again. Use new words for the blue words. You can use vocabulary from activity 4 and from page 204.

> ✓ **Checkpoint**
>
> What do you usually do on the weekends?

Vocabulary Log

Workbook page 149

Independent Practice CD-ROM

● Vocabulary

Weather

1 Read and listen.

_____

What's the weather like?

It's sunny.

It's cloudy.

It's raining.

It's snowing.

It's cold.

It's hot.

The weather is nice.

The weather is terrible.

2 Listen and repeat.

3 **PAIR WORK** Talk about the pictures above.

 What's the weather like today?

 It's sunny.

4 _Hot_ and _cold_ are antonyms. They have the opposite meaning of each other. Find the other antonyms.

hot — cold

cloudy — _____

nice — _____

Listening and Speaking

Talking About the Weather

1 Listen. What do Lily and Alberto say about the weather? Choose the correct words.

Lily	Alberto
b. hot	

1. Lily

2. Alberto

a. nice   **c.** terrible   **e.** sunny   **g.** raining

b. hot   **d.** cold   **f.** cloudy   **h.** snowing

2 Read and listen.

Dante: It's **hot and sunny** today. What do you want to do?

Ana: I want to **meet my friends**. What about you?

Dante: I want to **play basketball**.

Ana: OK. Talk to you later.

Dante: Bye.

3 Listen and repeat.

4 PAIR WORK Say the conversation again. Use new words for the blue words. You can use the vocabulary from page 204 and page 206.

5 PAIR WORK What's the weather like today in your city? What do you want to do today?

It's sunny today. I want to ride my bike.

✓ **Checkpoint**

What is the weather usually like where you live?

● Grammar

Present Continuous Tense

The **present continuous tense** tells about an action that is happening right now.

Present Continuous Statements		
subject pronoun	be	verb ending in -ing
I	am	
He / She / It	is	talk**ing**.
We / You / They	are	

You can use contractions with **be**.

I**'m** walk**ing**.   He**'s** walk**ing**.   We**'re** walk**ing**.

He is riding a bike.

 PAIR WORK Look at the pictures. Say what is happening.

✎ Writing Conventions

Spelling -ing *Spelling Rules*

1. Add **ing** to the end of most verbs.
talk ➜ talk**ing**   go ➜ go**ing**

2. For verbs that end in **e**, drop the **e** and add **ing**.
writ~~e~~ ➜ writ**ing**   rid~~e~~ ➜ rid**ing**

3. For verbs with one syllable that end in a vowel + a consonant, double the consonant and add **ing**.
shop ➜ shop**ping**   sit ➜ sit**ting**

Apply Add **ing** to the words.

1. walk   **2.** run   **3.** move   **4.** play   **5.** drive   **6.** swim

 Workbook
page 151

 Independent Practice
CD-ROM

● Grammar

Present Continuous Questions and Negative Statements

Present Continuous Questions
Am I **going** with you?
Is he **walking** to the bus stop?
What **are** you **doing?**
Where **is** he **going?**

Present Continuous Negative Statements
Put **not** between the form of **be** and the verb ending in **ing**.
I **am not walking** to the mall.

PAIR WORK Look at the pictures. What is the person doing?

Janet

play basketball

 Is Janet playing basketball?

No, she isn't playing basketball. She's playing soccer.

1. Sandy

drink water

2. Pat

listen to music

3. Jim

ride a bike

4. Robin

watch TV

5. Jo

play soccer

PAIR WORK Pretend you're doing something. Your partner guesses what you're doing.

Are you reading a book?

Yes, I am reading a book.

✓Checkpoint

1. When do you use the **present continuous tense?**
2. Give an example of a sentence with the present continuous tense.

● Word Study

Initial Blends: bl, cl, fl, sl, pl, gl

Phonemic Awareness

1 Listen and repeat.

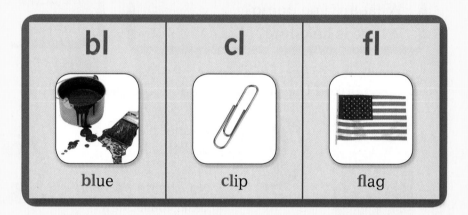

| bl | cl | fl |
| blue | clip | flag |

| sl | pl | gl |
| sleep | plate | globe |

Decoding

2 Listen. Write the missing letters.

1. ___ ad   3. ___ id   5. ___ ot

2. ___ at   4. ___ ed   6. ___ ap

3 Listen again and repeat.

4 Spell the words.

✓ Checkpoint

Read the words.

    plan
    flat
    glad
    blink
    clap
    sled

Decodable
Reader 23

● Word Study

Consonant Clusters: squ, spr, str, scr, spl

Phonemic Awareness

1 Listen and repeat.

squ	spr	str
square	spray	straw

scr	spl
screw	splash

Decoding

2 Read each letter. Listen and say each sound.

1. s | qu | i | d

2. s | p | r | i | ng

3. s | t | r | a | p

4. s | c | r | u | b

5. s | p | l | i | t

3 Listen again. Repeat. Put the sounds together.

✓Checkpoint

Read the words.

squad

spring

string

scrub

Decodable
Reader 24

Workbook
page 154

Independent Practice
CD-ROM

Word Study

Prefixes: un, dis, non, im

A **prefix** is a group of letters added to the beginning of a word. The word without the prefix is a **root word**. The prefix changes the meaning of the root word.

Prefixes	Examples
un = not	unfriendly, unfair
dis = not	disagree, dislike
non = not	nonfiction, nonfat
im = not	impossible, immature

1 **Read each word and definition.**

Word	Definition
unhappy	not happy
dislike	not like
nonstop	not stopping
imperfect	not perfect

2 **Use a dictionary. Look up the words in the chart. Make a sentence or a picture for each word.**

3 **Copy the sentences. Write the missing word from the chart above.**

1. Peter was unhappy with his bad test score.
2. The paper was ___ and had mistakes in it.
3. Juan ___ his job and wants to quit.
4. Many cities have ___ flights to Mexico City.

Decodable Reader 31

Workbook page 155

Independent Practice CD-ROM

Writing Assignment

Descriptive Paragraph

Writing Prompt

Write a short narrative about what your friends and family are doing. Use the present continuous tense in your descriptions.

Student Model

Lorena Cabaltera

Friday in the Park

It is four o'clock on Friday afternoon. It is a beautiful day here in Tampa. I am sitting on a bench in Sunshine park. Many of my friends are in the park, too. Paulo is riding his bike. Nora and Donna are eating ice cream. Manny is listening to music. What am I doing? I am doing my homework. I am writing a paragraph for my English class!

1. What are your friends and family doing? Make a list. Use a picture dictionary to find new words.

1. Paulo	riding a bike
2. Nora	eating ice cream
3. Donna	eating ice cream
4. Manny	listening to music

2. Write your paragraph. Use the model.

3. Use the **Writing Checklist** to check your paragraph.

4. Read your paragraph to the class.

Writing Checklist

1. I indented the first sentence of my paragraph.

2. I used the present continuous tense correctly.

3. I used periods, question marks, and exclamation points at the end of my sentences.

Workbook
page 156

Objectives

Reading Strategy
Identify sequence

Text Genre
Short story

Listening and Speaking
Retell the story in sequence

Literary Element
Plot

Writing Conventions
Punctuation: Quotation
  marks and commas

Writing
Narrative

Academic Vocabulary

identify | sequence

Academic Content

weather

● About the Reading

You are going to read a short story about a girl.
She is going to school. She is late.

● Use Prior Knowledge

Talk About Being on Time

Are you always on time? For example, if school
starts at 8:00, are you always at school by 8:00?

Look at the chart. Is it important to be on time
for these things? Copy the chart. Choose *very
important, important,* or *not important* for each.

	very important	important	not important
1. school	✔		
2. meeting with friends			
3. wedding			
4. birthday party			
5. movie			

● Vocabulary From the Reading

Learn, Practice, and Use Independently

Key Vocabulary

fall off

gate

holiday

late

run

watch

Learn Vocabulary Look at the pictures. Read the sentences. What do the **highlighted** words mean?

1. Be careful! Don't **fall off** your bike!

2. I can't enter the park. The **gate** is closed.

3. Today is a **holiday**. There's no school today.

4. School starts at 8:00, but it's already 8:10! He's **late**!

5. The boys **run** to school. They need to go fast.

6. She looked at the **watch** on her arm. It was 2:00.

Antonyms and Synonyms
Use a dictionary to find antonyms for **fall off** and **late**.
Find synonyms for **gate** and **run**.

Practice Vocabulary Complete the sentences with the correct Key Vocabulary words.

1. A ____ gives you the time.
2. Class starts at 9:30. It is 10:00. You are ____ .
3. To enter the school, you must go through a ____ .
4. January 1st is New Year's Day. It's a national ____ .
5. When you ride a bike, don't ____ and get hurt.
6. When people are late, they often ____ to go faster.

Multiple-meaning Words
Watch is a noun here. **Watch** is a verb with a different meaning on page 204 in **watch TV**.

Use Vocabulary Independently Write one sentence for each Key Vocabulary word. Read your sentences to a partner.

✓Checkpoint
1. Name two **holidays**.
2. Who has a **watch** in class?
3. Is there a **gate** outside your school?

Vocabulary Log

Workbook page 157

Independent Practice CD-ROM

● Academic Vocabulary

Vocabulary for the Reading Strategy

Word	Explanation	Sample Sentence	Visual Cue
identify *verb*	to notice or see something	The doctor **identified** the problem and helped the patient.	
sequence *noun*	the order of events	The **sequence** of events is the same every night—she comes home, does homework, eats dinner, and plays a game.	1. 4:00 Come home. 2. 4:15 Do homework. 3. 6:00 Eat dinner. 4. 7:00 Play a game.

Draw a picture or write a sentence for each word.

Build Vocabulary

Key words for sequence

- first
- then
- next
- at last
- finally

● Reading Strategy

Identify Sequence

Sequence is the order of events. It is the order things happen in a story. As you read "Rain, Rain, Rain!", **identify** the key **sequence** words. They help you understand when things happen.

● Text Genre

Short Story

A **short story** is a **narrative**. **Identify** these features of a narrative as you read "Rain, Rain, Rain!"

Narrative	
characters	people in the story
setting	time and place of the story
plot	what happens in a story with a beginning, middle, and end

✓**Checkpoint**

1. Talk about what you do every morning. Use key **sequence** words.
2. Think of a **short story**. Identify the characters, setting, and plot.

Vocabulary Log

Workbook pages 158, 159

Independent Practice CD-ROM

● Reading

Reading Focus Questions

As you read, think about these questions.

1. How does Faye feel about the rain?
2. Why is she trying to get to school fast?

Rain, Rain, Rain!

by Rob Waring and Maurice Jamal

1   "Oh, no! It's Monday today. And I have school," thinks Faye. She is looking at the rain. "I don't like the rain. And it's raining today." She thinks, "I don't want to go to school."

2   School starts at 9 o'clock. Now it's 8:20! She looks at the clock. "Oh no," she thinks. "I'm **late** for school!" Faye gets dressed. Then she eats breakfast quickly.

3   "Good morning, Faye," says her mother.

4   "Morning, Mom," she says.

5   Her mother says, "Please sit down, Faye."

6   "Sorry, Mom. I'm **late**," says Faye.

7   "Late? Where are you going?" asks her mother.

8   "School," she says.

9   "But Faye …," says her mother.

Reading Strategy

Identify sequence
What does Faye do after she gets dressed? What is the key **sequence** word?

10   "Sorry, Mom. I'm **late**. See you!" says Faye. Faye **runs** out of the house. Then, Faye gets on her bike.

11   Every day, Faye takes the train to school. She rides to the train station on her bike. She looks at her **watch**. She thinks, "I'm **late**. Oh, no! It's 8:35."

✔ Reading Check

1. **Recall facts** Where is Faye going?
2. **Understand plot** Why is Faye going fast?

Reading Strategy

Identify sequence
Faye **falls off** her bike and gets up. What happens after that? What is the key **sequence** word?

12   The rain is coming down. Faye is getting wet. A girl is walking a dog. Faye does not see the girl and the dog.

13   Faye **falls off** her bike. "Oh, no! My bike!" she says. Faye gets up. "I'm very **late**," she thinks.

14   Next, Faye pushes her bike to the station. She is cold and very wet. Faye puts her bike in the bike rack. She looks at the clock. It's now 8:45. Faye goes into the station.

15   "But where's the train?" she thinks.

16   A man says, "There are no trains today."

17   She sees a tree in front of the train. "Oh, no!" thinks Faye. "No trains today!" She looks at her **watch**. It's now 8:47. "What do I do?" she thinks. "School starts at 9 o'clock! How do I get to the school?"

18 Next, Faye **runs** to school. She's very cold and very wet.

19 A boy and girl are looking at Faye. "Why is she **running**?" they think.

20 Faye **runs** and **runs**. At last, she sees the school **gate**. She thinks, "Good! There's the school." She looks at her **watch**. It is 8:59. "Good, I'm not **late**," she thinks.

21 Finally, Faye gets to school. She sees something on the school **gate**. It says, "*No school today. School holiday.*"

22 "There's no school today. It's a school **holiday**. Oh, no!" she says.

Reading Strategy

Identify sequence
What happens after 8:59? What is the key **sequence** word?

✓ **Reading Check**

1. **Recall facts** What time does Faye get to the station?

2. **Explain** Why is there no train today?

3. **Understand character motivation** Why does Faye **run** to school?

Reading Comprehension Questions

Think and Discuss

1. **Recall facts** What time does Faye's school start?

2. **Recognize sequence of events** What happened after Faye got to the train station?

3. **Make inferences** What do you think Faye's mother wanted to tell her?

4. **Relate your experiences** How do you think Faye felt after she read the sign on the school gate? Have you ever had an experience like Faye's in "Rain, Rain, Rain!"? How did you feel?

5. **Revisit the Reading Focus Questions** Go back to page 217 and discuss the questions.

Listening and Speaking

Retell the Story in Sequence

1. Read the story aloud.

2. Imagine you are Faye. You just got home. Tell your story. Organize your story in the correct sequence. Use **sequence words**.

- first
- next
- second
- at last
- then
- finally

3. Show your feelings with your voice.

4. Listen to your partner tell you about Faye's day. Ask questions to get more information or explanations.

- Where were you?
- What did you do?
- When did you get to school?
- Why were there no trains?
- How did you get to school?

5. Answer your partner's questions with more details.

Phrases for Conversation

Asking About Sequence

What happened first?

What happened next?

What happened after that?

And then what happened?

Workbook page 160

Independent Practice CD-ROM

● Literary Element

Plot

The **plot** is what happens in a story. You can use a time line to help **identify** the plot. A time line lists the **sequence** of events. It answers: *What happened first? What happened next? What happened last?*

1. Copy the time line. Write the events of the story.

2. Use the time line to retell the plot.

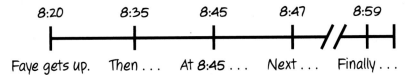

8:20   8:35   8:45   8:47   8:59

Faye gets up.   Then . . .   At 8:45 . . .   Next . . .   Finally . . .

✐ **Writing Conventions**

Punctuation *Quotation Marks and Commas*

Quotation marks— (" ") —show what people say. Put the first quotation mark where the speaker's words start. Put the other quotation mark where the speaker's words stop. Put a **comma**— (,) —between the quotation and the speaker.

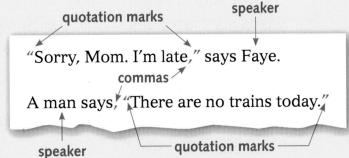

quotation marks   speaker

"Sorry, Mom. I'm late," says Faye.

commas

A man says, "There are no trains today."

speaker   quotation marks

Apply Find two examples of quotations in "Rain, Rain, Rain!" Write the quotations and circle the quotation marks and commas.

✓**Checkpoint**

1. What is a **plot**?
2. Add the correct punctuation: Joe says there is no school today.

Workbook
pages 161, 162

Independent Practice
CD-ROM

● Writing Assignment

Narrative

A narrative is a story. It can be real or imaginary.

Writing Suggestion

Use **sequence** in a narrative. **Sequence** helps you organize your writing.

Writing Prompt

Write a narrative about an after-school activity. Use the simple present tense, present continuous tense, and **sequence** words. Make sure your narrative has a beginning, a middle, and an end.

Write Your Narrative

1. Read the student model.

Student Model

Cheng Li-ying

Sasha Gets to Class

It is 3 o'clock. It is a cold, snowy Chicago afternoon. Sasha is going to his karate class after school. His class starts at 4 o'clock. He's usually a good karate student.

"I don't want to be late," thinks Sasha.

Sasha goes to the bus stop. It is snowing very hard. He waits and waits for the bus. The bus is late.

Finally, it arrives. Sasha gets a seat. He is happy.

The bus starts. Then, it stops. There is an accident!

"Oh, no!" thinks Sasha. "It's 3:35. My karate teacher is not happy when I am late."

The bus waits and waits. Finally, it starts again. It is 3:45.

At last, Sasha gets to his karate class. It is 3:59.

"You're always on time, Sasha. You are a good student," says his teacher. Sasha smiles.

2. **Brainstorm.** Write notes for your narrative. Give details about your characters, setting, and plot.

    a. Who is in the story?

    b. When does the story happen?

    c. Where does the story happen?

    d. What do the characters do first? What do they do next? What happens at the end?

    e. Describe the people, places, and things in your story.

3. **Write your narrative.**

    a. Use quotation marks for the words that people say.

    b. Use **sequence** words to show the order things happen.

4. **Revise.** Reread your paragraph. Add, delete, or rearrange words or sentences to make your paragraph clearer. Use the editing and proofreading symbols on page 493 to help you mark the changes you need to make.

5. **Edit.** Use the **Writing Checklist** to help you find problems and errors.

Writing Checklist
1. My narrative has characters, a setting, and a plot.
2. I used **sequence** words correctly.
3. I used the simple present tense and present continuous tense correctly.
4. I indented my paragraphs.
5. I capitalized the first word of each sentence.
6. I used quotation marks and commas correctly.

Progress Check

MILESTONESTRACKER

How well did you understand this chapter? Try to answer the questions. If necessary, go back to the pages listed for a review.

Skills	Skills Assessment Questions	Pages to Review
Vocabulary	What after-school activities can you name? What weather words can you name?	204–207
Grammar	When is the **present continuous tense** used? Say a sentence using the present continuous tense.	208–209
Writing Conventions	**Spelling**: What are the spelling rules for adding **ing** to a verb?	208
	Punctuation: When are **quotation marks** used? Where do the quotation marks and **comma** go in the sentence?	221
Word Study	What do these **prefixes** mean? • un, dis, non, im	212
Vocabulary From the Reading	What do these words and phrases mean? • **fall off**, **gate**, **holiday**, **late**, **run**, **watch**	215
Academic Vocabulary	What does **sequence** mean? What does **identify** mean?	216
Reading Strategy	How can **identifying sequence** help you understand a story?	216
Text Genre	What is the text genre of "Rain, Rain, Rain!"?	216
Reading Comprehension	What is "Rain, Rain, Rain!" about?	220
Listening and Speaking	**Phrases for Conversation**: What phrases can you use to talk about **sequence**?	220
Literary Element	What is a **plot**?	221

Assessment Practice

Read this story. Then answer Questions 1 through 4.

Saturday Morning

1   "Mom!" yells Nina. "It is Saturday and the weather is sunny. Can we go to the beach today?" She runs out of her bedroom and into the kitchen. Her mother is making pancakes. They smell good.

2   "Yes," says her mother. "But we need to be home before 4:00. We are having friends over for dinner. We can't be late." She puts two pancakes on Nina's plate.

3   "Did you write your report for social studies class?" asks her mother.

4   Nina nods her head. She answers, "I finished it yesterday."

5   "Good. I'm making lunch to take with us now," says Mom.

1 **Read this sentence from paragraph 2.**

> We can't be late.

What does <u>late</u> mean?

A tired

B not on time

C gone

D at home

2 **What does Nina do first?**

A run into the kitchen

B eat a pancake

C go to the beach

D finish her social studies report

3 **Which sentence has an example of the present continuous tense?**

A She runs out of her bedroom.

B They smell good.

C Her mother is making pancakes.

D Nina nods her head.

4 **What is the setting of this story?**

A Nina's kitchen on a Saturday morning

B Nina asks her mother to go to the beach.

C Nina and her mother

D Nina loves her mother.

 # Writing on Demand: Narrative Paragraph

Write a narrative paragraph about doing something fun outside in good weather. Use the simple present tense and present continuous tense in your narrative. **(20 minutes)**

Writing Tip

Before you write, decide how you will begin and end your narrative.

Objectives

Vocabulary
Clothing for all kinds of weather
Everyday objects

Listening and Speaking
Talking about clothing for weather
Giving reminders

Grammar
Imperatives
Object pronouns

Writing Conventions
Spelling: Compound words

Word Study
r-controlled vowel sounds

Writing
List of rules

● **Vocabulary**
Clothing for All Kinds of Weather

sunglasses
jacket
hat
scarf
gloves

umbrella
raincoat

coat

● Listening and Speaking

Talking About Clothing for Weather

1 Listen and repeat the words on page 226.

2 **PAIR WORK** Write the clothing words in alphabetical order. Draw a picture of the item next to each word.

3 Read and listen.

Matt: Good-bye! I'm leaving now.

Susan: It's **cold** today. Wear your **gloves**!

Matt: OK. See you later.

Susan: Bye.

4 Listen again. Repeat.

5 **PAIR WORK** Say the conversation again. Use new words for the blue words. You can use vocabulary from page 226. Talk about the following kinds of weather:

cold   hot   sunny   raining   snowing

> It's raining today.
> Take your umbrella!

√Checkpoint

1. What do you need when it rains?
2. What do you need when it is cold?

● Vocabulary
Everyday Objects

1 Read and listen.

helmet

sunscreen

wallet

keys

cell phone

backpack

2 Listen and repeat.

3 PAIR WORK **What do you take with you when you do these things?**

1. go shopping
2. go to school
3. ride your bike
4. go to the beach
5. go to a restaurant

> When I go shopping, I take my wallet and my cell phone.

● Listening and Speaking

Giving Reminders

1 **Read and listen.**

Kevin: Where are you going?

Cindy: I'm going to the beach.

Kevin: Don't forget your sunscreen.

Cindy: Don't worry. I won't!

2 **Listen and repeat.**

3  **PAIR WORK** **Talk about these activities. Remind your partner not to forget the things on page 228.**

1. going shopping
2. going out with my friends
3. going for a bike ride
4. going to school

4 **Listen. Which things did George and Jessica forget? Write G if George forgot it. Write J if Jessica forgot it. Write X if no one forgot it.**

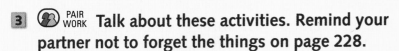

_____ 1. wallet

_____ 2. bag

_____ 3. cell phone

_____ 4. phone number

_____ 5. keys

5 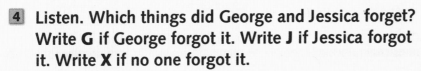 **PAIR WORK** **What things do you bring to school every day? Do you sometimes forget things?**

I always bring my backpack to school but sometimes I forget my keys.

✓**Checkpoint**

What do you bring when you go shopping?

Vocabulary Log

Workbook page 164

Independent Practice CD-ROM

● Grammar

Imperatives

Use the **imperative** to give orders, instructions, directions, or reminders. The imperative is like the simple present tense without the subject.

Simple Present Tense	Imperative
You close the door.	**Close** the door. (order)
You write your name.	**Write** your name. (instruction)
You turn left.	**Turn** left. (direction)
You wear a coat.	**Wear** a coat. (reminder)

Use an **exclamation point** (!) after a strong order.

Wear a hat!   Take a scarf!   Go to school!

To make a **negative imperative**, add **don't** before the imperative.

Imperative	Negative Imperative
Ride your bike.	**Don't ride** your bike.
Turn off the computer.	**Don't turn off** the computer.
Open the window.	**Don't open** the window.

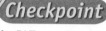 **PAIR WORK** **Choose one activity below. Tell your partner three things to do and three things not to do.**

1. going to the library
2. going for a bike ride
3. studying for a test

I'm going to the library.

Don't forget your library card. Turn off your cell phone in the library.

✓Checkpoint

1. When do you use the imperative?
2. Give an example of an imperative and a negative imperative.

Workbook
page 165

Independent Practice
CD-ROM

Object Pronouns

Pronouns are words that take the place of nouns.
Object pronouns take the place of object nouns.

             verb   preposition

Close the **door**.   Close **it**.   Give the book to **Sue**.   Give the book to **her**.

object noun   object pronoun   object noun   object pronoun

Object Pronouns	
I am hot. Give the water to **me**.	It is hot. Give the water to **it**.
You are hot. Keep the water with **you**.	We are hot. Give the water to **us**.
She is hot. Give the water to **her**.	They are hot. Give the water to **them**.
He is hot. Give the water to **him**.	

Rewrite the sentences with an object pronoun.

Example: Take <u>my scarf</u> with you. *Take it with you.*

1. Give the book to <u>Nancy</u>.
2. Tell <u>Jon</u> to wear gloves.
3. Take the keys from <u>Ty and Kim</u>.
4. Wear <u>gloves</u>. It's cold.

Prepositions
about   of
at   to
for   with
from

Writing Conventions

Spelling *Compound Words*

Sometimes two words go together to make one word.

back + pack = backpack
rain + coat = raincoat
sun + glasses = sunglasses

Apply Read the compound words. Find the two individual words. Match with the correct photo.

paintbrush   wheelchair   notebook   bathroom

✓Checkpoint

1. What **object pronoun** do you use for "I"?
2. What two words make up these **compound words**?
classroom
birthday
toothbrush

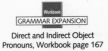

● Word Study

r-controlled Vowel Sounds

The letters **or** sometimes make different sounds. Be careful!

Phonemic Awareness

1 Listen and repeat.

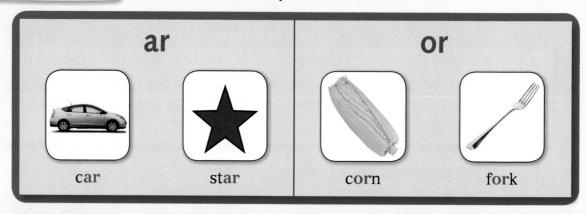

ar		or	
car	star	corn	fork

er	ir	ur	or
enter	bird	purse	color

Decoding

2 Listen. Choose the word you hear.

1. far	fur		**4.** ark	irk
2. are	or		**5.** barn	burn
3. wore	were		**6.** herd	word

3 Listen again and repeat.

4 Spell the words.

✓ Checkpoint

Read the words.
born
tar
turn

Decodable
Reader 26, 27, 28

Workbook
page 168

Independent Practice
CD-ROM

● Writing Assignment

List of Rules

> **Writing Prompt**
>
> Write a list of rules for your class. Use imperatives and negative imperatives in your list.

Writing Suggestion

Always think about the **audience** and **purpose** of your writing.

1. Read the student model.

Student Model

> ### Our Class Rules
>
> 1. Do your homework before class.
>
> 2. Come to class on time.
>
> 3. Don't run in the classroom.
>
> 4.

2. Decide who your audience is. Who is this list for? Think about the purpose of your writing. Why do you need a list of rules?

3. Write your list of class rules.

4. Share your list with another classmate. Make one list and present it to the class.

Writing Checklist

1. I used imperatives and negative imperatives correctly.

2. I used a period at the end of each sentence.

3. I numbered my list.

Objectives

Reading Strategy
Identify main idea and details

Text Genre
Textbook

Listening and Speaking
Give a weather report

Text Element
Maps

Writing
Letter

Academic Vocabulary

main idea | details

Academic Content

climate and weather maps

● About the Reading

You are going to read a lesson from a science textbook. It is about the weather.

● Use Prior Knowledge

Talk About Temperature

Temperature is how hot or cold something is. We use a thermometer to measure temperature. The United States uses Fahrenheit degrees. Most other countries use Celsius degrees.

thermometer

The freezing point of water is 32°F (thirty-two degrees Fahrenheit), or 0°C (zero degrees Celsius). The boiling point of water is 212°F (212 degrees Fahrenheit), or 100°C (100 degrees Celsius).

Match the Fahrenheit temperature with the correct Celsius temperature.

1. 68°F   **a.** 30°C

2. 86°F   **b.** 10°C

3. 0°F   **c.** 20°C

4. 50°F   **d.** 0°C

5. 32°F   **e.** -18°C

temp. = temperature

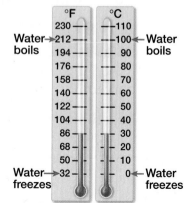

Vocabulary From the Reading

Learn, Practice, and Use Independently

Key Vocabulary

climate

polar

precipitation

storms

subtropical

tropical

Learn Vocabulary Read the sentences. Look at the **highlighted** words. Use the context (the words around the highlighted words) to find the meanings.

1. Northern Africa has a hot, dry **climate**. The temperature is usually hot and there isn't a lot of rain.

2. A **polar** climate, like the one in northern Alaska, never gets very warm. It is cold most of the year.

3. Washington State gets a lot of **precipitation**—rain where it's warm and snow where it's cold.

4. **Storms** bring heavy wind and rain or snow.

5. Florida has a **subtropical** climate. It's usually hot, but sometimes it's a little cool.

6. Hawaii is a **tropical** place. It's hot all year and has a lot of beautiful, green trees.

Practice Vocabulary What **climate** do the places have?

Houston, Texas
Climate: (1) ____
Jan. temp. = 63°F
Jul. temp. = 90°F

Vietnam
Climate: (2) ____
Jan. temp. = 86°F
Jul. temp. = 86°F

Antarctica
Climate: (3) ____
Jan. temp. = 20°F
Jul. temp. = -30°F

Use Vocabulary Independently Tell about a **climate** you know. Remember to use at least two Key Vocabulary words.

✓**Checkpoint**

1. Name a place that has a **tropical climate**.

2. Name a place that has a **subtropical climate**.

Vocabulary
Log

Workbook
page 170

Independent Practice
CD-ROM

● Academic Vocabulary

Vocabulary for the Reading Strategy

Word	Explanation	Sample Sentence	Visual Cue
main idea *noun*	the most important idea	The **main idea** of the lesson is about different **climates** in Africa.	Climates in Africa tropical desert subtropical polar
details *noun*	more information about the main idea	The lesson has many **details**. It talks about the desert and **tropical** and **subtropical climates** in Africa.	Climates in Africa tropical desert subtropical polar

Draw a picture or write a sentence for each word.

● Reading Strategy

Identify Main Idea and Details

The **main idea** is the most important idea in a reading. **Details** give more information about the **main idea**. As you read, identify the **main idea** and **details**.

● Text Genre

Textbook

"Weather and Climate" is a reading from a science textbook. Look at the features of a textbook.

Textbook	
headings	titles of sections
facts	true information
graphics	photos, graphs, charts
captions	information about a picture

✓Checkpoint

1. What is the **main idea** of a reading?
2. What does a **detail** give?
3. What **headings** can you find on pages 237–239?

Vocabulary Log

Workbook pages 171, 172

Independent Practice CD-ROM

● Reading

Reading Focus Questions

As you read, think about these questions.

1. How do you get information about the weather?
2. What kinds of weather does the United States have?

CHAPTER 1 **Weather and Climate**

» Weather Reports

1 "Dark clouds in the west—stay home and rest." This is a **popular** old expression about the weather. It means if you see dark clouds coming from the west, rain or **storms** are coming. Today, weather reports can give us very detailed information about the weather.

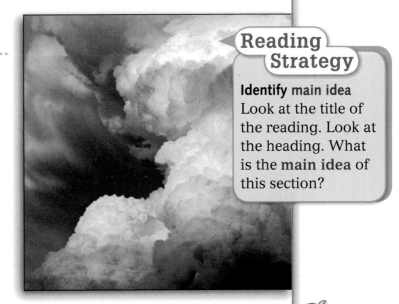

Reading Strategy

Identify main idea
Look at the title of the reading. Look at the heading. What is the **main idea** of this section?

2 You can get a weather report on TV, on the Internet, on the radio, or in the newspaper. On the radio, you might hear a weather report like this: "We will have sunny skies this morning. Around noon, a **storm** will move through, bringing heavy rain. Winds will be at about 8 **mph**. Temperatures will be in the 50s. There is a 30% chance of **precipitation** again tonight."

✓ **Reading Check**

1. **Recall facts** Where can we get weather reports?
2. **Make inferences** Does this weather report say it will rain?
3. **Understand author's purpose** What do dark clouds mean?

---

popular enjoyed or used by many people
mph miles per hour

» Weather Maps

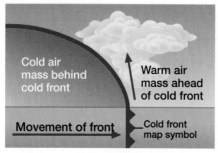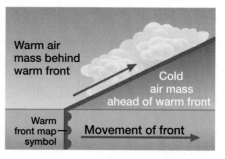

Fronts

3   What is a cold front? It starts with an area of cold air. This area of air is colder than nearby air. A warm front is an area of air that is warmer than nearby air. A cold front is a cold-air area pushing into a warm air area. A warm front is a warm-air area pushing into a cold-air area.

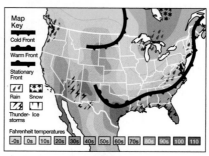

A weather map

Reading Strategy

Identify details What kinds of information can you find on a weather map?

4   Some weather maps show temperatures across a region. Some show fronts. Others display areas of high and low pressure. High and low pressure describes the pressure, or weight, of the air. Areas of high pressure (**H**) usually stop areas of low pressure (**L**). Low-pressure areas must go around areas of high pressure. Low pressures often bring **storms**.

» Weather and Climate

5   Weather can change from hour to hour. **Climate** changes more slowly. **Climate** is the **average** weather for an area over many years. An area's **climate** includes its average temperature and its average amounts of rain and snow.

Reading Strategy

Identify details What features are used to describe the **climate** of a place?

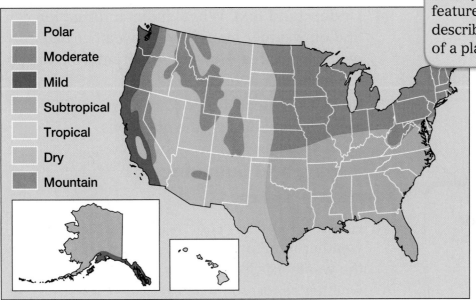

Polar
Moderate
Mild
Subtropical
Tropical
Dry
Mountain

Climate areas of the United States

6   The United States has more than one **climate**. It has dry, mild, **tropical**, **subtropical**, and other **climates**. Alaska is a state with a **polar climate**.

---

average (adj) usual or normal

Reading Check

1. **Recall facts** How often can weather change?

2. **Identify the main idea** What is the main idea of this section?

3. **Understand maps** How many **climates** does the United States have?

● Reading Comprehension Questions

Think and Discuss

1. **Recall details** What synonym does the writer use to help explain air "pressure"?

2. **Give the main ideas** What is the **main idea** of each page of the reading?

3. **Describe** What is the difference between a warm front and a cold front?

4. **Understand text** What kind of information can you find on weather maps? Find a weather map of your own city or area. How is it different from the ones in the reading?

5. **Revisit the Reading Focus Questions** Go back to page 237 and discuss the questions.

● Listening and Speaking

Give a Weather Report

1. Create a weather report with a partner. Draw a weather map for the United States and decide what the weather is like in other cities. Present your weather report to the class.

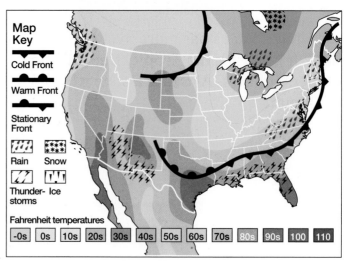

2. Organize your ideas before you present. Give details about the weather. Use weather vocabulary.

Phrases for Conversation

Reporting the Weather

Today will be rainy/ sunny/cloudy.

The high temperature this afternoon will be ____ degrees.

The low temperature tonight will be ____ degrees.

There is a ____ percent chance of **precipitation**.

Workbook
page 173

Independent Practice
CD-ROM

● Text Element

Maps

A **map** gives information about a place. Look at the two maps. The first map is a geographic map. It shows the U.S. state borders. The second map is a weather map. It gives information about temperatures and **precipitation**.

Both maps have a **key**. The key tells what colors and symbols on a map mean.

1. Write the abbreviations for five states on the Atlantic Ocean.

2. Look at the maps. What is the temperature in your area?

● Reading Fluency

Adjust Your Reading Rate: Scan to Locate Information

Scanning is reading fast. Look for key, or important, words to find information.

1. Read silently. Then answer the questions.

   a. Which chapter tells about stars?

   b. Which chapter tells about the moon?

A. Geographic Map

B. Weather Map

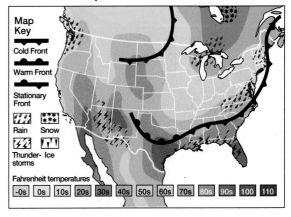

Earth Science
Table of Contents

2. Check your answers with a partner.

✓Checkpoint

1. What states border California?

2. On the map, what temperature is it in Illinois?

Workbook
page 174

Independent Practice
CD-ROM

Unit 3 • Chapter 2 **241**

Writing Assignment

Letter

Writing Suggestion

Choose a **main idea**. Use **details** to support (tell more about) the **main idea**.

Writing Prompt

Write a letter to your friend who is coming to visit you. Tell your friend what to bring to your house. Think about these questions.

- What kind of **climate** do you live in?
- What temperature is it in your area?
- What things do people need to bring?

Write Your Letter

1. Read the student model.

Student Model

Hi Jesse,

I am very happy that you are coming to visit me. In Seattle, it rains often, and the temperature is cool. It's about 65 degrees Fahrenheit. Bring your umbrella and hat for the rain. Also bring warm clothes. On rainy days, I like to go to the movies. Sometimes I read a book or listen to music. Remember to bring a book for rainy days. On sunny days, I like to ride my bike. My friend Julie gave me her bike. You can use it. Don't bring your bike to Seattle. Don't forget to bring your helmet!

See you soon,

Irina

2. **Brainstorm**. What kind of weather or **climate** do you have in your city? What can you do in the different kinds of weather? Use a graphic organizer to help you get ready.

Main Idea: kind of weather: _____
   Details:
   1. What we can do: _____
   2. What we need: _____

---

3. **Write your letter**. Write a **main idea** and two or three **details**.

4. **Revise**. Read your letter. Add, delete, or rearrange words or sentences to make your letter clearer. Use the editing and proofreading symbols on page 493 to help you mark the changes you need to make.

5. **Edit**. Use the **Writing Checklist** to help you find problems and errors.

Writing Checklist

1. I indented the first sentence.

2. I capitalized the first word of each sentence.

3. My paragraph has a **main idea**.

4. I used **details** to give more information about my **main idea**.

5. I used the imperative correctly to remind my friend what to bring.

Progress Check

MILESTONES TRACKER

How well did you understand this chapter? Try to answer the questions. If necessary, go back to the pages listed for a review.

Skills	Skills Assessment Questions	Pages to Review
Vocabulary	What clothing do you wear in hot weather? What do you need to bring with you to school?	**226–229**
Grammar	When are three times we use **imperatives**? What are the **object pronouns** for *he* and *we*?	**230** **231**
Writing Conventions	**Spelling:** Find the two words in *backpack* and *classroom*.	**231**
Vocabulary From the Reading	What do these words mean? • climate, polar, precipitation, storms, subtropical, tropical	**235**
Academic Vocabulary	What is a **main idea**? What are **details**?	**236**
Reading Strategy	How does identifying the **main idea** and **details** help you understand a reading better?	**236**
Text Genre	What is the text genre of "Weather and Climate"?	**236**
Reading Comprehension	What is "Weather and Climate" about?	**240**
Listening and Speaking	**Phrases for Conversation:** What phrases can you use to report the weather?	**240**
Text Element	What can you tell from reading a **weather map**? What can you tell from reading a **geographic map**?	**241**
Reading Fluency	How do you **scan** a text?	**241**

Assessment Practice

Read this story. Then answer Questions 1 through 4.

The Climate of Nevada

1   The state of Nevada is in the southwest United States. Las Vegas's climate is very dry. Most of the time, people in Las Vegas do not need raincoats!

2   It is also very hot in Nevada. Nevada has hot summers and warm winters. Look at the map. It shows Nevada in July. Each color shows the average temperature of an area. The key tells you what the colors mean.

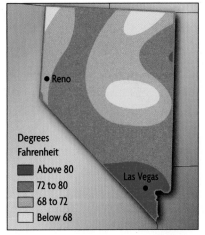

Degrees Fahrenheit
- Above 80
- 72 to 80
- 68 to 72
- Below 68

Average Temperature in Nevada

1 Read this sentence from paragraph 2.

> Las Vegas's climate is very dry.

What does <u>climate</u> mean?

A average weather over time

B how high above sea level

C polar

D temperature

2 What is the main idea of paragraph 1?

A Nevada is very dry.

B Nevada is in the southwest United States.

C Nevada is very hot.

D Nevada is a fun place to visit.

3 What is the average temperature in Reno in July?

A above 80 degrees Fahrenheit

B 72 to 80 degrees Fahrenheit

C 68 to 72 degrees Fahrenheit

D below 68 degrees Fahrenheit

4 Where would you find this selection?

A in a book of poems

B in a science textbook

C in a book of stories

D in a diary

Writing on Demand: Reminder Letter

Imagine you and a friend are going to visit Nevada. Write a letter to your friend. Tell your friend what clothes to pack. **(20 minutes)**

> **Writing Tip**
> Think about the climate of Nevada, and what you might need to wear while you are there.

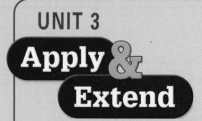

Apply & Extend

Objectives

Listening and Speaking
Paraphrase a story

Writing
Descriptive narrative

Word Study
Nonsense words

● Listening and Speaking Workshop
Paraphrase a Story

> **Topic**
>
> **Listen and retell a story.** Tell a story. Listen to your classmate's story. Then retell your classmate's story to another student.

1. **Brainstorm**
   Think about a time when weather affected an event or day. Talk about a personal experience or someone else's experience.

2. **Plan and Organize**
   Tell your story to a partner.
   a. Who is the story about? Describe the characters.
   b. Describe the setting.
   c. What actions happen during the story? What happens first? What happens next? Last?
   d. How does weather affect the events in the story?
   e. Why do you remember this event?

   Make sure you have enough information to tell the story clearly and in the correct order.

3. **Listen and Take Notes**
   Tell your story. Your classmate takes notes and asks questions.

   Listen carefully to your partner's story. Evaluate what you hear. Ask questions about things you don't understand.

   Take notes. Answer the questions a–e from step 2.

4. **Prepare**
   Write notes or draw pictures to help you retell the story. Make sure your notes are in order and answer your questions.

5. **Review Your Notes and Practice**

   Practice retelling your partner's story. You might make an audio recording. Then play the recording to hear how you sound. Be sure to speak slowly and clearly. Use your voice and body to show emotions and actions.

6. **Present**

   Paraphrase, or retell, your partner's story to another student. Be sure to speak clearly, use your voice to show emotion, and look directly at your audience. Use your notes or pictures to tell the story in the correct sequence. Use your body or hands to show actions.

7. **Evaluate**

   When you finish, ask your partner for feedback. Use the **Speaking Self-Evaluation** to evaluate your retelling of the story. Use the **Active Listening Evaluation** to evaluate your partner.

Speaking Self-Evaluation
1. I practiced retelling my partner's story and was prepared. I was relaxed when I retold it.
2. I described the story's setting and characters.
3. I retold the story's plot in the correct sequence.
4. I used my voice to show emotion.
5. I used my body and hands to show actions.
6. I spoke clearly and slowly.
7. I looked at my audience when I spoke.

Active Listening Evaluation
1. You described the story's characters and setting.
2. You retold the story's plot in a way that made sense and showed a sequence.
3. You used your voice to show emotion.
4. You used your body and hands to show actions.
5. You spoke clearly and slowly.
6. You looked at me when you spoke.
7. You could improve your retelling by _____.

Apply & Extend

UNIT 3

● Writing Workshop

Descriptive Narrative

In a **descriptive narrative**, you tell a story about a person, place, or thing.

> **Writing Prompt**
>
> Write about a storm or exciting weather event that you remember. Tell your story in the present continuous tense.

PREWRITE

1. Read the writing prompt and student model.
2. Think about these questions. Take notes.
    a. Imagine the event. What is happening?
    b. What is the weather like? Why is it memorable?
    c. In what sequence are things happening?
3. Write your plot in a time line. Use sequence words.

WRITE A DRAFT

1. Write a draft of your story. Visualize the details in your mind. Use adjectives to describe the weather and what is happening.
2. Tell what happens. Think about the sequence of events. Say what is happening and how you feel.
3. Conclude. Tell why the events were memorable.

Writing Suggestion

Make your story interesting by giving exact quotes. Remember to put quotations in their own paragraphs.

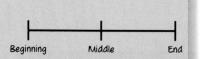

Beginning   Middle   End

Writing Suggestion

You can use a dictionary or thesaurus to find exact words that will paint a word picture for your reader.

Student Model

Jamal Martin

A Storm to Remember

Introduction

We do not often have snow where I live. But last year we had a real surprise. It was a big snowstorm.

Body

I am walking to school. The snow begins to fall. It is snowing very fast. The wind is blowing. Inside we are watching the snow fall. Snow is everywhere. All of the students are excited.

The principal makes an announcement. He says, "We are closing the school until Monday. The school buses are waiting to take you home."

My father is waiting for us at the bus stop. At home, my brother and I play in the snow. We are freezing and run inside.

The storm lasted for days. My brother and I still remember that storm and the winter fun we had.

REVISE

1. Review your narrative. Did you give descriptive details?
2. Give your narrative to a partner. Your partner uses the **Peer Review Checklist** to make suggestions.
3. Revise your draft. Add or delete sentences.
4. Use the editing and proofreading symbols on page 493.

EDIT

1. Use the **Revising and Editing Checklist** to evaluate your essay.
2. Fix your grammar, punctuation, and spelling.

Peer Review Checklist
1. The beginning of the story caught my interest in the introduction.
2. The story focuses on one event. The events are told in order.
3. The details and descriptions help me imagine the event.
4. You could improve your writing by ____.

Revising and Editing Checklist
1. My introduction is clear and states the main idea.
2. I included details and exact words in the body of the story.
3. My story has a conclusion.
4. The subjects and verbs agree.
5. I used the present continuous tense.

PUBLISH

1. Write your descriptive narrative again or use a computer.
2. Read your story aloud to a small group.

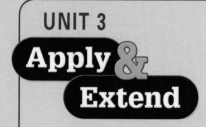

Apply & Extend

● Word Study Workshop

Nonsense Words

Onomatopoeia is a word used to make a sound. For example, we write "buzz" to show what sound a bee makes. Read "buzz" aloud. It sounds like a bee!

1. Read these sounds aloud. What do they sound like?

   a. mumble   **c.** splash   **e.** varroom

   b. hiss   **d.** ding-dong   **f.** click

2. Make your own words. Think of a sound. Write how it sounds. Ask your partner to read your word aloud. Did your partner make the right sound?

● Projects

Choose one or more of the following projects to explore the theme of Weather and Activities further.

PROJECT 1
Write a Descriptive Paragraph About an Outdoor Activity

1. Draw a picture of your favorite outdoor activity.

2. Write a descriptive paragraph about this activity. Explain why you enjoy the activity. Say what weather is best for this activity.

3. Read your paragraph to the class. Answer any questions your classmates have.

PROJECT 2
Create a Comic Strip About a Snowman

1. Imagine building a snowman on a sunny day. Draw a comic strip that shows what happens to the snowman. Talk with a partner about what other characters to include.

2. Work with your partner to make the comic strip. Write what the snowman and other characters say in speech bubbles.

3. Display your comic strip in the classroom.

PROJECT 3
Describe How Weather Affected Your Plans

1. Think of a time when weather affected you. What plans did you have? What happened with the weather? How did the weather make you change your plans? What did you finally do? Write notes about your experience.

2. Look at your notes and decide how to tell the story. Organize your notes into the following categories:

    a. Setting: Where were you? Describe it.

    b. Characters: Who was with you? Describe them.

    c. Plot: Put the actions into a sequence.

3. Draw pictures to illustrate your story.

4. Tell your story to the class. Show your pictures.

● Independent Reading

Explore the theme of Weather and Activities further by reading one or more of these books.

Weather Words and What They Mean by Gail Gibbons, Holiday House, 1992.

This book explains where weather comes from. It explains the words used to talk about weather. Terms include those used with temperature, air pressure, moisture, and wind.

Wild Weather Days by Katie Marsico, Children's Press, 2006.

This book introduces wild weather words. Each wild weather setting is described and has photos.

Tornado by Betsy Cromer Byars, HarperCollins, 1996.

Waiting out a tornado in a storm cellar becomes a time to share stories. Each chapter tells a story about Tornado the dog.

> **Milestones Intro Reading Library**
>
> ***Bad Dog? Good Dog*** by Rob Waring and Maurice Jamall, Heinle, 2006.
>
> ***The Bear's Mouth*** by Rob Waring and Maurice Jamall, Heinle, 2006.
>
> ***No, You Can't*** by Rob Waring and Maurice Jamall, Heinle, 2006.

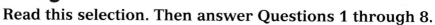

Milestones to Achievement

● Reading

MILESTONES TRACKER

Read this selection. Then answer Questions 1 through 8.

1   "Dad, I'm leaving now," says Felipe. "I'm riding my bike to the park." Felipe is wearing shorts and a T-shirt. He grabs his helmet and walks toward the door.

2   "Wait a minute," says Dad. "The weather isn't good for biking." He points to the window. Rain is falling, and the trees are moving from the wind.

3   Felipe looks at his shorts and shirt. Then he looks out the window. He says, "It is difficult to ride a bike with an umbrella. I guess I'm not riding my bike to the park."

4   Felipe goes to his room and waits for the rain to stop. First he does his homework. Next, he picks up his books and papers, and puts them in his backpack. Then he listens to some music. Finally, the rain stops, and the sun comes out.

5   Felipe walks down the stairs and into the living room. "OK, Dad, now I am really going to the park!" he says.

6   Dad says, "OK. Don't forget your helmet."

7   Felipe gets his bike. He puts on his helmet and rides to the park. His friends are at the park. They look at the football field. It is wet. The field is full of mud. "I don't know if I want to play mud football," says Felipe's friend Jake.

8   "I don't know," says Felipe. "Mud football sounds like a lot of fun."

9   "Yes, the football sounds fun," agrees Jake. "But my angry grandmother when she sees the mud on my clothes is not fun."

10   "Yes," agrees Felipe. "Let's play basketball instead."

1 Which sentence is an example of the present continuous tense?

A Felipe goes to his room and waits for the rain to stop.

B He points to the window.

C Rain is falling, and the trees are moving from the wind.

D They look at the football field.

2 Which sentence describes the plot of this story?

A Felipe wants to ride his bike and listen to music.

B The story takes place at Felipe's house and at the park.

C The main character of the story is Felipe.

D Felipe changes his plans twice because of the rain.

3 Which sequence word tells you that Felipe picks up his room after he does his homework?

A Then C Finally

B Next D When

4 What is the main idea of paragraph 4?

A Felipe listens to music.

B Felipe does his homework.

C Felipe waits for the rain to stop.

D Felipe cleans his room.

5 Read this sentence from paragraph 2.

> The weather isn't good for biking.

What does <u>weather</u> mean?

A what it is like outside

B the time of day

C the setting of the story

D the clothing you wear

6 Which sentence contains an imperative?

A "Wait a minute," says Dad.

B Rain is falling, and the trees are moving from the wind.

C It is wet.

D Finally, the rain stops, and the sun comes out.

7 Why does Jake play basketball?

A He likes basketball better than football.

B He does not want to get muddy.

C He does not have a football.

D He does not think there are enough people to play football.

8 Which word from the story is a compound word?

A helmet C umbrella

B window D basketball

 # Writing on Demand: Narrative Paragraph

Write a narrative paragraph about a time you had to change your plans because of bad weather. **(20 minutes)**

Writing Tip
Make a list of what happens in your narrative. Organize the sequence of events.

At Home

Talk About the Theme

1. Look at the photos. What do you see?
2. What things make a place a home?

Theme Activity

Some people live in houses. Others live in apartments. What is important in a home? What things does a home need? Make a list as a class.

255

Objectives

Vocabulary
Rooms in your home
Furniture

Listening and Speaking
Talking about rooms in
  your home
Describing rooms

Grammar
Plural nouns
Irregular plural nouns
A, an, some, any

Writing Conventions
Spelling: Regular plural
  nouns

Word Study
Silent e
Vowel digraph: -oo- and u
Suffixes: er, or, ist

Writing
Descriptive paragraph

● **Vocabulary**
Rooms in Your Home

living room

kitchen

dining room

bathroom

bedroom

garage

closet

● Listening and Speaking

Talking About Rooms in Your Home

1 Listen and repeat the words on page 256.

2 Draw a map of your home. Label the rooms. Use the words on page 256.

3 Talk about what you do in the rooms of your house. Complete the sentences below.

1. I watch TV in the ____.
2. I eat dinner in the ____.
3. I cook in the ____.
4. I wash in the ____.
5. I sleep in the ____.
6. I hang my clothes in the ____.
7. I read in the ____.
8. I do my homework in the ____.

I sleep in the bedroom.

4 Read and listen.

Lori: Where do you **eat dinner**?

Don: We **eat dinner** in the **dining room**. How about you?

Lori: We eat in the **kitchen**.

Don: Where do you **study**?

Lori: I **study** in my **bedroom**.

Don: I do, too!

5 Listen again. Repeat.

6 Say the conversation again. Use new words for the blue words. You can use vocabulary from page 256 and activity 3.

✓ Checkpoint

1. Where do you study?
2. Where do you eat breakfast?

Vocabulary Log

Workbook page 175

Independent Practice CD-ROM

● Vocabulary
Furniture

1 Read and listen.

kitchen

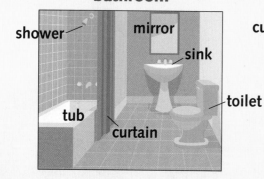

cabinet
sink
refrigerator
table
oven
chair

living room

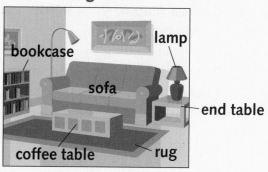

bookcase
lamp
sofa
end table
coffee table
rug

bathroom

shower
mirror
sink
toilet
tub
curtain

bedroom

curtain
window
pillow
dresser
desk
bed

2 Listen and repeat.

3 Copy and write items in the chart.

bed
sofa
desk
mirror
pillow
curtain
rug
bookcase
TV
dresser
table

kitchen	bedroom	bathroom	living room	dining room
	bed			

4 PAIR WORK **Compare your chart with a partner's chart.**

I have a bookcase in my bedroom but you don't.

Listening and Speaking
Describing Rooms

1 **Read and listen.**

Jorge: What is in your bedroom?

Miki: In my bedroom, there is a bed and there is a desk. There are also many books. What about you?

Jorge: In my bedroom, there are two beds and a dresser.

2 **Listen and repeat.**

Use **there is** with one noun. Note: **there is** = **there's**	**There is** a desk. **There is** an end table. **There's** one chair.
Use **there are** with two or more nouns.	**There are** two chairs. **There are** four pillows.

3 **PAIR WORK** **Practice the conversation in activity 1. Use new words for the blue words. You can use the words on page 256 and page 258.**

> Remember to use **a** before singular nouns that begin with a consonant. Use **an** before singular nouns that begin with a vowel.

4 **Listen. Which objects does Jada talk about?**

In Jada's bedroom	Not in Jada's bedroom
2 beds	desk

✓**Checkpoint**

1. What is in your kitchen?
2. What is in your bedroom?

Vocabulary Log

Workbook page 176

Independent Practice CD-ROM

● Grammar

Plural Nouns

A **noun** is a person, place, or thing. A noun can be **singular** (only one) or **plural** (two or more). To make regular nouns plural, add **s** or **es** to the end of the noun.

Regular Plurals
1. Add **s** to the end of most words.   one desk → two desk**s**   a telephone → four telephone**s**
2. Add **es** if the word ends with **s, x, z, sh,** or **ch**.   one dish → six dish**es**
3. Change the **y** to **i** and add **es** if the word ends in a **consonant + y**.   one story → four stor**ies**

Remember, when you make the noun plural, you need to change the <u>verb be</u> and <u>pronouns</u>, too.

singular	plural
is was	are were
this that	these those
he, she, it	they

1 **Make each sentence plural.**
Example: This is a curtain. → *These are curtains.*

1. That is a coffee table.   **3.** That is his rug.

2. This is a new couch.   **4.** She is a nice lady.

Some nouns are **irregular** in the **plural**. You must learn these words.

Nouns with Irregular Plurals	
Singular Noun	**Plural Noun**
man, woman	men, women
person	people
child	children
foot, tooth	feet, teeth
deer, fish	deer, fish

2 **Make each sentence plural.**
Example: This is a tooth. → *These are teeth.*

1. He is a gentleman.   **3.** This is a fish.

2. She is a child.   **4.** That is a mouse.

Workbook
page 177

Independent Practice
CD-ROM

A, An, Some, Any

With nouns, we often use **a**, **an**, **some**, and **any**.
- Use **a** or **an** for **singular nouns**.
- Use **some** or **any** for **plural nouns**.
  - Use **some** for **positive statements**.
  - Use **any** for **negative statements** and **questions**.

	Singular Nouns	Plural Nouns
positive statements	Use **a** or **an**. I have **a** couch. There is **an** oven.	Use **some**. I have **some** chairs. There are **some** pillows.
negative statements	Use **a** or **an**. I don't have **a** table.	Use **any**. I don't have **any** rugs. There aren't **any** ovens.
questions	Use **a** or **an**. Do you have **a** dresser? Is there **an** armchair?	Use **any**. Do you have **any** chairs? Are there **any** pillows?

3 Complete these sentences with **a**, **an**, **some**, or **any**.

1. There aren't ____ rugs in the living room.
2. Hiro needs ____ refrigerator for his kitchen.
3. Do you have ____ curtains for your new house?
4. There are ____ pillows on the couch.

✏ Writing Conventions

Spelling *Regular Plural Nouns*

1. Add **s** if the word ends in **vowel + o**.
   radio ➜ radio**s**   stereo ➜ stereo**s**
2. Add **es** if the word ends in **consonant + o**.
   tomato ➜ tomato**es**   potato ➜ potato**es**
3. Change the **f** to **v** and add **s** if the word ends in **fe**.
   life ➜ li**ves**   wife ➜ wi**ves**
4. Change **f** to **v** and add **es** if the word ends in **f**.
   half ➜ hal**ves**   loaf ➜ loa**ves**

Apply Make these words plural.

1. patio   2. wolf   3. knife   4. mosquito

> ✓ **Checkpoint**
>
> Make these sentences plural.
> a. She is a lady.
> b. He is my child.
> c. That is my knife.

Word Study

Silent e

Phonemic Awareness

Some words end with a consonant followed by *e*.
In these words, the *e* is **silent**. Do not say it. Words that
end in **silent e** usually have a long vowel sound.

1 Listen and repeat.

plate   slide   rose   cube

Decoding

2 Listen to the pair of words.

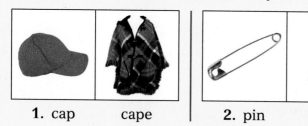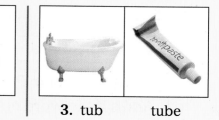

1. cap   cape   **2.** pin   pine   **3.** tub   tube

3 Listen again and repeat.

4 Say the word. Then add **e**. Say the new word.

1. cut   cut ____   **3.** not   not ____

2. kit   kit ____   **4.** tap   tap ____

5 Spell and say the words in activity 4.

Decodable
Reader 33

● Word Study

Vowel digraph: -oo- and u

Phonemic Awareness

These vowels have the same sound, even though the spellings are very different.

1 **Listen and repeat.**

oo

hood   wool

Note: **ould** in *should* and *could* makes the same sound as -oo- and u.

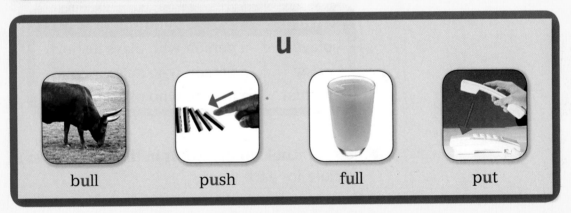

u

bull   push   full   put

Decoding

2 **Listen. Find the -oo- sounds in each sentence.**
1. He pulled the wool cap.
2. She could put her foot there.
3. The cook shook the wooden bowl.
4. They pulled and pushed.

3 **Listen again and repeat.**

✓Checkpoint

Read these words.
late
hose
foot
pull
would

Decodable Reader 39

Workbook page 180

Independent Practice CD-ROM

● Word Study

Suffixes: er, or, ist

A **suffix** is a group of letters you can add to the end of a word. The suffix changes the meaning of the root word. You need to change the spelling of some words to add a suffix.

Suffix	Examples
er = person or thing that does something	teach**er**, work**er**, comput**er**
or = a person who does something	doct**or**, visit**or**
ist = a person who does something	pian**ist**, dent**ist**

1 Read each word and definition.

Word	Definition
play**er**	a person who plays a sport
act**or**	a person who acts
pian**ist**	a person who plays piano

2  **PAIR WORK** Look up the words in the chart. Make a picture for each word.

3 Copy the sentences. Write the missing word from the chart above.

Example: The _dentist_ looked at Lamar's teeth.

1. The students use a ⬚ to do their homework.
2. The ⬚ in that movie is very good.
3. We listened to the ⬚ at the concert for hours.
4. Who is your favorite soccer ⬚?

✓**Checkpoint**
A violin is for playing music. What is a *violinist*?

Workbook page 181

Writing Assignment
Descriptive Paragraph

> **Writing Prompt**
>
> Look around a room in your home or classroom. Write a paragraph about objects in the room.

1. Read the student model.

Student Model

Jamil Ali

In My Kitchen

In my kitchen there is a table with three chairs. Of course, there is an oven and a refrigerator. There is one sink. There are some cabinets with dishes in them. There is a small rug near the sink. There is a door to the dining room. There are two windows over the sink. The windows have yellow curtains. My family is very big, so we cannot eat in the kitchen at the same time. We eat in the dining room.

2. What is in the room? Make a list. Use a picture dictionary to find new words.
3. Write your paragraph. Use the model.
4. Use the **Writing Checklist** to check your paragraph.

Writing Checklist
1. I indented the first sentence of my paragraph.
2. I spelled regular and irregular plural nouns correctly.
3. I used a, an, some, and any correctly.

Objectives

Reading Strategy
Recognize cause and effect

Text Genre
Myth

Listening and Speaking
Act out a story

Literary Elements
Problem and solution

Writing Conventions
Spelling homophones: two, to, too

Writing
Short story

Academic Vocabulary

cause | effect

Academic Content

myths

● About the Reading

You are going to read a short story from ancient Greece. The Greek civilization lasted from 750 BC to 146 BC. This story explains why spiders make webs.

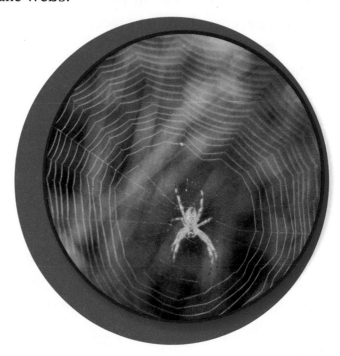

● Use Prior Knowledge

Talk About Contests

People enter contests to see who is the best. For example, a spelling bee is a contest in which students spell words. The contest is to see who is the best speller in the class, school, or even country. There are contests for many different things. There are school contests, sports contests, and even eating contests!

1. **GROUP WORK** List some contests you know.

2. Tell your group about a contest you, a relative, or friend entered. This is an informal discussion. Relax and be yourself as you talk.

3. Tell the class if you won a contest.

Vocabulary From the Reading
Learn, Practice, and Use Independently

Key Vocabulary

angry
behave
contest
spider
weave

Learn Vocabulary Look at the pictures. Read the sentences. Look at the **highlighted** words. What do these words mean?

1. Mary became **angry** because someone broke a window.

2. The students **behave** very well when a visitor comes to class.

3. The boys had a running **contest**. Joe won.

4. The **spider** made a web.

5. The Mayans **weave** beautiful cloth.

Synonyms and Antonyms
Use a thesaurus or dictionary to find synonyms and antonyms for **angry**.

Practice Vocabulary Fill in the blanks with Key Vocabulary words.

1. A ____ crawled into the house.
2. We had a ____ to find out who could read fastest.
3. I want to yell and scream when I get ____ .
4. The teacher was happy to see the students ____ well in class.
5. She likes to ____ and make beautiful cloth.

Use Vocabulary Independently PAIR WORK Work with a partner. Make a sentence using a Key Vocabulary word. Take turns.

✓Checkpoint
1. Tell about something that makes you **angry**.
2. What kinds of **contests** does your school have?

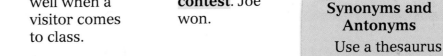

Vocabulary Log | Workbook page 183 | Independent Practice CD-ROM

Unit 4 • Chapter 1 **267**

Academic Vocabulary
Vocabulary for the Reading Strategy

Word	Explanation	Sample Sentence	Visual Cue
cause *noun*	a reason something happens	The **cause** of the accident was a loose nail.	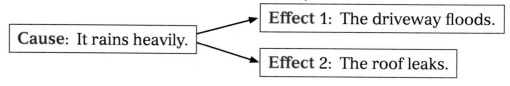
effect *noun*	the result of something else	The **effect** of his hard work was he passed his test easily!	

Draw a picture or write a sentence for each word.

Reading Strategy
Recognize Cause and Effect

Cause is the reason something happens. **Effect** is what happens because of the **cause**. It can be a good or bad thing. There can be one or more **effects**.

Cause: It rains heavily. → **Effect 1:** The driveway floods.

→ **Effect 2:** The roof leaks.

> fiction *(n.)* 1. stories that a writer imagines; not true stories. 2. *(adj.)* something not real.

Dictionary Entry

Text Genre
Myth

A **myth** is a story. It is not true. Myths usually explain why something is the way it is in nature. Characters in myths may have special powers.

Myth	
characters with special powers	people in myths can often do things that real people can't do
explanation	a reason why something in nature is the way it is

✓ Checkpoint

1. What comes first, the **cause** or **effect**?
2. What do **myths** explain?

Vocabulary Log

Workbook page 184, 185

Independent Practice CD-ROM

● Reading

Reading Focus Questions

As you read, think about these questions.

1. What are Athena's special powers?
2. What does Arachne learn about saying she is the best **weaver**?

THE STORY OF
Arachne

1   This myth is from a long time ago. It is more than two **thousand** years old. Back then, people in **Greece** had stories about different **gods and goddesses** with special powers. Athena was the goddess of wisdom. Athena was also the best **weaver** in the world.

---

thousand = 1,000

Greece the name of a country

gods and goddesses immortal beings that have powers humans do not have

Reading Check

1. **Recall facts**
   How old is this myth?

2. **Make inferences**
   Why does Athena have special powers?

2   The story begins with a young woman named Arachne. She lived in Greece and she loved to **weave**. She was very good at **weaving**. She could **weave** beautiful pictures into her cloth.

Reading Strategy

Recognize cause and effect What **caused** Arachne to think she was special?

3   Many people told Arachne how much they liked her work. She started to think she was very special. Then she began to **brag**. Arachne said, "I am the best **weaver** in the world. I am even better than Athena."

4   Athena heard what Arachne said. She went to talk to Arachne. She dressed up like an old lady. Arachne did not know it was Athena. Athena told Arachne, "You should not say you are better than a goddess. You might make Athena **angry**."

5   Arachne did not stop bragging. She told the old lady, "I am not afraid of Athena. If I see her, I will tell her I am a better **weaver**!"

---

brag to tell others you are the best at something

6 Athena became **angry**. She showed Arachne who she really was. Then Athena said, "You can only say you are a better **weaver** if you can beat me in a **weaving contest**."

7 They had a **weaving contest**. Athena **wove** a cloth with pictures of gods and goddesses doing good to humans. Arachne **wove** a picture of gods and goddesses **behaving** badly.

8 Arachne's pictures made Athena even more **angry**. She turned Arachne into a **spider**. Arachne and her children and her grandchildren could only **weave spider** webs for all of time. This story explains where **spiders** came from and why they **weave** webs.

Reading Strategy

Recognize cause and effect What was the **effect** of Arachne's bragging?

✓ **Reading Check**

1. **Recall facts** How did Athena dress to go talk to Arachne?

2. **Understand character motives** Why does Athena say they should have a **weaving contest**?

3. **Make predictions** What will Arachne do now that she is a **spider**?

● Reading Comprehension Questions

Think and Discuss

1. **Recall facts** What does Arachne love to do?

2. **Cause and effect** Why did Athena and Arachne have a **weaving contest**?

3. **Make inferences** Why do you think Arachne's picture made Athena more **angry**?

4. **Relate to prior knowledge** Do you think a **contest** was the best way to solve the problem? What are some other possible ways to fix the problem?

5. **Revisit the Reading Focus Questions** Go back to page 269 and discuss the questions.

● Listening and Speaking

Act Out a Story

 **PAIR WORK** Retell the story of Arachne to your class.

1. With a partner write the most important idea of each paragraph. Example: *Athena was a Greek goddess and the best **weaver** in the world.*

2. Change the sentences to present tense and first person. Example: *Athena: I am a Greek goddess and the best **weaver** in the world.*

3. Use Key Vocabulary words and words from the text to get your meaning across.

4. Think about language to get feelings or tone across. For example, how can you show Arachne's pride? How can you show Athena's anger?

5. Act out "The Story of Arachne." One reads what Athena says. The other person reads what Arachne says.

6. Present the story to the class. Show what happens in the story. Read your new sentences.

Phrases for Conversation

Showing How Characters Feel

I'm the best!
I'm better than you.
I don't like that.
I'm really **angry** now!

Workbook
page 186

Independent Practice
CD-ROM

● Literary Elements

Problem and Solution

In many stories there is a **problem**. A problem makes the story interesting. We read because we want to find the **solution**.

A solution is what stops the problem. Sometimes the solution is not happy, but it stops the problem.

In "The Story of Arachne," the problem is Arachne and Athena both believe they are the best **weaver** in the world. The solution is Athena turns Arachne into a **spider**.

Think of a problem from your life or a story you know. Tell your partner what the problem was and what the solution was.

Writing Conventions

Spelling *Homophones: two, to, too*

Read these words aloud: **to**, **too**, **two**. They are homophones. They sound the same but have different spellings and meanings.

Homophones	Sentence
two = 2 (number)	I have **two** pillows.
to = part of a verb = preposition	You need **to** eat. She went **to** the store.
too = also	He has a book. I have a book, **too**.

Apply Write the sentences with the correct word. Check your spelling.

1. There are ____ couches in the room.

2. There is a dresser in the room, ____ .

3. Go ____ the kitchen.

4. I don't have any lamps. I need ____ buy some.

5. I have ____ buy a mirror, ____ .

✓ Checkpoint

Is the **solution** in "The Story of Arachne" a happy solution?

Workbook
page 187, 188

Independent Practice
CD-ROM

● Writing Assignment

Short Story

Writing Prompt

Write an alternative ending to "The Story of Arachne." Read the story again. Find a different way to solve the problem. Write a new ending. Remember:

- A myth tells about something in nature. Your new ending for "The Story of Arachne" should tell why **spiders weave**.
- Characters can have special powers.

---

1. **Read the student model.**

An essay is a group of paragraphs about the same topic. The first paragraph is the **introduction**. The introduction tells what the story or essay is about. It sometimes introduces the problem.

The middle paragraphs are **body paragraphs**. They give more information about the topic. Each paragraph has a new main idea. In your essay, your body paragraphs will give the solution.

The last paragraph is the **conclusion**. Your conclusion should give the explanation.

2. **Brainstorm.** Decide how a new ending will change the story's message. What new message do you want to give?

3. **Plan.** Write notes for your new ending.

   a. What is the problem?

   b. What is a possible solution to the problem?

   c. Why do **spiders weave**?

Title:
Introduction: What is the problem?
Body: What is the solution to the problem?
Conclusion: Why do **spiders weave**?

4. **Write your new ending.** Use your notes.

Benito Muñoz

The New Story of Arachne

Athena and Arachne had a problem. Athena said she was the best weaver and Arachne said she was the best, too. They had a weaving contest. Athena started to weave first. Arachne watched Athena. Arachne saw that Athena really was a better weaver.

Arachne had an idea. The contest finished. Athena's cloth had pictures of the gods and goddesses. It was great! Arachne showed her cloth. She made a picture of Athena. Athena was teaching humans and animals how to weave. It made Athena look very beautiful.

Arachne showed Athena her cloth. She said, "I am sorry. I know now that you are a better weaver." Athena wasn't angry. She gave Arachne power to talk to the animals. Athena said to Arachne, "You are a very good weaver. You can teach the animals how to weave."

Introduction:
Introduce the idea. State the problem.

Body paragraph:
What happened

Conclusion:
Explanation

5. **Revise.** Reread your paragraph. Add, delete, or rearrange words or sentences to make your paragraph clearer. Use the editing and proofreading symbols on page 493 to help you mark the changes you need to make.

6. **Edit.** Use the **Writing Checklist** to help you find problems and errors.

Writing Checklist

1. My ending tells why **spiders weave**.

2. I spelled regular and irregular plurals correctly.

3. I wrote three paragraphs with three to four sentences.

Progress Check

How well did you understand this chapter? Try to answer the questions. If necessary, go back to the pages listed for a review.

Skills	Skills Assessment Questions	Pages to Review
Vocabulary	What rooms are in a house? What is in your living room?	**256–259**
Grammar	When do you use a **plural noun**? What are **irregular plural nouns**?	**260–261**
Writing Conventions	**Spelling:** What are the spelling rules for making regular plurals? **Spelling:** Write a sentence for *two*, *to*, and *too*.	**260** **273**
Word Study	What do these suffixes mean: **er, or, ist**?	**264**
Vocabulary From the Reading	What do these words mean? • **angry, behave, contest, spider, weave**	**267**
Academic Vocabulary	What is a **cause**? What is an **effect**? Which comes first?	**268**
Reading Strategy	Which is the **cause** and which is the **effect** in this sentence? He got an A+ on his math test because he studied very hard all week.	**268**
Text Genre	What is the text genre of "The Story of Arachne"?	**268**
Reading Comprehension	What is "The Story of Arachne" about?	**269–272**
Listening and Speaking	**Phrases for Conversation:** What phrases can you use to show how characters feel?	**272**
Literary Elements	What is the **problem** in "The Story of Arachne"? What is the **solution**?	**273**

Assessment Practice

Read this myth. Then answer Questions 1 through 4.

Anansi the Spider

1   Anansi the spider put some yams in his oven. When the yams were cooked, he was ready to eat. Then Anansi heard Turtle at the door. Turtle said, "I am hungry!" Anansi did not want to share his yams. He said, "Turtle, wash your hands before you eat." Turtle walked slowly to the river. Anansi quickly ate his dinner. Finally, Turtle returned. He saw there was no dinner left. Turtle was angry.

2   A few days later, Anansi went to see Turtle. Turtle lived at the bottom of the river. Anansi tried to dive down to Turtle's house but he floated back up. Then Anansi had an idea. He put stones in his coat pockets. He sank to the bottom of the river. Turtle said, "Anansi, you cannot eat with your coat on." Anansi took off his coat. He floated back up to the top of the river. Turtle ate all the food.

1 Read this sentence from paragraph 1.

> Anansi the spider put some yams in his oven.

Why did Anansi put the yams in the oven?

A to store them   C to wash them

B to hear them   D to cook them

2 How does Anansi try to solve a problem in paragraph 2?

A He puts stones in his coat pockets.

B He goes to visit Turtle.

C He takes his coat off.

D He dives to the bottom of the river.

3 In paragraph 2, what is the effect of putting stones in his pockets?

A Turtle ate the food.

B Turtle lived at the bottom of the river.

C Anansi sank to the bottom of the river.

D Anansi floated back up.

4 What is the genre of this text?

A poem   C myth

B textbook   D letter

Writing on Demand: Alternative Ending

Read the story about Anansi again. Write an alternative ending in which Anansi and Turtle eat together. Include details about the meal. Explain where and what they ate.
(20 minutes)

> **Writing Tip**
> Make notes to yourself about what you want to say. Then check your notes as you write.

Objectives

Vocabulary
Food and drinks
Other foods and dishes

Listening and Speaking
Talking about food and drinks
Saying what you have and need

Grammar
Count and noncount nouns

Writing Conventions
Punctuation: Commas in a series

Word Study
Long a

Writing
Descriptive essay

● **Vocabulary**
Food and Drinks

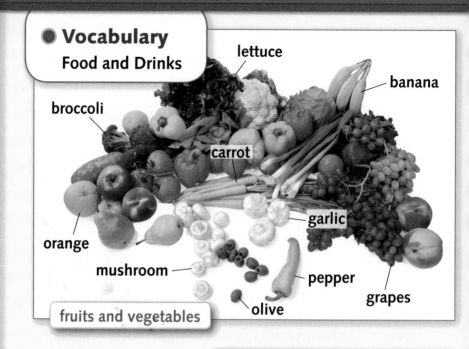

lettuce
banana
broccoli
carrot
garlic
orange
mushroom
pepper
grapes
olive

fruits and vegetables

bread
cereal
pasta
rice

grains

meat
cheese
egg

proteins

chicken
fish
ground meat
beef

meat

juice
milk
water
lemonade

drinks

Part A

● **Listening and Speaking**

Talking About Food and Drinks

1 Listen and repeat the words on page 278.

2  PAIR WORK Tell your partner which foods on page 278 you like and which foods on page 278 you don't like.

3 Read and listen.

Tammy: Dad, what's for **dinner**?

Father: We're having **chicken** and **mushrooms**.

Tammy: What else are we having?

Father: What do you want?

Tammy: Can we have some **pasta**?

Father: No, we don't have any **pasta**. How about **rice**?

Tammy: Great!

Build Vocabulary
breakfast = morning meal
lunch = noon meal
dinner = evening meal

4 Listen again. Repeat.

5 PAIR WORK Say the conversation again. Use new words for the blue words. You can use vocabulary from page 278.

√ Checkpoint

Draw three foods and two drinks. Label each one.

● Vocabulary

Other Foods and Dishes

1 **Read and listen.**

dishes = plate, bowl
silverware = fork,
   knife, spoon

2 **Listen and repeat.**

3  **PAIR WORK Look at the picture. Answer these questions.**

> What do you
> eat in a bowl?

> I eat cereal
> in a bowl.

1. What do you eat in a bowl?
2. What do you drink in a glass?
3. What do you eat with a fork?
4. What do you eat with a spoon?

Prepositions
Notice these
prepositions.
  in a bowl
  in a glass
  on a plate
  with a knife

4 **PAIR WORK Look at the picture again. Ask your partner these questions. Your partner will answer. Take turns.**

> What do you
> put butter on?

> I put butter
> on pasta.

1. What food do you put butter on?
2. What food do you put salsa on?
3. What food do you put salt on?
4. What food do you put ketchup on?

- ## Listening and Speaking
Saying What You Have and Need

1 **Read and listen.**

Jorge: Do we need any **eggs**?

Father: No, we have some **eggs**. But we don't have any **milk**.

Jorge: OK. We need **milk**. I'm writing a list.

Father: Great! We also need some **rice**.

Jorge: OK. It's on the list!

2 **Listen and repeat.**

3  **PAIR WORK Practice the conversation in activity 1. Use new words for the blue words. You can use vocabulary on page 278 and page 280.**

4 **Listen. What things do Anita and David have? What things do they need? Write H if they have the food. Write N if they need it.**

_____ 1. rice	_____ 5. sugar
_____ 2. beans	_____ 6. oil
_____ 3. apples	_____ 7. butter
_____ 4. chicken	_____ 8. eggs

Build Vocabulary

soup

sandwich

salad

✓Checkpoint

What things do you need to make a sandwich?

Vocabulary Log

Workbook
page 190

Independent Practice
CD-ROM

Unit 4 • Chapter 2   **281**

● Grammar

Count and Noncount Nouns

Count Nouns
an egg / 2 eggs
one apple / 3 apples
a pear / 6 pears
Noncount Nouns
rice
milk
some butter

English has two kinds of nouns: **count** and **noncount**.

- **Count nouns** are things you can count. They have a singular form and a plural form.
- **Noncount nouns** are things you cannot count.
  1. things that are too small to count = rice or sugar
  2. liquids = milk or water
  3. things that are too large to be for one person = bread or butter

1 **PAIR WORK Are these things count or noncount?**

1. oil
2. orange
3. cheese
4. tomato
5. juice

Review rules for **a**, **an**, **some**, **any** on page 261.

In Unit 4, Chapter 1, you learned about **a**, **an**, **some**, and **any**. Here are some more rules with count and noncount nouns.

- Use **a** or **an** with singular count nouns:

  I have **a sandwich**. I need **an apple**.

- Use **some** with plural count nouns:

  I have some **apples**. I need some **eggs**.

- Use **some** with noncount nouns:

  I have some **rice**. I need some **milk**.

- Use **any** with count and noncount nouns:

  I don't have any **beans**. Do you have any **sugar**?

2 Complete these sentences with **a**, **an**, **some**, or **any**.

1. I don't have ____ sugar.
2. Tara needs ____ orange for the salad.
3. Does Juan have ____ rice?
4. Robert wants ____ butter for his bread.
5. We have ____ sandwiches for lunch.

Workbook
page 191

Independent Practice
CD-ROM

Use a singular verb *be* with a noncount noun.

Example: There **is** some milk in the refrigerator.

3 **Complete the sentences with is or are.**

1. There _____ some apples on the table.
2. There _____ some rice in the bowl.
3. There _____ an orange on the plate.
4. There _____ a banana with the fruit.
5. There _____ three grapes left.

4 **PAIR WORK** **Write a list of foods and drinks you like. Decide if they are count or noncount.**

Count Nouns	Noncount Nouns
apples beans	pizza milk

5 **Make a sentence for each item in the list. Use there is or there are.**

Examples: *There are some apples on the table.*
There is some pizza.

✎ Writing Conventions

Punctuation *Commas in a Series*

Remember to use commas (,) for items in a series:

We need some sugar, butter, ketchup, and mustard.

There are some peaches, apples, and bananas.

Apply Write these sentences with commas.

1. We need some bread an apple and some milk.
2. There is some butter milk and sugar on the table.
3. There is some ketchup mustard and oil on the sandwich.

✓Checkpoint

1. Name 3 **count nouns**. Use them in sentences.
2. Name 3 **noncount nouns**. Use them in sentences.

GRAMMAR EXPANSION
Quantifiers,
Workbook page 193

Workbook
page 192

Independent Practice
CD-ROM

Unit 4 • Chapter 2   **283**

● Word Study

Long a

Phonemic Awareness

1 Listen and repeat.

> Remember that the **e** is silent!

rake	lemonade	lake
tail	rain	braid
hay	tray	weigh

Decoding

2 Listen. Choose the word you hear.

1. man	mane		**4.** pain	pan
2. ate	at		**5.** land	lay
3. pal	pale		**6.** say	sand

3 Listen again and repeat.

✓ **Checkpoint**

Read these words.
  train
  neighbor
  stay
  late
  bait

Decodable
Reader 42

Workbook
page 194

Independent Practice
CD-ROM

Writing Assignment
Descriptive Essay

> **Writing Prompt**
>
> What kinds of foods do people like?

1. Read the student model.

Phuong Nguyen

Pedro's Favorite Foods

Today, Pedro and I talked about food. He told me what he likes to eat. The food he eats at home is delicious.

Pedro's family eats a lot of rice, vegetables, and meat. Pedro's favorite food is fish. He eats fried fish, baked fish, and even fish soup! He says the perfect dinner is fish and rice.

The food Pedro told me about sounds delicious. I also think it sounds healthy. I want to go to Pedro's house for dinner some time.

2. Interview a classmate. Ask questions. Take notes.
Examples: What do you usually eat at home?
Do you like vegetables?

3. Write your essay.

4. Revise. Read your essay. Add, delete, or rearrange words or sentences to make your paragraphs clearer. Use the editing and proofreading symbols on page 493 to help you mark the changes you need to make.

5. Edit. Use the **Writing Checklist** to help you find problems and errors.

Writing Checklist

1. I used correct count and noncount nouns.

2. I used commas in a series.

3. I gave my opinion in the conclusion.

Objectives

Reading Strategy
Take notes

Text Genre
Expository text

Listening and Speaking
Asking clarifying questions

Text Elements
Photos and illustrations

Reading Fluency
Repeated reading

Writing
Process

Academic Vocabulary

| notes | graphic organizer |

Academic Content

United States history

● About the Reading

You are going to read an expository text. This expository text gives information about symbols of the United States.

● Use Prior Knowledge

Use Symbols

A symbol is a person, object, or event that stands for something else. For example, flags are symbols of each country. $ is a symbol for dollar or sometimes people use it as a symbol for money.

1. **PAIR WORK** Match the symbols below with the meaning.

Symbol	Meaning
1. ¢	a. and
2. &	b. percent (in 100)
3. #	c. at
4. %	d. number
5. @	e. cents

2. Think of symbols you use in math class. Copy the chart. Add symbols and meanings.

Math Symbols	
+	add
−	subtract

Vocabulary From the Reading
Learn, Practice, and Use Independently

Key Vocabulary

liberty

monument

national

represent

symbol

Learn Vocabulary Read the sentences. Use the context to find the meaning of the **highlighted** words.

1. People in the United States have **liberty**. They are free to do many things.
2. There is a **monument** in the middle of the town. It is a statue of Abraham Lincoln.
3. The **national** government makes laws for the whole country.
4. When I think of winter, I think of snow and ice. Snow and ice **represent** winter to me.
5. A green light is a **symbol** that means "go."

Practice Vocabulary Complete the sentences with Key Vocabulary words.

Example: If you can do what you want, you have __liberty__ .

1. A picture of a cloud on a weather map is a ____ that means it is cloudy outside.
2. The rose is the ____ flower of the United States.
3. The city built a ____ in the park.
4. A sign on the road showing a picture of a tent can ____ a place to camp.

Use Vocabulary Independently 👥 PAIR WORK Write a paragraph that uses the Key Vocabulary words. Share your paragraph with a partner.

✓**Checkpoint**

1. Describe a **monument** that you know.
2. What are some things that **represent** the beginning of the school year?

Vocabulary Log

Workbook page 196

Independent Practice CD-ROM

Unit 4 • Chapter 2   **287**

● Academic Vocabulary

Vocabulary for the Reading Strategy

Word	Explanation	Sample Sentence	Visual Cue
notes *plural noun*	short written reminders of what you have read or heard	Brad takes **notes** when he reads his homework.	
graphic organizer *noun*	a way to picture information	Lin drew a **graphic organizer** of the main ideas.	

Draw a picture or write a sentence for each word.

● Reading Strategy

Take Notes

Take **notes** on paper as you read.
- **Identify what you read.** Write the title, chapter, and page number.
- **Take notes.** Write down the important ideas.
- **Use your own words.** Do not copy from the book.
- **Keep notes short.** Do not write sentences.
- **Draw** a **graphic organizer** to help you organize.

● Text Genre

Expository Text

nonfiction *(n.)* stories, books, and articles about real people and events.

Dictionary Entry

"**Symbols** of the United States" is **expository text**. Expository text is a form of nonfiction writing.

Expository Text	
subject	what the text is about
facts	true information
explanations	tell how someone does something
captions	words under a picture or illustration to explain what it is

✓**Checkpoint**

1. Why should you take **notes**?
2. Is a story about a talking eagle **expository text**? Why or why not?

Vocabulary Log

Workbook pages 197, 198

Independent Practice CD-ROM

Reading

Reading Focus Questions

As you read, think about these questions.

1. What are some **symbols** of the United States?
2. How are the American flag and the Statue of **Liberty** alike?

Symbols of the
United
States

1   The United States has many **national symbols** to **represent** the ideas of the country. Like other countries, the American flag **represents** the United States to its **citizens**. Some other **symbols** of the United States are the bald eagle and the Statue of **Liberty**. **Symbols** bring people in a country together. They are things that all people in the United States share.

2   What do you think about when you see an American flag? Some people might think of freedom. Other people think of being strong. Most people think of the U.S. government or the **Pledge of Allegiance**. Even the shapes on the flag are **symbols**. The 13 stripes on the flag **represent** the first 13 colonies, which later became the first 13 states. The 50 stars **represent** the 50 states.

---

citizen a person who lives in and belongs to a place
Pledge of Allegiance a promise to be loyal and faithful to the laws of the country

Reading Strategy

Take notes What are some **symbols** of the United States?

Reading Check

1. **Recall facts** Name a **symbol** of the U.S.

2. **Think and search** What do people think when they see the U.S. flag?

3. **Predict** How might the U.S. flag change if there is a new state?

Reading Strategy

Take notes Write down the **symbols** listed on this page. What do they **represent**?

3   Another famous **symbol** of the United States is the bald eagle. It became the country's **national** bird in 1782. The **founders** of the U.S. government wanted a **national** bird that would **represent** the United States. Benjamin Franklin wanted the turkey to be the **national** bird. The turkey is from North America. However, the other leaders wanted a **symbol** that would make people think of strength. They chose the bald eagle because they thought it looked powerful.

4   The Statue of **Liberty** is an important **symbol** to many people in the United States. It was a gift from France. The finished statue was put up in 1886. **Immigrants** saw the statue when they came to the United States. It meant freedom and a new life.

5   Here are some other **symbols** of the United States:

1 The **Liberty** Bell

6   The **Liberty** Bell rang when the leaders of the new United States signed the **Declaration of Independence**. It is in Philadelphia, PA. It is a **symbol** of freedom and independence.

The **Liberty** Bell was first rung in 1776.

2 Uncle Sam

7   Uncle Sam is a **symbol** of the U.S. government. He is a man with a white beard. He wears red, white, and blue.

Uncle Sam often walks in **parades**.

founder a person who begins or sets up something for the first time

immigrant a person who has come to live in a country from another country

Declaration of Independence the document U.S. leaders signed to say they did not want to be a part of England's government

parade event where people walk in the street, as a celebration

③ The Capitol

8   The Capitol building is a very large building. The founders of the U.S. government wanted the building to look powerful to people visiting the United States for the first time. People make laws for the United States in the Capitol building.

The Capitol is a building in Washington, D.C.

Reading Strategy

Take notes Write down the symbols listed on this page. What do they represent?

The Washington Monument is in Washington, D.C.

④ The Washington Monument

9   The Washington Monument was built for George Washington. George Washington was the first president of the United States. It is tall and represents strength.

⑤ The Great Seal

10   The Great Seal is a special design that the founders of the United States made. It has a picture of a pyramid and an eye on one side. The other side shows an eagle. Remember the eagle represents freedom and power.

The Great Seal is on the one-dollar bill.

Reading Check

1. Recall facts Where is the Liberty Bell?
2. Think and search What happens at the Capitol building?
3. Make inferences Why do you think Uncle Sam wears red, white, and blue?

Reading Comprehension Questions

Think and Discuss

1. **Recall facts** What is the **national** bird of the United States?

2. **Identify sequence** Which **symbol** did the U.S. have first: the Statue of **Liberty** or the **Liberty** Bell?

3. **Draw conclusions** Why do **symbols** bring people together?

4. **Understand captions** How does the caption under the photo of Uncle Sam help you understand where we see him?

5. **Revisit the Reading Focus Questions** Go back to page 289 and discuss the questions.

Listening and Speaking

Ask Your Partner Clarifying Questions

 **PAIR WORK** Role play an interview.

1. One person plays the role of a television reporter.

   • Look at your **notes**. Think of wh- questions you can ask about the American **symbols**.

   • Look at the reading. What questions are answered in the reading? Write the questions down as **notes**.

2. Another person plays the role of an expert on **symbols**.

   • An expert is a person who knows a lot about something.

   • Look at the reading again. Create a **graphic organizer** for each U.S. **symbol**.

3. The reporter asks questions to the expert. Ask questions if you don't understand.

4. When you answer questions, give more information. Give more details.

5. Role-play your interview in front of the class.

Phrases for Conversation

Asking Clarifying Questions

Who is . . .?

Why is . . . an important **symbol**?

How do **symbols** bring people together?

What did France give to the United States?

Where can you find . . . ?

Workbook page 199

Independent Practice CD-ROM

● Text Elements

Photos and Illustrations

A **photo** is a photograph of a real object. An **illustration** is an artist's drawing. Photos or illustrations are also called pictures.

The words next to or below the photo or illustration are the **caption**. A caption explains what the picture is or where it is from.

Photos and illustrations make a reading more interesting. Also, they can give important points. Use photos and illustrations to understand the main idea of a text.

Look at the photos in "**Symbols** of the United States." How do the captions help you understand the text?

The Liberty Bell was first rung in 1776.

● Reading Fluency

Repeated Reading

Reading something two or three times helps you build fluency and comprehension (or understanding). Reading something again is called **repeated reading**.

1. With a partner, read the first two paragraphs of the text "**Symbols** of the United States." (See page 289.) Your partner listens for errors. Your partner also times your reading.

2. After you read, your partner tells you how long it took you to read. Your partner also tells you what mistakes or errors you made.

3. Reread the two paragraphs three times. Each time you reread, try not to make errors and try to read faster. Also think about your rhythm and intonation.

4. Now your partner reads and you listen for errors. Write down the errors you hear. Time how long your partner takes to read.

> **✓Checkpoint**
>
> Look at the **caption** on page 291. Where is the Capitol building?

Workbook
page 200

Independent Practice
CD-ROM

● Writing Assignment

Process

Writing Suggestion

Think about the steps. Put the steps in order. Number each step. Make sure each step has the facts you need to do it.

> **Writing Prompt**
>
> Write a description of how to make something that looks like a **symbol** of the United States. It can be some kind of food, a drawing, a model, a piñata, or anything else you can think of!

1. Read the student model.

Student Model

Luisa Hernandez

How To Make a Star Hanging

1. Get the following things:
   a) a piece of red, blue, and white paper
   b) white glue or a glue stick
   c) yarn or string
   d) scissors
   e) a quarter (dated before 1999)
2. Cut out a large red star, a medium blue star, and a small white star. The white star must be bigger than a quarter.
3. Place the quarter on the table with the Great Seal up.
4. Place the white paper on top of the quarter.
5. Rub a pencil across the paper on the quarter. See the Great Seal on the paper.
6. Glue the white star on the blue star. Glue the blue star on the red star.
7. Make a hole in the top of the red star.
8. Put the string or yarn through the hole.
9. Tie the two ends of the string together. Your hanging is finished!

2. **Brainstorm.** Think of some **symbols** of the United States. What do they look like? Write **notes** in a **graphic organizer**.

American flag	Liberty Bell	Eagle
red, white, and blue rectangle, flat	brown round	brown and white many sides

3. **Organize your information.** Think about how to make it. Write **notes** with your ideas.

4. **Write your list.** Write each step of the process. Number each step. Make sure each step has all the facts you need to complete it.

5. **Revise.** Read your list. Add, delete, or rearrange steps to make the process clear. Use the editing and proofreading **symbols** on page 493 to help you mark the changes you need to make.

6. **Edit.** Use the **Writing Checklist** to help you find problems and errors.

Writing Checklist
1. I numbered each step of the process.
2. I wrote the steps in the correct order.
3. I included all the facts necessary to complete each step.
4. I used imperatives to begin each step.
5. I wrote each step in complete sentences.

Progress Check

MILESTONESTRACKER

How well did you understand this chapter? Try to answer the questions. If necessary, go back to the pages listed for a review.

Skills	Skills Assessment Questions	Pages to Review
Vocabulary	What foods and drinks do you like?	278–281
Grammar	Give two examples of **count** and **noncount nouns**.	282–283
Writing Convention	**Punctuation:** What punctuation do you use when you list things in a series?	283
Vocabulary From the Reading	What do these words mean? • **liberty, monument, national, represent, symbol**	287
Academic Vocabulary	What is a **note**? What is a **graphic organizer**?	288
Reading Strategy	Why is it important to take **notes**?	288
Text Genre	What is the text genre of "**Symbols** of the United States"?	288
Reading Comprehension	Name three **symbols** from "**Symbols** of the United States."	289–291
Listening and Speaking	**Phrases for Conversation:** What questions can you ask to clarify information?	292
Text Elements	What does a **caption** tell about a **photo** or an **illustration**?	293
Reading Fluency	How does reading a passage again help your reading rate?	293

Assessment Practice

Read this expository text. Then answer Questions 1 through 4.

Thanksgiving

1   The early Americans had a big dinner in 1621. This was the first Thanksgiving. Thanksgiving was made a national holiday in 1863. Most families eat a big meal that day.

2   A turkey is the symbol of a Thanksgiving meal. The early Americans had turkey. They also had fish and deer meat. They ate peas, squash, and onions. They did not have any potatoes. They had some dried fruits, such as grapes, plums, and cherries. They ate different kinds of nuts. Pilgrims ate these foods with spoons, knives, and their fingers! They did not have any forks.

A Thanksgiving meal

---

1 **Read this sentence from paragraph 2.**

> A turkey is the symbol of a Thanksgiving meal.

What does <u>symbol</u> mean?

A a kind of food

B something that stands for something else

C something you eat with

D a big meal or feast

2 **What food was not in the early Americans' meal?**

A grapes   C potatoes

B nuts   D peas

3 **Which word is a noncount noun?**

A turkey   C meat

B potato   D spoon

4 **What was the author's purpose for writing this article?**

A to write about personal feelings

B to give information to readers

C to persuade readers

D to entertain readers

Writing on Demand: Describing a Process

    Write a paragraph describing what is in your favorite food. List the things that go into the food. Also explain what tools you will need. **(20 minutes)**

> **Writing Tip**
>   Draw a graphic organizer. Put each item into the graphic organizer. Then add details.

Apply & Extend

Objectives

Listening and Speaking
Tell a legend

Media
Analyze media messages in television commercials

Writing
A step-by-step guide

● Listening and Speaking Workshop

Tell a Legend

A **legend** is a very old story. It often tells how a problem was solved a long time ago.

> **Topic**
>
> Deliver a narrative presentation of a legend. Tell about the characters and the plot of a legend that you know.

1. **Choose a Legend**
   Choose a legend you know. It can be from another country. If you don't know a legend, ask your teacher for ideas or look for "legends" online.

2. **Brainstorm**
   Answer these questions in your presentation.
   a. Where does the story begin?
   b. Who are the main characters? Describe them.
   c. What is the problem? What is the solution?
   d. What happens at the end of the story?

3. **Plan**
   Make visuals to help explain the main points.

4. **Prepare**
   Write one note card for each focus question. Practice your presentation. Ask a partner to listen to your presentation and tell you how to improve. Listen to and help your partner.

5. **Present**
   Present your legend to the class. Use your visuals.

6. **Evaluate**
   Use the **Speaking Self-Assessment** to evaluate your presentation. Use the **Active Listening Assessment** to evaluate your classmates' presentations.

Speaking Self-Assessment	Active Listening Assessment
1. I practiced and was prepared.	1. You spoke at the right speed—not too slowly and not too quickly.
2. I told the story in the order of time when things happened.	2. The story was interesting.
3. I spoke clearly and loudly enough.	3. I think _____ was the most interesting part.
4. I looked at the audience.	4. You could improve your presentation by _____ .

Media Workshop

Analyze Media Messages in Television Commercials

Television commercials use sounds, music, color, and animation to deliver messages. The messages are for the people watching.

1. Watch television commercials. Choose two. Think about these questions as you watch. Write your answers.

    a. How does the commercial deliver its message? Does it use sounds? Music? Color? Animation?

    b. What do you notice most?

    c. What is the message of the commercial? What does it want you to do?

    d. Do you like the commercial? Why or why not?

2. Work in a small group. Tell your group about the commercials. Share your answers.

3. In your group, plan and prepare a commercial. Choose a product and a message. Decide which elements to use in the commercial—colors, sounds, music, or animation.

4. Practice your commercial. You may want to videotape your commercial.

5. Present your commercial to the class.

Apply & Extend

Writing Suggestion

Act out or pretend to do the activity. What do you need? What are the steps?

Writing Suggestion

A thesaurus gives you words with similar meanings. Look up a word you know and find other words that are similar.

● Writing Workshop

A Step-by-Step Guide

In a **step-by-step guide**, you explain how to do something.

> **Writing Prompt**
>
> Write a step-by-step guide. You can tell how to play a game, or explain how something works. Give each step. Use nouns to talk about what you need. Use verbs to explain the steps of the activity.

PREWRITE

1. Read the Writing Prompt and student model.
2. Think about these questions. Take notes.
   a. What activity do you want to explain?
   b. What things do you need to do the activity?
   c. What do you do first, second, third, etc.?

WRITE A DRAFT

1. The introduction tells what the activity is.
2. In the second part, write the steps in order. Use nouns to identify the things you need or use.
3. The conclusion identifies the activity and says why you should try it.

Student Model

Title ⟶   Hector Valasquez

How to Ride a Bicycle

Introduction

Many kids ride their bicycles to school. I like to ride my bicycle with my friends. It is easy and fun to do. It's also good exercise.

Include the things you need.

Include steps.

Body

You need a bicycle and a helmet. The helmet protects your head. First, you put on the helmet. Then, you sit on the seat of the bicycle with your feet on the ground. You hold the handles. Next, you put your right foot on the pedal. Push on the pedal and pull your left foot onto the other pedal. After that, push with your left foot and then right foot. Try to go straight, turn, and stop.

You need to practice. You can ride in the park or on the sidewalk. Sometimes you may fall, but soon it is easy and you will have fun.

REVISE

1. Review your step-by-step guide. Are your steps in order?
2. Exchange your guide with a partner. Your partner uses the **Peer Review Checklist** to make suggestions. Use the editing and proofreading symbols on page 493.
3. Revise your draft. Make changes to make the steps clearer.

EDIT

1. Use the **Revising and Editing Checklist** to evaluate your essay.
2. Fix any errors in grammar, spelling, and punctuation.

Peer Review Checklist
1. There is a title.
2. The first part says what the guide is about.
3. There are steps in order in the guide.
4. The guide helps me understand how to do an activity.
5. You could improve your writing by ____ .

Revising and Editing Checklist
1. My guide has a title.
2. I have clear steps in the guide.
3. I put the steps in order.
4. I used capital letters and punctuation correctly.
5. I spelled plural nouns correctly.
6. I used commas in a series correctly.

PUBLISH

1. Write your guide in your best handwriting or use a computer. You can add drawings or photos to show the steps you describe in your guide.
2. Read your essay to the class. Pause after each step.
3. As a class, choose one or two activities you want to try. Listen to or read the directions in your classmate's guides and do what you are told.

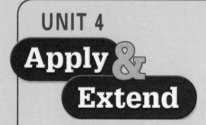
● Projects

Choose one or more of the following projects to explore the theme of At Home further.

PROJECT 1

Write a Description of a Room

1. Find a magazine picture of a room you like.
2. Make a list of objects that are in the room. Use a picture dictionary to find the names of objects.
3. Write sentences about the objects in the room.
4. Show your picture to the class. Read your sentences. Answer questions from your classmates.

PROJECT 2

Draw, Write, Read, and Draw Again

1. Work in a small group. Draw a room. Draw objects in the room. Color your drawing.
2. Write a step-by-step guide. Tell how to draw your room. Explain:
   - What is in the room?
   - Where are the objects?
   - What color is everything?
   - Is there anything special about the room?
3. Exchange directions with another group.
4. Together, read and follow the directions and draw the new room.
5. Compare your new drawing with the other group's drawing. Compare their new drawing with your original drawing.
6. Talk about the directions you wrote. What was clear or not? How can you improve the directions?

PROJECT 3

Plan a Monument

A monument is a symbol of a person, group, or event.

1. Choose an important person, group, or event.
2. Plan a monument.
   a. Who or what is the monument for?
   b. Where do you want the monument?
   c. What will you name the monument?
   d. Is there a message on the monument?
   e. Why did you choose this monument?
3. Draw a picture of your monument.
4. Present your monument to the class.

● Independent Reading

Explore the theme of At Home further by reading one or more of these books.

Home to Medicine Mountain by Chiori Santiago, Children's Book Press, 1998.

Two Native American brothers move hundreds of miles away from their home to a government school.

Ruby Holler by Sharon Creech, Joanna Colter Books, 2002.

Thirteen-year-old twins lose their parents. They are in an orphanage. They feel alone and sad. Then Sairy and Tiller take the twins into their family.

Wagon Wheels by Barbara Brenner, HarperCollins, 1993.

The Muldi family leaves the South after the Civil War. They travel west to make a new home. The book is based on a true story.

Greek Myths by Geraldine McCaughrean, Margaret K. McElderry Books, 1992.

This book tells many myths of ancient Greece.

> **Milestones Intro Reading Library**
>
> *Old Boat, New Boat* by Rob Waring and Maurice Jamall, Heinle, 2006.
>
> *Who's Best?* by Rob Waring and Maurice Jamall, Heinle, 2006.
>
> *The Shipwreck* by Rob Waring and Maurice Jamall, Heinle, 2006.

Milestones to Achievement

● Reading

Read this expository text. Then answer Questions 1 through 8.

Mount Rushmore

1   Mount Rushmore is a national monument. It is in South Dakota. It is a symbol of the first 150 years of U.S. history.

2   The mountain has the faces of four great U.S. presidents. Workers cut the faces into it. More than 400 people worked on the project. It was started in 1927. It took 14 years to make. The faces are 500 feet above the ground. Each day the workers climbed to the top. They climbed 506 steps.

3   The presidents on the monument are George Washington, Thomas Jefferson, Theodore Roosevelt, and Abraham Lincoln. Each president's face is 60 feet tall. Their noses are 20 feet long. Their mouths are 18 feet wide. Their eyes are 11 feet across!

4   Washington's head was finished first. Next, Jefferson's head was finished. Then, Lincoln's head was finished. Roosevelt's head was finished last.

5   George Washington was our first president. He helped start our new country. Thomas Jefferson was our third president. He also helped write the Declaration of Independence. Theodore Roosevelt was our 26th president. He was a war hero. He also made many new parks. Abraham Lincoln was our 16th president. He was president during the Civil War. He freed the slaves. This made many people angry.

George Washington, Thomas Jefferson,
Theodore Roosevelt, Abraham Lincoln

1 Find the word that has the same sound as the underlined letter in mon<u>u</u>ment.

A cut   C tube

B pull   D four

2 What is a question you can ask about paragraph 2?

A How many people worked on the monument?

B What presidents are on the monument?

C Which president was finished first?

D Where is the monument located?

3 Read this sentence from paragraph 5.

> This made many people angry.

What does <u>angry</u> mean?

A scared   C mad

B happy   D lonely

4 Which sentence tells what Lincoln did to cause people to be angry?

A He freed the slaves.

B He was president during the Civil War.

C He helped start our new country.

D He made many new parks.

5 Look at the caption on the picture. Which president has a moustache?

A George Washington

B Thomas Jefferson

C Theodore Roosevelt

D Abraham Lincoln

6 What problem did the 506 steps solve?

A The presidents' noses were too small.

B Washington's head was finished first.

C The workers needed to get to the top of the monument.

D Too many people worked on the project.

7 Which sentence has an irregular plural?

A Each day the workers climbed to the top.

B Workers cut the faces into it.

C Their noses are 20 feet long.

D It took 14 years to make.

8 Which sentence is correct?

A The monument is on a mountain.

B The monument has any faces on it.

C Is there an head of Washington on the mountain?

D Is there some presidents on the mountain?

 Writing on Demand: Describe a Process

Write an expository paragraph about how to do your favorite hobby. Describe the materials that you will need.
(20 minutes)

> **Writing Tip**
> Be sure to break your process down into steps. Put the steps in the order in which they have to happen.

Florence Nightingale
nurse

Franklin D. Roosevelt
U.S. president

Michelle Kwan
athlete

Albert Einstein
scientist

Frida Kahlo
artist

Cesar Chavez
political activist

Important
People

Talk About the Theme

1. Look at the pictures. Are you familiar with these people?
2. Are you familiar with any other famous people? Who?

Theme Activity

Work with a partner. Look at these words. Choose words to describe the people in the photos.

rich   famous   strong   caring
intelligent   brave   creative

Mae Jemison
astronaut

Yo-Yo Ma
musician

Objectives

Vocabulary
Occupations
Tools and equipment

Listening and Speaking
Talking about occupations
   and workplaces
Describing people at work

Grammar
Adjectives and adverbs

Writing Conventions
Spelling: Making adverbs

Word Study
Vowels: long o, long i
Prefixes: pre, post, re

Writing
Descriptive narrative

● Vocabulary
Occupations

A **cashier** takes money and gives change.

A **police officer** protects people.

A **chef** prepares and cooks food.

A **doctor** takes care of sick people.

A **firefighter** fights fires.

A **mail carrier** delivers mail.

A **hairstylist** cuts and styles hair.

A **construction worker** builds houses and buildings.

● Listening and Speaking

Talking About Occupations and Workplaces

1 Listen and repeat the sentences on page 308.

2 Where does each person work? Match the occupation on page 308 with the place below.

The cashier works at Big Dollar Supermarket.

1. Big Dollar Supermarket
2. Anthony's Hair Design
3. Fire Station Number 22
4. the Precinct 5 Police Station
5. Washington Hospital
6. Panama Restaurant
7. the Westside Post Office
8. the Hillside construction site

3 Read and listen.

Emily: What do you do?

James: I'm a cashier.

Emily: Oh, really? Where do you work?

James: I work at Big Dollar Supermarket.

4 Listen again. Repeat.

5 **PAIR WORK** Say the conversation again. Use new words for the blue words. Use vocabulary from page 308 and activity 2.

✓Checkpoint
1. Who builds houses?
2. What does a police officer do?

Vocabulary Log   Workbook page 201   Independent Practice CD-ROM

● Vocabulary
Tools and Equipment

1 Read and listen.

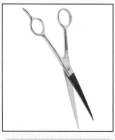    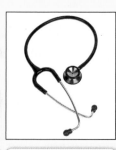

| scissors | a flashlight | a cash register | a clipboard | a stethoscope |

| a fire extinguisher | tools | utensils |

2 Listen and repeat.

Use **too** or **also** when you want to say something is the same.

She is a doctor.

He is a doctor, **too**.

or

He is **also** a doctor.

3 PAIR WORK Tell your partner who uses the tools and equipment. Use the job titles from page 308.

 A police officer uses a flashlight.

A firefighter uses a flashlight, too.

4 What other tools and equipment do these people use? Look in a dictionary to find new words.

 A firefighter also uses a water hose.

Vocabulary Log

Listening and Speaking
Describing People at Work

1 Listen and repeat.

Adjectives to Describe Employees		
punctual	polite	caring
hardworking	friendly	patient
creative	organized	reliable

employee (n.) someone who works for a person, company, or government.

Dictionary Entry
(See page 485.)

2 PAIR WORK **Describe good workers.**

Students need to be punctual and hardworking.

3 Listen. Match the person with the correct job.

1. Alicia   **a.** doctor
2. Keiran   **b.** chef
3. Jose   **c.** cashier
4. Wendy   **d.** teacher

4 Listen again. What adjectives are used to describe the employees? Write two words from activity 1 for each person.

5 Read and listen.

Harry: What does Keiran do?
Camilla: He's a doctor.
Harry: Is he a good doctor?
Camilla: Yes, he is caring and reliable.

6 Listen and repeat.

7 PAIR WORK **Say the conversation again. Use new words for the blue words.**

✓Checkpoint
What utensils does a chef need?

Vocabulary Log   Workbook page 202   Independent Practice CD-ROM

● Grammar

Adjectives

Adjectives describe **nouns**. They come before the noun they describe.

> She has an **interesting** job.   I don't like **cold** weather.

1 **Make sentences using adjectives and nouns.**

Examples: hard / test   *It is a hard test.*
           happy / lady   *She is a happy lady.*

1. sad / child   **3.** cold / milk   **5.** hot / water
2. fun / class   **4.** large / shirt   **6.** nice / man

Adjectives are often used after verbs like **be, feel, look,** and **seem.**

> My job <u>is</u> **interesting.**   The weather <u>feels</u> **cold.**
> This book <u>looks</u> **good.**   The men <u>seem</u> **angry.**

2 **Make sentences from the words in activity 1. Use be, feel, seem,** or **look.**

Examples: hard / test   *The test was hard.*
           happy / lady   *The lady feels happy.*

Adverbs

Adverbs tell how something is done.

> Tom walked home **sadly.**   The teacher told us **nicely.**

Many adverbs can be made by adding **-ly** to the end of adjectives.

> slow → slowly   careful → carefully
> nice → nicely   warm → warmly

Some adverbs are the same as their adjectives.

> fast → fast

Some adverbs are irregular.

> good → well

Workbook
page 203

Independent Practice
CD-ROM

1 **Write each sentence. Underline the adverb.**

Example: Ahn spoke with the people <u>politely</u>.

1. Scott opened the door slowly.

2. Natalie plays the piano badly.

3. The construction worker is working carefully.

4. Christine danced well.

5. Lauren ate dinner quickly.

2 **Rewrite the sentences in activity 1. Use these adverbs.**

Example: Ahn spoke with the people <u>nicely</u>.

terribly	hungrily	beautifully
carefully	~~nicely~~	patiently

**Writing Conventions**

Spelling *Making Adverbs*

1. To make many adjectives into adverbs, just add **-ly**:

   quick ➔ quick**ly**   slow ➔ slow**ly**

2. For adjectives ending in **vowel + l**, be careful to spell with **-lly** at the end:

   careful ➔ careful**ly**   successful ➔ successful**ly**

3. For adjectives ending in **-le**, take away the **e** and add **y**:

   simple ➔ simp**ly**   terrible ➔ terrib**ly**

4. For adjectives ending in **consonant + y**, change the **y** to **i** and add **-ly**:

   happy ➔ happ**ily**   lazy ➔ laz**ily**

Apply Change these adjectives into adverbs.

1. sad   **2.** angry   **3.** beautiful   **4.** warm

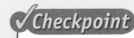**Checkpoint**

1. Make two sentences with the words **cold** and **water**.

2. Make a sentence with an adverb.

GRAMMAR EXPANSION
Adverbs,
Workbook page 205

Workbook
page 204

Independent Practice
CD-ROM

Unit 5 • Chapter 1   **313**

● Word Study

Vowel: Long o

Phonemic Awareness

1 **Listen and repeat.**

home	nose	rose
snow	goat	road

Decoding

2 **Listen. Find the long o sounds in each phrase.**

1. no toll on this road
2. a stone's throw from here
3. don't know Tom
4. most know her
5. drove past the old post
6. go up the pole slowly

3 **Listen again and repeat.**

Decodable
Reader 44

Word Study

Vowel: Long i

1 Listen and repeat.

ice   kite   fly

slide   website   night

Decoding

2 Listen. Find the **long i** sounds in each sentence.

1. I slide on the ice.
2. High tide is at nine.
3. He drives for miles.
4. She flies here at night.
5. It's fine, not tight.
6. Her kite is on the slide.

3 Listen again and repeat.

✓Checkpoint

Read these words.

nose
boat
tow
might
try
line

Decodable
Reader 45

Workbook
page 206

Independent Practice
CD-ROM

● Word Study

Prefixes: pre, post, re

A **prefix** is a group of letters added to the beginning of a word. The word it is added to is the **root word**. A prefix has its own **meaning**, and makes new words with the root word.

Prefixes	Examples
pre = before	**pre**fix, **pre**heat, **pre**record
post = after	**post**test
re = again	**re**group, **re**tell

1 Read each word and definition.

Word	Definition
prepaid	something that is paid for before it is used or received
postgame	something that happens after a sports game
redecorate	decorate a house again, for example, changing the wall color or furniture

2 Write the sentences with the correct word from the charts.

1. A _prefix_ is a group of letters at the beginning of some words.

2. The ____ will show the teacher if you learned the new words.

3. You have to ____ the food before you eat it.

4. Sam heard Lisa's story and he ____ it to Pete.

5. After the football game, there was a ____ meeting for the team.

3 **PAIR WORK** Look up the meaning of the other example words at the top of the page. Write a definition for each. Read your definitions to a partner.

✓**Checkpoint**

1. What does **reread** mean?

2. What does **preteach** mean?

Decodable Reader 43

Workbook page 207

Independent Practice CD-ROM

● Writing Assignment

Descriptive Narrative

> **Writing Prompt**
>
> Write a short narrative about a person you know. Use adjectives and adverbs in your description.

1. Read the student model.

Student Model

Jamie Leung

My Uncle Frank

   My Uncle Frank is an interesting person. He is very smart. He speaks several languages very well. He knows English, Cantonese, German, and Spanish. Those are very different languages but he reads, writes, and speaks all of them fluently. He is a professor at a university. He is a popular teacher. He teaches English literature. He lives in Chicago, Illinois. His house is filled with books. I like to look at Uncle Frank's library. He lets me borrow books frequently. I like my Uncle Frank very much.

2. Brainstorm. Who do you want to write about?
  a. What is the person like? Write some adjectives.
  b. What does the person do? Write some verbs.

3. Write your paragraph. Use the model.

4. Use the **Writing Checklist** to check your paragraph.

Adjectives to describe the person	Verbs to describe what the person does

Writing Checklist

1. I indented the first sentence in my paragraph.

2. I used adjectives and adverbs correctly.

3. I used correct spelling and punctuation.

Objectives

Reading Strategy
Ask information questions

Text Genre
Play

Listening and Speaking
Perform a play

Literary Elements
Figurative language: Similes

Writing Conventions
Capitalization for creative works, organizations, historical periods, and special events

Writing
Autobiography

Academic Vocabulary

when, why, where questions

Academic Content

drama

● About the Reading

You are going to read a play about Rosa Parks. She is famous for helping African Americans in the 1950s. At that time, many places in the United States were segregated—African Americans and white Americans did things separately. For example, laws made them go to separate schools and even drink from separate water fountains.

● Use Prior Knowledge

Learn About Civil Rights

A right is something you are allowed to do by law. For example, U.S. citizens have the right to vote when they are 18 years old.

Civil rights leaders work for equality. Susan B. Anthony fought for the civil rights of women. Martin Luther King Jr. and Rosa Parks fought for the civil rights of African Americans. César Chávez fought for the civil rights of Latinos.

Make a KWL (Know, Want to know, Learned) chart like the one here. Copy the chart. Complete the first and second columns with a partner. At the end of the chapter, complete the third column.

KWL Chart		
What I <u>K</u>now about civil rights	What I <u>W</u>ant to know about civil rights	What I <u>L</u>earned about civil rights

● Vocabulary From the Reading
Learn, Practice, and Use Independently

Key Vocabulary

community

court

elect

fare

fingerprints

Learn Vocabulary Look at the pictures. Match the words with the correct definition.

1. **community**

2. **court**

3. **elect**

4. **fare**

5. **fingerprints**

a. choose someone for something by voting for him or her

b. a group of people, such as those in a town, or with similar interests

c. a place where decisions are made about people who may have broken the law

d. prints from small lines on your fingers

e. money you pay to ride a bus, train, or taxi

Homophones
Fare and **fair** sound the same but are spelled differently and have different meanings.

If you hear **fare** or **fair**, use the context of the sentence to determine which word the person is saying.

Practice Vocabulary Write the correct Key Vocabulary word in the sentences.

1. At the police station, the police take a picture and get the ▆▆ of anyone who they think broke the law. Then the person goes to ▆▆ to decide if he or she broke the law.

2. The city raised the bus ▆▆ from $1 to $2, so the people in that ▆▆ feel angry. They will ▆▆ a leader to go and speak to the city about this problem.

Use Vocabulary Independently Write one sentence for each Key Vocabulary word. Read your sentences to a partner.

✓Checkpoint
Give a definition for each Key Vocabulary word. Use your own words.

Vocabulary Log

Workbook page 209

Independent Practice CD-ROM

● Academic Vocabulary

Vocabulary for the Reading Strategy

Phrase	Explanation	Sample Sentence	Visual Cue
when question	asks about time	"When did it happen?"	
why question	asks about a reason	"Why did he come?"	
where question	asks about a place	"Where did they go?"	
noun phrases			
Draw a picture or write a sentence for each word.			

● Reading Strategy

Ask Information Questions While You Read

Questions that begin with **when, why, where, what,** and **who** are examples of information questions. Ask questions as you read and find the answers.

● Text Genre

Play

A **play** is a story presented to an **audience**. Plays have characters, a setting, and plot.

Play	
audience	people who watch a play
scene	part of a play that happens at one time
lines	what the actors say
stage directions	notes in the play that tell the actors how to speak and move
narrator	a person who gives the scene and background information
character	a person in a play

✓Checkpoint

1. Give an example of a **when, why,** and **where** question.

2. Name some famous plays.

Vocabulary Log

Workbook pages 210, 211

Independent Practice CD-ROM

● Reading

Reading Focus Questions

As you read, think about these questions.

1. What is the problem?
2. Why did African Americans decide not to ride the bus?

Enter Rosa Parks

by Emily Dendinger

Setting	1950s. Montgomery, Alabama.		
Characters	Narrator 1	Bus Driver	Suzy
	Narrator 2	Raymond Parks	Police Officer 1
	Rosa Parks	E. D. Nixon	Police Officer 2

Prologue

1 NARRATOR 1: Welcome to Montgomery, Alabama. It is 1955.

2 NARRATOR 2: The city is segregated. If black people ride the bus, they have to sit in the back. If the bus is full, they have to give their seats to white people.

3 NARRATOR 1: Tonight that is going to change. Enter Rosa Parks.

4 (ROSA PARKS, a 42-year-old black woman, enters with several others, and they stand at the bus stop.)

5 NARRATOR 2: Rosa and her husband are in the National Association for the Advancement of Colored People, or **NAACP**. They believe segregation laws are wrong.

6 NARRATOR 1: But tonight she is not thinking about that. Tonight she is tired of **giving in**. Her feet are like **lead**. She just wants to go home.

7 (The bus arrives. ROSA PARKS and others get on.)

---

giving in doing what other people want instead of what you want
lead a very heavy metal
NAACP a famous civil rights group in the United States

Reading Strategy

Ask information questions What kind of **when** question can you ask about the setting of this play?

✓ Reading Check

1. **Recall facts** Where is the setting of the play?
2. **Explain** What does the word *that* in paragraph 3 mean?
3. **Predict** What do you think will happen next?

Scene 1: The bus

8   BUS DRIVER: This stop Cleveland Avenue!

9   *(The doors open, and some people get off while others get on. The bus fills up quickly.)*

"Segregated Bus" by Tony Vaccaro/Getty Images

10   BUS DRIVER: Hey, **y'all** in the back! I need those seats.

11   *(A few black people give their seats to white people. ROSA PARKS moves to the window. One white man is still standing.)*

12   BUS DRIVER: Hey, lady, didn't you just hear what I said? Are you going to give up your seat or not?

13   ROSA PARKS: Yes, I heard you. And no, I'm not going to give up my seat.

14   BUS DRIVER: Well, then I'm going to have you **arrested**.

15   ROSA PARKS: You may do that.

16   *(The BUS DRIVER gets off the bus to find a police officer.)*

17   POLICE OFFICER 1: This man said you didn't give up your seat.

18   ROSA PARKS: That is correct.

19   POLICE OFFICER 2: I'm sorry, lady, but I'm afraid you're under arrest. Please come with us.

20   *(ROSA stands. One POLICE OFFICER picks up her purse and another POLICE OFFICER takes her shopping bag. The three exit the bus.)*

---

y'all short for "you all": a common word in the southern part of the United States; it means the same as the plural form of "you"

arrested taken to a police station because a person has done something against the law

Scene 2: The police station, later that night

21 NARRATOR 1: They take Rosa to the police station. First, they take her **fingerprints**. Then they take her picture.

22 NARRATOR 2: Finally, they let her make a telephone call.

23 ROSA PARKS: (on the phone) Hi, Mama, it's me… So I guess you've already heard… No, I'm fine. They arrested me because I didn't give up my seat… I know that, but just because it is the law doesn't mean it's right.

24 (RAYMOND PARKS and civil rights leader E. D. NIXON enter, led by an OFFICER.)

25 ROSA PARKS: Hey, listen, Mama, I need to speak to Raymond and…. Oh, **never mind**. He's here.

26 (ROSA hangs up.)

27 RAYMOND PARKS: Rosa! Are you okay? Did anyone hurt you?

28 ROSA PARKS: No, I'm fine.

29 RAYMOND PARKS: What were you thinking?

30 ROSA PARKS: I don't know. I just got so tired of having to do what they say all the time. **There is no good reason** for segregation laws.

31 E. D. NIXON: You're right, there isn't.

---

never mind it's OK; it doesn't matter

there is no good reason we shouldn't have

Reading Strategy

Ask information questions What kind of **why question** can you ask about Rosa Parks's arrest?

Identification, Rosa 2001
by Colin Bootman

Reading Check

1. **Recall facts** Who does Rosa try to call from the police station?

2. **Explain** Why does Raymond say "What were you thinking?"

3. **Understand character motivation** Why did Rosa Parks decide not to stand up on the bus?

32 RAYMOND PARKS: Rosa, do you remember Mr. E. D. Nixon from the NAACP? Mr. Nixon paid your **bail money**.

33 ROSA PARKS: Yes, of course. Thank you for that, Mr. Nixon. Unfortunately, I still have to go to **court** on Monday morning.

34 E. D. NIXON: You did a very brave thing tonight, Mrs. Parks.

35 ROSA PARKS: I only did what I thought was right.

36 E. D. NIXON: There are a lot of people who feel the same as you do. Tomorrow there is a meeting among the leaders of the black **community**. We are going to do something to end bus segregation.

37 ROSA PARKS: What do you mean?

38 E. D. NIXON: What happened to you tonight could have happened to any black person. People are ready to do something. We are going to stop riding the buses.

39 NARRATOR 1: A bus **boycott** by the black people of Montgomery, Alabama is planned for Monday.

Reading Strategy

Ask information questions What why questions can you ask about what E. D. Nixon says?

Empty bus during boycott

40 NARRATOR 2: The black leaders in the community meet the next day. They **elect** a young black minister named Martin Luther King Jr. to be their leader.

41 NARRATOR 1: The Women's Political Council makes 35,000 pamphlets. They give them to people around the city, asking black people not to ride the buses Monday morning.

42 NARRATOR 2: Black taxi drivers agree to charge ten cents to black riders, which is the same **fare** as the bus.

---

bail money money paid to get a person out of jail while he or she waits for a court date

boycott an action where many people decide to stop using something

Scene 3: Monday morning

⁴³ NARRATOR 1: It's Monday morning at the Montgomery courthouse.

⁴⁴ NARRATOR 2: Enter Rosa Parks.

⁴⁵ *(ROSA PARKS enters stage left wearing a black dress and hat, ready to appear in* **court**. *At the same moment, a group of African Americans enter stage right. Adults are walking to work, and students are walking to school. SUZY, a little girl, stays behind.)*

⁴⁶ SUZY: Excuse me, but are you Mrs. Rosa Parks?

⁴⁷ ROSA PARKS: Yes, I am.

⁴⁸ SUZY: I'm not riding the bus to school today because of you, and my family isn't either. We want to help. I'm sorry you were arrested.

⁴⁹ ROSA PARKS: It's okay. Sometimes bad things need to happen before anything changes.

⁵⁰ SUZY: Good luck to you today, ma'am. You're a real hero.

⁵¹ ROSA PARKS: Not at all. You run along to school, dear.

⁵² *(Enter E. D. NIXON.)*

⁵³ E. D. NIXON: They're ready for you, Mrs. Parks.

⁵⁴ *(ROSA PARKS and E. D. NIXON start to exit.)*

⁵⁵ SUZY: **They've messed with the wrong one now!**

(CURTAIN)

They've messed with the wrong one now! The police have arrested someone who isn't afraid to fight back.

Rosa Parks

> **Reading Strategy**

Ask information questions What kind of **why question** can you ask about what Suzy says?

✓ **Reading Check**

1. **Recall facts** Where is Rosa Parks on Monday morning?
2. **Explain** Why are Suzy and her family not riding the bus today?
3. **Understand genre features** How do the directions, such as those in paragraph 45, help you understand the play?

● Reading Comprehension Questions

Think and Discuss

1. **Recall facts** What organization does E. D. Nixon belong to?

2. **Understand plot** Which people helped organize the bus boycott?

3. **Recognize character traits** Read paragraphs 48–51 again. Do you think Rosa Parks thinks she is really a hero? Why or why not?

4. **Identify mood** Read what Suzy says on page 325. How do you think she feels about Rosa Parks?

5. **Revisit the Reading Focus Questions** Go back to page 321 and discuss the questions.

● Listening and Speaking

Perform a Play

Perform the play *Enter Rosa Parks* in your class.

1. Decide where, when, who, and what.
   a. Decide who will play each character.
   b. Decide where and when you will practice.
   c. Decide what props you need. Props are things actors use onstage.

2. Practice the play.
   a. Think like your character. How does your character feel?
   b. Listen to the audio. Listen to the expression.

3. Perform the play.
   a. Speak with expression.
   b. Speak loudly and clearly.
   c. Use your face and hands to show expression.

Phrases for Conversation

Organizing a Production

Who wants to be Rosa Parks?
Where should we practice the play?
When should we practice?

Workbook
page 212

Independent Practice
CD-ROM

● Literary Element

Figurative Language: Similes

Authors sometimes use **figurative language** in their writing. Figurative language can help the reader see or feel what's happening in the reading. A **simile** is one kind of figurative language. Similes use the words *like* or *as* to compare things. The author uses one in paragraph 7 of *Enter Rosa Parks*.

Her feet are like lead. ➔ Her feet are very heavy, because she is tired.

Many similes use animals to describe what people are like.

She is as brave as a lion.   He is as quiet as a mouse.

What similes do you know? Make a list.

Writing Conventions

Capitalization *Creative Works, Organizations, Historical Periods, and Special Events*

Use capital letters for each word in creative works: titles of books, names of plays, famous works of art, names of songs, and so on.

Enter Rosa Parks   *We Shall Overcome*

Use capital letters for names of groups and organizations. Use capital letter for historical periods and special events.

African American Civil Rights Movement

Martin Luther King Jr. Parade

Do not capitalize the words *the* or *a/an*, prepositions (*for, to, on*, etc.), or conjunctions (*and, but, or*) unless they are the first word in the title or event.

Apply Work with a partner. List 2 creative works, organization names, historical periods, and special events. Share with the class.

✓Checkpoint

1. What is a **simile**?
2. What words does a simile use?

Workbook
page 213

Independent Practice
CD-ROM

● Writing Assignment
Autobiography

Writing Suggestion

Use a **topic sentence** in each paragraph.

> **Writing Prompt**
>
> Write an autobiography. An autobiography is a story about your life that you write yourself.

1. Read the student model.

Student Model

Simon Velazquez

My Autobiography

I was born in Los Angeles, California, in 1996. Until I was five years old, my family and I lived in Los Angeles. We lived in a small apartment. When I was five years old, we moved to our own house in San Diego, California.

When I was six years old, I started school at Franklin Elementary in San Diego. My favorite class was art. I like to draw and paint. At home, I painted many pictures of my house and of my family. After school I rode my bike every day.

2. Brainstorm. Think of the actions and events in your life that you want to include in your autobiography. When did they happen? Where did they happen? Why did they happen? Who was there? How did they happen?

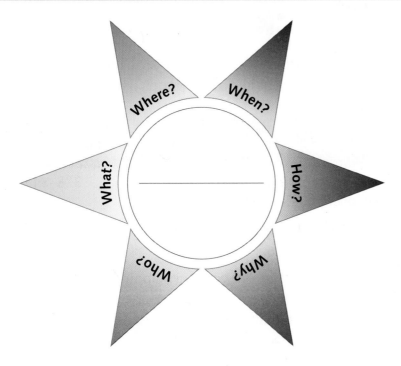

3. **Write your autobiography.**

4. **Revise.** Read your autobiography. Add, delete, or rearrange words or sentences to make your writing clearer. Use the editing and proofreading symbols on page 493 to help you mark the changes you need to make.

5. **Edit.** Use the **Writing Checklist** to help you find problems and errors.

Writing Checklist
1. I wrote a topic sentence for each paragraph.
2. I used the correct verb tenses.
3. I used adverbs and adjectives.
4. I indented each paragraph.
5. I wrote neatly and clearly.

How well did you understand this chapter? Try to answer the questions. If necessary, go back to the pages listed for a review.

Skills	Skills Assessment Questions	Pages to Review
Vocabulary	What words and expressions can you use to talk about people's occupations and workplaces?	**308–311**
Grammar	Give examples of adjectives and adverbs in sentences.	**312–313**
Writing Conventions	**Spelling:** What spelling rules did you learn about for adverbs? Give examples.	**313**
	Capitalization: What capitalization rules did you learn about? Give examples.	**327**
Word Study	What do these prefixes mean? • pre-, post-, re-	**316**
Vocabulary From the Reading	What do these words mean? • community, court, elect, fare, fingerprints	**319**
Academic Vocabulary	What do where question, when question, and how question mean?	**320**
Reading Strategy	What are examples of information questions?	**320**
Text Genre	What is the text genre of *Enter Rosa Parks*?	**320**
Reading Comprehension	What is *Enter Rosa Parks* about?	**326**
Listening and Speaking	**Phrases for Conversation:** What phrases can you use to talk about performing a play?	**326**
Literary Elements	Give an example of a simile.	**327**

Assessment Practice

Read a passage from a play. Answer Questions 1 through 4.

The Jackson Sit-In

1   NARRATOR: The year is 1963. This is a restaurant in Jackson, Mississippi. The community is segregated. African Americans have to eat at tables in the back.

2   *(Anne, Pearlena, and Memphis sit in the front of the restaurant.)*

3   CASHIER: I can't take your order. This table is for whites only.

4   ANNE: We are not leaving. We want service.

5   MEMPHIS: We are good people. We aren't different from you. We only want service.

6   *(Angry people throw food at the characters. They are afraid but they stay at the table.)*

7   NARRATOR: In the past, the police arrested many African Americans. That didn't happen this time. Anne, Pearlena, and Memphis stayed in the restaurant.

1 **Read this sentence from paragraph 1.**

> The community is segregated.

What does <u>community</u> mean?

A people in a restaurant

B a group of people in a town

C people who eat different foods

D a group of people who do not speak to each other

2 **What part of speech is the underlined word?**

> They were <u>afraid</u> but they stayed at the table.

A verb   C noun

B adjective   D pronoun

3 **What adjective best describes Anne, Pearlena, and Memphis?**

A reliable   C punctual

B angry   D patient

4 **Why does this play have a narrator?**

A to make it interesting

B to tell when the play begins

C to explain who the characters are

D to explain these events in history

Writing on Demand: Autobiography

Write about a time when you felt important. Use adjectives to describe the people around you. Use adverbs to describe your own actions. **(20 minutes)**

> **Writing Tip**
> Ask questions. When and where did this story happen? Why did it happen? How did the story begin and end?

Objectives

Vocabulary
Abilities
Problems and advice

Listening and Speaking
Talking about abilities
Giving advice

Grammar
Can and should

Writing Conventions
Capitalization and
punctuation in place
names

Word Study
Vowels: long e

Writing
Advice letter

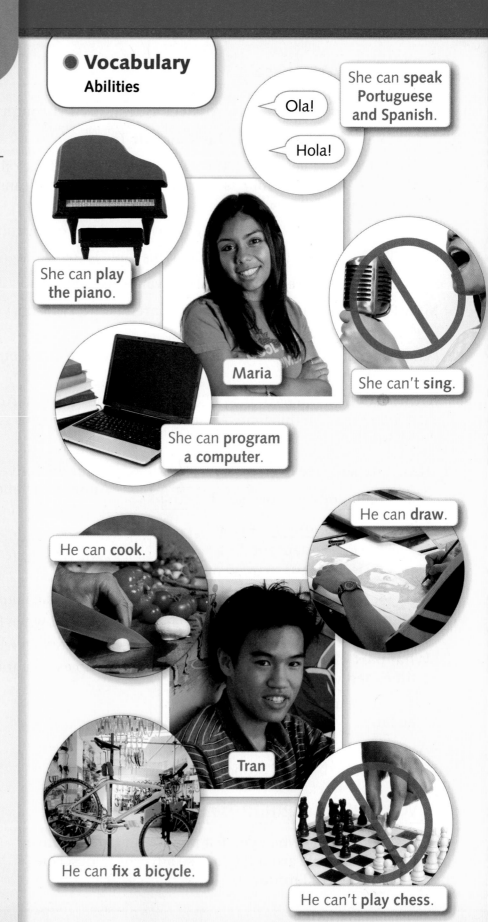

● Vocabulary
Abilities

She can **play the piano**.

Ola!

Hola!

She can **speak Portuguese and Spanish**.

Maria

She can't **sing**.

She can **program a computer**.

He can **cook**.

He can **draw**.

Tran

He can **fix a bicycle**.

He can't **play chess**.

● Listening and Speaking
Talking About Ability

1 Listen and repeat the sentences on page 332.

2 Who can do the activities listed on page 332?

Maria can play the piano.

Tran can draw.

3 Listen. Can the people do these things?
Answer *yes* **or** *no*.

1. Can Gavin sing?
2. Can Camilla play tennis?
3. Can Tyler play the piano?
4. Can Mercedes speak Spanish?

4 Read and listen.

Marta: Can you **cook**?

Ken: Yes, I can. What about you?

Marta: No, I can't.

5 Listen again. Repeat.

6  PAIR WORK **Say the conversation again. Use new words for the blue word. Use vocabulary from page 332.**

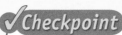
✓Checkpoint

1. Name three things you can do.
2. Name something you can't do.

● Vocabulary

Problems and Advice

1 Listen and say these sentences.

1. My tooth hurts.

2. I lost my phone.

3. I forgot my workbook at home.

4. I need some information for my report.

2 What advice would you give the people above?

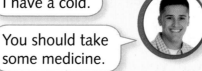

I have a cold.

You should take some medicine.

a. You should tell the teacher.

b. You should check on the Internet.

c. You should go to the school "Lost and Found."

d. You should see a dentist.

3 PAIR WORK Practice. Use the information above.

I forgot my workbook at home.

You should tell the teacher.

● Listening and Speaking
Giving Advice

1 **Listen. What advice does each person give?**

1. He lost his keys.
   - ____ **a.** He should check "Lost and Found."
   - ____ **b.** He should check in your locker.

2. She has a terrible headache.
   - ____ **a.** She should take some medicine.
   - ____ **b.** She should see the school nurse.

3. He needs to study for the math test.
   - ____ **a.** He should practice in the computer lab.
   - ____ **b.** He should go to the library.

4. She forgot her books at home.
   - ____ **a.** She should call someone at home.
   - ✓ **b.** She should tell the teacher.

2 **Read and listen.**

Kelli: What's wrong?

Ramon: I lost my keys.

Kelli: Maybe you should go to the school "Lost and Found."

Ramon: That's a good idea.

3 **Listen and repeat.**

4 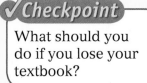 **PAIR WORK Say the conversation again. Use new words for the blue words. Talk about these problems and solutions.**

1. forgot my gym bag / call someone at home
2. have a fever / see a doctor
3. going for a bike ride / put on some sunscreen
4. can't find my watch / check your locker

√ Checkpoint
What should you do if you lose your textbook?

Vocabulary Log

Workbook page 216

Independent Practice CD-ROM

● Grammar

Can

Use **can** to talk about abilities.

Question		
Modal	**Subject**	**Base verb**
Can	I / you / he / she / it / we / they	sing?

Affirmative statement	I can sing.
Negative statements	He can't sing.
	You cannot sing.

<table>
<tr><td>Multiple-meaning Word

Can is a modal verb to talk about abilities.

Can is also a noun. It's a metal cylinder used to hold soup or food.</td></tr>
</table>

1 **Write answers that are true for you.**

Example: Can you speak Spanish?
> Yes, I can speak Spanish.

1. Can you draw pictures?
2. Can you swim?
3. Can you fix a bike?
4. Can you sing well?
5. Can you run fast?
6. Can you cook?

Should

Use **should** to give advice or solutions to problems.

Question		
Modal	**Subject**	**Base verb**
Should	I / you / he / she / it / we / they	tell the teacher?

Affirmative statement	I should study.
Negative statements	He shouldn't get up.
	You should not get up.

Workbook
page 217

Independent Practice
CD-ROM

2 PAIR WORK **Ask your partner questions using should and these words. Your partner answers.**

Should I exercise every day?

Yes, you should.

1. buy my sister a gift for her birthday
2. do my homework after school
3. eat popcorn for lunch
4. watch TV all day Saturday
5. eat breakfast every day
6. play computer games every night

Writing Conventions

Capitalization and Punctuation *Place Names*

Use capital letters for names of cities, states, and countries.

Boston (city)   **California** (state)   **Mexico** (country)

Use two-letter capital abbreviations for state names.

FL = Florida   **TX** = Texas   **NY** = New York

Use commas to separate cities and states and cities and countries.

I was born in Naples, FL.   Her dream is to go to Paris, France.

Apply Write these sentences with capital letters and commas.

1. I want to visit san francisco ca.
2. The letter was from brooklyn ny.
3. Julia is from guadalajara mexico.
4. My family is moving to miami fl.

✓Checkpoint

1. What is one thing you **can** do? What is one thing you **can't** do?
2. What **should** you do if you feel sick at school?

● Word Study

Vowel: Long e

Phonemic Awareness

1 Listen and repeat.

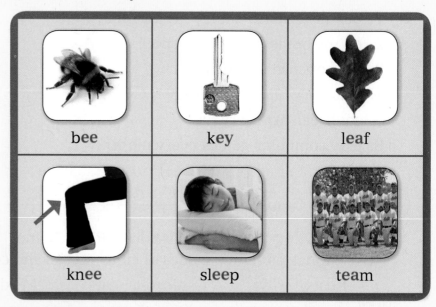

bee	key	leaf
knee	sleep	team

Decoding

2 Listen. Find the **long e** sounds in each sentence.

1. Please clean the screen.
2. Keep your feet off the seat.
3. Let the tea steep.
4. The team is here this week.
5. Get some lean meat.
6. Sleet freezes fast.

3 Listen again and repeat.

✓*Checkpoint*

Read these words.

bead

seem

hockey

Decodable
Reader 47

Workbook
page 220

Independent Practice
CD-ROM

● Writing Assignment

Advice Letter

> **Writing Prompt**
>
> Write an advice letter. Use *should*.

1. Read the problem.
   I am tired all day. I'm sleepy at class and at home.
2. Read the student model. The writer gives advice.

Student Model

> March 3, 2009
>
> Dear Sleepy,
>
>   Teenagers need a lot of sleep. You should sleep more than eight hours every night. What time are you going to bed? You should go to bed early. You said you want to exercise. Try exercising for twenty minutes before dinner. You should eat healthy foods. You shouldn't eat chocolate or sugar. These things will keep you awake. I hope this helps you!
>
> Sincerely,
> Teen Advice

3. Write an advice letter for one of these problems.
   a. I can't do my math homework. It's too hard.
   b. I can't dance, and the school dance is coming soon.
   c. I don't have enough money to buy my mom a birthday gift.

Writing Checklist
1. I used a greeting and wrote the date.
2. I closed with "Sincerely,".
3. I used *should* and *can* correctly.

Workbook
page 221

CHAPTER 2

Part B

Objectives

Reading Strategy
Summarize

Text Genre
Biography

Listening and Speaking
Retell details about a
person's life

Text Element
Figurative language:
Metaphors

Reading Fluency
Choral reading

Writing
Summary

Academic Vocabulary

summarize

topic sentence

Academic Content

A Famous Native American

● About the Reading

You are going to read a biography about a
famous Native American man named Sequoyah.

● Use Prior Knowledge

Understand Writing Systems

Most languages have their own writing
system. English uses an alphabet of 26 **letters**.
Other languages use different alphabets. Some
languages have no writing system. In these
cultures, people pass down their history and
stories by spoken word.

1. Look at the list of languages. Do they use the
   same alphabet as English? Talk about them with
   your partner.

Arabic	Hmong	Russian
Chinese	Korean	Spanish
Haitian Creole	Portuguese	Vietnamese

2. Can you write any of these alphabets? If you
   can, show the class.

Vocabulary From the Reading
Learn, Practice, and Use Independently

Learn Vocabulary Read the sentences. Look at the **highlighted** words. Find the definition on the right.

1. Ask Mairo to fix the bike. He has the **ability** to do it.
2. John crashed his car. He had a terrible **accident**.
3. Huong **adopted** the new plan and started using it on Monday.
4. Her **invention** is very useful.
5. The dance event had many Native Americans present. Each person belongs to a large **tribe**.

a. They are members of a community.
b. He can fix a bike.
c. She decided to use the new plan.
d. Something bad happened to him and his car.
e. The new thing she made can be used by many people.

Practice Vocabulary Write each sentence with the correct vocabulary words.

1. The new ____ increased car safety and helped prevent a lot of ____ .
2. The early European American of New England ____ many of the farming practices of the Wampanoag Native American ____ .
3. She has the ____ to make many people listen to her.

Use Vocabulary Independently PAIR WORK Test your partner. Give a definition for each Key Vocabulary word. Use your own words. Your partner says the word.

Vocabulary Log

Workbook page 222

Independent Practice CD-ROM

Academic Vocabulary

Vocabulary for the Reading Strategy

Word	Explanation	Sample Sentence	Visual Cue
summarize *verb*	give the main points of a story or article	I don't have time to read the whole report. Can you **summarize** it for me?	Biography A biography contains important information about events and actions in that person's life. • things that happen in a person's life • things a person does • when things happen in a person's life • the order that things happen
topic sentence *noun*	a sentence that gives the main idea of a paragraph	The **topic sentence** is usually the first sentence in a paragraph.	The topic sentence is usually the first sentence in a paragraph. I don't have time to read the whole report. Can you summarize it for me?

Draw a picture or write a sentence for each word.

Reading Strategy

Summarize

When you **summarize** something, you make it shorter. You only give the important ideas. First look at the **topic sentence** to find the main idea. Then look through the text for other important details.

Text Genre

Biography

A **biography** is about another person. It gives important information about events and actions in that person's life.

Biography	
events	things that happen in a person's life
actions	things a person does
dates	when things happen in a person's life
sequence	the order that things happen

✓Checkpoint

1. What is a **summary**?
2. Name a famous person whose **biography** you have read or seen on TV.

Vocabulary Log

Workbook pages 223, 224

Independent Practice CD-ROM

Reading

Reading Focus Questions

As you read, think about these questions.

1. Who was Sequoyah?
2. What was Sequoyah's gift to the Cherokee people?

SEQUOYAH
FATHER OF THE WRITTEN CHEROKEE LANGUAGE

1   This is a story of a man who gave his people a wonderful gift–the **ability** to read and write their own language. His name was Sequoyah. He was born around 1776 in Tuskegee, Tennessee, near the Tennessee River.

Reading Strategy

Summarize Who is this text about? What did he do?

2   Sequoyah, also known as George Gist, was the son of an English **fur trader** named Nathaniel Gist. His mother, Wu-teh, was a member of the Paint Clan, part of the Cherokee **tribe**–one of the largest groups of Native American people.

Reading Check

1. **Recall facts** When was Sequoyah born?
2. **Describe** Who are the Cherokees?

---

fur trader a person who exchanges the skin of animals, used to make coats or hats, for money or other things

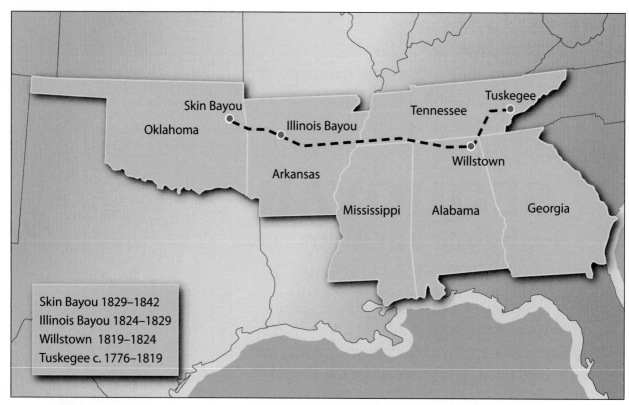

Skin Bayou 1829–1842
Illinois Bayou 1824–1829
Willstown 1819–1824
Tuskegee c. 1776–1819

Sequoyah's homesites

Reading Strategy

Summarize How did Sequoyah spend his early life?

3   Sequoyah grew up as a Cherokee, learning the old ways of **trapping** and trading furs. When he was only twelve years old, he had an **accident** while he was hunting. Because of his **accident** he could not walk or hunt very well. Instead, he became very good at making things out of silver.

4   Years later, Sequoyah married a Cherokee woman and had a family. He and his family moved to the northern part of the state of Alabama. There he worked as a **silversmith**.

---

trapping catching animals
silversmith someone who makes useful things out of silver

5   Sequoyah never learned to read or write English. He saw many white men **making marks** on paper and using these papers to read and communicate. Some Native Americans called these "talking leaves."

6   For the next twelve years, Sequoyah worked hard to make a system of reading and writing for the Cherokee language. He finally made a list of 86 letters. Each of the letters was used for one syllable in the Cherokee language.

Reading Strategy

Summarize What did Sequoyah **invent**?

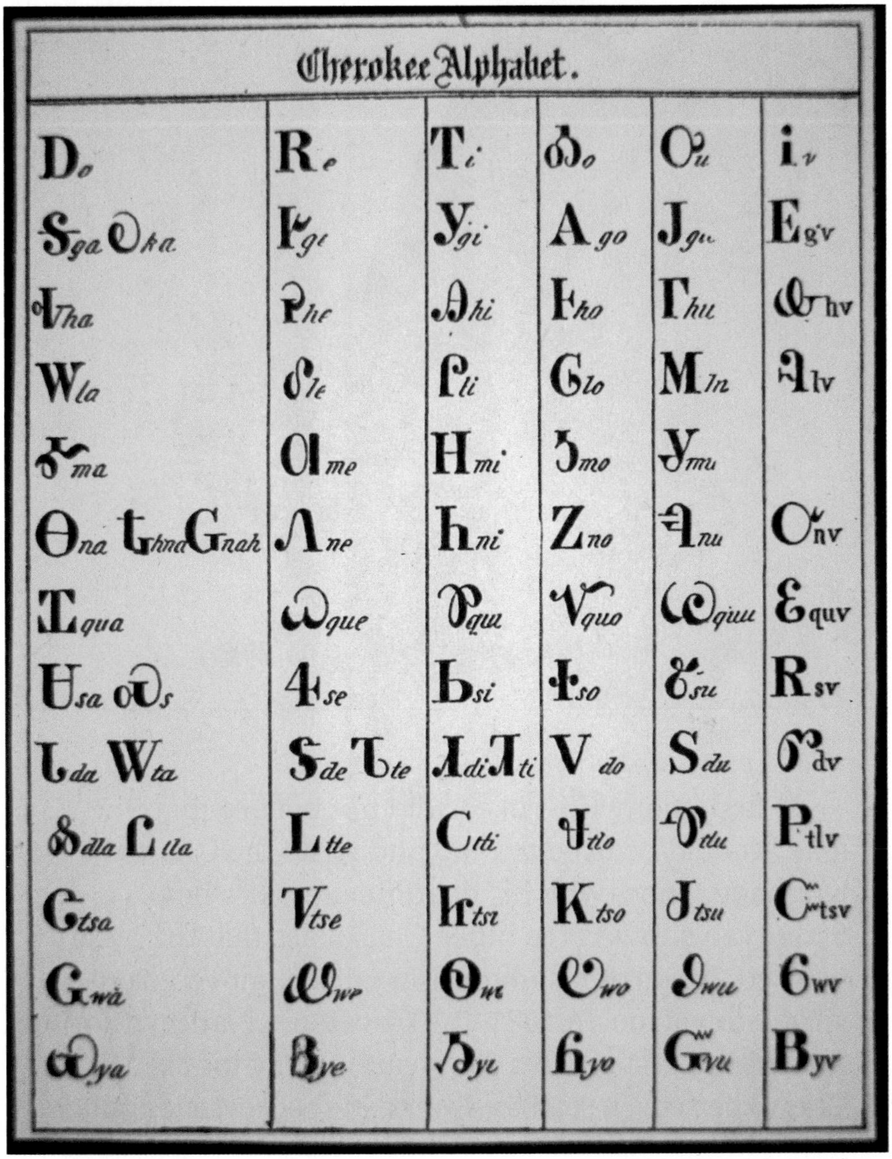

Cherokee Alphabet.

Reading Check

1. **Recall facts** What did Native Americans call written English?
2. **Describe** How many symbols are in the Cherokee writing system?

making marks writing letters

Reading Strategy

Summarize How did Sequoyah's **invention** help Cherokees?

7   At first, many Cherokees did not believe that the letters could be used to read and write the Cherokee language. Then, with his daughter Ayoka's help, Sequoyah showed the other Cherokees that the letters worked. News of his **invention** quickly moved from village to village. In 1821, the **Cherokee Nation adopted** his writing system. In a few years, finally thousands of Cherokees could read and write in their own language.

Cherokee Nation Native Americans have nations with their own government and laws in addition to those of the United States.

8   In 1828, the Cherokee National Council started to print the first Cherokee newspaper in the United States. It was called *Tsa la gi Tsu lehisanunhi*, or *Cherokee Phoenix*. It had information both in English and in the Cherokee language.

9   For the rest of his life, Sequoyah worked to help other Native Americans, both in the Cherokee Nation and in other **tribes**. He wanted to make a writing system to help other Native American **tribes** to read their own languages.

Reading Strategy

Summarize How did Sequoyah spend the rest of his life?

10   Sequoyah died around 1843 in Mexico. He was looking for other Cherokees who had moved there, and wanted to bring them back to the Cherokee Nation. He wanted to see all Cherokees living together in one place.

11   Today the Cherokee language is one of the few Native American languages that is still growing. His gift of a writing system is still seen as a wonderful thing in the hearts and minds of the Cherokee people.

Reading Check

1. **Recall facts** When did Sequoyah die?

2. **Make inferences** What was special about the *Cherokee Phoenix*?

● Reading Comprehension Questions

Think and Discuss

1. **Recall facts** When did Sequoyah live?

2. **Describe** Who was Sequoyah?

3. **Relate to prior knowledge** Why do you think there are 86 letters in the Cherokee alphabet?

4. **Understand genre features** Why is it important to have a writing system for one's language?

5. **Revisit the Reading Focus Questions** Go back to page 343 and discuss the questions.

Phrases for Conversation

Use Signpost Words and Time Expressions

First / Next / After that / Finally . . .
In 1776 / In 1843 . . .
When he was 12 years old . . .
Several years later . . .

● Listening and Speaking

Retell Details About a Person's Life

Summarize Sequoyah's life by retelling the important details of his life.

1. List the important details from Sequoyah's life. You can use the list below to help you. Write complete sentences with the correct information from the biography.

   - Born in ___ .
   - Raised as a ___ .
   - Had an **accident** ___ .

   - Worked as a ___ .
   - **Invented** ___ .
   - Died in ___ .

2. Add two details.

3. **PAIR WORK** With a partner, decide what are the most important details. Take notes. Use vocabulary from the text.

4. Organize your notes in sequence of time (chronological order). Present the beginning, middle, and end of Sequoyah's life.

5. Practice your **summary**. With your partner, practice reading your notes.

6. **PAIR WORK** Present your **summary** to the class.

Workbook
page 225

Independent Practice
CD-ROM

● Text Element

Figurative Language: Metaphors

A **metaphor** describes one thing by comparing it with another thing. If someone can sing very well, you might call the person "a songbird." If someone is very good at doing something, you might call the person "a genius."

In the biography of Sequoyah, the title calls him the "father of the written Cherokee language." This is another example of a metaphor. What does it mean when we say that he was a "father" in this way?

Here are some other examples of metaphors. With a partner, talk about what each one means.

1. Elizabeth was **boiling** mad when she heard the news.

2. As Paul watched the scary movie, he was **frozen** in his seat.

3. When her family needed her help, Sarah was a **rock**.

4. Todd's fingers **flew** over the keys of the piano.

● Reading Fluency

Choral Reading

When you listen to someone read fluently, you learn how to be a more fluent reader.

1. Your teacher will read a paragraph from a reading in this chapter.

    a. Follow along silently as your teacher reads.

    b. Pay attention to your teacher's pacing (speed), expression, and intonation (level and sound of voice).

2. Your teacher will read the paragraph again.

    a. Read aloud with your teacher and the class.

    b. Try to use your teacher's pacing, expression, and intonation.

✓Checkpoint

1. What is a **metaphor**?
2. Give an example of a metaphor.

Workbook
page 226

Independent Practice
CD-ROM

● Writing Assignment

Summary

> **Writing Prompt**
>
> Write a **summary** of the biography "Sequoyah: Father of the Written Cherokee Language." Make sure it has a beginning, a middle, and an end.

1. Read the student model.

Student Model

Claudia Bautista

Summary of "Sequoyah: Father of the Written Cherokee Language"

"Sequoyah: Father of the Written Cherokee Language" is a biography about a famous Native American. It tells about the life of Sequoyah, a Native American man from Tennessee. He invented a written language for the Cherokee Nation.

Sequoyah was born in Tennessee. He was a trapper and trader. When he was a child, he had an accident and couldn't hunt anymore. He made things from silver instead. Later, he married a Cherokee woman and moved to Alabama.

Sequoyah is famous for inventing a system for reading and writing the Cherokee language. Before that, it was an oral language only. At first people didn't think it would work, but Sequoyah and his daughter showed people that it would work and it quickly became the adopted alphabet for the whole Cherokee Nation. Sequoyah died in 1843.

2. **Brainstorm.** Write notes for your **summary**.

    a. What is the main idea for the opening paragraph?

    b. What are the main ideas for Sequoyah's childhood?

    c. What are the main ideas of Sequoyah's **invention**?

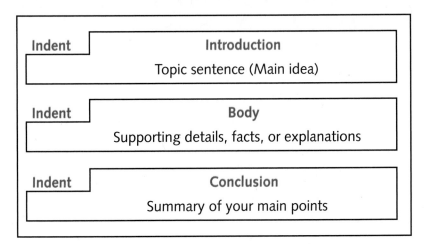

Indent — **Introduction**
Topic sentence (Main idea)

Indent — **Body**
Supporting details, facts, or explanations

Indent — **Conclusion**
Summary of your main points

3. **Write your summary.**

4. **Revise.** Read your paragraph. Add, delete, or rearrange words or sentences to make your paragraph clearer. Use the editing and proofreading symbols on page 493 to help you mark the changes you need to make.

5. **Edit.** Use the **Writing Checklist** to help you find problems and errors.

Writing Checklist
1. I indented my paragraphs.
2. I capitalized the first word of each sentence.
3. My **summary** has a beginning, a middle, and an end.

6. **Publish.** Make your autobiography into a book. Design a cover. Give it a title.

Progress Check

How well did you understand this chapter? Try to answer the questions. If necessary, go back to the pages listed for a review.

Skills	Skills Assessment Questions	Pages to Review
Vocabulary	What kinds of things can you do? What kinds of advice did you learn about?	**332–335**
Grammar	How do you make statements with *can*? How do you make statements with *should*?	**336–337**
Writing Conventions	**Capitalization and Punctuation:** What capitalization and comma rules did you learn for place names?	**337**
Vocabulary From the Reading	Can you make a sentence with each of these words? Give examples. • **ability**, **accident**, **adopted**, **invention**, **tribe**	**341**
Academic Vocabulary	What do **summarize** and **topic sentence** mean?	**342**
Reading Strategy	What do you do when you **summarize** something?	**342**
Text Genre	What do you find in a biography?	**342**
Reading Comprehension	What was "Sequoyah: Father of the Written Cherokee Language" about?	**348**
Listening and Speaking	**Phrases for Conversation:** Can you retell details of a person's life? What phrases help you?	**348**
Text Element	What is a metaphor?	**349**
Reading Fluency	How does reading aloud help you read?	**349**

Assessment Practice

Read this biography. Then answer Questions 1 through 4.

Ellen Ochoa

1   Ellen Ochoa was born in California in 1958. She also went to college in California. Ellen has many abilities. She is an inventor. She made three inventions.

2   In 1990, NASA picked Ellen to be an astronaut. She was the first Hispanic woman picked. She went on three space flights. She was in space more than 700 hours.

3   Ellen's first space flight was in 1993. She flew on the space shuttle. She studied the sun. The sun was a light in the dark sea of space. In 1999, she flew in space again. The space shuttle took supplies to the Space Station. Her last space flight was in 2002. Ellen still works for NASA. She is a smart and brave woman.

1 **Read this sentence from paragraph 1.**

> She made three inventions.

What does <u>invention</u> mean?

A a thing to make people happy

B a science experiment

C a new thing that someone makes

D something that is a special event

2 **Which sentence best summarizes Ellen Ochoa's life?**

A She studied the sun.

B Her last space flight was in 2002.

C She is an inventor.

D She is a smart and brave woman.

3 **Which sentence uses a metaphor?**

A She has many abilities.

B The sun was a light in the dark sea of space.

C She was in space more than 700 hours.

D Ellen's first space flight was in 1993.

4 **What does a biography tell about?**

A how to make or do something

B what happened in your life

C what happened in a person's life

D a story that is not true

 Writing on Demand: Biography

    Write a short biography about a family member. Write about the person's life. Include a metaphor. **(20 minutes)**

> **Writing Tip**
> Make a list of ideas and circle words you want to include.

Apply & Extend

Objectives

Listening and Speaking
Present a poem orally

Media
Compare a book and a movie

Writing
Informational text

● Listening and Speaking Workshop
Present a Poem Orally

> **Topic**
>
> Give a dramatic interpretation of a poem. Choose a poem about an important person. Practice and present your reading to a group.

1. **Choose the Selections**
   Find a poem about a famous person who interests you. Visit the library or look online for poems about famous people.

2. **Brainstorm**
   Think about these focus questions.
   a. What does the poem say about the person?
   b. Is there rhyme, rhythm, alliteration, or repetition in the poem?
   c. Where are good places in the text to pause?
   d. What words or phrases do you want to stress?

3. **Plan**
   Copy the poem. Use slash marks (/) to mark places to pause. Underline the parts to stress. Prepare a few questions for your listeners. For example: "What did you like?"

4. **Prepare**
   Read the selection aloud several times. You might make an audio recording. Then play the recording to hear how you sound. Ask a partner to listen to you. Ask your partner how to improve. Help your partner prepare.

5. **Present**
   Present your oral reading to a group. Pause at the places you chose. Change your voice to stress key words. Speak clearly. Ask your listeners the questions you prepared.

6. **Evaluate**
   Use the **Speaking Self-Evaluation** to evaluate your oral reading. Use the **Active Listening Evaluation** to evaluate your classmates' presentations.

Speaking Self-Evaluation	Active Listening Evaluation
1. I practiced the reading and was prepared. I relaxed when I read.	1. The reading held my interest. I learned more about _____.
2. I stressed key words in the reading.	2. You read each selection with the correct pitch, tempo, and tone.
3. I spoke clearly and slowly enough.	3. You read the stressed and unstressed syllables correctly. You read the _____ (rhymes, repeated sounds) well.
4. I looked at my audience when I spoke.	4. You could improve your oral reading by _____.
	5. The purpose of the listening was clear.

● Media Workshop

Compare a Book and a Movie

Some people are so famous that there are many stories about them. Sometimes the same story is told in different ways. There are stories in books and also in movies. However, books and movies often do not tell the story in the same way.

1. Find a video and a book about the same famous person in the school or public library. At the library, look for movies in the documentary section.

2. Read the book. Ask questions as you read. Take notes.

3. Then watch the movie. Ask questions before you see the movie. Take notes.

4. Think about these questions.

   a. How is the movie different from the book? Are the facts the same? Is the story told differently?

   b. Do you think the movie or the book is more interesting? Why?

5. Tell your class about your comparison.

● Writing Workshop

Informational Text

> **Writing Prompt**
>
> Write an informational text about a famous person. Tell why the person is important. Write details about events in the person's life.

PREWRITE

1. Read the student model.
2. Choose an important person. Here are some ideas.

   a. Diego Rivera
   b. Helen Keller
   c. Martin Luther King Jr.
   d. Maya Lin

   e. Marie Curie
   f. Sally Ride
   g. Mahatma Gandhi
   h. Mathew Henson

3. Use library books, encyclopedias, and the Internet to research the person. Use the index to find the subject. Take notes on your research.

   a. Where and when was the person born?
   b. Where did the person grow up? What people, places, or things affected him or her?
   c. What job did/does he or she have?
   d. Why is the person important? What did/does he or she do to become famous?

WRITE A DRAFT

1. Include headings in each section.
2. Give information on the person's early life.
3. Give information on the person's adult life.
4. Give information about why this person is important.
5. Use adjectives to help the reader visualize the person.

Student Model

Clara Barton

Early Life

   Clara Barton was born on December 25, 1821, in Massachusetts. Her mother taught her at home. Clara was very shy. She was a good student. Her brother was sick often. She took care of him.

Clara's Work

Clara started teaching when she was 17 years old. She taught for ten years. Then Clara moved to Washington, D.C. Then the Civil War started.

Clara wanted to help the soldiers. Women couldn't go on the battlefield. She took medicine to the wounded soldiers. She asked people for help. People sent supplies. She traveled with army ambulances. She took care of the sick soldiers.

Why Clara Barton Is Important

She started the American Red Cross after the Civil War. The Red Cross helps people when fires, floods, hurricanes, tornadoes, or earthquakes happen.

REVISE

1. Make sure your text tells the story of the person. Include headings to help your reader find information.

2. Ask your partner to use the **Peer Review Checklist** to review your text. Your partner will make suggestions.

3. Revise your draft. Add, delete, or rearrange sentences to make your ideas clearer. Use the editing and proofreading symbols on page 493.

EDIT

1. Use the **Revising and Editing Checklist.**

2. Fix errors in grammar, spelling, and punctuation.

Peer Review Checklist
1. Your text has a title and headings.
2. You used adjectives and adverbs.
3. You gave details and descriptions.
4. You could improve your writing by ____.

Revising and Editing Checklist
1. My text has a title and headings.
2. I told why the person is important.
3. I included sensory details about people, places, and things.
4. I used adjectives and adverbs.

PUBLISH

1. Write your informational text in your best handwriting. Or use a computer and do a spell and grammar check.

2. Display your informational text in class.

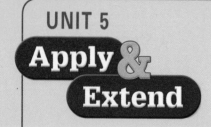

Projects

Choose one or more of the following projects to explore the theme of Important People further.

PROJECT 1
Internet Research

1. Use the Internet to find information about a famous person you admire.
2. Take notes on what you learn. Organize your notes.
3. Share your information with a partner. Look at your notes to remember ideas only. Do not read your notes. Speak naturally.

PROJECT 2
Write a Journal Entry

1. With a partner, brainstorm a list of famous people.
2. Choose one person from your list. Find an interesting event from that person's life.
3. Pretend you are that person. Write a journal entry.
   a. The journal entry should be based on facts.
   b. Include specific details about the event and the person's experiences.
   c. Include details about what you think his or her personal feelings about the event were.
4. Share your journal entry with the class or a group.

PROJECT 3
Asking Questions

1. Imagine you have a chance to interview ten important people.
2. You can ask each person just one question.
3. Make a list of the ten people you would interview.
4. Next to each name, write a question to ask. Example: George Washington: What was it like to be the first president of a new nation?
5. Share your list of names and questions with a partner.

PROJECT 4
Cities Named for Presidents

1. Work in a small group. Find a list of U.S. presidents.
2. Each group member picks a different president.
3. Use an atlas. An atlas is a book of maps.
4. Find cities or towns named for the presidents.
5. List each state and the names of the towns.
6. Share your list with another group.

● Independent Reading

Explore the theme of Important People further by reading one or more of these books.

In Their Own Words Series: Sitting Bull by Peter Roop and Connie Roop, Scholastic Paperbacks, 2002.
Sitting Bull spent most of his life trying to protect his people. He was a proud father and brave warrior.

Ballot Box Battle by Emily Arnold McCully, Knopf, 1996.
Cordelia learns about courage and the value of education. The book tells about Elizabeth Cady Stanton's attempt to vote in the 1880 elections.

The Wright Brothers at Kitty Hawk by Donald J. Sobol, Scholastic Paperbacks, 1987.
This biography tells about Orville and Wilbur Wright's attempts to build an airplane.

Helen Keller by Margaret Davidson, Scholastic Paperbacks, 1989.
Helen Keller became deaf and blind at an early age. With the help of Annie Sullivan, her teacher, she learned to talk and read. She even graduated from college with honors!

In Their Own Words Series: Pocahontas by George Sullivan, Scholastic Reference, 2002.
Pocahontas grew up as the favorite daughter of the Native American chief of the Powhatan tribe.

> **Milestones Intro Reading Library**
>
> *I Always Win!* by Rob Waring and Maurice Jamall, Heinle, 2006.
>
> *Trouble at the Zoo* by Rob Waring and Maurice Jamall, Heinle, 2006.
>
> *Quiz Night* by Rob Waring and Maurice Jamall, Heinle, 2006.

● Reading

Read this biography. Then answer Questions 1 through 8.

1   Thomas Edison was born in Ohio in 1847. He wanted to know about everything. He always asked questions. His mother could not answer all his questions. He tried to find the answers himself. Once he sat on some eggs. He was trying to hatch them. Another time he caused an accident. It burned the family's barn. His family was very angry.

2   Edison had many jobs. First, he sold newspapers at age 12. Next, he worked for the telegraph office. He sent messages over wires. Then Edison went to New York when he was 22 years old. He had no money. He looked for a job during the day. He slept in a room at a gold company. He watched everything around him closely. A machine at the company broke. Edison fixed it. The owners gave him a job. He made some changes to the machine. The company paid him $40,000 for his invention. Finally, he started the American Telegraph Works in New Jersey.

3   Edison built a workshop in Menlo Park, New Jersey. It was a beehive of work. He and his employees made many inventions there. He and his team worked to invent a light bulb that would last a long time. They tried many things and nothing worked well. Finally he tried something new. The light bulb stayed on for nearly 200 hours.

4   Then Edison worked to make a power system so people could use the light bulbs. In 1882 he turned on a switch. A community in New York City had electric lights for the first time. Inside the homes, it was as bright as day.

1 Read this sentence from paragraph 1.

> Another time he caused an accident.

What does <u>accident</u> mean?

A something bad that happens

B a special event

C a thing to make people happy

D a useful thing

2 What was Edison's first job?

A sending messages

B making inventions

C fixing machines

D selling newspapers

3 Which of the following sentences contains a signpost word?

A Next, he worked for the telegraph office.

B He always asked questions.

C A machine at the company broke.

D The light bulb stayed on for nearly 200 hours.

4 What is a question you can ask about paragraph 2?

A Who did Edison meet at his first job?

B Where did Edison invent a long lasting light bulb?

C Why did Edison leave the telegraph job?

D What jobs did Edison have?

5 Which sentence contains a metaphor?

A First, he sold newspapers at age 12.

B It was a beehive of work.

C He wanted to know about everything.

D He looked for a job during the day.

6 Which sentence contains a simile?

A Inside the homes, it was as bright as day.

B He watched everything around him closely.

C Once he sat on some eggs.

D First, Thomas sold newspapers at age 12.

7 Which is the correct way to make <u>angry</u> into an adverb?

A angryly   C angrily

B angrylly   D angrilly

8 Which adjective describes Edison?

A creative   C polite

B friendly   D punctual

Writing on Demand: Advice Letter

Imagine Edison came to you for advice. What should he do with the money he made from his invention? Write your advice to him in a letter. Include details. **(20 minutes)**

Writing Tip
Don't forget to put all the parts of a letter in your writing.

Community

Talk About the Theme

1. Look at the pictures. Which one looks more like your town?
2. What is the same as your town? What is different?

Theme Activity

List places in your town or neighborhood. What kind of places do you like to go to?

As a class, make a list of all the places you thought of.

Objectives

Vocabulary
Places in the community
Giving directions

Listening and Speaking
Talking about locations around town
Giving directions around town

Grammar
Comparative adjectives

Writing Conventions
Spelling: Comparative adjectives with -er

Word Study
Diphthongs: oi, oy
Suffixes: ful, less, able, ish
Suffixes: ion, ous, ness

Writing
Personal narrative

● Vocabulary
Places in the Community

People eat in a **restaurant**.

People watch movies at a **movie theater**.

People visit the **park** to have fun.

People go to the **bookstore** to buy books.

People buy music at a **music store**.

People visit the **community center** to meet other people.

People go to the **shopping mall** to buy things.

People shop at a **clothing store**.

Listening and Speaking
Talking About Locations Around Town

1 Listen and repeat the sentences on page 364.

2 Look at the map. Listen and repeat the sentences below.

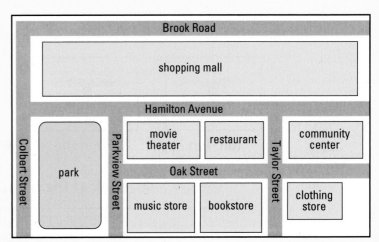

1. The movie theater is **in front of** the shopping mall.

2. The community center is **across from** the restaurant.

3. The shopping mall is **on** Hamilton Avenue.

4. The bookstore is **between** the music store and the clothing store.

5. The restaurant is **beside** the movie theater.

6. The clothing store is **on the corner of** Taylor Street and Oak Street.

3 Make new sentences with the blue words in activity 2. Use the map.

4 Read and listen.

Patti: Where did you go last night?

Joan: I went to the **bookstore**.

Patti: Do you mean the one on **Oak Street**?

Joan: Yes, **next to** the music store.

Patti: What did you do there?

Joan: I **bought a new book**.

5 Listen again. Repeat.

6 PAIR WORK Say the conversation again. Use new words for the blue words. Use the places on the map above.

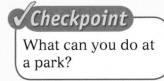

Checkpoint
What can you do at a park?

Vocabulary Log

Workbook page 227

Independent Practice CD-ROM

Unit 6 • Chapter 1 **365**

● Vocabulary

Giving Directions

1 Look at the pictures. Listen and repeat.

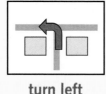

turn left

turn right

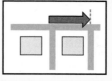

walk one block

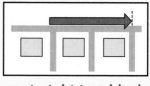

go straight two blocks

2 Look at the map. Listen and read the directions.

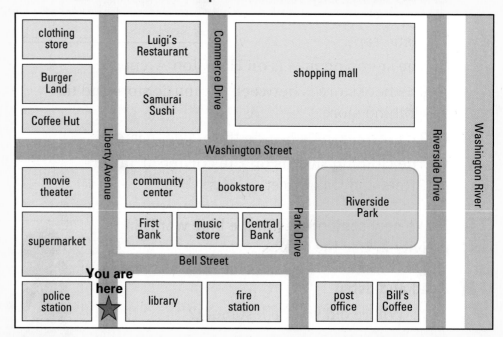

> Go straight two blocks on Liberty Avenue. Turn right onto Washington Street. Walk down Washington Street almost one block. It's on your right. It's on the corner of Washington Street and Park Drive.

3 PAIR WORK **Practice. Give directions from the police station to:**

1. the post office
2. the shopping mall
3. Samurai Sushi
4. Coffee Hut

● Listening and Speaking

Giving Directions Around Town

1 Listen. Which directions do you hear? Choose the letters.

1. **a.** about a block   **c.** turn right
   b. about two blocks   **d.** on the right

2. **a.** on the corner   **c.** on your left
   b. at that corner   **d.** turn left

3. **a.** turn left at Commerce   **c.** go past Samurai Sushi
   b. it's on Commerce   **d.** go left at Samurai Sushi

2 Read and listen.

Elijah: Do you know how to get to the music store?

Rose: Yes. Walk straight down Liberty Avenue. Turn right onto Bell Street. Walk about half a block. The music store is on your left.

Elijah: Thanks.

Rose: You're welcome.

3 Listen and repeat.

4  **PAIR WORK** Practice the conversation above. Use the map on page 366. Give directions:

1. from Central Bank to Samurai Sushi
2. from the music store to Burger Land
3. from the supermarket to Riverside Park
4. from the community center to the post office

✓ *Checkpoint*

Give directions from the school to a place you like to go.

Vocabulary Log

Workbook page 228

Independent Practice CD-ROM

● Grammar

Comparative Adjectives

Use **comparative adjectives** to compare two things.

The red dress is **cheap**.
The blue dress is **cheaper than** the red dress.

Use the comparative adjective and **than** when talking about both things in the same sentence.

The red dress is <u>cheaper</u> **than** the blue dress.
The blue dress is <u>more</u> <u>expensive</u> **than** the red dress.

For most one-syllable adjectives or two-syllable adjectives add the suffix **-er**.

new → The movie theater is **newer than** mall.
small → The park is **smaller than** the mall.

Writing Conventions

Spelling *Comparative Adjectives with -er*

1. Add **er** to the end of most adjectives.
   cheap → cheap**er**   fast → fast**er**
2. For adjectives that end in **e**, add **r**.
   nice → nice**r**
3. For one-syllable adjectives that end in a vowel + a consonant, double the consonant and add **er**.
   hot → hot**ter**   big → big**ger**
4. For adjectives that end in **y**, change the **y** to **i** and add **er**.
   pretty → prett**ier**   funny → funn**ier**

Apply Change the adjectives to comparative adjectives.

1. hungry   **2.** old   **3.** simple   **4.** sad   **5.** happy   **6.** short

 Workbook
page 229

 Independent Practice
CD-ROM

For most adjectives with two syllables, and all adjectives with more than two syllables, use the word **more** in front of the adjective.

expensive ➜ The red dress is **more expensive** than the blue dress.

important ➜ A community center is **more important** than a mall.

A few adjectives are irregular in the comparative form. You should learn these forms.

good ➜ This mall is **better**.
bad ➜ My old bag was **worse than** this one.

1 Write the following sentences. Change the adjectives in parentheses into comparative adjectives.

1. The old movie theater was (terrible) than this one.

2. This book is (scary) than the one you bought at the bookstore.

3. This restaurant is (good) than the one downtown.

4. This music store is (expensive) than the other one.

5. New York is (cold) than Miami in the winter.

2 **PAIR WORK Find several objects around your classroom. Use comparative adjectives to compare them.**

 This desk is taller than that one.

Ms. Morgan's desk is wider than mine.

Show your list of comparisons to other groups. Who found the most comparisons in the class?

> ✓ **Checkpoint**
> 1. How do you make **comparative adjectives**?
> 2. Make a sentence with a **comparative adjective**.

● Word Study

Diphthongs: oi and oy

Phonemic Awareness

1 Listen and repeat.

oi

coin   oil   boil

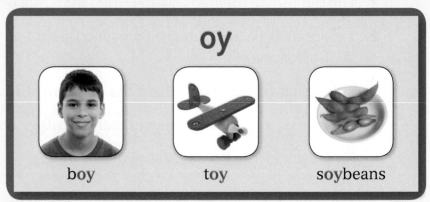

oy

boy   toy   soybeans

Decoding

2 Listen. Find the oi or oy sounds in each sentence.

1. I toil in the boiling sun.
2. The boy hoisted his toy.
3. I enjoy soy sauce.
4. Broil it with a little oil.

3 Listen again and repeat.

✓Checkpoint

Read these words.

     soil

     coil

     coy

     enjoy

Decodable
Reader 55

Workbook
page 232

Independent Practice
CD-ROM

● Word Study

Suffixes: ful, less, able, ish

Remember, a **suffix** is a group of letters added to the end of a word. The word it is added to is the root word. A suffix has its own meaning, and makes a new word with the root word.

Suffixes	Examples
ful = full of	care**ful**, forget**ful**, hope**ful**
less = without	care**less**, hope**less**, help**less**
able = can be done	predict**able**, enjoy**able**, wash**able**
ish = like, in the same way as	fool**ish**, child**ish**

Read each word and definition.

Word	Definition
peace**ful**	full of peace
thought**less**	without thought
tax**able**	can be taxed
redd**ish**	looking similar to the color red

Copy the sentences. Write the missing word from the charts above.

Example: May is __hopeful__ that she did well on her
        test. She studied a lot.

1. After the war, a ____ agreement was signed.
2. It was ____ of Juan to forget her birthday again!
3. This is a very ____ movie. It's my favorite.
4. Mr. Smith is 30 years old but sometimes he is very ____ and makes a lot of noise.
5. Clothing is ____ in some states but some states don't tax clothes.

✓Checkpoint

What does *erasable* mean?

What does *thoughtful* mean?

Word Study

Suffixes: ion, ous, ness

Sometimes a **suffix** changes the part of speech of the root word. For example, a suffix can be used to change verbs into nouns, verbs into adjectives, nouns into adjectives, or adjectives into nouns.

Suffixes	Parts of Speech	Examples
ion (sion, ition, ation)	verbs ➔ nouns	collect**ion**, expan**sion**, present**ation**, reserv**ation**
ous (eous, ious)	nouns ➔ adjectives	fam**ous**, nerv**ous**, env**ious**, courag**eous**
ness	adjectives ➔ nouns	kind**ness**, happi**ness**, weak**ness**

Read each word and definition.

Word	Definition
attract**ion**	the feeling of being attracted to someone or something
danger**ous**	having the ability to cause danger
serious**ness**	the quality of being serious

1 Complete the sentences with words from the charts.

Example: My father has a large stamp collection from around the world.

1. I made a _____ for the restaurant so they will save a table for us.
2. Look at Stu smile. His _____ is so easy to see.
3. That's a very _____ painting. Everyone knows it.

2 PAIR WORK Use a dictionary. Look up the meaning of the other example words in the charts. Write a definition for each. Read your definitions to a partner.

✓Checkpoint

What part of speech are each of these words?

conclusion
silliness
glamorous

Workbook page 233

Independent Practice CD-ROM

● **Writing Assignment**

Personal Narrative

Writing Suggestion

Use **ago** to talk about how far in the past something happened:

He went to Paris five years **ago**.

> **Writing Prompt**
>
> Write a narrative. Compare your life now to five years ago. Use comparative adjectives.

1. Read the student model.

Student Model

> Andre Donovan
>
> #### My Life Now and Five Years Ago
>
> I am now fifteen years old. Five years ago, I was ten years old. My life was very different. I lived in another house then. It was smaller than my house now. My family is bigger now too. My younger brother was born two years ago.
>
> My middle school was closer to my home than my high school is. I have more homework now, and my classes are harder. My classes are more interesting now, too.
>
> My life five years ago was simpler than it is now, but I like my life. I'm happier now than I was when I was ten.

2. Brainstorm. How is your life different now compared to five years ago? Make a list.

3. Write your personal narrative. Use the model.

4. Use the **Writing Checklist** to check your writing.

Writing Checklist

1. I indented the first sentence in my paragraphs.

2. I used comparative adjectives correctly.

3. I used correct spelling and punctuation.

Objectives

Reading Strategy
Understand characters

Text Genre
Folktales and fables

Listening and Speaking
Compare and contrast
stories

Literary Element
Moral

Writing Conventions
Punctuation: Parentheses
and commas

Writing
Comparative essay

Academic Vocabulary

trait | motive

Academic Content

folktales and fables

● **About the Reading**

You are going to read two traditional stories. One is a folktale from Korea, and the other is a fable from Greece.

● **Use Prior Knowledge**

Talk About Traditional Stories

Every culture has traditional stories. Parents tell them to their children. There are two common features in these stories.

1. They all happened a long time ago.

2. At the end of the story, everyone is happy.

Here are some common phrases:

Beginning	Ending
Once upon a time . . .	They lived happily ever after.
Long, long ago . . .	
A long time ago . . .	And they all lived happily ever after.

Some stories are told in different parts of the world, but with different names. **Cinderella** is one of the world's most famous fairy tales. In France, it is *Cendrillon*. In Denmark, it is called *Aschenputtel*. In ancient Greece and Egypt, it is *Rhodopis*. In Korea, it is *Kongji*. In Africa, it's *Mufara's Beautiful Daughters*. In Spanish, it is *La Cenicienta*.

PAIR WORK With your partner, tell the story of Cinderella, or another fairy tale you know.

Vocabulary From the Reading
Learn, Practice, and Use Independently

Key Vocabulary

barn

beak

field

grain

net

stream

Learn Vocabulary Look at the pictures. Match the words with the correct definition.

1. barn

2. beak

3. field

4. grain

5. net

6. stream

a. rice, corn, wheat, and barley, for example
b. a small river
c. something used to catch animals, like fish or birds
d. a bird's mouth
e. a place where farmers grow things
f. a place farmers keep their hay

Practice Vocabulary Complete the sentences with Key Vocabulary words.

1. Catching birds is not easy. Their ____ are very sharp. You need a strong ____ .

2. After the farmers take their ____ from their ____, they put it in a ____ to keep it dry.

3. I was walking near the ____ and I saw a small boat on the water.

Use Vocabulary Independently PAIR WORK Draw a picture for each vocabulary word. Your partner says what it is.

✓ Checkpoint

1. Give an example of a **grain**.
2. What can you keep in a **barn**?

Vocabulary Log

Workbook page 235

Independent Practice CD-ROM

● Academic Vocabulary

Vocabulary for the Reading Strategy

Word	Explanation	Sample Sentence	Visual Cue
trait *noun*	characteristic or quality that someone has	The main character has good **traits**. She is hardworking and kind.	
motive *noun*	reason for doing something	Ted's **motive** for eating was he was hungry.	

Draw a picture or write a sentence for each word.

● Reading Strategy

Understand Characters

Most stories have different kinds of characters. As you read, decide what **traits** characters have by what they say or do. Are they kind, mean, good, or bad?

As you read, look for each character's **motive**. Why do the characters do what they do?

● Text Genre

Folktales and Fables

Folktales and **fables** are types of traditional stories. A **folktale** is a timeless story that is usually passed on orally among a group of people. A **fable** is usually a story with animals as the **characters**. There is often a lesson in these stories. This lesson, or message, is a **moral**.

Folktales and Fables	
characters	people, or animals, in a story
moral	a message, or a lesson, that you can learn from the story

✓**Checkpoint**

1. What might **motive** a person to help a stranger?
2. Name a character from a famous story and list two **traits** that character has.

Vocabulary Log

Workbook page 235, 237

Independent Practice CD-ROM

● Reading

Reading Focus Questions

As you read, think about these questions.

1. What is the moral in each of the two stories?
2. Which story do you like better? Why?

Real Brotherly Love

A Korean Folktale

1   Once upon a time there lived two brothers. The brothers loved each other very much, and always took care of one another.

2   Every day they worked from morning until night, getting as much **grain** as possible from their **fields**.

3   One late **autumn** evening, after their work in the **fields** was done, the older brother said to his wife, "Younger Brother got married last month. He has many **bills** to pay. I think I will put a bag of rice in his **barn**."

◀ Reading Strategy

Understand characters
What **motivated** Older Brother to put rice in Younger Brother's barn?

✓ Reading Check

1. **Recall facts** At what time of year does this story take place?
2. **Understand characters** What character **trait** does the art show?

---

autumn fall (season)
bills money you have to pay for things or services you buy

Reading Strategy

Understand characters
What **traits** does the older brother have?

4   "Oh, that's a good idea," said his wife.

5   "But please don't tell him," said the older brother. "If he knows I put the rice there, he will never take it."

6   So, late that night the older brother took a bag of rice to the younger brother's **barn**.

7   The next day, while looking at his own **barn**, he found something strange. "I took a bag of rice to Younger Brother's house last night, but I still have the same number of bags in my **barn**. How did that happen?"

8   He decided to take another bag of rice to his brother's **barn** that night. But the next morning, he found the same number of bags in his **barn** again! "This is very strange," he thought.

9   That night he tried again. He carried a large bag of rice on his shoulder, and walked down the **path** to his younger brother's house. In the bright moonlight, he could see another person coming down the path. He was carrying something on his shoulder too.

10   "Younger Brother!" the man cried. "What are you doing?"

11   "I was worried about you, Older Brother," said the man. "Your family is larger than mine. I thought you needed more rice."

12   The two brothers quickly realized that they had been taking rice to each other. They laughed about what had happened. "It is good to have a brother like you," they both said. And they lived happily ever after.

Reading Strategy

Understand characters
How does the author show that both brothers have generous **traits**?

✔

Reading Check

1. **Recall facts** Where did the brothers see each other?

2. **Understand plot** Why was the younger brother carrying rice for the older brother?

----
path a small road

The Ant and the Dove

A Fable by **Aesop**

1   Once upon a time, an ant was looking for water on a very hot day. "I am so thirsty," she thought. After walking for some time, she found a **stream**.

2   To reach the water, the ant had to climb up on a **blade** of grass. As she bent down to reach the water, she slipped off the grass and fell into the **stream**.

3   Luckily, a dove sitting on a **branch** nearby saw the ant. The dove quickly used his **beak** to cut a leaf from the tree. He dropped the leaf into the **stream** near the ant. The ant grabbed onto the leaf, and slowly climbed onto it. The ant, sitting on top of the leaf, safely rode to the side of the **stream**.

4   "Thank you, dove!" shouted the ant, in her tiny voice. But her voice was so small that the dove could not hear it.

Reading Strategy

Understand characters What **motivated** the ant to say thank you?

Aesop a famous author of hundreds of fables from ancient Greece
blade a long flat piece
branch part of a tree that a bird can sit on

5　　Soon after that, a **birdcatcher** came and stood near the tree where the dove was resting. "What a beautiful dove," he thought. "I must have it!"

6　　The birdcatcher carefully took out his **net**. He quietly walked toward the branch where the dove was sitting.

7　　Just then, the ant saw the birdcatcher. "Watch out, dove!" she cried. But of course the dove could not hear her tiny voice.

8　　"How can I help the dove?" she thought. "The birdcatcher is much larger than I am."

9　　Then the ant knew what she could do. She ran as quickly as she could. She climbed up on the birdcatcher's boot, and she bit him on the leg.

10　　"Ow!" cried the birdcatcher. The pain in his leg made him drop his **net**. The dove heard the noise and flew away.

Reading Strategy

Understand characters
What is one **trait** the ant has?

11　　The dove never knew how the little ant helped him. But the ant was happy that she was able to do something for the dove. Both the ant and the dove lived happily ever after.

Reading Check

1. **Recall facts** What did the birdcatcher use to try to catch the dove?

2. **Understand characters** Why did the ant think she could not help the dove at first?

3. **Understand plot** Why did the ant bite the birdcatcher?

---

birdcatcher a person whose job is catching birds

Reading Comprehension Questions

Think and Discuss

1. **Recall facts** Who is the author of "The Ant and the Dove"?

2. **Compare and contrast** How are the two stories similar? How are they different?

3. **Understand the message** What is the message in each of the two stories?

4. **Present an opinion** Which of the stories did you like better? Why?

5. **Revisit the Reading Focus Questions** Go back to page 377 and discuss the questions.

Listening and Speaking

Compare and Contrast Stories

There are similarities between "Real Brotherly Love" and "The Ant and the Dove." There are also differences.

1. **PAIR WORK** With your partner copy the chart. Show what is the same or different. Think about the plot and setting. Think about the characters' **traits** and **motives**.

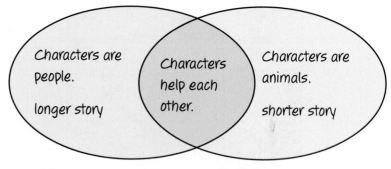

Characters are people.

longer story

Characters help each other.

Characters are animals.

shorter story

"Real Brotherly Love"   "The Ant and the Dove"

2. Present your list to the class. One person presents the similarities and the other person presents the differences. Remember to stay on topic. If you are talking about similarities, don't mention differences.

3. Use vocabulary from the story to make your point.

Phrases for Conversation

Comparing and Contrasting

The characters in **both** stories are helpful.

The first story has people for characters **but** the second story has animals.

"Real Brotherly Love" is **longer than** "The Ant and the Dove."

Workbook
page 238

Independent Practice
CD-ROM

● Literary Element

Moral

A **moral** is a lesson or message in a story. Traditionally, people taught lessons to children by telling fables. For example, many people know Aesop's fable "The Turtle and the Rabbit." In this story the slow turtle wins a race with a fast rabbit because the rabbit is lazy and sleeps during the race and the turtle never stops walking. The moral of this story is *slow and steady wins the race*. The message is we should never quit. We should work hard and in the end, we will win.

As you read, look for the author's message to find a moral. For example, what is the moral of "Real Brotherly Love"?

Writing Conventions

Punctuation *Parentheses and Commas*

Parentheses give extra information or an explanation in a reading. Sometimes you can use commas instead of parentheses. Here are some examples:

"The Ant and the Dove" (by Aesop) is a famous fable.

"The Ant and the Dove," by Aesop, is a famous fable.

Apply Find the extra information in each sentence. Then write each sentence with parentheses. Write each sentence again with commas.

1. My sister Liza is coming to visit.

2. Ms. Carroll an actress from the 1960s was in a show called *Julia*.

3. Boca Insurance on Center Street is where he works.

4. Color television the first invention of its kind was soon found in many homes.

5. His art show the third one this year brought in people from all over.

> ✓**Checkpoint**
>
> What is the moral of "The Ant and the Dove"?

Workbook
pages 239, 240

Independent Practice
CD-ROM

● Writing Assignment

Comparative Essay

> **Writing Prompt**
>
> Write an essay comparing the stories you read in this chapter: "Real Brotherly Love" and "The Ant and the Dove."

1. Read the student model.

Student Model

Reynaldo Marasigan

Comparison of "Real Brotherly Love" and "The Ant and the Dove"

"Real Brotherly Love" is a Korean folktale. "The Ant and the Dove" is a Greek fable by Aesop. They are from different countries. The characters of the two stories are very different. In "Real Brotherly Love," the characters are two brothers. They are people and they know and love each other. However, in "The Ant and the Dove," the two characters do not know each other before the story begins. They are not family and they do not love each other.

However, the morals of the stories are similar. In both stories, the main characters try to help each other. In "Real Brotherly Love," the two brothers help each other but they don't know the other brother is helping also. In "The Ant and the Dove," the dove helps the ant first and then the ant helps the dove. The dove never knows the ant helped him. The moral of both stories is to help others and they might help you someday. You might not know they are helping you.

2. **Brainstorm.** Write notes for your comparison. Use the chart you made on page 382 to help you list the similarities and differences of the stories. Include information about the characters, the setting, the plot, and the moral of the two stories.

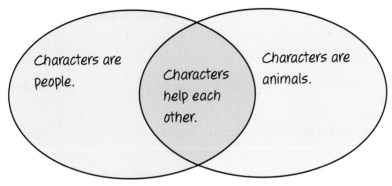

Characters are people.

Characters help each other.

Characters are animals.

"Real Brotherly Love"   "The Ant and the Dove"

3. **Organize your ideas.**

　1. First paragraph

　　a. Topic Sentence

　　b. Similarities

　2. Second paragraph

　　a. Differences

　　b. Restate topic sentence

4. **Write your comparison.**

5. **Revise.** Read your report. Add, delete, or rearrange words or sentences to make your report clearer. Use the editing and proofreading symbols on page 493 to help you mark the changes you need to make.

6. **Edit.** Use the **Writing Checklist** to help you find problems and errors.

Writing Checklist
1. I indented my paragraphs.
2. I capitalized the first word of each sentence.
3. My essay has some similarities and some differences.

Progress Check

MILESTONESTRACKER

How well did you understand this chapter? Try to answer the questions. If necessary, go back to the pages listed for a review.

Skills	Skills Assessment Questions	Pages to Review
Vocabulary	What places do you know in the community? Give directions.	364–367
Grammar	Give examples of **comparative adjectives** in sentences.	368–369
Writing Conventions	**Spelling:** Make the following adjectives comparative: happy, young, mad, nice.	368
	Punctuation: How do you use parentheses and commas for showing additional information? Give examples.	383
Word Study	What do the suffixes **ful, less, able,** and **ish** mean?	371
	What do these suffixes do? **ion, ous, ness**	372
Vocabulary From the Reading	What do these words mean? • **barn, beak, field, grain, net, stream**	375
Academic Vocabulary	What do **trait** and **motive** mean?	376
Reading Strategy	What questions do you ask to **understand** a **character**?	376
Text Genre	What are the text genres in this chapter?	376
Reading Comprehension	What happens in "Real Brotherly Love"?	377–379
	Retell the story "The Ant and the Dove."	380–381
Listening and Speaking	**Phrases for Conversation:** What phrases can you use to compare and contrast stories?	382
Literary Element	What is the **moral** of "Real Brotherly Love" and "The Ant and the Dove"?	383

Assessment Practice

Read this fable. Then answer Questions 1 through 4.

The Crow and the Water

1   Once upon a time, a crow flew to a farmer's field. It was thirsty. The crow saw a glass of water sitting on a table. It flew to the table. When it reached the glass, there was only a little water at the bottom of the glass. The crow could not reach the water.

2   First, the crow thought for a while. Then it flew off and picked up a stone. The crow carried the stone back to the table in its beak. Next, the crow dropped the stone into the glass. The crow dropped more and more stones into the glass. The water got higher and higher. The crow said, "Now I can reach the water." It drank and drank. Finally, the crow was not thirsty.

1 **Read this sentence from paragraph 2.**

> The crow carried the stone back to the table in its beak.

What does <u>beak</u> mean?

A a bird's wing

B a bird's foot

C a bird's back

D a bird's mouth

2 **What adjective describes a character trait of the crow?**

A smart   C sad

B brave   D angry

3 **What is the moral of the fable?**

A Act first and ask questions later.

B Think before you act.

C Take what you can get.

D Fight for what you believe.

4 **What words show that this story is a fable?**

A Once upon a time . . .

B First, the crow thought for a while.

C . . . dropped the stone into the glass.

D . . . the crow was not thirsty.

Writing on Demand: A Fable

Write your own fable. Give details that show the main character's traits. Make sure the fable has a moral. **(20 minutes)**

> **Writing Tip**
> Make a graphic organizer. Write the moral you want to teach in the center. Write ideas of how to teach the moral around the center.

Objectives

Vocabulary
Neighborhood places
Famous places and
attractions

Listening and Speaking
Talking about chores and
errands
Giving reasons

Grammar
Superlative adjectives

Writing Conventions
Punctuation: Colons

Word Study
Diphthongs: ow, ou

Writing
Descriptive essay

● Vocabulary
Neighborhood Places

People go to the **pharmacy** when they feel sick.

People borrow books from the **library**.

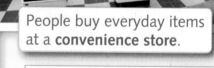

People buy everyday items at a **convenience store**.

People mail things at the **post office**.

People wash their clothes at a **laundromat**.

People keep their money in a **bank**.

People buy gasoline for their cars at a **gas station**.

● Listening and Speaking
Talking About Chores and Errands

1 Listen and repeat the sentences on page 388.

2 Where can you do each of these things? Match the activity with the place on page 388.

return some
books

buy some
stamps

pick up some
bandages

buy some
water

put air in my
bicycle tires

do some
laundry

3 Read and listen.

I'm going to the post office because I have to buy some stamps.

> Use **because** when giving a reason.
> Why is he going to the bank?
> He is going to the bank **because** he needs to get money.

4 Listen again. Repeat.

5 PAIR WORK Say the sentence in activity 3. Use new words for the blue words. You can use vocabulary from page 388 and activity 2.

✓**Checkpoint**
1. Why do people go to the bank?
2. Why do people go to the post office?

● Vocabulary

Famous Places and Attractions

1 Listen and say these phrases about places to visit.

see the
Pyramids

go to Miami
Beach

visit the Statue
of Liberty

go on a safari

see the Great
Wall of China

see the
Mona Lisa

Florida
Egypt
Kenya
France
China
New York

2 PAIR WORK **Where can you do each of the things above?
Ask a partner.**

Where can
you see the
Pyramids?

In Egypt.

● Listening and Speaking

Giving Reasons

1 Listen. Where does each person want to go?
Choose the correct place.

Places	
1. a. India	**b.** Italy
2. a. Chile	**b.** China
3. a. New York	**b.** New Orleans
4. a. Alaska	**b.** Australia

2 Listen again. What reason does the person give for
wanting to go there?

Reasons			
a. mountains	**b.** music	**c.** weather	**d.** food

3 Read and listen.

Kelli: Where would you like to go someday?

Reynaldo: I'd like to go to Brazil.

Kelli: Why?

Reynaldo: Because I want to see Rio de Janeiro.

4 Listen and repeat.

5 **PAIR WORK** Say the conversation again. Use new
words for the blue words. You can use places from
page 390.

6 **PAIR WORK** Tell your partner where <u>you</u> want to go,
and why.

✓ Checkpoint

1. Where can you
go to the beach?

2. Where do you
want to visit?

● Grammar

Superlative Adjectives

Use **comparative adjectives** to compare two things. To compare more than two things use **superlative adjectives**. Always use **the** before a superlative adjective.

The Mississippi River is **long**.
The Yellow River is **longer** than the Mississippi River.
The Nile is **the longest** river in the world.

For most one-syllable or two-syllable adjectives add the suffix **-est**.

Forming Superlative Adjectives with -est	
tall ➜ the tall**est**	add **est**
nice ➜ the nice**st**	ends in **e**; add **st**
pretty ➜ the pretti**est**	ends in **y**; change to **i** and add **est**
hot ➜ the hot**test**	for single syllable words that end in consonant-vowel-consonant; **double** the last consonant and add **est**

For most adjectives with two or more syllables, use the words **the most** in front of the adjective.

Forming Superlative Adjectives with Most	
interesting ➜	This is **the most interesting** museum in the city.
important ➜	The capitol building is **the most important** building in the city.

A few adjectives are irregular in the superlative form. You should learn these forms.

good ➜ My mother is a **good** cook.
My father is a **better** cook **than** my mother.
My grandmother is **the best** cook.

bad ➜ The bank on Central Street is **bad**.
The bank across from the library is **worse**.
This is **the worst** bank in the city.

Workbook
page 243

Independent Practice
CD-ROM

1 Write sentences about something you know. Use the superlative form of the adjectives below.

Example: tall
The Empire State Building is the tallest building in New York.

1. smart
4. good
2. bad
5. delicious
3. interesting

2 **PAIR WORK** **Make questions about your sentences and ask your partner.**

What is the tallest building in New York?

The Empire State Building is the tallest building in New York.

Writing Conventions

Punctuation *Colons*

Use a **colon** (:) when you are going to announce something, or write a list of things, at the end of a sentence.

Here are the items I need at the supermarket**:** some milk, some eggs, and a loaf of bread.

He gave me what I really wanted**:** a vacation.

Apply Write these sentences. Use a colon in each sentence.

1. I have everything my backpack, my books, and my workbook.

2. She sent me something yesterday a book of poems.

3. Everyone is coming to the party Jane, Maria, and Robert.

4. Japan has so many things to see old temples, great museums, and beautiful parks.

> **✓Checkpoint**
>
> 1. How do you make **superlative adjectives**?
> 2. Make two sentences with superlative adjectives.

GRAMMAR EXPANSION
Superlative Adverbs,
Workbook page 245

Workbook
page 244

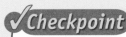
Independent Practice
CD-ROM

Unit 6 • Chapter 2   **393**

Word Study

Diphthongs: ow, ou for /ow/

Phonemic Awareness

1 Listen and repeat.

ow

cow   town   flower

ou

cloud   house   couch

Decoding

2 Listen. Find the /ow/ sounds in each sentence.

1. I hear loud shouts from the crowd.
2. I found it on the ground.
3. How can she be proud?
4. The spout points down.

3 Listen again and repeat.

Decodable
Reader 54

Workbook
page 246

Independent Practice
CD-ROM

✓Checkpoint

Read these words.
    shout
    chowder
    south
    mouse
    shower

Writing Assignment
Descriptive Essay

> ### Writing Prompt
>
> Write about the best or worst place you visited.
> Use superlative adjectives.

1. Read the student model.

Leonardo Valderrama

The Best Vacation

I visited Chicago, IL last year and it was the best vacation. The first reason Chicago was the best place was because it was good to see my family. I enjoyed talking to my aunt, uncle, and cousins and telling them my stories. The other reason I enjoyed my vacation was because my cousin and I went to the tallest building in Chicago: the Sears Tower. We saw the city from the top and it was beautiful. I hope that some day I can go to Chicago again. I had a very good time there. It was the best vacation. I enjoyed many things there so I want to go again.

2. What was the best or worst place you visited? Give reasons why it was good or bad.

3. Use descriptive adjectives and examples to help your audience imagine the place.

4. Write your essay.

Writing Checklist

1. I capitalized the names of places.

2. I used superlative adjectives correctly.

3. I used **because** to give reasons.

Part B

Objectives

Reading Strategy
Identify the author's
purpose and audience

Text Genre
Informational text

Listening and Speaking
Give an opinion

Text Element
Index

Reading Fluency
Reading words in chunks

Writing
Book report

Academic Vocabulary

inform | audience

Academic Content

The U.S. Constitution

● About the Reading

You are going to read an excerpt from a social studies textbook about the United States Constitution.

● Use Prior Knowledge

Talk About the Job of the Government

What is the job of the government? Here is a list of possible jobs:

- Protect the country
- Take care of people
- Protect people's rights
- Do what is best for the majority of people
- Keep people safe

1. Brainstorm. What other things should a government do?

2. Look at your list. Which do you think is the most important? The second most important? Write your list in order of most to least important.

3. **PAIR WORK** Show your new list to your partner. Tell your partner why you put the items in the order you did.

● Vocabulary From the Reading
Learn, Practice, and Use Independently

Key Vocabulary

allowed

amendment

approve

document

vote

war

Learn Vocabulary Read the sentences. Use the context to find the meaning of the **highlighted** words. Write what the words mean.

1. You're not **allowed** to skateboard there. You can't skateboard anywhere in the park.
2. John gave us an **amendment** to change the plan. We made his change.
3. The managers **approve** of our idea. We can do it.
4. All of the information is written in this **document**. Please keep this paper safe.
5. Everyone's **vote** is important. Please raise your hand if you agree.
6. Some people feel **war** is never an answer. Too many people are hurt and die.

Practice Vocabulary Read the sentences. Write the Key Vocabulary word that has the same meaning as the underlined phrase.

1. Some people think it is wrong for countries to fight each other.
2. There are several changes to the plan here.
3. My mother agreed with our plan so we can do it now.
4. Even one person's choice can decide who becomes the new leader.
5. You can enter that room.
6. You can find what you need on this piece of paper.

Use Vocabulary Independently Write a paragraph. Use all of your vocabulary words in the paragraph.

✓Checkpoint

1. Name one thing you need your teacher's **approval** to do.
2. Name two things you are not **allowed** to do in school.

Vocabulary Log

Workbook page 248

Independent Practice CD-ROM

● Academic Vocabulary

Vocabulary for the Reading Strategy

Word	Explanation	Sample Sentence	Visual Cue
inform *verb*	to give information or facts to someone	The principal **informed** the students there was a school concert on Thursday.	
audience *noun*	a person or people who read something an author has written	The **audience** for this book is teenagers, but adults like to read it too.	

Draw a picture or write a sentence for each word.

● Reading Strategy

Identify the Author's Purpose and Audience

entertain *(v.)* to amuse or make people happy.

persuade *(v.)* to lead people to believe or do something.

Dictionary Entries

The author's **purpose** of a textbook is to **inform** students. Other reasons for writing are to entertain or persuade.

Authors think about who will read the text. An author writes differently for different **audiences**.

● Text Genre

Informational Text: Textbook

A **textbook** has these features.

Textbook	
title	the name of a chapter or text
heading	the name of a part of the text
time line	a graphic that shows when things happen
maps	illustrations that show where things happen
index	a list that shows where to find specific words or topics

✓ Checkpoint

1. What kind of **audience** reads this book?
2. What is the **purpose** of this book?

Vocabulary Log

Workbook page 249, 250

Independent Practice CD-ROM

● Reading

Reading Focus Questions

As you read, think about these questions.

1. Why is the United States Constitution important?

2. What are some of the changes to the Constitution that have changed America?

CHAPTER

1

The United States Constitution
Our Most Important Document

◆ **What the Constitution Does**

1   The Constitution is the most important **document** in the U.S. government. All laws come from this **document**. Each state has its own constitution, too, but the United States Constitution has more power.

2   The Constitution also set up the United States government that we know today. There are three branches, or parts, of government: legislative, executive, and judiciary. The writers of the Constitution made the government this way so that no single person or group could have too much power.

3   The legislative branch, which includes the Congress, makes the laws. The executive branch, which includes the president and vice-president of the United States, makes sure that the laws are followed. The judiciary branch, which includes the Supreme Court, looks at laws and decides whether they agree with the Constitution.

> **Reading Strategy**
>
> **Identify the author's purpose and audience** Is this text written to **inform** or entertain? How do you know?

> ✔
> ## Reading Check
>
> 1. **Recall facts** Which has more power: state constitutions or the United States Constitution?
>
> 2. **Describe** What are the three branches of American government?

◆ **Writing the Constitution**

⁴   The Constitution was written in 1787. At that time, the new American government was having some problems. Many people wanted to make a **document** that would help them set up a better government.

⁵   From May to September of 1787, a group of people worked together to write the Constitution. These people were called the Framers. This group included many important people in American history, such as George Washington, James Madison, and Benjamin Franklin.

⁶   The summer of 1787 was very hot, and writing the Constitution was not easy. Many people wanted different things. Some people did not like the Constitution then because they said it did not include a list of people's rights. The Framers agreed that they would send the Constitution to the states for **approval** first. They promised they would add a list of rights later, after the Constitution was **approved**.

⁷   In 1787, there were only thirteen states. They only needed nine of the thirteen states to **approve** the Constitution. Finally, nine states approved the **document**, and a new U.S. government was born.

Reading Strategy

Identify the author's purpose and audience Why do you think the author included a time line in the reading?

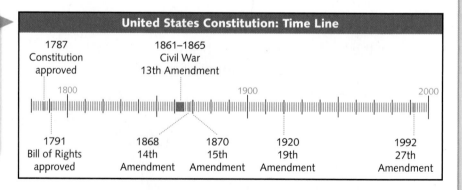

United States Constitution: Time Line

1787 Constitution approved	1861–1865 Civil War 13th Amendment			
1800		1900		2000
1791 Bill of Rights approved	1868 14th Amendment	1870 15th Amendment	1920 19th Amendment	1992 27th Amendment

◆ The Bill of Rights

8   One of the most important things about the Constitution is that it can be changed. These changes are called **amendments**. As of 2007, there were 27 **amendments** to the Constitution.

9   After the Constitution was first **approved**, many people wanted to add a list of people's rights to the **document**. Ten rights were **approved** by the states in 1791, and they became the first **amendments** to the Constitution. These **amendments** are called the Bill of Rights.

◆ The Right to Free **Speech**

10   One of the most important rights in the Bill of Rights is the right to free speech. Americans can say or write anything they want about the government, or any of the people in the government. They will not be arrested because of what they say.

◆ Other Important Rights

11   Another important right is freedom of **religion**. Americans can believe in any religion they want. They can also decide not to have any religion. The Constitution protects these rights.

12   The Bill of Rights talks about many other important rights. The government cannot make you let **soldiers** stay in your house. If the police want to come into your house to look for something, they cannot do it without a good reason. If you are arrested, you do not have to say anything against yourself. These are just some of the rights that are listed in the Bill of Rights.

---

speech something you say (or write) to others
religion a system of spiritual beliefs in a god or gods
soldier someone who is in the army or other service

Reading Strategy

Identify the author's purpose and audience Why do you think the author used headings for each of the sections in this reading?

✓ Reading Check

1. **Recall facts** How many **amendments** have been made to the U.S. Constitution?

2. **Describe** What is the Bill of Rights?

◆ The End of Slavery

13   Besides the Bill of Rights, there have been many other important **amendments** to the Constitution. When the Constitution was written, there were many slaves in America. The slaves had been brought over from Africa. After several years, many people started to say that **slavery** was wrong. They wanted to end slavery.

14   However, many people in the southern United States did not want to end slavery. Slaves were important for them to run their businesses. They were afraid that without slaves, they would lose money.

15   When Abraham Lincoln was elected president in 1860, many people in the South were angry. President Lincoln was against slavery. The states in the South decided to make their own country: the Confederate States of America (CSA).

16   In the North, the United States of America did not want the CSA to break away from the USA. From 1861–1865 there was a terrible **war** called the American Civil **War**. More than 600,000 people died. The North won the **war**, and the CSA was not **allowed** to break away.

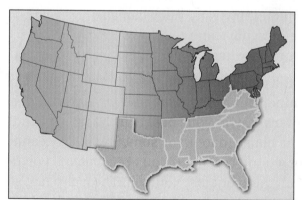

The Confederate States of America, shown in light orange

---

slavery the practice of owning other people, and making them work for you

Reading Strategy

Identify the author's purpose and audience Why do you think the author included a map?

17   At the end of the **war**, however, one good thing happened. The 13th **Amendment** to the Constitution (1865) ended slavery in the entire country. Then the 14th **Amendment** (1868) said that every person born in the United States was a full **citizen**. The 15th **Amendment** gave African Americans the right to **vote** (1870).

18   Even with these new rights, African Americans still saw a lot of **discrimination**. For 100 years after the end of slavery, there were still many laws that separated African Americans from white Americans. Today, those laws are gone, and now all Americans have the same rights, no matter what the color of their skin is.

◆ **Women's Right to Vote**

19   In the early days of the United States, women were not **allowed** to be in the government. They also could not **vote**. Men had all of the power in the government, and women had none.

20   That changed in 1920. With the 19th **Amendment**, American women finally got the right to **vote** in all elections. Now many women have important jobs in the U.S. government.

◆ **The Future of the Constitution**

21   Many changes have been made to the Constitution since it was **approved** in 1787. More changes will probably come. It is the job of the government and of the people to make sure that this **document** helps protect the rights of all Americans, so that the United States can continue to take care of its citizens in the future.

---

citizen someone who is **allowed** to live in a particular country because he or she was born there, or because the country has legally accepted him or her

discrimination treating two groups of people differently

Reading Strategy

Identify the author's purpose and audience Why do you think the author only mentioned a few of the 27 **amendments** in the Constitution?

✔

Reading Check

1. **Recall facts** When did women get the right to **vote**?

2. **Make inferences** Why do you think the author says "more changes will probably come"?

● Reading Comprehension Questions

Think and Discuss

1. **Recall facts** Why is the United States Constitution important?

2. **Evaluate information** What are some of the changes to the Constitution that have changed America?

3. **Make inferences** Why do you think it was so difficult to write the Constitution?

4. **Present an opinion** Do you think it is important for Americans to read and understand the Constitution? Why or why not?

5. **Revisit the Reading Focus Questions** Go back to page 399 and discuss the questions.

● Listening and Speaking

Give an Opinion

U.S. school students learn about the U.S. Constitution in school, but very few American citizens read the whole U.S. Constitution. Most people in the United States believe the Constitution is the most important **document** of the whole government. Do you think we should all read it?

1. As a class, list reasons why U.S. citizens should read the U.S. Constitution.

2. As a class, list reasons why most citizens don't read the Constitution.

3. **PAIR WORK** Give your opinion. Do you think it is important for all Americans to read the U.S. Constitution? Give reasons.

4. Listen to your classmates. What is the purpose of their speeches? Are your classmates trying to inform, persuade, or entertain the audience?

Build Vocabulary

When people know they should do something but don't, the reason they give for not doing it is called an **excuse**.

Phrases for Conversation

Giving an Opinion

In my opinion, reading the U.S. Constitution is important because . . .

I think that people don't need to read the U.S. Constitution because . . .

I believe . . .

Workbook page 251

Independent Practice CD-ROM

● Text Element

Index

Textbooks usually have an **index** in the back of the book. An index lists page numbers where specific information can be found. Topics are listed in alphabetical order by key words or phrases.

1. Where can you find information on the U.S. Constitution?

2. Where can you find details about civil rights heroes?

civil rights, 281, 285–288, 304–307
    heroes, 306–307
    movement, 304–307
Civil **War**, American, 188–197
civilization, Native American, 32–35, 45, 123–125, 349–350
colonies, original thirteen, 120–135
Confederate States of America, 192–193
Congress, U.S., 532–540
Constitution, U.S., 483–499
    Framers and, 487–489
    approval of, 491–495
Continental Congress, 142
Court, U.S. Supreme, 557–559
    and state courts, 558
CSA *see* Confederate States of America

● Reading Fluency

Reading Words in Chunks

Good readers do not read word by word. They read words in "chunks." Chunks are groups of words that go together. Finding phrases and reading them together helps you understand better.

1. Look at the underlined phrases in the passage.

Many changes have been made to the Constitution since it was approved in 1787. More changes will probably come. It is the job of the government and of the people to make sure that this document helps protect the rights of all Americans, so that the United States can continue to take care of its citizens in the future.

---

2. Listen to your teacher read the passage. Can you hear the chunks?

3. Read the passage aloud to your partner twice. Think about pace as you read.

4. Rate yourself. How well did I read the paragraph?
I read the words in chunks. ❑ Yes ❑ No
I read the words at the correct pace. ❑ Yes ❑ No

✓ **Checkpoint**

1. What is an **index**?
2. Where is the **index** of this book?

Workbook
page 252

Independent Practice
CD-ROM

● Writing Assignment
Book Report

> **Writing Prompt**
>
> What is the most important book or **document** you have read? Give reasons why it is important.

1. Read the student model.

Student Model

Brynna Epperly

The Most Important Book

The book <u>Stone Fox</u> by John Reynolds Gardiner is the most important book to me. It is important to me because it is about helping family and other people. I think this book is important for everybody because it shows the best way to treat other people.

I like this book because I understand how Willy feels. The person I love the most is my grandfather and I am sad when he is sick. I try my hardest to help him. Willy knows that it is his job to take care of his grandfather. Also, at the end of the book, Stone Fox understands you have to help strangers, too. This is an important lesson because it means you should help everyone. That is the best thing to do.

I think that this book is the most important book about friendship. I think everybody should read this book because they can learn the best way to help other people. Everyone can learn more about being good to family, friends, and strangers, too.

2. **Brainstorm.** What is the best book or paper you have read? Did you read it in school or at home? Did you read it in English?

3. **Organize your ideas.**

   1) Opening paragraph

      a) Topic sentence: _____

   2) Body paragraph

      a) What happened in the book: _____

      b) Reason it is important to you: _____

         example: _____

   3) Conclusion

      a) Restate topic sentence: _____

      b) Give a reason it is an important book: _____

4. **Write your book report.**

5. **Revise.** Read your book report. Add, delete, or rearrange words or sentences to make your paragraphs clearer. Use the editing and proofreading symbols on page 493 to help you mark the changes you need to make.

6. **Edit.** Use the **Writing Checklist** to help you find problems and errors.

Writing Checklist
1. I used correct superlative adjectives.
2. I used **because** correctly.
3. I gave good reasons.
4. I gave my opinion.

Progress Check

MILESTONES TRACKER

How well did you understand this chapter? Try to answer the questions. If necessary, go back to the pages listed for a review.

Skills	Skills Assessment Questions	Pages to Review
Vocabulary	What are some places in your neighborhood? What kinds of errands do you run?	**388–391**
Grammar	How do you make **superlative adjectives**? What are they used for?	**392–393**
Writing Conventions	**Punctuation:** When do you use a **colon**?	**393**
Vocabulary From the Reading	Can you make a sentence with each of these words? Give examples. • **allowed**, **amendment**, **approve**, **document**, **vote**, **war**	**397**
Academic Vocabulary	What do **inform** and **audience** mean? Extra: What do **entertain** and **persuade** mean?	**398**
Reading Strategy	What do you do when you identify the author's **purpose** and **audience**?	**398**
Text Genre	What do you find in a textbook?	**398**
Reading Comprehension	What is the U.S. Constitution? What are some important **amendments**?	**399–404**
Listening and Speaking	**Phrases for Conversation:** What phrases can you use to give an opinion?	**404**
Text Element	What is an **index**? How do you use it?	**405**
Reading Fluency	What is **chunking**?	**405**

Assessment Practice

Read this passage from a textbook. Then answer Questions 1 through 4.

How Local Government Works

1   A city council is a group of people. They lead the city or town government together. One member of the city council is elected as the president.

2   The group meets once a month. They decide what to do about local matters. People who live in the community can come to these meetings. They can give their opinions.

3   Imagine a man has a plan to build a shopping mall. He explains his plan to the city council. He gives them documents that tell about his plans. Council members and community members can ask questions. They can say why they like or don't like the plan. Then, the city council votes. They can approve the plan or not. They decide what is best for the city.

1 Read the sentence from paragraph 3.

> They can approve the plan or not.

What does **approve** mean?

A agree with

B write a letter about

C change

D help with

2 Which sentence best describes the author's purpose?

A to teach about local government

B to entertain

C to persuade the audience to go to city council meetings

D to teach a lesson

3 Which sentence uses a superlative adjective correctly?

A The group meets once a month.

B They can give their opinions.

C They decide what is best for the city.

D They can say why they like or don't like the plan.

4 Where might you find this reading?

A in a book of folktales and fables

B in a book of short stories

C in a social studies book

D in a poetry book

 Writing on Demand: Descriptive Essay

Write a descriptive paragraph about the best holiday your family celebrates. Include details such as special foods that you eat or special things you do. **(20 minutes)**

Writing Tip
Brainstorm ideas before you begin writing.

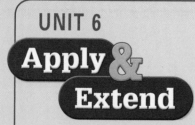

Apply & Extend

Objectives

Listening and Speaking
Deliver a dramatic presentation of a story

Media
Compare a television news story and a newspaper article

Writing
A newspaper article

● Listening and Speaking Workshop
Deliver a Dramatic Presentation of a Story

> **Topic**
>
> Deliver a dramatic presentation of a story or event from your community. Use dialog lines to act out your story. Use props as part of your presentation.

1. **Choose a Story or Event**
   Work in a small group. Choose a story or event in a community.

2. **Brainstorm**
   Think about the people in the story.
   a. Who are the main people? Where are they?
   b. What adjectives can you use to describe them?
   c. What do they do?
   d. What do they say to each other?
   e. What happens at the beginning, middle, and end of the story?

3. **Plan**
   As a group, decide who will play each character in your presentation. Write the words your character will say. Think about what props you can use.

4. **Prepare and Practice**
   Practice your presentation. Use your voice to show the feelings of your character. Memorize your lines. Ask another group to listen to your presentation and tell you how to improve. Listen to the other group. Help them.

5. **Present**
   Present your story to the class.

6. **Evaluate**
   Ask the class for feedback. Use the **Speaking Self-Evaluation**. Use the **Active Listening Evaluation** to evaluate and discuss your classmates' presentations.

Speaking Self-Evaluation	Active Listening Evaluation
1. I practiced the story and was prepared.	1. You spoke at the right speed—not too slowly and not too quickly.
2. I used tone, tempo, and pitch to show the character's feelings.	2. The story was interesting. I learned about ____.
3. I spoke clearly and loudly enough.	3. I understood the feelings of the character.
4. I looked at the audience when I spoke.	4. I think ____ was the most interesting part of your presentation.
	5. You could improve your presentation by ____.

Media Workshop

Compare a Television News Story and a Newspaper Article

A television news show and a newspaper can report the same story or event. Compare a television news report and a newspaper article about the same event or story.

1. Watch a television news show. Choose a story that is interesting. Take notes about the story. Ask questions as you watch. Write your answers.

   a. What is the main idea of the story?

   b. Who is in the story?

   c. Who tells the story?

   d. What happens?

   e. What is the purpose of this story?

2. Find a newspaper article about the same event. Take notes and answer the same questions from activity 1.

3. Work in a small group. Discuss the stories. How were the answers to the questions the same? How were they different?

4. Discuss what you found with the class.

Writing Workshop

Write a Newspaper Article

A **newspaper article** reports details on important events.

> **Writing Prompt**
>
> Imagine that you are a newspaper reporter during an important event in history. Write an article. Tell who, what, where, when, why, and how about the event.

Writing Suggestion

Close your eyes and imagine you are at the event. What sounds do you hear? Do you smell anything? What do you see? How do you feel? Use sensory adjectives to describe the event.

PREWRITE

1. Read the student model.
2. Think about these questions. Take notes.
   a. What event are you reporting?
   b. Who was at the event?
   c. What happened?
   d. Where did it happen?
   e. When did it happen?
   f. Why did it happen?
   g. How did it happen? What caused the event?
3. Make a chart. Use an encyclopedia or the Internet to find more details.

WRITE A DRAFT

1. Tell what happened and where it happened.
2. Give details about the event: who was there, when it was.
3. Use comparative and superlative adjectives.
4. Tell why the event was important.

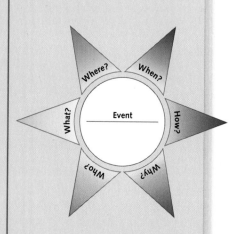

Student Model

Include who and what.

Title

Nati Petrova

Americans Walk on the Moon

Introduction

Today, two American astronauts walked on the moon. They were Neil Armstrong and Edwin Aldrin.

They traveled to the moon on the Apollo 11 mission. It was a dangerous mission. On July 20, 1969, they called Earth on a radio. They reported that everything was OK. They took pictures of themselves walking on the moon. They used a large spaceship to go to the moon and then a smaller spaceship to go down to the moon.

They picked up some rocks for the scientists on Earth. They will fly back to Earth soon. People will learn a lot about the moon from their trip.

Include details.

Body

Conclusion

REVISE

1. Review your article. Did you answer all the questions?
2. Ask your partner to use the **Peer Review Checklist.**
3. Use the editing and proofreading symbols on page 493.
4. Revise your draft. Add or delete sentences. Add details.

EDIT

1. Use the **Revising and Editing Checklist** to evaluate your article.
2. Fix any errors in grammar, spelling, and punctuation.

Peer Review Checklist
1. The article has a title.
2. You told what happened and who was there. You gave details.
3. The article tells me about an important event.
4. You could improve your writing by ____ .

Revising and Editing Checklist
1. My article has a title.
2. I have descriptive details.
3. I answered these questions: what, who, where, when, why, how.
4. I spelled comparative and superlative adjectives correctly.

PUBLISH

1. Write your article in your best handwriting or use a computer. If you use a computer, do a spell and grammar check.
2. Find a picture or photo on the Internet about the event. Print it and put it with your article.
3. Read your article to the class.

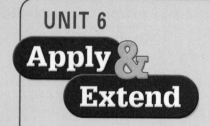

UNIT 6

Apply & Extend

● Projects

Choose one or more of the following projects to explore the theme of Community further.

PROJECT 1
Write a Book Report

1. Read a new book. Your teacher can help you find an appropriate book.
2. Take notes about the book: main ideas, characters, setting, sequence of events, and problem/solution.
3. Use your notes to write a book report.
4. Draw a picture to show your favorite event.
5. Read your report and share your picture with the class. Answer questions from your classmates.

PROJECT 2
Compare Stories

1. Read two stories by the same author. You may choose two stories from the Milestones Intro Reading Library by Rob Waring and Maurice Jamall.
2. Compare the stories. Use a Venn diagram like the one you made on page 382.
3. Compare characters, plot, and settings.

PROJECT 3
Make a Community Places Poster

1. Work in a small group. Copy the chart below on poster paper.

Places in Our Community				
	Supermarket	Park	Post Office	Library
Name				
Address				
Days it is open				
Time it opens and closes				
What you can do there				

2. Complete the chart with information from your community. Use the Internet or telephone book for names.

3. Present and display your poster for the class.

PROJECT 4
Plan a New Building for Your Community

1. Work with a partner. Think of a new place you want in your community: a restaurant, a movie theater, a park.

2. Make a picture of the building or place.

3. Pick a name for the place.

4. Put the address and hours it is open on the picture.

5. Answer these questions:
   a. Who will go to this place?
   b. What will people do there?
   c. Why did you choose this place?

6. Present your building to the class. Tell why it is needed in your community.

● Independent Reading

Explore the theme of Community further by reading one or more of these books.

Fair Weather by Richard Peck, Dial, 2001.
In 1893, Rosie and her family travel from their farm in Illinois to Chicago. They go to the World's Columbian Exposition.

If You Traveled on the Underground Railroad by Ellen Levine, Scholastic Paperbacks, 1993.
In this book, you find questions and answers about the underground railroad. You learn what it was, when it was, and how people used it to help slaves in the United States escape to the North.

The Day It Snowed Tortillas by Joe Hayes, Cinco Puntos Press, 2004.
This folktale and other tales from New Mexico are full of magic and fun.

Hoot by Carl Hiaasen, Random House, 2002.
Roy and his new friend are worried about some owls. They try to stop a huge construction project to save the trees and forest where the owls live.

> **Milestones Intro Reading Library**
>
> *Slam Dunk for Mark* by Rob Waring and Maurice Jamall, Heinle, 2006.
>
> *Go Jimmy Go!* by Rob Waring and Maurice Jamall, Heinle, 2006.
>
> *Singer Wanted* by Rob Waring and Maurice Jamall, Heinle, 2006.

Milestones to Achievement

● Reading

Read this fable. Then answer Questions 1 through 8.

The Little Red Hen

1   One day, a little red hen found some grain near the barn. She took it home. She showed the grain to her friends (the cat and the duck) because they liked wheat bread.

2   "Will you help me plant this wheat?" the red hen asked her friends. "No," they replied. "It is time for our nap." The little red hen went to the corner of a field and she planted the wheat herself.

3   The little red hen knew that wheat does not grow without water. She went back to her friends. "Who will help me water the wheat?" she asked. "Not I," said the cat. "I am busy cleaning my paws." "Not I," said the duck. "I am busy washing my feathers." The little red hen carried water from the stream and she watered the wheat herself.

4   Then, it was time to pick the wheat. The little red hen went back to her friends. "Can you help me pick the wheat?" she asked. "Oh, not today," they both replied. "We are busy listening to music." The little red hen walked to the field and picked the wheat herself.

5   The little red hen knew that a miller down the road could grind her wheat into flour. It was a long walk to the mill and she did not want to walk alone. "Can you walk with me to the mill?" she asked the cat and the duck. "Sorry, no," they said. "We are too tired to walk that far." So the little red hen walked to the mill by herself.

6   Finally, the little red hen walked home with her flour. She did not ask her friends if they wanted to help her bake the bread. She saw they were watching television. When the bread came out of the oven, the cat and the duck came into the kitchen. "Can we have some bread?" they asked. "Anyone who helped to plant the wheat, water it, pick it, take it to the mill, and bake the bread can have some," responded the little red hen. And she ate the bread herself. Later, she took some to the miller. He thought it was very good bread.

1 Read this sentence from paragraph 3.

> The little red hen carried water from the stream and she watered the wheat herself.

What does <u>stream</u> mean?

A a home   C a small river

B a farm   D a school

2 Which of the adjectives below best describes the little red hen?

A hard-working   C careless

B lazy   D foolish

3 What character trait best describes the cat and the duck?

A helpful   C thoughtless

B enjoyable   D famous

4 How might the story end if the hen's friends had helped her?

A The hen ate all the bread.

B They all ate the bread together.

C The whole town ate the bread.

D The miller ate all the bread.

5 What is the moral of this fable?

A Weather is important for crops.

B You must work to get what you want.

C It is better to do things yourself.

D Don't ask friends to help you.

6 Paragraph 5 tells you

A why the little red hen went to the miller's alone.

B the directions to go to the miller's house.

C how long it is to the miller's house.

D what cat and duck did at the miller's house.

7 In paragraph 1, *the cat and the duck* is in parentheses. What is another way to write this sentence?

A She showed, the grain, to her friends the cat and the duck because they liked wheat bread.

B She showed the grain, to her friends the cat and the duck, because they liked wheat bread.

C She showed the grain, to her friends, the cat and the duck because they liked wheat bread.

D She showed the grain to her friends, the cat and the duck, because they liked wheat bread.

8 Where should the miller go if he wants to send a thank-you card to the little red hen?

A the post office   C a bank

B the library   D a gas station

Writing on Demand: Descriptive Essay

Write a description of your community. Tell where your community is located and what the town is like. Tell what businesses are there. **(20 minutes)**

> **Writing Tip**
> Before you start writing, draw a word web. Use the word web to organize your ideas.

Shopping

Talk About the Theme

1. Look at the photos. Where are the people?
2. What are they buying?

Theme Activity

With a partner, make a list of stores you know. Then, with the class, list the things you can buy in those stores.

CHAPTER 1

Part A

Objectives

Vocabulary
Shopping for clothing
Questions and answers for shopping

Listening and Speaking
Talking about shopping
Using shopping questions and answers

Grammar
Using will to talk about the future
Questions with will

Writing Conventions
Spelling words with qu

Word Study
u as /yu/
The /oo/ sound
Words with multiple meanings

Writing
Personal narrative

● Vocabulary
Shopping for Clothing

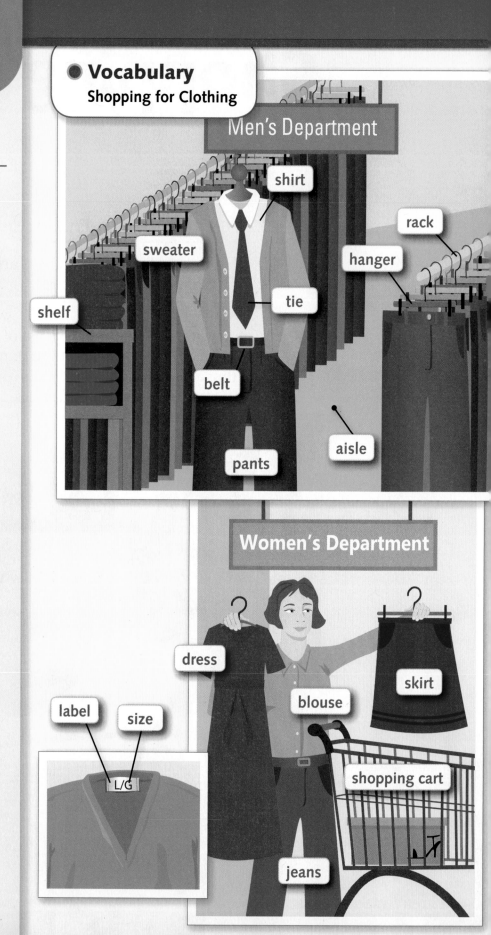

Men's Department

shirt
rack
sweater
hanger
tie
shelf
belt
aisle
pants

Women's Department

dress
skirt
blouse
label
size
L/G
shopping cart
jeans

Part A

● Listening and Speaking
Talking About Shopping

1 Listen and repeat the words on page 420.

2 PAIR WORK **What are you wearing? Tell your partner.**

3 Read and listen.

Salesclerk: Can I help you?

Alex: Yes. Where are the jeans?

Salesclerk: Teen's jeans are in the Men's Department—in aisle 17.

Alex: Thank you.

4 Listen again. Repeat.

5 PAIR WORK **Say the conversation again. Use new words for the blue words. Use vocabulary from page 420.**

6 Read and listen.

Nina: Excuse me, where can I find a black skirt?

Salesclerk: They are on this rack. What size do you need?

Nina: I need a medium.

Salesclerk: Here you go. Do you need a blouse to go with it?

Nina: No, thank you. This is fine.

Salesclerk: Let me know if you need any more help.

7 Listen again. Repeat.

8 PAIR WORK **Say the conversation again. Use new words for the blue words.**

Build Vocabulary

Sizes

XS = extra small

S = small

M = medium

L = large

XL = extra large

✓Checkpoint

1. In which department can you find ties and belts?

2. What size is an XXL?

Vocabulary Log   Workbook page 253   Independent Practice CD-ROM

● Vocabulary
Questions and Answers for Shopping

1 **Read and listen.**

Where can I try these on?

They're too big.

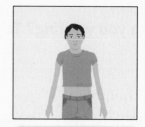

It's too small.

Do you have this in another size?

Do you have this in another color?

I'll take it.

Can I return these?

2 **Listen and repeat.**

3 **PAIR WORK** **Work with a partner. Decide what to ask or say.**

Example: You are looking for a pair of large pants.
You can only find size small.

Do you have these in large?

1. You want to see if a shirt fits you.
2. You try on a pair of shoes. Your feet hurt.
3. You see white socks. You want black socks.
4. You buy a blouse for your mother. You are not sure she will like it.

● Listening and Speaking
Using Shopping Questions and Answers

1 **Read and listen.**

Customer: Excuse me, **can I return this shirt?**

Salesclerk: Of course. What is the problem?

Customer: It's **too small.**

2 **Listen and repeat.**

3 PAIR WORK **Say the conversation again. Use new words for the blue words. You can use vocabulary from pages 421 and 422.**

4 **Listen to the conversation between a mother, her daughter, and a salesclerk. Answer the questions.**

1. What is the girl trying on?

2. What is the problem?

3. What color is the new dress?

4. Will the girl take it?

5 PAIR WORK **Role-play your own conversation. One person is a customer. The other is a salesclerk or cashier.**

Build Vocabulary

Cleaning Clothing

machine wash

hand wash

dry clean

✓Checkpoint

You have tried on ten pairs of jeans. Finally you find a pair that fits you. What do you say?

Vocabulary Log

Workbook page 254

Independent Practice CD-ROM

● Grammar

Using Will to Talk About the Future

The **future** is time that has not happened yet. It can be later today, or tomorrow, or a long time from now. For the future, use **will** or **will not** before the verb.

Using Will to Talk About the Future	
Affirmative	**Negative**
I will run.	I will not walk.
He will dance.	He will not sing.
We will study.	We will not watch TV.
They will shop.	They will not pay later.

1 Use will or will not to make each sentence future.

Example: Rebecca tries on clothes.
  Rebecca will try on clothes.

1. Mary runs every day.
2. Steven didn't buy shoes.
3. I didn't shop there.
4. My brothers bought shirts.

Questions with Will

To make yes/no questions with **will**, use **will** before the subject and verb. Answer with **will** or **won't**.

Yes / No Questions with Will			Short Answers with Will
Will	I/you he/she/it we/they	shop?	Yes, he will.
			No, you won't.

2 PAIR WORK **Answer the questions.**

1. Will you go shopping tonight?
2. Will your teacher give you homework?
3. Will you buy a friend something this weekend?

Workbook
page 255

Independent Practice
CD-ROM

Look at some wh- questions you might use with **will**.

Wh- Questions with Will	
Who will I see at the mall?	You will see Jim and Pat.
What will you get?	I will get some shoes.
Where will he go shopping?	He will go to the mall.
When will she try it on?	She will try it on tonight.
How will we know if our shoes fit?	We will try them on.
Why will they return it?	They will return it because it's too small.

3 **Read the answers below. Write a question.**

Example: They'll go to the movies.
           Where will they go?

1. Susan will be home at 8:00 tonight.

2. I'll do my homework.

3. He'll look for a blue T-shirt because his other shirt
   is too small.

4. They'll meet Joan and Cathy.

5. I'll try on this shirt.

✎ Writing Conventions

Spelling *Words with* qu

When you use the letter **q**, it is usually followed by the letter **u** and
another vowel. The letters **qu** are pronounced /kw/, for example: **qu**estion

quiet   **qu**ack   li**qu**id   **qu**een   e**qu**als

Apply Use the words above to complete the sentences.
Spell the words correctly.

1. Shhh! Please be ____ . The baby will wake up.

2. I don't understand. I will ask a ____ .

3. Two plus four ____ six.

4. Milk is a ____ .

✓ Checkpoint

Make sentences
with **will** and **won't**.
Use the verbs wash,
wear, and try on.

GRAMMAR EXPANSION

More Wh- Questions with
will, Workbook page 257

Workbook
page 256

Independent Practice
CD-ROM

Unit 7 • Chapter 1   **425**

● Word Study

Vowel: u as /yu/

Phonemic Awareness

1 **Listen and repeat.**

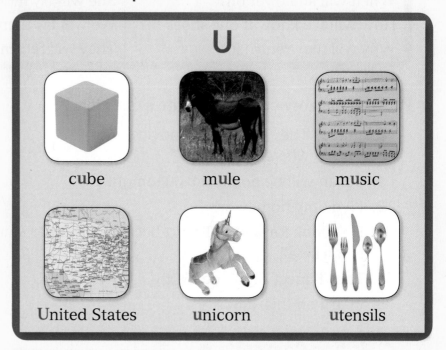

U

cube   mule   music

United States   unicorn   utensils

Decoding

2 **Listen. Find the /yu/ sounds in each sentence.**

1. I use a saddle on my mule.
2. Unicorns are cute.
3. How many humans live in the United States?
4. Utensils are useful when you eat.
5. Do you want ice cubes in your drink?
6. The huge fire made bad fumes.

3 **Listen again and repeat.**

✓ Checkpoint

Read these words.

cute

use

united

Decodable
Reader 49

● Word Study

The /oo/ Sound

Phonemic Awareness

The /oo/ sound is different from the /yu/ sound. The /oo/ sound can be spelled different ways.

1 **Listen and repeat.**

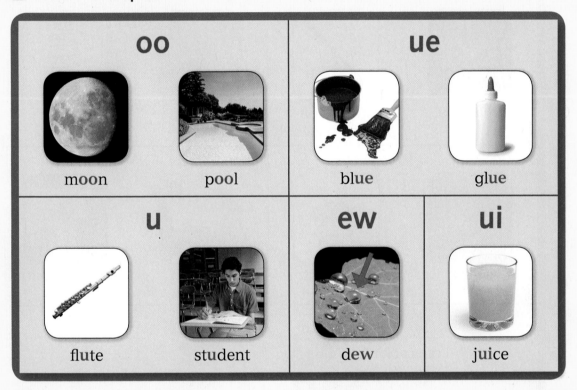

oo — moon — pool

ue — blue — glue

u — flute — student

ew — dew

ui — juice

2 **Listen again and repeat.**

Decoding

3 **Listen. Circle the word with the /oo/ sound in it.**

1. moon / mule
2. cute / dude
3. puny / pool
4. student / human

4 **Listen again. Repeat all the words. Make the /yu/ sounds different from the /oo/ sounds.**

✓**Checkpoint**

Read these words.

grew

room

blue

Decodable
Reader 51

Workbook
page 258

Independent Practice
CD-ROM

Unit 7 • Chapter 1 **427**

● Word Study

Words with Multiple Meanings

Many words in English are spelled and pronounced the same but have more than one meaning. Look at the words below. Do you know both meanings?

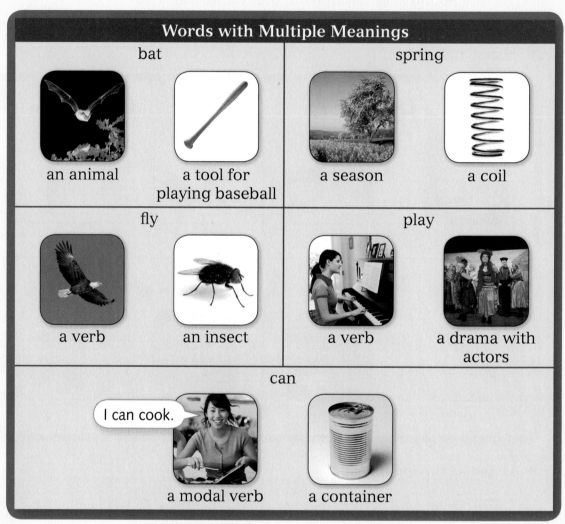

Words with Multiple Meanings

bat
an animal | a tool for playing baseball

spring
a season | a coil

fly
a verb | an insect

play
a verb | a drama with actors

can
I can cook. — a modal verb | a container

Read each sentence. Decide which answer has the same meaning as the <u>underlined word</u>.

1. Mary <u>can</u> sing well.
   a. modal verb **b.** a container

2. We saw a <u>play</u> on Thursday.
   a. a verb **b.** a drama

3. The <u>fly</u> sat on the window.
   a. a verb **b.** an insect

4. It's a lovely <u>spring</u> day.
   a. a season **b.** a coil

Workbook
page 259

Independent Practice
CD-ROM

● Writing Assignment

Personal Narrative

> **Writing Prompt**
>
> Write a personal narrative about what you will do this weekend.

1. Read the student model.

_____
Student Model

Felicidade Coimbra

My Weekend Plans

This weekend I will see my friends on Friday. I will go to the library on Saturday. I will shop on Sunday.

On Friday night, I will see my best friend Shannon. We will try on each other's clothes. We share clothing. We are the same size. On Saturday afternoon I'll go to the library. I will look for a book I need for class.

On Sunday, I will read my book. In the afternoon I'll go shopping with my mother. I won't buy a lot of things but I will buy a new pair of sneakers for gym class.

It will be a fun weekend. I won't be bored because I have so much to do! I will see my friends. I will go to the library and I will go to the mall. And of course, I will do my homework and start my book report!

2. List what you will do this weekend.

3. Write your essay.

4. Revise. Reread your essay. Use the editing and proofreading symbols on page 493 to help you mark the changes you need to make.

5. Edit. Use the **Writing Checklist** to help you find problems and errors.

Writing Checklist

1. I have only one main idea in each paragraph.

2. I have an introduction, body paragraph, and conclusion.

3. I used **will** to talk about the future.

Workbook
page 260

Objectives

Reading Strategy
Recognize fact and opinion

Text Genre
Persuasive text

Listening and Speaking
Change the point of view

Literary Element
Key words

Writing Conventions
Capitalizing and punctuating titles

Writing
Letter to the editor

Academic Vocabulary

fact	opinion
persuade	

Academic Content

news
health

● About the Reading

You are going to read a newspaper article called "Get Healthy!" The writer wants children and teens to be more active and eat better foods.

● Use Prior Knowledge

Talk About the News

News is important new events and ideas. It is called the **news** because new things happen every day.

1. What information do you find in a newspaper? Copy and complete the chart.

print or online newspaper

sports

2. Do you read a newspaper? Where are some other places people get news? Make a list.

3. 🔲 PAIR WORK Tell a partner. How do you or your family get the news?

● Vocabulary From the Reading
Learn, Practice, and Use Independently

Key Vocabulary

expert

fitness

healthy

physical

weight

Learn Vocabulary Look at the pictures. Read the sentences. Look at the **highlighted** words. What do these words mean?

1. These **experts** have studied thousands of children and teens.

2. Make **fitness** fun.

3. Exercise keeps adults **healthy**, too!

4. People who get plenty of **physical** activity sleep better at night.

5. Doctors say that people who stay at a healthy **weight** have fewer health problems.

Antonyms
What prefix could be added to "healthy" to mean "not healthy"?

Practice Vocabulary Complete the sentences with Key Vocabulary words.

1. My doctor said I was ____ .
2. My dad writes down my height and ____ every year.
3. My mom exercises at the ____ center.
4. Rory and Joe are ____ in rock climbing.
5. Doing lots of ____ activity keeps your body in shape.

Use Vocabulary Independently **PAIR WORK** Give a definition of a Key Vocabulary word. Your partner says what word you are defining.

✓Checkpoint

1. What is the best way to stay **healthy**?
2. Are you an **expert** at anything? What is it?

Vocabulary Log

Workbook page 261

Independent Practice CD-ROM

Academic Vocabulary

Vocabulary for the Reading Strategy

Word	Explanation	Sample Sentence	Visual Cue
fact *noun*	something that is true	It is a **fact** that it rained 30 inches here last month.	Big Book of Facts
opinion *noun*	a belief or idea	In my **opinion**, my team is the best baseball team.	

Draw a picture or write a sentence for each word.

Reading Strategy

Recognize Fact and Opinion

> Remember, the author's purpose in writing might be to inform, entertain, or persuade.

As you read, look for **facts** or **opinions**. **Facts** are true for everyone. **Opinions** can be different from person to person.

Writers use **facts** to **persuade**—to get you to agree with their **opinion**. Remember, it is still the writer's **opinion**. Don't forget to form your own **opinion** as you read!

Text Genre

Persuasive Text

You will read an **editorial**. An editorial is a persuasive news article.

Persuasive Text	
author's opinion	what the author believes or thinks is the right thing to do
facts	data or information to support the author's **opinion**
instructions	tell the audience what to do based on the **facts** given

✓**Checkpoint**

1. Does everyone have the same **opinion**?
2. Why does **persuasive** text have **facts**?

Vocabulary Log

Workbook pages 262, 263

Independent Practice CD-ROM

Reading

Reading Focus Questions

As you read, think about these questions.

1. What is the writer's **opinion** about exercise?

2. What is the writer trying to persuade the audience to do?

The Daily News

Get Healthy!

1   Teenagers, the *Daily News* has some bad news for you. You're probably not eating right or getting enough exercise.

2   This bad news comes from doctors and scientists. These **experts** studied thousands of children and teens. All of their reports seem to say the same thing. Kids and teenagers today need to eat better and be more **physically** active.

Reading Strategy

Recognize fact and opinion What is the writer's **opinion** about teens today?

✔ Reading Check

1. **Find the main idea** What do reports say about kids and exercise?

2. **Note details** How many children and teens have these **experts** studied?

3. **Express personal opinions** Do you agree with these **experts**? Are kids and teens today not **healthy**?

Reading Strategy

Recognize fact and opinion Find a fact in this paragraph. Find an opinion.

3   The American Academy of Pediatrics is the largest group of children's doctors. These **experts** on children's **health** wrote a report called *Active Healthy Living*. It says children and teens need 60 minutes of **physical** activity every day to stay **healthy**. But their research shows kids and teens exercise far less than 20 minutes a day.

4   Only 3 percent of the kids were active for an hour a day. Three percent is 3 out of every 100 kids. That means that the other 97 kids need more exercise.

5   Teens are gaining **weight**. Today most teenagers are at least one size larger than teens were 20 years ago. Even clothing sizes have changed. Did you know that a small today used to be a medium in the 1980s?

6   Why is this bad news? It's bad because too little exercise means you are missing a lot of good things in life. Exercise helps in two main ways.

7   First, exercise helps your body. **Physical** activity can make your body strong. It can also keep you at a **healthy weight**. Doctors say that people who stay at a **healthy weight** have fewer **health** problems.

8   Next, exercise can help your mind. People who get plenty of **physical** activity might worry less and sleep better at night. You may even learn better in school. Students who are **healthy** can listen and understand better in class.

9   The news is not all bad, however. We have some good news, too. You can change your life and be more active at any point. It's never too late. An article called "How to Limit Tube Time and Get Moving" gives these ideas:

10   • **Step away from the screen.** Doctors call watching TV or playing video games screen time. You should have no more than two hours of screen time a day. You will enjoy life more if you live it instead of watching it!

Reading Strategy

Recognize fact and opinion Find one **fact** and two **opinions** in this paragraph.

11   • **Start slowly.** An hour a day can seem like a long time. Start with 10 minutes of new activities every day. Add more as you get stronger. Think about walking. Take the stairs instead of the escalator. You will feel **healthier**.

12   • **Make fitness fun.** Find a sport you like. It doesn't need to be the traditional sports of basketball, soccer, or baseball. Those are all great sports and if you like them, play them. However, you can also try hiking, skateboarding, or even rope jumping. If you enjoy the sport, you will do it.

13   • **Choose food carefully.** Help your family shop for **healthy** food. Read the labels. Look for **healthy** foods. Eat lots of fruits and vegetables. Stop buying soft drinks and junk foods. You will feel better if you eat right.

Reading Check

1. **Recall facts** How long do most teens exercise every day?

2. **Draw conclusions** Why does the writer say that 97 percent of kids need more exercise?

3. **Make predictions** What will happen when kids who do not exercise grow up?

14   • **Exercise with others.** Find a friend or family member to exercise or play with you. You will have more fun and it helps keep you responsible for going.

● Reading Comprehension Questions

Think and Discuss

1. **Recall** facts What happens to people who stay at a **healthy weight**?

2. **Identify audience** Who does the writer believe are main readers of "Get **Healthy**!"? How do you know?

3. **Evaluate the author** Does this writer think that exercise **experts** are right about kids and exercise? How can you tell?

4. **Make judgments** How would this article be different if it was written for parents instead of teens?

5. **Revisit the Reading Focus Questions** Go back to page 433 and discuss the questions.

● Listening and Speaking

Change the Point of View

A **character** is a part of a story. A **narrator** is not in the story. A newspaper article is usually told by a narrator, or a writer outside of the situation.

1. **PAIR WORK** Who tells the news story "Get **Healthy**!"? Are they characters or a narrator? How can you tell?

2. Retell the story from the point of view of a character. Retell the facts by a person in the situation.

   a. Decide if your character will be an **expert**, parent, or teenager.

   b. Decide how the point of view will change.

3. **GROUP WORK** Retell the story to some classmates. Talk about your experience as your character. Do not say who you are. Your classmates will guess if you are an **expert**, parent, or teenager.

4. As you listen to your classmates, decide if each classmate is trying to persuade or inform you.

5. As you listen to your classmates, decide what is each speaker's opinion and what are the facts. Do you agree with the speaker's opinion?

Phrases for Conversation

Giving an Opinion

I think that (children should exercise more).

I believe that (my teenagers get enough exercise).

I can see that (I spend too much time in front of the television).

Workbook
page 264

Independent Practice
CD-ROM

Literary Element
Key Words

Key words are the important words. They tell you the main ideas of the text. Key words are often used at the beginning of a text. The writer may explain what a key word means. Words that are repeated are usually key words. Read the following from "Get **Healthy**!"

Key Word: **Health**

> The American Academy of Pediatrics is the largest group of children's doctors. These experts on children's **health** wrote a report called *Active **Healthy** Living*. It says children and teens need 60 minutes of physical activity every day to stay **healthy**. But their research shows kids and teens exercise far less than 20 minutes a day.

Writing Conventions

Capitalization and Punctuation *Titles*

The **title** is the name of something. Follow these rules for writing the title of an article, book, magazine, or newspaper.

1. For all titles: **Capitalize** the first word and all the important words.

2. For the title of an article: Put **quotation marks** around the title.

3. For the title of a book, magazine, or newspaper:

- If you are handwriting, **underline** the title.
- If you use a computer, put the title in **italics**.

Title of an Article	Title of a Book, Magazine, or Newspaper
"Get Healthy!" ↑ ↑ Capitalize	The Daily News *The Daily News* ↖ ↑ ↗ Capitalize

Apply

1. Look in paragraph 3 of "Get **Healthy**!" Find a title.

2. Is the title in paragraph 3 an article? How can you tell?

✓ Checkpoint
What are the most important words in a text called?

● Writing Assignment

Letter to the Editor

> **Writing Prompt**
>
> Write a letter to the editor of *The Daily News*. The editor is the person who wrote "Get **Healthy**!" Tell the editor your **opinion** about kids and exercise.

1. Read the student model.

Student Model

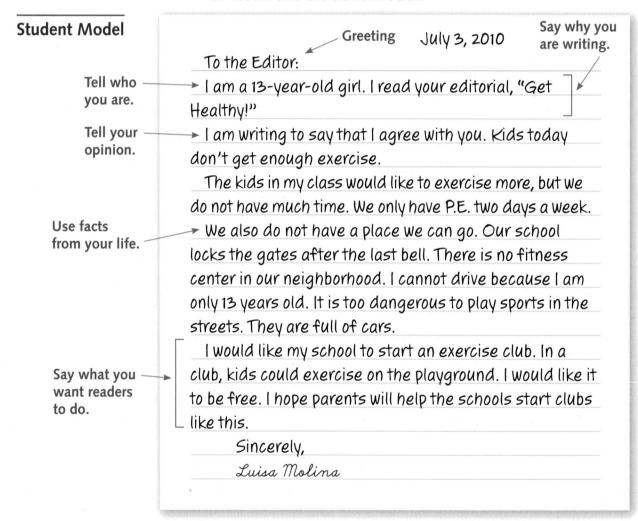

Greeting

July 3, 2010

Say why you are writing.

To the Editor:

Tell who you are. → I am a 13-year-old girl. I read your editorial, "Get Healthy!"

Tell your opinion. → I am writing to say that I agree with you. Kids today don't get enough exercise.

The kids in my class would like to exercise more, but we do not have much time. We only have P.E. two days a week.

Use facts from your life. → We also do not have a place we can go. Our school locks the gates after the last bell. There is no fitness center in our neighborhood. I cannot drive because I am only 13 years old. It is too dangerous to play sports in the streets. They are full of cars.

Say what you want readers to do. → I would like my school to start an exercise club. In a club, kids could exercise on the playground. I would like it to be free. I hope parents will help the schools start clubs like this.

Sincerely,
Luisa Molina

2. **Plan your letter.**
   - Reread "Get **Healthy**!"
   - What is your **opinion** about exercise and kids?
   - What do you want readers to do and think?
   - Think of **facts** about exercise in your life.

3. **Write your letter.**
   - Start with a greeting.
   - Tell who you are.
   - Say why you are writing.
   - Explain your **opinion**.
   - Use **facts** to support your **opinion**.
   - Say what you want people to think or do.
   - Sign your name.

4. **Revise.** Reread your letter. Add, delete, or rearrange words or sentences to make your paragraph clearer. Use the editing and proofreading symbols on page 493 to help you mark the changes you need to make.

5. **Edit.** Use the **Writing Checklist** to help you find problems and errors.

Writing Checklist
1. My letter includes a greeting with a colon.
2. I say who I am and why I am writing.
3. I tell my **opinion** and use **facts** to support it.
4. I tell what I want people to think or do.
5. I used punctuation and capitalization for titles.
6. I signed my letter.
7. I wrote the date.

Progress Check

How well did you understand this chapter? Try to answer the questions. If necessary, go back to the pages listed for a review.

Skills	Skills Assessment Questions	Pages to Review
Vocabulary	What shopping questions and statements can you say?	420–424
Grammar	How do you form the **future tense**?	424–425
Writing Conventions	**Spelling:** What letter usually follows *q*?	425
	Punctuation and Capitalization: What punctuation do you use with titles of articles? Which words of a title do you capitalize?	437
Word Study	What are multiple meaning words? Give an example.	428
Vocabulary From the Reading	What do these words mean? • **expert**, **fitness**, **healthy**, **physical**, **weight**	431
Academic Vocabulary	What is a **fact**? What is an **opinion**?	432
Reading Strategy	How do you know if a writer is giving **facts** or **opinions**?	432
Text Genre	What is the text genre of "Get **Healthy**!"?	432
Reading Comprehension	What is the main **opinion** of "Get **Healthy**!"?	433–436
Listening and Speaking	**Phrases for Conversation:** What phrases can you use to give your **opinion**?	436
Literary Element	What are key words?	437

Assessment Practice

Read this article. Then answer Questions 1 through 4.

The Dangers of Diets

1   When people worry about their weight, they may decide to go on a diet. Experts warn that diets can be harmful. Skipping meals is a bad way to lose weight. Your body needs the good things in foods. Diet pills are another bad idea. Diet pills can harm your body.

2   What can you do to stay at a healthy weight? First, eat healthy foods, not junk food. Then, add more physical activity to your day. You will feel good about yourself.

1 Read this sentence from paragraph 1.

> Experts warn that diets can be harmful.

What does <u>experts</u> mean?

A people who have a lot of money

B people who know a lot

C people who love food

D people who enjoy playing sports

2 Which sentence contains a fact?

A What can you do to stay at a healthy weight?

B Then add more physical activity to your day.

C Your body needs the good things in foods.

D First, eat healthy foods, not junk food.

3 According to paragraph 1, why is taking diet pills a bad idea?

A They can harm your body.

B Your body needs the things in foods.

C They cost a lot of money.

D They help you stay at a healthy weight.

4 Where might you find this text?

A in a story

B in a play

C in a letter

D in a newspaper

Writing on Demand: Personal Narrative

Write a personal narrative that tells what you will do on your birthday. **(20 minutes)**

> **Writing Tip**
> Make a list of things you will do on your birthday. Use your list to write.

Objectives

Vocabulary
Money
Prices

Listening and Speaking
Talking about buying things
Using shopping questions
and statements

Grammar
Future with going to

Writing Conventions
Spelling common
homophones

Word Study
The /aw/ sound

Writing
Descriptive paragraph

Vocabulary
Money

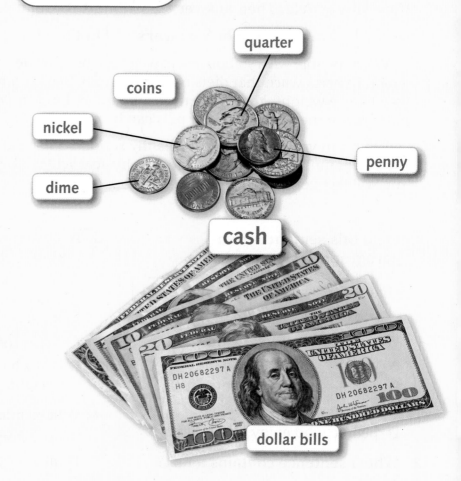

quarter

coins

nickel

penny

dime

cash

dollar bills

credit card

giftcard

gift card

ATM/debit card

● Vocabulary

Prices

1 Listen and repeat the words on page 442.

2 **PAIR WORK** Draw some coins and bills. Your partner says how much money is shown.

3 Read and listen.

| The **price tag** gives the **regular price**. |

| The sweaters are on **sale**. They are **half-off**. That's a **bargain**. |

| The **coupon** says I get $10 off. The **sale price** will be $10 less. |

| You get **change** back when you pay cash. |

| The store gives you a **receipt** when you buy something. |

| The price is high. The pants are **too expensive**. |

4 Listen and repeat.

5 Copy and complete the sentences. Check your spelling.

1. You saved $25.00. The jeans you want are $60.00. The jeans are too ▢▢▢▢▢▢▢▢▢▢ .

2. A cashier gives you a r▢▢▢▢▢▢ with your ch▢▢▢e.

3. She has a ▢▢▢p▢▢ for $5.00 off. It's such a b▢▢▢▢▢▢ .

✓**Checkpoint**

1. The price of a shirt is $27.99. You give the clerk $30.00 in cash. Will you get change back?

2. What does the price tag give you?

● Listening and Speaking

Talking About Buying Things

We read $3.75 as "three dollars and seventy-five cents" or "three seventy-five."

1 Read the prices aloud.

1. $76.50
2. $11.99
3. $36.50
4. $2.19
5. $19.49

2 Read and listen.

Rose: Do you have any **coins**?

Anna: I have **three quarters, a dime, two nickels, and four pennies.** How much is that?

Rose: That's **99 cents.**

3 Listen again. Repeat.

4 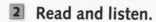 **PAIR WORK** Say the conversation again. Use new words for the blue words. You can use vocabulary from pages 442 and 443.

5 Listen. Copy the chart. Write the price for each item.

sandwich	fruit salad	carton of milk	muffin

6 **PAIR WORK** Listen again. Answer the questions.

1. How much money does the lunch cost?
2. How much money does Amaya have?

● Listening and Speaking
Using Shopping Questions and Statements

1 Read and listen.

Julia:	Excuse me, there is no price tag on **this shirt**. How much does it cost?
Salesclerk:	The price is $15.
Julia:	Is it **on sale**?
Salesclerk:	Yes, $15 is the **sale price**. The **regular price** is $30. It's **half off**.
Julia:	It's a bargain! I'll take it.
Salesclerk:	How will you pay?
Julia:	Can I pay with **a gift card**?
Salesclerk:	Certainly.
Julia:	Good. Here it is.
Salesclerk:	Thank you. Here's your **receipt**.

2 Listen and repeat.

3 🔲 PAIR WORK Say the conversation again. Use new words for the blue words. You can use vocabulary from pages 442 and 443.

4 🔲 PAIR WORK Role-play your own conversation. One person is a customer. The other is a salesclerk or cashier.

✓Checkpoint

1. How do you say this price: $14.99?

2. Name two different ways to pay for something.

● Grammar
Future with going to

Remember: to talk about the future you can use **will** + verb. Another way to talk about the future is to use **be** + **going to** + verb.

Tran **will pay** with cash.	→	Tran **is going to pay** with cash.
Olga **will buy** a sweater.	→	Olga **is going to buy** a sweater.
Martin **will use** a coupon.	→	Martin i**s going to use** a coupon.

Remember, the verb **be** changes with the subject.

I am going to buy a book.	**We are** going to buy a book.
You are going to buy a book.	**You are** going to buy a book.
He / She / It is going to buy a book.	**They are** going to buy a book.

Complete sentences with the correct form of be + going to. Use the verb in parentheses ( ).

Example: Peter will shop for shoes tonight.
He _is going to go_ to the mall. (go)

1. Nancy will help her father tonight. They ____ the stove. (fix)

2. Jin Hock will go to the movies. He ____ *Dragonfly*. (see)

3. I will visit my aunt. I ____ dinner at her house. (eat)

4. My parents and I will go shopping tonight. We ____ clothes. (buy)

Workbook
page 269

Independent Practice
CD-ROM

PAIR WORK **Ask your classmates what they are going to do tonight. Make a list.**

I'm going to do my math homework.

Julianna is going to do her math homework. I'm going to eat dinner.

✒ **Writing Conventions**

Spelling *Common Homophones*

Homophones are words that sound the same when you say them, but are spelled differently and mean different things. Look at the words below.

Good-bye!

by
close to or near

buy
to purchase

bye
part of good-bye

sale
lowered price

sail
a part of a boat that catches wind

Apply Copy and complete the sentences with a homophone.

1. I need to ____ some pencils. (by / buy / bye)

2. The pencils are ____ the pens and paper. (by / buy / bye)

3. I'm glad the sweaters are on ____ . (sale / sail)

4. The ____ opened in the wind. (sale / sail)

5. ____ ! See you tomorrow. (By / Buy / Bye)

✓**Checkpoint**

Look at the sentences. Change each one to a form of **be** + **going to** + verb.

1. Susana will buy a dress on sale.

2. Nguyen and Kim will use coupons.

3. I will keep my receipt.

Word Study
The /aw/ Sound

Phonemic Awareness

1 Listen and repeat.

> There are many ways to write the /aw/ sound!
>
> For example, **ought** in bought and thought and **aught** in taught also have the /aw/ sound in them.

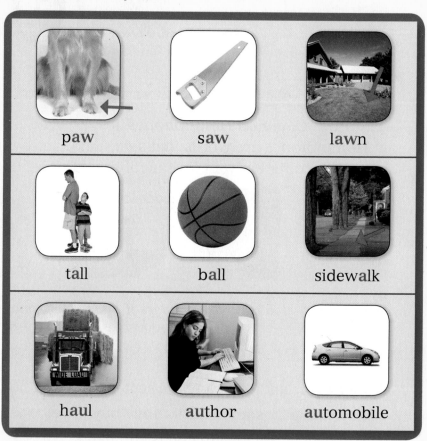

paw   saw   lawn

tall   ball   sidewalk

haul   author   automobile

Decoding

2 Listen. Choose the word you hear.

1. mall   mail   5. caw   cow
2. raw   ray   6. jay   jaw
3. brawny   brainy   7. vault   vat
4. can   call   8. cat   caught

3 Listen again and repeat.

✓ Checkpoint

Read these words.

- thaw
- talk
- brought
- wall
- auto

Decodable Reader 56

Workbook page 272

Independent Practice CD-ROM

● Writing Assignment
Descriptive Paragraph

> **Writing Prompt**
>
> List five classmates. What do you think they are going to do when they go shopping? Be specific. Write your best guess for each one. Use the future tense with **will** or **going to**.

1. Read the student model.

> Bojan Belic
>
> ### My Classmates
> I have many interesting classmates. Because I know them, these are my guesses of what they will buy. Susana likes animals and she has many pictures of animals in her locker. I think that she is going to buy a dog. However, Antoine is always talking about movies. He knows all the actors' names, so I think that he will buy a DVD.

2. Think of a classmate. Write a sentence that describes that person. Then write a sentence that tells what you think he or she will buy. Write about five classmates.

3. Share your paragraph with the class.

Writing Checklist
1. I used **will** + verb correctly.
2. I used **going to** + verb correctly.
3. I used **I think** to start the sentences that have my guesses.

Objectives

Reading Strategy
Make and confirm predictions

Text Genre
Informational text: Web article

Listening and Speaking
Make a radio advertisement

Text Elements
Headings and signpost words

Reading Fluency
Paired reading

Writing
Persuasive e-mail

Academic Vocabulary

confirm | prediction

Academic Content

math for money

● About the Reading

You are going to read a Web article. It gives information about math used for money. The article lets you practice money skills.

● Use Prior Knowledge

Talk About How You Use Money

1. How do people get money? What things do people use money to buy?

2. Write things you want to buy in a chart. Then write how much you think you would pay for these things.

What I Want to Buy	How Much I Would Pay

3. **GROUP WORK** Share your chart with the class. Talk with classmates about how you earn money. Do you work at jobs, such as babysitting or delivering newspapers? Do your parents give you cash?

Vocabulary From the Reading
Learn, Practice, and Use Independently

Learn Vocabulary Read the sentences. Use the context to find the meaning of the **highlighted** words.

1. Nora is making a **budget** to plan her money so she knows how much she can spend.
2. I will wait until the store offers a lower-price **discount** on sweaters to buy one. The lower price will save me money.
3. Jason needs enough money every day to pay his **expenses**: lunch money and bus fare.
4. The number of eighth graders absent today was 20 out of 100, or 20 **percent**.
5. The cell phone's **value** is $90.

Multiple-meaning Words

Budget and **discount** are nouns here. Use a dictionary to find the definition for the verb form of these two words.

Practice Vocabulary Complete the sentences with Key Vocabulary words.

1. Nila put $100 in her ____ for clothing.
2. Neena's ____ at the movies are tickets and popcorn.
3. The ____ on the price of the jeans was 50 ____ . They were half off.
4. The new book is worth $25. Its ____ is $10 if it's used.

Use Vocabulary Independently PAIR WORK Work with a partner. Write a sentence for each Key Vocabulary word. Read your sentences to another pair.

✓Checkpoint

Complete these sentences with a Key Vocabulary word.

1. What ____ of students in your class have brown hair?
2. I need to plan a ____ so I know how much I can spend on school supplies.
3. Stores that always offer a ____ have low prices.

Vocabulary Log   Workbook page 274   Independent Practice CD-ROM   Unit 7 • Chapter 2   **451**

Academic Vocabulary

Vocabulary for the Reading Strategy

Word	Explanation	Sample Sentence	Visual Cue
confirm *verb*	prove that something is true	Researchers studied teen shoppers to **confirm** that those who learned money math were smarter shoppers.	
prediction *noun*	a guess about what will happen in the future	Many educators have made the **prediction** that teens who learn money math will become smarter shoppers.	

Draw a picture or write a sentence for each word.

Reading Strategy

Make and Confirm Predictions

A **prediction** is something you guess will happen. Look at photos, charts, graphs, titles, and headings to make **predictions** about the reading.

If you find your guess is correct, you **confirm** the **prediction**. As you read, make **predictions** about what comes next. Continue reading and **confirm** if your **predictions** are correct.

> You may change, or modify, your **prediction** as you continue to read and find new information.

Text Genre

Informational Text: Web Article

"Money Math for Kids" is an informational Web article. Look for these features in an informational text.

Informational Text	
headings	what each section is about
facts	true information
predictions	things the Web site tells you will happen if you follow instructions
instructions	statements that tell you what to do

✓ Checkpoint

1. What does an informational Web article give you?
2. What are predictions?

Vocabulary Log

Workbook pages 275, 276

Independent Practice CD-ROM

● Reading

Reading Focus Questions

As you read, think about these questions.

1. What kinds of money math do you need to know?
2. How does having a **budget** help you?

Money Math for Kids

http://www.moneymathforkids.com/

MONEY MATH for Kids

1   Many adults have a hard time dealing with money. Don't let that happen to you. Learn money math now!

2   If you play all the games at *Money Math for Kids*, you'll learn math skills many adults don't know. Here at *Money Math for Kids*, you will learn how to

- recognize U.S. coins and bills and write their **values**.

- give and get correct change.

- calculate **percentages** to find **discounts**.

- make yourself a **budget**.

- and much, much more!

Name That Coin!

3   Name the coins shown.

Write the **value** of each coin.

CLICK HERE TO
CHECK YOUR ANSWERS

**Reading
Strategy**

Make and **confirm
predictions** What
prediction is in
this paragraph?

✓
Reading Check

1. **Recall facts**
   What coins are
   in the photo?
2. **Think and
   search** How do
   you check your
   answers?
3. **Make inferences**
   Why do you
   need to know
   coin **values**?

Reading Strategy

Make and confirm predictions Read the heading. Make a prediction about what you will learn about. Then look at the text to confirm or modify your prediction.

Money Math for Kids

http://www.moneymathforkids.com/

It's All About Change

4   If you ever plan to use cash to buy or sell anything, you need to know how to give and get change. Answer the questions below to find out what you already know. When you check your answers, you can get more information if you need it.

5   You buy a snack and get these coins back. How much change did you get? Write the total **value** of the coins.

76¢

6   Which coin combination matches the price on this price tag? Can you find another combination that matches the price tag?

7   You buy something that costs $2.59 and give the salesclerk three $1 bills. How much change should you get back? The clerk gives you four coins in change. What coins did you get back?

CLICK HERE TO CHECK YOUR ANSWERS

◄ ► ↻ ✖ ♥ http://www.moneymathforkids.com/

What Is Percent?

8

- When you understand **percent**, you will be able to figure out the sale price of an item.

- **Percent** is a part, or portion, of one hundred.

- There are 100 squares in the grid. 20 squares are colored.

- 20 parts out of 100 parts are colored. We can write this as 20/100.

- When the second, or bottom, number in a fraction is 100, you can write the first number as a **percent**.

- The symbol for **percent** is %.

- So the **percent** of the grid that is colored is 20%.

What **percent** of a dollar is a dime? Hint: Change both to cents.

9
In a **survey** of 100 teens, 53 said they liked shopping at the local mall on weekends. What **percent** of teens like shopping at the mall?

10
If 17 **percent** of teens say they never wear jeans to school, what **percent** do wear jeans to school? Hint: How many total **percent** are there? Subtract the **percent** of teens who never wear jeans from the total **percent**.

CLICK HERE TO
CHECK YOUR ANSWERS

survey when people are asked questions and their answers are recorded

▲

▼

> ## Reading Strategy
>
> **Make and confirm predictions** What prediction do you see in this list? What do you need to do to make this prediction come true?

> ## ✓ Reading Check
>
> 1. **Recall facts** What is the symbol for **percent**?
> 2. **Think and search** Which is the larger number: 10% or 20%?
> 3. **Understand numbers** In a survey of 100 sixth-graders, 7 said they had never shopped at a mall. What **percent** of the students have never shopped at a mall?

Reading Strategy

Make and confirm predictions What prediction can you make about this section of the Web article? Read the section to confirm your prediction.

◄ ▶ ℃ ✕ ♥   http://www.moneymathforkids.com/

Which Discount Is Better?

11   A **discount** lowers the price of an item. The **discount** rate is usually expressed as a **percent**. The sale price is the price of the item after the **discount** is subtracted.

12   **Calculate a Discount**

Follow these steps to find the **discount** and the sale price:

① At first, use the equation *Regular Price x **Discount Rate** = **Discount***.

You can express the **discount** rate as a fraction. For example, if the **discount** rate is 10%, the **discount** rate would be 10/100. Multiply the regular price and the **discount** rate to find the **discount**.

② Then, use the equation *Regular Price – **Discount** = Sale Price*.

③ Finally, subtract the **discount** from the regular price. This is the sale price.

13   The regular price of a book is $15.00. The book is 10% off. How much money will you save by buying the book on sale?

How much do you save if the book is 20% off?

14   The regular price of the red sweater is $30.00. It is on sale for 10% off. How much will you pay for the red sweater?

15   The regular price of the blue sweater is $50.00. It is on sale for 50% off. How much will you pay for the blue sweater? Which sweater is a better buy? Why?

CLICK HERE TO CHECK YOUR ANSWERS

http://www.moneymathforkids.com/

What Is a Budget?

16 • A **budget** is a plan for what you do with money. If you don't have a **budget**, you will not use your money wisely.

• A **budget** should balance the money you have with the money you spend. If you **budget**, you will be able to buy the things you need.

• A **budget** has **expenses** that are things you need to buy. These are called fixed **expenses**. For example, school lunches and bus fares are fixed **expenses**. They are items you need.

• A **budget** also has **expenses**, such as clothing and entertainment, that you buy occasionally. These are flexible **expenses**. They are items you want but do not need. Know the difference between what you need and want.

• Fixed **expenses** are the most important. As a result, you should think about them first. Then you know how much money is left for flexible **expenses**.

A Sample Budget

17 When you plan a **budget**, make sure the items you buy cost less than the amount of money you have. In this **budget**, Elena has $50.00.

Things I Need	Things I Want	$ for Needs	$ for Wants
new shoes for gym class		$25.00	
poster board for project		$ 1.75	
	concert ticket		$15.00
school lunches		$20.00	
bus pass		$ 3.00	
	a new sweater		$18.00

18 What should Elena buy?

CLICK HERE TO CHECK YOUR ANSWERS

Reading Strategy

Make and confirm predictions What prediction does the Web article make about how a **budget** will help?

Reading Check

1. **Recall facts** What is a **budget**?

2. **Think and search** What are things you need to buy called?

3. **Make inferences** If you buy too many after-school snacks, you will not have enough money for a bus pass. Which should you buy? Why?

Reading Comprehension Questions

Think and Discuss

1. **Recall facts** What is the title of the Web article?

2. **Identify main ideas** What are the main ideas in the reading?

3. **Make inferences** Why do you think this Web article was written?

4. **Relating to prior knowledge** What information did you already know? What did you learn? Answer the questions in the text.

5. **Revisit the Reading Focus Questions** Go back to page 453 and discuss the questions.

Listening and Speaking

Make a Radio Advertisement

 PAIR WORK Make an advertisement for the radio.

1. Decide what you want your audience to do. Do you want them to buy something or do something?

2. Think about what makes a good ad on the radio. Do you like music or rhyming jingles?

3. Write your advertisement. Practice with your partner.

4. Present your advertisement to the class.

5. After you heard all of the advertisements, say what you liked about the advertisements. What did the other groups want you to do? Did they want you to buy something or do something else?

Phrases for Conversation

Persuasive Language

You should buy this because . . .
We are the best because . . .

Build Vocabulary

A **jingle** is a little song used in advertising.

Workbook
page 277

Independent Practice
CD-ROM

● Text Elements

Using Headings and Signpost Words to Make Predictions

Headings help you **predict** the content of the text. When you see a heading that says "Name That Coin!" you can make a **prediction** that the following text will be about identifying coins.

Signpost words also help you make **predictions**. Signpost words are words that tell you something different is coming or hint at what happens next. Some examples are **but**, **now**, **at first**, **for example**, **as a result**, and **on the other hand**.

---

12   **Calculate a Discount**

    Follow these steps to find the **discount** and the sale price:

signpost words

① **At first**, use the equation *Regular Price x **Discount** Rate = **Discount***.

② You can express the **discount** rate as a fraction. **For example**, if the **discount** rate is 10%, the **discount** rate would be 10/100. Multiply the regular price and the **discount** rate to find the **discount**.

---

1. Look at the heading before you read. Make a **prediction** about the text.

2. Look at the signpost words. Make **predictions** about what will come next.

● Reading Fluency

Paired Reading

PAIR WORK Work with a partner to improve your fluency.

1. You and a partner read paragraphs 1 and 2 of "Money Math for Kids" (on page 453) silently.

2. Your partner reads the paragraphs out loud three times.

3. During the third reading, take notes on your partner's errors. After the reading, give suggestions.

4. Now, you read aloud and your partner takes notes.

✓Checkpoint

1. Find a different heading in the informational Web site. How does it help you make a **prediction** about the text?

2. Look at "What Is a **Budget**?" on page 457. What are two signpost words you find there?

Workbook
page 278

Independent Practice
CD-ROM

● Writing Assignment

Persuasive E-mail

Writing Suggestion

Think about the math you need before you write.

Writing Prompt

Your class is planning a party. Your group is in charge of the decorations. You have a budget of $25.00 for decorations. Write an e-mail to your group members with suggestions.

---

1. Read the student model.

Student Model

Build Vocabulary

Decorations are things to make the room look good for a party.

From: Anya
Date: November 13, 2007 11:17 AM
To: Kate, Luis, Baxter
Subject: Decoration Budget

Dear Kate, Luis, and Baxter,

Our group is going to decorate the classroom. I think we should hang shiny ribbons in the doorway. Students will walk through them to come in. We should put big posters on the walls. We should hang streamers from the lights. On every desk, we can have a bag of treats.

We have $25.00 to spend. Here is the budget I suggest:

25 shiny ribbons (25 cents each x 25 = $6.25)	$ 6.25
15 sheets of poster paper (5 cents each x 15 = $.75)	$ .75
6 rolls of streamers ($1 each x 6 = $6.00)	$ 6.00
24 treat bags (25 cents each x 24 = $6.00)	$ 6.00
Treats	$ 6.00
Total Decoration Budget	$25.00

Our teacher has tape we can use to hang up the shiny ribbons, big posters, and streamers. We have markers in class that we can use to draw the pictures. If we use those supplies, we will save money. The party store is having a sale on streamers, too. They are half off. I wrote the sale price in the budget.

Please write back and tell me if you like this plan, or if you have some other ideas.

Anya

2. **Plan your budget.**

   - Think of the decorations you would like.

   - Figure out how much the decorations will cost. Make sure it is $25.00 or less.

   - Decide what to tell your group. List ways you can save money. Tell what items you already have that you can use.

   - Be sure to include a **prediction** about the decorations or the **budget**.

3. **Write your e-mail.** Tell your group members your plan, and include a chart of your **budget**.

4. **Revise.** Read your e-mail. Add, delete, or rearrange words and sentences to make your paragraphs clearer. Use the editing and proofreading symbols on page 493 to help you mark the changes you need to make.

5. **Edit.** Use the **Writing Checklist** to help you find problems and errors.

Writing Checklist
1. I capitalized the first word in each sentence.
2. I used periods, question marks, and exclamation points at the end of my sentences.
3. I used *will* or *going to* to talk about the future.
4. I made a **prediction**.

Progress Check

How well did you understand this chapter? Try to answer the questions. If necessary, go back to the pages listed for a review.

Skills	Skills Assessment Questions	Pages to Review
Vocabulary	What ways can you pay for something you buy? What does it mean when something is on sale?	**442–445**
Grammar	How do you use **going to** to talk about the future? Write two sentences that use this form.	**446–447**
Writing Conventions	**Spelling:** What are homophones? Give an example.	**447**
Vocabulary From the Reading	What do these words mean? • **budget, discount, expenses, percent, value**	**451**
Academic Vocabulary	What is a **prediction**? How do you **confirm** a **prediction**?	**452**
Reading Strategy	What parts of a reading can you use to make and **confirm predictions**?	**452**
Text Genre	What is the text genre of "Money Math for Kids"?	**452**
Reading Comprehension	What is "Money Math for Kids" about?	**453–458**
Listening and Speaking	What are some questions you can ask about **discounts**?	**458**
Text Elements	How do **headings** and **signpost words** help you make **predictions**?	**459**
Reading Fluency	How does paired reading help your reading rate?	**459**

Assessment Practice

Read this Web article. Then answer Questions 1 through 4.

Start Saving!

1   It is never a bad time to start saving money. Do you have a job? Do you babysit, deliver newspapers, or mow lawns? If so, you can start saving. Make a budget. Your budget will help you decide how much you will save each month.

2   You can keep your money in a bank. Are you going to open a savings account? Then look for one that pays you interest. Interest is a percent of the money you have in the account. For example, your bank might pay 1% interest. If you have $500 in the account, the bank will pay you $5.00.

---

1 **Read this sentence from paragraph 1.**

> Your budget will help you decide how much you will save each month.

What does <u>budget</u> mean?

A   a plan for using money

B   a way to make more money

C   a list of things you want to buy

D   a savings account

2 **What signpost words are in paragraph 2?**

A   look for   C   at first

B   going to   D   for example

3 **Which prediction can you make based on the title of this article?**

A   The article will be about food.

B   The article will be about interest.

C   The article will be about saving money.

D   The article will be about banks.

4 **This passage teaches readers**

A   how to make a budget.

B   how to save money.

C   how to calculate interest.

D   how to find a job.

 ## Writing on Demand: Descriptive Paragraph

Think about a person in your family. Write a paragraph telling what you think he or she is going to do this weekend. Include details. **(20 minutes)**

> **Writing Tip**
> Start your paragraph with "I think." Use the words *going to* and *will* in your paragraph.

Objectives

Listening and Speaking
Give a descriptive presentation

Media
Examine and compare sales advertisements

Writing
Formal letter

Person	Gift	Amount	Reason
my sister	earrings	$75.00	She likes jewelry.
1.			
2.			
3.			
4.			
5.			

● Listening and Speaking Workshop

Give a Descriptive Presentation

> **Topic**
>
> Imagine you have $500 to buy things for other people. Make a presentation that describes what gifts you are going to buy.

1. **Brainstorm**

   Make a list of who you want to buy things for. Then write your gift ideas.

   Compare your answers with your classmates. Did you choose any of the same people and gifts?

2. **Plan**

   - Think of an introduction. Explain you won $500, and you are going to use it to buy gifts for five people.

   - Organize your presentation by person. Fill out the chart. For each person, say what gift you are going to buy, how much you will spend, and why you are choosing that gift.

   - Think of a conclusion. Tell how planning what gifts to buy for different people made you feel.

3. **Prepare**

   Copy your chart onto poster board. Use the poster when you present. Practice your presentation. Point to the information in the chart.

4. **Present**

   Make your presentation to the class. Speak clearly and look directly at your classmates. Use your poster to present.

5. **Evaluate**

   Ask your classmates for feedback. Use the **Speaking Self-Evaluation** to evaluate your presentation. Use the **Active Listening Evaluation** to evaluate your classmates' presentations.

Speaking Self-Evaluation	Active Listening Evaluation
1. I practiced my presentation and was prepared. I was relaxed.	1. You described the people you are going to buy for and the gifts you will buy.
2. I described what I am going to buy for each person, why, and how much it will cost.	2. You talked about five different people.
3. I showed my poster.	3. You used a poster.
4. I spoke clearly and slowly.	4. You spoke clearly and slowly.
5. I looked at my classmates when I spoke.	5. You looked at your audience.
	6. You could improve your presentation by ____.

⬤ Media Workshop

Examine and Compare Sales Advertisements

Advertisements try to persuade you to buy something. Advertisements in magazines and newspapers are called **print** advertisements. Advertisements on radio and television are called **nonprint** advertisements. Advertisements contain some facts, but they also contain opinions. It is important to evaluate an advertisement and see what is fact and what is opinion.

1. Find an interesting advertisement in a newspaper or magazine. Write down two facts from the advertisement. Write down two opinions.

2. Watch television or listen to the radio until you hear an advertisement for a similar product. Write down two facts you hear. Then write down two opinions.

3. Compare and contrast the two advertisements.
   - How do the facts help persuade you to buy something? Do the two advertisements have similar facts?
   - How do the opinions help persuade you to buy something? Do the two advertisements have similar opinions?

4. Share your comparison with the class.

Apply & Extend

Writing Suggestion

Write legibly. Use cursive or joined italic. Make sure your letter has margins and that you have spaces between letters in a word and words in a sentence.

Facts	Opinions
Many students need library books to do homework.	The library is a nice, quiet place to study.

Examples	Predictions
I use the library every week.	Students won't be able to do some homework assignments.

● Writing Workshop

Write a Formal Letter

Write a **formal letter** to someone you do not know well. Use polite language. Address the person by his or her title and family name.

> **Writing Prompt**
>
> To save money, your principal wants to close the school library. Write a letter. Give your principal reasons to keep it open. Persuade the principal. Predict what will happen if the library closes.

PREWRITE

1. Read the writing prompt and student model carefully.
2. Ask questions. Take notes.
   a. What is your opinion? Show why it is important to keep the library open.
   b. How do students use the library? Give examples.
   c. What will happen if the library closes?
3. Write your ideas in a chart.

WRITE A DRAFT

1. Write a draft of your letter. Include the date.
2. Explain the problem and make a request.
3. Give facts, opinions, examples, and predictions to persuade the principal to keep the library open.
4. End with a **closing** and your **signature**.

Student Model

Introduction: tells the problem and makes a request

Body: includes facts, opinions, and predictions

Date

April 18, 2010

Dear Ms. Buendía: ← Greeting

    I heard that the school library will soon be closed. I am writing to ask you to please keep it open!

    Many students use the library at school. It is a quiet place to study. The library is a good place to find answers to questions. And it doesn't cost any money! Some students do not have the money to buy books.

I think that many students need a place to study. There will be nowhere for them to find answers. They will not be able to find books to read. They will have to spend money to buy books.

Please keep the library open. I know many students are going to be sad if it is closed. Thank you for your help!

Sincerely, — **Closing**

Iran Nguyen ← **Signature**

REVISE

1. Read your draft.
2. Ask your partner to use the **Peer Review Checklist** to review your work. Use the editing and proofreading symbols on page 493.
3. Revise your draft. Add, delete, or change sentences.

EDIT

1. Use the **Revising and Editing Checklist.**
2. Fix errors in grammar, punctuation, and spelling.

Peer Review Checklist

1. The letter describes a problem and makes a request in the **introduction**.
2. The **body** of the letter gives facts and opinions to persuade the reader. It predicts what will happen if the problem is not solved.
3. You could improve your writing by _____.

Revising and Editing Checklist

1. I identify the problem and a solution.
2. My letter includes facts and opinions to persuade the reader.
3. I included a date, a greeting, a closing, and a signature.
4. I used *going to* and *will* to talk about the future.

PUBLISH

1. Write your formal letter again. Write neatly.
2. Display your letter in class.

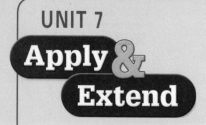

Apply & Extend

● **PROJECTS**

Choose one or more of the following projects to explore the theme of Shopping and Money.

PROJECT 1
Create a Plan for a Lemonade Stand

1. You want $20.00 to buy something. You will sell lemonade. Figure out how much the lemonade will cost and how many cups you need to sell to earn $20.00.

2. Copy and fill in the chart to figure your costs.

	20 cups	50 cups	100 cups
Cost of ingredients: lemons, sugar, water, paper cups			

3. You can sell one cup of lemonade for 50 cents. Figure out how much money you will earn. Then subtract the costs above to find your profit.

4. Write a plan that describes how many cups of lemonade you need to sell in order to earn $20.00.

PROJECT 2
Create an Advertisement for a Shopping Mall

1. Imagine the perfect shopping mall. Who will shop there? What kinds of stores will it have?

2. Work with a partner to brainstorm ideas to make your mall interesting. Make a list of facts about the mall. Write your opinions about these facts.

3. Decide what kind of ad you want to create. It can be a print, radio, or television ad. Work together to write your advertisement. Predict why shoppers will like your mall.

4. Act out your television ad or display your print ad for the class.

PROJECT 3
Use the Internet to Learn About Money in Different Countries

1. Work in a group of three people. Think of three different countries you want to visit. Use a map.

2. Each person in the group will choose one country. A country's money is called its **currency**. In the United States, *dollars* are the currency. Use the Internet to find information about currency in the country you chose.

Country	Name of the currency that is used there	100 U.S. dollars = how much of that currency?
Mexico	peso	1,070 pesos

3. Write a description of a trip to the country. What will you do there? How much currency will you need to bring?

4. Share your description with the class.

● Independent Reading

Explore the theme of Shopping and Money by reading one or more of these books.

Let's Exercise by Alice B. McGinty, Rosen Publishing Group, 1997.

This book teaches basic exercises. It tells why they are important. It will teach you how to stay active.

The Girl with 500 Middle Names by Margaret Peterson Haddix, Simon and Schuster, 2001.

Janie's parents move away from the city. They want her to go to a better school. She learns there are more important things than money.

Stone Fox by John Reynolds Gardiner, HarperCollins, 1980.

Little Willy joins the National Dog Sled Races. He wants to win money to save his grandfather's farm. But to win he must beat Stone Fox.

> **Milestones Intro Reading Library**
>
> *The Golden Monkey* by Rob Waring and Maurice Jamall, Heinle, 2006.
>
> *The New Guitar* by Rob Waring and Maurice Jamall, Heinle, 2006.
>
> *My Mom, the Movie Star* by Rob Waring and Maurice Jamall, Heinle, 2006.

Milestones to Achievement

● Reading

Read this Web article. Then answer Questions 1 through 8.

Get Healthy on a Budget

1   Are you trying to save money? Do you want to get more exercise? You don't have to go to an expensive gym. You don't have to spend money on fitness DVDs.

2   **Walk or Ride**
    One way to get more physical activity is to walk or ride a bike. If you usually use a car or bus to get to school, try riding your bike instead. If you want to go to a friend's house, walk. In many places, a bus ride can cost $1.00 or more. So walk or ride a bike. You will get exercise, and you will save some cash!

3   **Enjoy Nature**
    You don't have to be an expert on birds, flowers, or trees to enjoy a walk in the park. Get away from the TV or computer screen and go outside! Walk in the park and listen to the birds. Pick up trash at the park. Find colorful flowers and leaves with your little sister. As a result, you will get the exercise you need for free!

4   **Help Out at Home**
    Did you know that doing chores is good exercise? For example, doing laundry, mowing the lawn, and cleaning floors are great ways to stay healthy. Your family is going to ask you to help anyway. You can make them happy and exercise at the same time.

1 Read this sentence from paragraph 1.

> You don't have to go to an expensive gym.

What word helps you understand the cost of going to a gym?

A You   C expensive

B have   D gym

2 Read this sentence from paragraph 2.

> One way to get more physical activity is to walk or ride a bike.

Find the word that has been divided into syllables correctly.

A phy-sic-al   C ph-ysi-cal

B phys-i-cal   D phy-si-cal

3 Read this sentence from paragraph 1.

> You don't have to spend money on fitness DVDs.

What does <u>fitness</u> mean?

A movies   C heavy

B expensive   D exercise

4 What is one way to get exercise?

A watch TV

B play computer games

C clean the floor

D do your homework

5 How can you get exercise and make your family happy?

A help with chores

B ride the bus to school

C give your mother a hug

D spend money on DVDs

6 Which heading tells you that the next paragraph will be about walking?

A Get Healthy on a Budget

B Walk or Ride

C Enjoy Nature

D Help Out at Home

7 Which signpost words are used in paragraph 4?

A going to ask you

B did you know

C for example

D make them happy

8 Which sentence is an example of the future tense?

A You will get exercise, and you will save some cash!

B Did you know that doing chores is good exercise?

C Walk in the woods and listen to the birds.

D You can make them happy and exercise at the same time.

Writing on Demand: Persuasive E-mail

Your guardian is going shopping. Write him or her an e-mail to say what you want.

> **Writing Tip**
> Include reasons why you want a gift. What reasons will persuade your guardian to buy it?

MILESTONES HANDBOOK

Grammar Reference

○ Nouns

- **Nouns** name a person, place, or thing.
- **Singular nouns** are nouns that name one person, place, or thing.
- **Plural nouns** are nouns that name more than one person, place, or thing.

Regular Plural Nouns

Singular	Plural	Spelling Rule
book	book**s**	most nouns: add **-s**
bus lunch	bus**es** lunch**es**	nouns that end in **s, ch, sh, x,** or **z**: add **-es**
baby family	bab**ies** famil**ies**	nouns that end in a **consonant + y**: change the **y** to **i** and add **-es**
loaf knife	loa**ves** kni**ves**	nouns that end in **f** or **fe**: change the **f** or **fe** to **-ves**

Irregular Plural Nouns

Some nouns are irregular in the plural form.

Singular	Plural	Singular	Plural
man	**men**	child	**children**
woman	**women**	person	**people**
foot	**feet**	tooth	**teeth**
deer	**deer**	fish	**fish**

Possessive Nouns

- To show possession with **names** and **singular nouns,** use an apostrophe + **s** (**'s**).
- To show possession with **plural nouns ending in s,** use only an apostrophe (**'**).
- To show possession with **irregular plurals,** use an apostrophe + **s** (**'s**).

Statement	Sentence with Possessive Noun
Sara has a nice apartment.	Sara**'s** apartment is nice.
The boy has a TV in his room.	The boy**'s** TV is in his room.
The girls have a big bedroom.	The girls**'** bedroom is big.
The men have blue hats.	The men**'s** hats are blue.

Count and Noncount Nouns

- **Count nouns** are nouns you can count. They are singular or plural.
- You use **a, an, the,** or a number with count nouns.

  I have **one egg.** I have **12 carrots.**

  I made **a salad.** I made it with **a tomato** and **an onion. The salad** was delicious.

- **Noncount nouns** can't be counted. They are singular. Don't use **a, an,** or numbers.

  I like **juice.** I eat **cheese.** I always drink **milk.**

Compound Nouns

A **compound noun** is two words joined to form a new word.

tooth + brush = toothbrush

back + pack = backpack

bed + room = bedroom

Articles

There are three articles: **a, an,** and **the.** Articles are used with nouns.

Indefinite Articles: a, an

- Use **a** and **an** with singular and plural count nouns when the noun is indefinite.
- Use **a** before a word beginning with a consonant sound.
- Use **an** before a word beginning with a vowel sound.

  I have **a** cousin and **an** uncle in Chicago.

Definite Article: the

- Use **the** before a specific noun.

  I do not usually like rice, but **the** rice your mother makes is great.

- Use **the** before names of:

regions of countries that are directions	I live in **the** South.
mountains, lakes, and islands that are plural	We go camping in **the** Rockies.
	The Caribbean Islands are beautiful.
large bodies of water and deserts	**The** Pacific is the largest ocean.

- Do not use **the** before names of:

continents, countries, states, cities	South America is very large.
	Miami is in Florida.
exception: the United States	I live in **the** United States.
mountains, lakes, and islands that are singular	Mount McKinley is in Alaska.
	My aunt is from Puerto Rico.

⃝ Pronouns

A **pronoun** takes the place of a noun or refers to a noun.

> <u>My brother</u> is sick today. **He** has a cold.

Subject Pronouns

- **Subject pronouns** take the place of subject nouns.
- They do the action in a sentence.

Subject Pronoun	Sentence	Subject Pronoun	Sentence
singular		**plural**	
I	**I** am a teacher.	we	**We** are at school.
you	**You** are a student.	you	**You** are students.
he	**He** is Toni.	they	**They** are in the library.
she	**She** is Maya.		
it	**It** is my pen.		

Object Pronouns

- **Object pronouns** take the place of object nouns.
- They show to whom something happened or who received something.
- They come after a verb or preposition.

Object Pronoun	Sentence	Object Pronoun	Sentence
singular		**plural**	
me	Min likes **me.**	us	They live next door to **us.**
you	Fatima works with **you.**	you	Ben helps **you** on Mondays.
him	Cosima knows **him.**	them	The teacher helps **them** every day.
her	Javier is walking with **her.**		
it	Victor bought **it.**		

Possessive Pronouns

Possessive pronouns tell who owns or has something.

> Is that Ana's book or **mine**?

Possessive Pronoun	Sentence	Possessive Pronoun	Sentence
singular		**plural**	
mine	This book is **mine.**	ours	That car is **ours.**
yours	**Yours** is on the table.	yours	Where did you park **yours?**
his	Matteo is reading **his.**	theirs	They brought **theirs** last week.

○ Adjectives

- **Adjectives** describe nouns.
- Adjectives can come before nouns: I have **brown** hair.
- Adjectives can come after the verb **be:** My hair is **brown.**

Possessive Adjectives

Possessive adjectives tell who something belongs to. They come before nouns.

This is Carla. This is **her** classroom.

Possessive Adjective	Sentence	Possessive Adjective	Sentence
singular		**plural**	
my	I am a student. **My** name is Matt.	**our**	We are in school. **Our** teacher is Mr. Dunn.
your	You are a teacher. **Your** class is in Room 21.	**your**	You are good students. **Your** grades are excellent.
his	Sam is a student. **His** teacher is Mrs. Martin.	**their**	Mrs. Ho and Mr. Dunn are teachers. **Their** students are in class.
her	Meg is in class. **Her** books are here.		
its	The computer is in the office. **Its** screen is on.		

Comparative Adjectives

Comparative adjectives compare two things.

Adjective	Comparative	Spelling Rule
tall	tall**er**	most one-syllable adjectives: add **-er**
dry happy	dr**ier** happ**ier**	one- and two-syllable adjectives that end in **y**: change the **y** to **i** and add **-er**
careful difficult	**more** careful **more** difficult	two or more syllable adjectives: put **more** in front of the adjective

Irregular comparatives

good / **better**
bad / **worse**

Superlative Adjectives

Superlative adjectives compare three or more things.

Adjective	Superlative	Spelling Rule
tall	**the** tall**est**	most one-syllable adjectives: add **-est**
dry happy	**the** dr**iest** **the** happ**iest**	one- and two-syllable adjectives that end in **y**: change the **y** to **i** and add **-est**
careful difficult	**the most** careful **the most** difficult	two or more syllable adjectives: put **most** in front of the adjective

Irregular superlatives

good / **the best**
bad / **the worst**

Prepositions

Prepositions and the words that follow them can tell *where, when,* and *how* something happens.

> She is playing **in** the park. (where)
> They go to school **at** 7:00. (when)
> Mary walks **with** energy. (how)

Common Prepositions		
about	below	of
above	between	on
against	by	over
around	for	through
at	from	to
before	in	under

Conjunctions

- **Conjunctions** can join words, phrases, or clauses (parts of a sentence with a subject and a verb).

Use these conjunctions: **and, or, but, so.**

> <u>Maria did her homework</u> **and** <u>I helped her</u>.

Adverbs

- **Adverbs** describe verbs, adjectives, or other adverbs. They often answer the question "how?" Many adverbs end with **-ly.**

> The man spoke **softly.**
> The audience was **surprisingly** large.

They can also answer the question "how often?"

Frequency adverbs				
always	usually	often	sometimes	never
100%				0%

Interjections

- **Interjections** are words that express strong feelings.
- They are often followed by an exclamation mark.

> **Hooray!** It's snowing.

○ Verbs

A **verb** is an action word.

Simple Present Tense

Use the **simple present** tense to tell about an action that generally happens or is true now.

Simple Present Tense of *be*	
singular	**plural**
I **am** a teacher.	We **are** at school.
You **are** a student.	You **are** students.
He **is** Toni.	They **are** in the library.
She **is** Maya.	
It **is** my pen.	

Contractions

I am = I'm
you are = you're
he is = he's
she is = she's
it is = it's
we are = we're
they are = they're

Simple Present Tense of Regular Verbs				
affirmative		**negative**		
subject	**verb**	**subject**	**verb**	
I You We They	**read.**	I You We They	**do not**	**read.**
He She It	**read<u>s</u>.**	He She It	**does not**	**read.**

Contractions

do not = don't
does not = doesn't

Simple Past Tense

Use the **simple past** tense of a verb to tell about an action that happened in the past.

Simple Past Tense of *be*

Simple Past Tense of *be*	
singular	**plural**
I **was not** sad.	We **were not** teachers.
You **were not** sad.	You **were not** hungry.
He **was not** old.	They **were not** short.
She **was not** my sister.	
It **was not** a fish.	

Contractions

was not = wasn't
were not = weren't

Simple Past Tense of Regular Verbs

- Add **-ed** or **-d** to form the simple past tense of a regular verb.
- There is only one form for past tense verbs (except **be**).
- Contraction: **did not = didn't**

Verb	Simple Past Tense	Sentence	Negative Sentence
play	play**ed**	Natalie **played** basketball last week.	Natalie **did not play** basketball last week.
exercise	exercise**d**	I **exercised** yesterday.	I **did not exercise** yesterday.

Simple Past Tense of Irregular Verbs

Irregular verbs have special forms.

Verb	Simple Past Tense	Sentence	Negative Sentence
do	**did**	You **did** your homework.	You **did not do** your homework.
have	**had**	She **had** a backpack.	She **did not have** a backpack.
go	**went**	He **went** to band practice.	He **did not go** to band practice.
say	**said**	She **said** it's two o'clock.	She **did not say** it's two o'clock.

Present	Simple Past	Present	Simple Past	Present	Simple Past	Present	Simple Past
be	was/were	feel	felt	make	made	sit	sat
begin	began	find	found	meet	met	sleep	slept
break	broke	fly	flew	pay	paid	speak	spoke
buy	bought	get	got	put	put	spend	spent
come	came	give	gave	read	read	stand	stood
cost	cost	go	went	ride	rode	swim	swam
cut	cut	have	had	run	ran	take	took
do	did	hit	hit	say	said	teach	taught
drink	drank	keep	kept	see	saw	tell	told
drive	drove	know	knew	sell	sold	think	thought
eat	ate	leave	left	send	sent	wear	wore
fall	fell	let	let	sing	sang	write	wrote

Present Continuous Tense

- The **present continuous** form of a verb tells about an action happening right now.
- The present continuous uses **am, is,** or **are** and a main verb.
- You add **-ing** to the end of the main verb.

Present Continuous Tense					
affirmative			**negative**		
I	**am**		I	**am not**	
He She It	**is**	walk**ing.**	He She It	**is not**	walk**ing.**
We You They	**are**		We You They	**are not**	

Contractions

I am = I'm
you are = you're
he is = he's
she is = she's
it is = it's
we are = we're
they are = they're

Present Continuous: *-ing* Spelling Rules

Present Continuous: *-ing* Spelling Rules	
rule	**examples**
Add **-ing** to the end of most verbs.	ask → ask**ing** go → go**ing**
For verbs that end in **e,** drop the **e** and add **-ing.**	dance → danc**ing** invite → invit**ing**
For verbs with one syllable that end in a vowel + a consonant, double the consonant and add **-ing.**	stop → sto**pping** run → ru**nning**
Do not double the consonant **w, x,** or **y.**	draw → draw**ing** fix → fix**ing** play → play**ing**
Double the consonant for verbs with two syllables that end in a consonant + vowel + consonant, with the stress on the last syllable.	begin → begi**nning** admit → admi**tting**
Do not double the consonant for verbs with two syllables that end in a consonant + vowel + consonant if the stress is *not* on the last syllable.	listen → listen**ing** open → open**ing**

Future Tense

The **future tense** describes events in the future.

Future with *will*

- One way to show the future tense is to use **will** before the main verb.
- Use **will** with all subject nouns and pronouns.

Future Tense with *will*	
affirmative	**negative**
I **will** go to the mall tonight.	I **will not** go to the mall tonight.
You **will** go at noon.	You **will not** go at noon.
He **will** buy a hat tomorrow.	He **will not** buy a hat tomorrow.
She **will** go next Tuesday.	She **will not** go next Tuesday.
It **will** be fun.	It **will not** be fun.
We **will** pay now.	We **will not** pay now.
They **will** use a credit card.	They **will not** use a credit card.

Affirmative Contractions

I will = I'll
you will = you'll
he will = he'll
she will = she'll
it will = it'll
we will = we'll
they will = they'll

Negative Contraction

will not = won't

Future with *going to* + verb

- You can also show the future time by using **be** + **going to** before the main verb.
- This is more informal than **will.**

Future Tense with *be + going to*	
affirmative	**negative**
I **am going to** go to the mall tonight.	I **am not going to** go to the mall tonight.
You **are going to** go at noon.	You **are not going to** go at noon.
He **is going to** buy a hat tomorrow.	He **is not going to** buy a hat tomorrow.
She **is going to** go next Tuesday.	She **is not going to** go next Tuesday.
It **is going to** be fun.	It **is not going to** be fun.
We **are going to** pay now.	We **are not going to** pay now.
They **are going to** use a credit card.	They **are not going to** use a credit card.

Imperatives

- Use the **imperative** to give instructions, directions, or orders.
- The imperative is like the simple present without a subject.
- Strong orders end with an exclamation point (**!**).

Imperatives		
simple present	**imperative**	**negative imperative**
You open your books.	**Open** your books.	**Do not (Don't) open** your books.
You turn left.	**Turn** left!	**Do not (Don't) turn** left!

○ Complete Sentences

- A sentence is a group of words. The words express a complete thought.
- A complete sentence has a subject and a verb.
- The subject tells who or what the sentence is about. The subject can be a noun or a pronoun.
- The verb tells about the subject.
- A complete sentence begins with a capital letter.
- A complete sentence ends with a punctuation mark:
  a period (**.**), a question mark (**?**), or an exclamation point (**!**).

Complete Sentences	Incomplete Sentences
My brother is in your math class.	Julien your brother. (no verb)
She needs a pen.	Exercises every day. (no subject)

Subject-Verb Agreement

- The **subject** and **verb** in a sentence must **agree** in number.
- When a subject is singular, the verb must be a singular form.
- When the subject is plural, the verb must be a plural form.

Subject-Verb Agreement	
singular subject + singular verb	**plural subject + plural verb**
She is a doctor.	**They are** teachers.
The man cook<u>s</u> breakfast every day.	**The children cook** dinner on the weekend.

Agreement with Compound Subjects

- A **compound subject** has two or more parts.
- The subjects are combined with conjunctions, such as **and** and **or.**
- If the conjunction is **and,** the verb is usually plural.
  <u>Alex and Bob</u> **play** soccer.
- If the conjunction is **or,** the verb agrees with the subject closest to the verb.
  A pen or <u>a pencil</u> **is** required.
  A book or <u>two notebooks</u> **are** required.

Declarative Sentence

- A **declarative sentence** states (or "declares") an idea, fact, or information.
- A declarative sentence usually ends in a period (**.**).
  My grandmother is a wise woman.

Interrogative Sentence

- An **interrogative sentence** asks a question.
- An interrogative sentence usually ends in a question mark (**?**).
- An interrogative sentence can ask for a *yes/no* answer or for specific information.
  Do you like tacos? (Answer: *yes* or *no*)
  Where were you born? (Answer: a specific place)

Imperative Sentence

- An **imperative sentence** gives an order or command.
- An imperative sentence does not include a subject. It uses the base form of the verb.
- An imperative sentence ends in a period (**.**) or an exclamation point (**!**).

    Please shut the door.   Be careful!

Exclamatory Sentence

- An **exclamatory sentence** shows strong feeling.
- An exclamatory sentence ends in an exclamation point (**!**).

    I really like my English class!   Hurry up! We're late.

◯ Question Types

- There are two types of questions: *yes/no* **questions** and **information questions.**

Yes/No Questions with *be*

Simple Present

To ask *yes/no* questions with **be,** put **am, is,** or **are** before the subject.

Present Continuous

- To ask *yes/no* questions with **be,** put **am, is,** or **are** before the subject.
- Use the **-ing** form of the verb after the subject.

Simple Past

- To ask *yes/no* questions with **be,** put **was/were** before the subject.
- Use the base form of the verb after the subject.

Future

- To ask *yes/no* questions with **be,** put **will** before the subject.
- Use the base form of the verb after the subject.

		Yes/No Questions with *be*	
	statement	*yes/no* **question**	**short answer**
Simple Present	The kitchen **is** big.	**Is** the kitchen big?	Yes, it **is.** No, it **isn't.**
	The rooms **are** small.	**Are** the rooms small?	Yes, they **are.** No, they **aren't.**
Present Continuous	She **is being** serious.	**Is** she **being** serious?	Yes, she **is.** No, she **isn't.**
Simple Past	The window **was** open.	**Was** the window open?	Yes, it **was.** No, it **wasn't.**
	The doors **were** closed.	**Were** the doors closed?	Yes, they **were.** No, they **weren't.**
Future	You **will be** here tomorrow.	**Will** you **be** here tomorrow?	Yes, I **will.** No, I **won't.**
	My parents **will be** busy this weekend.	**Will** my parents **be** busy this weekend?	Yes, they **will.** No, they **won't.**

Yes/No Questions with Verbs Except *be*

Simple Present
- Put **do** or **does** before the subject. Use the base form of the verb after the subject.

Present Progressive
- Put **am, is,** or **are** before the subject. Use the **-ing** form of the verb after the subject.

Simple Past
- Put **did** before the subject. Use the base form of the verb after the subject.

Future
- Put **will** before the subject. Use the base form of the verb after the subject.

Yes/No Questions with Other Verbs			
	statement	**yes/no question**	**short answer**
Simple Present	He **likes** the house.	**Does** he **like** the house?	Yes, he **does.** No, he **doesn't.**
	They **study** in the kitchen.	**Do** they **study** in the kitchen?	Yes, they **do.** No, they **don't.**
Present Continuous	You **are sitting** in the living room.	**Are** you **sitting** in the living room?	Yes, I **am.** No, **I'm not.**
	She **is learning** how to drive.	**Is** she **learning** how to drive?	Yes, she **is.** No, she **isn't.**
Simple Past	You **ate** in the kitchen.	**Did** you **eat** in the kitchen?	Yes, I **did.** No, I **didn't.**
	You **read** a book in the living room.	**Did** you **read** a book in the living room?	Yes, we **did.** No, we **didn't.**
Future	He **will graduate** in 2010.	**Will** he **graduate** in 2010?	Yes, he **will.** No, he **won't.**
	We **will have** a test on Friday.	**Will** we **have** a test on Friday?	Yes, we **will.** No, we **won't.**

Information Questions

- Information questions start with a question word. Another name for information questions is **wh- questions** because most question words begin with **wh- (who, what, when, where, why, how).**
- The answer to an information question is a specific piece of information.

	Question Word	**Helping Verb**	**Subject**	**Main Verb**	
Simple Present	Who	do	you	see	in the picture?
Simple Past	What	did	you	see	at the museum?
Present Continuous	Why	are	you	watching	the movie?
Future	Where	will	you	see	your friends?

How to Use a Dictionary and a Thesaurus

How to Use a Dictionary

A good dictionary is an important reference tool. A dictionary can tell you the meaning of a new word, when and where to use a word, and how to pronounce the word.

A dictionary can be a book, on CD-ROM, and online.

Features of a Dictionary

- Word entries are in alphabetical order from A to Z.
- An entry starts with a headword. The headword shows how the word is broken into syllables.
- After the headword, you will find the pronunciation and syllable stress. Dictionaries use symbols to represent sounds. These symbols help you say the word. The pronunciation also shows which syllable is stressed.
- Next, you'll find grammar information. For each word or meaning there is an abbreviation that tells you the part of speech—noun, pronoun, adjective, verb, adverb, preposition, conjunction, or interjection.
- Next is the definition—what the word means. If there is more than one meaning, they are numbered.
- Entries sometimes have an example sentence.
- Some dictionaries also have the origin of the word. The origin is where it came from.
- Some dictionaries also have synonyms (words with similar meanings) and antonyms (words with opposite meanings).

pronunciation

part of speech

definition

mile•stone /ˈmaɪlˌstoʊn/ *n.*
1 a marker, such as a stone that indicates the distance in miles: *Many years ago, the main road between Boston and New York had milestones next to it.* **2** an important achievement, event: *Getting her college degree was a milestone in her life.*
[from Old English]
synonym accomplishment, achievement, event

example sentence

origin

synonym

How to Use a Thesaurus

A thesaurus is another important reference tool.
- A thesaurus gives synonyms—words that have the same or similar meanings.
- Many thesauruses also have antonyms—words that have opposite meanings.
- A thesaurus may also include related words or concepts.
- Thesauruses are available as a book, on CD-ROM, and online.
- Use a thesaurus to help you use new vocabulary and make your writing more interesting.

sympathy *n.*
1 understanding, concern. *antonym* indifference **2** accord, support of someone/something. *antonym* hostility
Related words humanity, kindness, pity

synonyms

antonym

related words

MILESTONES HANDBOOK Spelling

Spelling Rules

i before *e* except after *c* or when pronounced *ay*

- **i** before **e:** fri**e**nd, bri**e**f, ni**e**ce, fi**e**rce
- after **c:** rec**ei**ve, c**ei**ling
- pronounced *ay:* **ei**ght, n**ei**ghbor, w**ei**gh, th**ei**r

q and *u*

- Always put the letter **u** after the letter **q: qu**ick, **qu**estion, **qu**iz.

Suffixes

- When adding a suffix that begins with a vowel: drop a final silent **-e.**
  combine / combin**ation**   remove / remov**able**
- When adding a suffix that begins with a consonant: keep the final silent **-e.**
  achieve / achiev**ement**   care / car**eful**
- When adding a suffix to a one-syllable word that ends in vowel + consonant: double the consonant.
  hit / hi**tting**   stop / sto**pped**
- Change a final **y** to **i,** except when adding **-ing.**
  day / da**ily**   try / tr**ied**   play / play**ing**

Adverbs

- To make many adjectives into adverbs, just add **-ly:**
  quick / quick**ly**   slow / slow**ly**
- For adjectives ending in **vowel + l,** be careful to spell with **-lly** at the end:
  careful / carefu**lly**   successful / successfu**lly**
- For adjectives ending in **le,** take away the **e** and add **-y:**
  simple / simp**ly**   terrible / terrib**ly**
- For adjectives ending in **consonant + y,** change the **y** to **i** and add **-ly:**
  happy / happ**ily**   lazy / laz**ily**

○ Homophones

- **Homophones** are words that have the same pronunciation but different spellings and meanings.

Homophone	Example
two = 2 (number)	I have **two** pillows.
to = part of a verb = preposition	You need **to** eat. She went **to** the store.
too = also	He has a book. I have a book, **too.**
you're = you are	**You're** a teacher.
your = possessive adjective	**Your** bag is blue.
it's = it is	**It's** two o'clock.
its = possessive adjective	The desk is broken. **Its** leg is broken.
they're = they are	**They're** students.
their = possessive adjective	**Their** parents are happy.
there = place	Put your bag over **there.**
by = close or near	Your book is **by** the door.
buy = to purchase	Sally will **buy** a notebook.
bye = part of good-bye	**Bye!** I'll see you tomorrow.
sale = lowered price	The book was on **sale.**
sail = part of the boat that catches wind	The **sail** blew in the wind.

Syllabication

- A **syllable** is a unit of pronunciation.
- A syllable contains only one vowel sound.
- A word can have one or more syllables.
- Dividing words into syllables helps you learn how to pronounce them.

Closed Syllables

- A closed syllable ends in a consonant.
- A closed syllable has one vowel.
- The vowel sound in a closed syllable is short.
  sat, run, nap/kin, **sub**/ject

Open Syllables

- An open syllable ends in a vowel.
- The vowel sound in an open syllable is usually long.
  me, no, she, mu/sic, **ta**/ble, **o**/pen

Final -e Syllables (VCe)

- A final **-e** syllable ends in a vowel (V), a consonant (C), and a final **-e.**
- The final **-e** is silent and makes the earlier vowel long.
  make, cute, hope a/**lone,** in/**side**

Vowel Digraphs (Vowel Teams)

- A vowel digraph (or vowel team) is when two vowels together form one vowel sound in the same syllable.
- The vowel sound in a vowel digraph syllable is long.
  boat, meat, ex/**plain,** re/**peat, sea**/son

r-Controlled Vowels

- **r**-controlled vowels contain a vowel followed by an **r.**
- The vowel sound is affected by the **r.**
- When dividing a word into syllables, the vowel and the **r** usually stay in the same syllable.
  car, her, bird, but/**ter,** en/**ter, per**/son

Consonant + -le

- A common syllable spelling pattern is a consonant + **-le.**
- The **e** is silent.
- The syllable appears at the end of a word.
  ta/**ble,** cir/**cle,** ti/**tle**

Prefixes and Suffixes

Common Prefixes

- A **prefix** is a group of letters added to the beginning of a word.
- The word it is added to is called the **root word.**
- The prefix changes the meaning of the root word.

Prefix	Example
un- = not	**un**friendly, **un**fair
dis- = not	**dis**agree, **dis**like
non- = not	**non**fiction, **non**fat
im- = not	**im**possible, **im**mature
pre- = before	**pre**fix, **pre**heat, **pre**record
post- = after	**post**test
re- = again	**re**group, **re**tell
over- = above	**over**head projector

Common Suffixes

- A **suffix** is a group of letters added to the end of a root word.
- A suffix changes the meaning or part of speech of the root word.

Suffix	Used . . .	Example
-er, -or	person or thing that does something	teach**er**, work**er**, act**or**, visit**or**
-ist	a person who does something	pian**ist**, dent**ist**
-ful	full of	care**ful**, forget**ful**, hope**ful**
-less	without	care**less**, hope**less**, help**less**
-able	can be done	predict**able**, enjoy**able**, wash**able**
-ish	like, in the same way as	fool**ish**, child**ish**
-ion	to make verbs into nouns	collect**ion**, expans**ion**, presenta**tion**, reserva**tion**
-ous	to make nouns into adjectives	fam**ous**, nerv**ous**, envi**ous**, courage**ous**
-ness	to make adjectives into nouns	kind**ness**, happi**ness**, weak**ness**
-ly	to make adjectives into adverbs	quick → quick**ly** She walked **quickly** to her car.
-er	to make a comparative adjective	cheap → cheap**er** This dress is **cheaper** than that one.
-est	to make a superlative adjective	tall → tall**est** This is the **tallest** building in the city.

Punctuation

Period (.)

Declarative Sentence	A statement is called a declarative sentence. Put a period at the end of a declarative sentence.	Today is the first day of school**.**
Abbreviations	An abbreviation is a short form of a word. Abbreviations always have a period at the end.	Tuesday → Tues**.** inch → in**.**

Question Mark (?)

Questions	A question is also called an interrogative sentence. You put a question mark at the end of a question.	What is your name**?** Are you going to the party**?**

Exclamation Point (!)

Exclamations and Emphasis	An exclamation point at the end of a sentence shows strong feelings. Use exclamation points with the imperative for emphasis.	The burrito was delicious**!** Don't eat the lettuce**!** I didn't wash it yet.

Comma (,)

Items in a Series	You put a comma after each item in a series. A series has three or more items.	I have a <u>pen</u>**,** a <u>pencil</u>**,** and a <u>book</u>.
In Dates	Use a comma after the day in a date.	September 13**,** 2009
In Addresses	Use a comma before an apartment number. Use a comma after a city.	126 First St.**,** Apt. 3A Santa Ana**,** CA 92701
In Letters	Use a comma after the greeting and the closing in a friendly letter.	Dear Aunt Mary**,**

Apostrophe (')

Contractions	An apostrophe takes the place of missing letters in contractions.	it is → it**'**s he will → he**'**ll
Possessives	An apostrophe + **s** indicates possession. If the word is singular and ends in **s,** add **'s.** If the word is plural and ends in **s,** just add an apostrophe.	the girl**'**s book Lois**'**s book the boys**'** house

Quotation Marks (" ")

Quotations	Quotation marks show what people say. You put quotation marks where the speaker's words start and stop. Put a comma between the quote and the speaker of the quote.	"Let me clean the car," Ramón said. Ramón said, "Let me clean the car."
Titles	Use quotation marks for titles of articles in newspapers and magazines, poems, songs, and short stories.	Did you read the article "New Park Opens" in *The Daily News?* My favorite poem is "The Road Not Taken," by Robert Frost.

Parentheses (( ))

Extra Information	Parentheses are curved signs that give extra information or an explanation in a reading.	You use it to access (make use of) hundreds of Web sites.

Colon (:)

In Time	Use a colon to separate hours from minutes.	10:15 A.M. 9:33 P.M.
In Letters	In a business letter, use a colon after the greeting.	Dear Mr. Best:
A List	Use a colon to introduce a list.	Kim enjoys lots of physical activities: hiking, swimming, soccer, and baseball.

◯ Italics

- When using a computer, use *italics* in the situations below.
- When using handwriting, use <u>underlining</u>.

For Emphasis	Use italics for words you want to emphasize.	Do you *really* want to go?
Titles of Documents	Use italics for titles of documents, newspapers, magazines, books, and movies.	*The Constitution* *The Sunday News* *Fun Magazine* *The Pearl*
Foreign Words	Use italics for foreign words in an English sentence.	In Turkish, the first two numbers are *bir* and *iki*.

Capitalization

First Word in Sentence	Use a capital letter for the first word in a sentence.	**A** word problem uses words and data.
First Word in a Quoted Sentence	Use a capital letter for a quotation that is a complete sentence. Do not use a capital letter for the second part of a quoted sentence that is interrupted.	He said, "**W**e are leaving at 4:00." "We are leaving," he said, "at 4:00."
Pronoun "I"	The subject pronoun **I** always has a capital letter.	**I** am Mario.
Proper Nouns	The names of the days and months always have capital letters. The names of people always have capital letters.	My birthday is **T**uesday, **M**arch 24th. My father's name is **I**brahim.
Nationalities, Languages, Academic Courses, Organizations, Holidays, Historical Events, and Special Events	Use capital letters for the names of nationalities, languages, academic courses, organizations, holidays, historical events, and special events.	**A**merican **S**panish **A**lgebra I **T**he **A**merican **R**ed **C**ross **F**ourth of **J**uly **B**attle of **G**ettysburg **W**inter **C**oncert
Specific Places and Geographical Names	Use capital letters for street names. Use capital letters for the names of cities, states, and countries. Use capital letters for the names of mountains, rivers, lakes, and oceans.	**F**ifth **A**venue, **E**ast **S**treet **S**acramento, **C**alifornia **U**nited **S**tates the **R**ocky **M**ountains, the **H**udson **R**iver, **L**ake **E**rie, the **P**acific **O**cean
Titles of Works	Capitalize the first word and the important words in the titles of books, magazines, newspapers, works of art, and musical compositions.	*The Circuit* *Scientific Magazine* *Community Newspaper* *Mona Lisa* "**S**ymphony **N**o. 5"

Editing and Proofreading Symbols

Symbol	Meaning
⌐H	insert a paragraph indent
ᴎ	transpose (move around) letters, words, or sentences
Sp	check spelling
∧	insert word, words, or punctuation mark
ꝋ	delete/take out
ˆ	insert a comma
⊙	insert a period
⌃	insert a semicolon
⊙	insert a colon
⌄⌄ ⌄⌄	insert quotation marks
≡	make a capital
⌿	make lowercase
#	insert a space
⌒	close up the space

Revising and Editing

○ Revising and Editing Checklist

1. **Development of Ideas/Content**
   a. Did I choose an appropriate form of writing (e.g., personal letter, letter to the editor, poem, report, narrative) for my purpose?
   b. Is the purpose of my writing clear?
   c. Is my writing focused on the topic?
   d. Did I support my ideas with details, facts, examples, and explanations?
   e. Did I write appropriately for my audience?

2. **Organization**
   a. Is my writing clear?
   b. Do I have a strong, interesting beginning to get the reader's attention?
   c. Did I maintain a focus?
   d. Do my ideas progress logically?
   e. Do I have a strong ending that summarizes my topic?

3. **Sentence Structures**
   a. Are my sentences complete? Do they have a subject and a verb?
   b. Did I use declarative, interrogative, imperative, and exclamatory sentences appropriately?

4. **Paragraph Structure**
   Single Paragraph
   a. Does my paragraph have a topic sentence?
   b. Did I support my topic sentence with facts and details?

   Multi-Paragraph
   a. Did I provide an introductory paragraph?
   b. Did I establish and support a central idea with a topic sentence at or near the beginning of the first paragraph?
   c. Did I include supporting paragraphs with simple facts, details, and explanations?
   d. Did I provide details and transitional expressions that link one paragraph to another in a clear line of thought?
   e. Did I conclude with a paragraph that summarizes the points?

5. **Grammar and Usage (see pages 473–484)**
   a. Is my writing in the right tense (for example, present or past tense)?
   b. Did I use subject pronouns and object pronouns correctly?
   c. Did I use the pronouns *she*, *her*, or *hers* for women and girls, and *he*, *him*, or *his* for men and boys?
   d. Do my verbs agree with their subjects? Did I use singular verb forms with singular subjects and plural verb forms with plural subjects?
   e. Did I use articles, nouns, adjectives, and compound words correctly?
   f. Did I use correct verb forms (regular and irregular) and appropriate verb tenses?

6. **Writing Conventions**
   Form
   a. Did I write my name and the date?
   b. Did I write a title and underline it?
   c. Did I leave margins at the top and bottom and on both sides of the paper?
   d. Did I use correct spacing between letters in words and words in a sentence?
   e. Did I indent the first line of each paragraph?
   f. Did I use my best handwriting, or did I create an attractive computer presentation?

   Spelling
   a. Did I check the spelling of all words?
   b. If I wrote my paper on a computer, did I use the spell check?

   Punctuation and Capitalization
   a. Did I punctuate each sentence with the right punctuation mark (., ?, !)?
   b. For direct speech, did I use quotation marks and commas correctly?
   c. Did I use apostrophes correctly in contractions and possessives?
   d. Did I start each sentence with a capital letter?

The Research Process

The Research Process

STEP 1 Identify a topic.

Choose a topic that is specific, not general. It is difficult to research and write about a general topic.

General Topic	Specific Topics
Rain Forests	The Climate of Rain Forests
	Ways to Save the Rain Forests

STEP 2 Frame a central question or questions about your topic.

Your questions guide your research. As you find out information, write new questions and revise your original questions, as necessary.

STEP 3 Use references.

Find out more about your topic by using a variety of reference resources.

Reference	Description	How to Use It
computer catalog	database of all books in the library	Type in keywords to find books and other references related to your topic. Ask the librarian for help, if necessary.
books	books with information related to your topic	Look at the table of contents, preface, appendix, and index to locate content related to your topic. Also look at citations, end notes, and bibliographic entries that provide more information.
encyclopedias	collection of articles on thousands of topics; often include illustrations, photos, charts, and maps	Print encyclopedias: Topics are in alphabetical order; they often have cross-references to related topics. CD-ROM or online encyclopedias: Type in keywords related to your topic, then click on the articles; links within the articles indicate cross-references.
atlas	collection of maps that show location of places or other features, such as geographic, economic, or political features	Print atlas: Look at the table of contents or index to locate information related to your topic. CD-ROM or online atlas: Type in keywords related to your topic, then click on the link.
almanac	yearly publication that includes lists, tables, and brief articles relating to a topic	Print almanac: Look at the table of contents or index to locate information related to your topic. CD-ROM or online almanac: Type in keywords related to your topic, then click on the link.

Reference	Description	How to Use It
dictionary	list of words in alphabetical order with pronunciation, part of speech, meanings, and often word origins	Print dictionary: Look up the word alphabetically; use the headwords (words at the top of the page) to guide you. CD-ROM or online dictionary: Type in the word.
thesaurus	dictionary of synonyms (words with the same or similar meanings); often includes antonyms (words with opposite meanings)	Print thesaurus: Look up the word alphabetically; use the headwords (words at the top of the page) to guide you. CD-ROM or online thesaurus: Type in the word.
magazine	a small weekly or monthly publication that includes articles, stories, essays, and photos	Use an electronic database at the library to locate magazines with articles about your topic. Use the table of contents of the magazine to find the article. Current issues are usually on display. Older ones will be in the electronic archives.
newspaper	a daily or weekly print paper containing news articles	Use an electronic database at the library to locate articles about your topic. Current issues are usually on display. Older ones will be in the electronic archives.
Internet	a computer network of electronic information on all kinds of topics	Type keywords into a browser. Scan the links to find sites that seem useful.

STEP 4 Take notes on note cards.

Note cards help you keep track of the information you find and its sources.

Use note cards to organize this information.

a. Follow the format below to record the information that answers your questions.

b. Paraphrase or summarize the information from your source. Use your own words.

c. If you cite words directly from the source, you must use quotation marks.

d. Provide the complete source information. See page 498 for how to cite sources.

TOPIC: _____

Question: _____
(What do you want to know?)

Paraphrase or summarize your source:
OR **"Quote" your source:**

    Source:

Citations for Reference Sources	
reference	**how to cite**
book	Author. <u>Title of Book</u>, City of Publication: Publisher, Year. **Example:** Roper, Edward R., <u>Rain Forest</u>, New York: Omni Publishing, 1998.
encyclopedia	Author of Article, "Title of Article." <u>Title of Book</u>. City of Publication: Publisher, Year. **Example:** Alpert, Louis C., "Inca." <u>Encyclopedia Americana</u>, International Edition. 1999.
magazine or newspaper	Author of Article. "Title of Article." <u>Title of Magazine or Newspaper</u> Date: Page(s). **Example:** Tyler, Dawn. "On the Sands." <u>Hawaii Living</u> February 1998: 20–23.
Internet article	Creator's Name (if given). "Title of Article." <u>Web Page Title</u>. Institution or Organization. Date of access. <URL address>. If you cannot find the information, use the Web address as the citation. **Example:** Likakis, Angela. "The World of Science." <u>Science News</u>. Science Resource Center. InfoSci. February 28, 1998. <http://infosci.thinkgroup.com/itweb/boston_massachusetts>

STEP 5 Write your research paper.

a. Organize your note cards in logical sequence.

b. Create an outline from your notes.

c. Use your outline to draft your paper.

d. Revise and edit your paper. Use the Revising and Editing Checklist on page 494.

e. Use visuals.

STEP 6 Create a title page, table of contents, and bibliography.

a. The first page should include the title of your research paper, centered on the page. Write your name and the date in the bottom right-hand corner.

b. At the beginning of your research paper, make a "Table of Contents" to show the organization.

c. At the end of your paper, start a new page with the title "Bibliography."

d. In your bibliography, list all your references. Use the correct citation format. List your references in alphabetical order.

Technology Guide

○ The Computer

You can use a computer to help you work. You can also use a computer to help you find information. A computer is made up of **hardware** and **software.** Hardware is the part of the computer that you can touch. Software is the instructions that make the computer work.

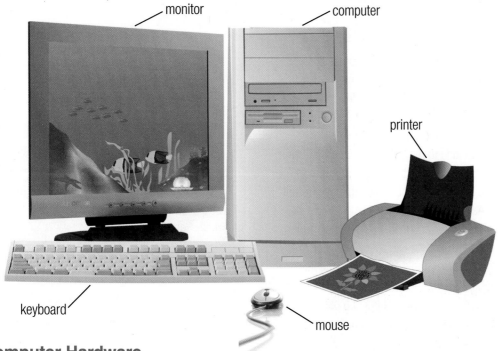

monitor
computer
printer
keyboard
mouse

Computer Hardware

1. The most important part of a computer is the box that contains the computer's memory. Your information is stored in the computer's memory.
2. You give information to the computer by typing on a keyboard or by clicking a mouse.
3. You see the information on the monitor. The monitor looks like a television screen.
4. You can use a printer to print the information on paper.

Computer Software

Software is made to do a special kind of job. For example, there is software that helps you write and edit your writing (word processing). There is software that makes it easy to create presentations. Other software lets you find information on the Internet. These pieces of software are also called **programs** or **applications.**

○ Word Processing

A word processing program is a tool for writing. You can use it to:

- correct mistakes, move text around, and add or delete text
- do spelling and grammar checks to help you find and correct errors
- find synonyms by using a thesaurus in the program
- create visuals
- choose text features such as **boldface type** and *italic type*

How to Create a Document

Anything that you write in a word processing program is called a **document.**

1. Make sure that the computer is on.
2. Find the **icon** (the little picture) for your word processing program on the screen.
3. Use the mouse to move the arrow onto the word processing icon and click on the program to open it. Different computers do this in different ways. Ask someone to help you.
4. When the program opens, you can start typing.
5. You can learn how to use special keys on the keyboard. For example, if you press the key marked **Tab** when you are at the beginning of a line, the computer will make a paragraph indent. The **Shift** keys make capital letters.
6. Look at the icons in this illustration. You can click on these icons with the mouse to make special effects such as **bold** or *italic* type. (The icons on your program might be different from these.)
7. VERY IMPORTANT: The computer will not "remember" your work by itself. You have to save it to the computer's memory. There is a Save icon that will make the computer do this. When you click on the Save icon the first time, the computer will ask you to name your document. As you write, save your work often.
8. When you have finished your first draft, use the spelling and grammar checks to find and fix errors. You can add text features and visuals if you like. Print your work or send it to someone by e-mail.

tab—makes a paragraph indentation

shift—makes capital letters

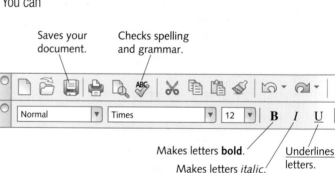

Saves your document.

Checks spelling and grammar.

Normal | Times | 12 | **B** *I* <u>U</u>

Makes letters **bold**.

Makes letters *italic.*

Underlines letters.

⬭ Technology Presentations

Using media such as video, graphics, and slides on a computer can make your oral presentations clearer and more interesting.

STEP 1 Plan the media parts of your presentation.

1. Plan, organize, and prepare your presentation. Take notes on how technology could help make your points.
    a. Is there a video that would help show your idea? Could you make one?
    b. Would music add to your presentation? What kind? Where can you get it?
    c. Should you show charts and visuals on the computer?
2. Make note cards. Use one card for what you will say and another card for the technology parts. Put the cards in order.

Card 1 My speech	Card 2 Media	Card 3 My speech
Sports Important in our community Most people like some kind of sport Introduce video	Play video of sports scenes in town	Sports are fun. Teamwork Healthy

STEP 2 Prepare the media parts of your presentation.

1. Find or create the images and sounds that you want to use.
    Look in the "Clip Art" section of your software or scan art or photos into your program.
2. If available, use the presentation software on your computer to organize the images and sounds.

STEP 3 Practice your presentation.

1. Practice your technology presentation.
2. Ask a partner to watch your presentation and help you.

STEP 4 Give your technology presentation to your audience.

1. Set up your equipment early to be sure that everything is working.
2. After your presentation, ask the audience to give you feedback.

How to Use the Internet

Key Definitions

Internet	millions of computers connected together to exchange information
Web sites	locations on the Internet
browser	software that lets you see Web sites
keywords	words that describe a topic
link	takes you to another Web site or to another place on the same Web site when you click your mouse on it

address bar—
Type Web
addresses here.

search box—
Type your
keywords here.

Click here
to start
your search.

Do Research on the Internet

1. Open your browser. Ask your teacher or a classmate how to do this.
2. Type keywords for your topic in the "search" box. Click on the button that says "go" (or "start" or "search").
3. Look at the list of Web sites that comes up on the screen. Choose one of the sites that seems interesting and click on it.
4. On a Web site, there are pages of information. Sometimes there are links to take you to other Web sites.
5. If you already know the exact address of a Web site, you can type it into the address bar. For example, http://visions.heinle.com.

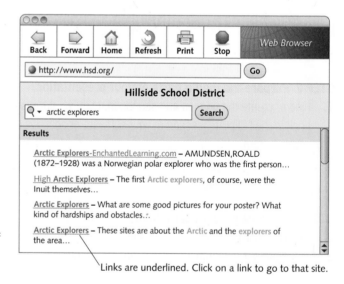

Links are underlined. Click on a link to go to that site.

Use Information from the Internet

Many Web sites have good information. Others may have mistakes, or they may tell only one side of an issue. You must evaluate the information that you find on the Internet. Ask your teacher or another adult for suggestions of sites that you can trust. Use other resources to check the information you find on the Internet.

○ **How to Use E-Mail**

Key Definitions

e-mail	software that lets you type a message and send it to someone else who has e-mail
e-mail address	where the e-mail system sends the message
inbox	a list of who sent you messages and what the messages are about

Read an E-Mail Message

1. Open the e-mail program. Ask your teacher or a classmate how to do this. See if there are any new messages in your inbox.

2. Open a message. Programs do this differently. Usually you double click the mouse on the message.

3. Read the message.

4. If you want to keep the message, do not do anything. The computer will save it in your inbox. If you want to discard the message, click on the "delete" button on the toolbar.

5. To send an answer back, click on the "reply" button. Write your message and click "send."

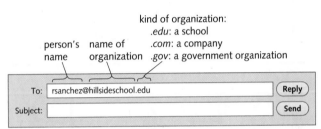

kind of organization:
.*edu*: a school
.*com*: a company
.*gov*: a government organization

person's name · name of organization

To: rsanchez@hillsideschool.edu   Reply
Subject: Send

Send an E-Mail Message

1. Open your e-mail program.

2. On the toolbar, click on the "new message" button.

3. Type in the address of the person you are writing to.

4. Type in a subject that tells what the message is about.

5. Type your message.

6. Click on the "send" button.

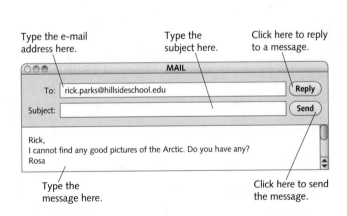

Type the e-mail address here.   Type the subject here.   Click here to reply to a message.

MAIL

To: rick.parks@hillsideschool.edu   Reply
Subject: Send

Rick,
I cannot find any good pictures of the Arctic. Do you have any?
Rosa

Type the message here.   Click here to send the message.

○ Print Letters

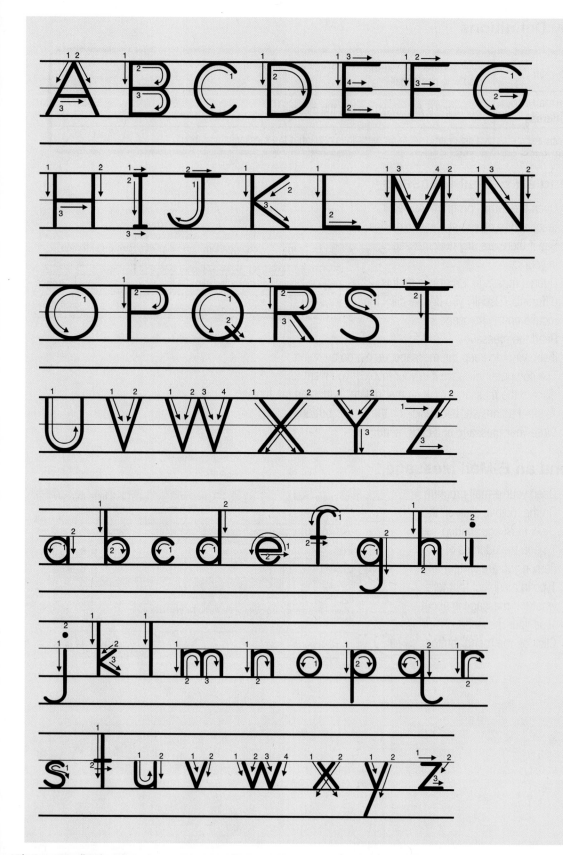

○ Cursive Letters

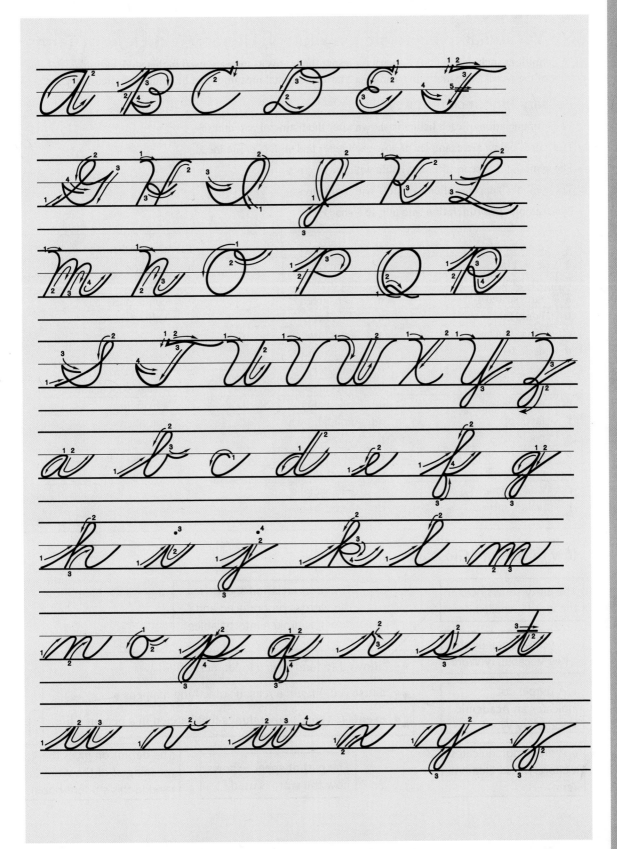

Glossary

Key Vocabulary, Academic Vocabulary, Literary/Text Element Terms

The definitions included in this Glossary represent the words as they are used in this student book. Many of the words have multiple meanings. These additional meanings can be found in a dictionary.

Glossary Pronunciation Key

• The pronunciation of each listing is shown after the listing in parentheses.

• The words below are examples of how each letter and sign is pronounced.

• The symbol (′) appears after a syllable with heavy stress.

  The symbol (′) appears after a syllable with light stress.

  For example: **pronunciation** (prə nun′sē ā′shən)

a	map, flag	**k**	keys, sink	**ŦH**	the, mother
ā	gate, play	**l**	library, animal	**u**	run, son
ä	art, barn	**m**	math, room	**ü**	school, rude
â	fare, scared	**n**	nice, green	**ŭ**	could, pull
b	book, tub	**ng**	sing, hang	**v**	value, weave
ch	chair, teacher	**o**	hot, closet	**w**	watch, shower
d	desk, bald	**ō**	motive, polar	**y**	yes, employer
e	net, pen	**ô**	war, story	**z**	zip, stanza
ē	heal, scene	**ŏ**	fall, cause	**zh**	visual, conclusion
ėr	nurse, germ	**oi**	soil, annoy	**ə**	a in ability
f	fact, sofa	**ou**	proud, brown		e in liberty
g	go, bag	**p**	pillow, lamp		i in pencil
h	helmet, holiday	**r**	ruler, hair		o in dictionary
i	miss, image	**s**	sunny, class		u in injury
ī	wise, rhyme	**t**	time, weight		
j	jacket, subject	**th**	theme, truth		

How to Use the Glossary

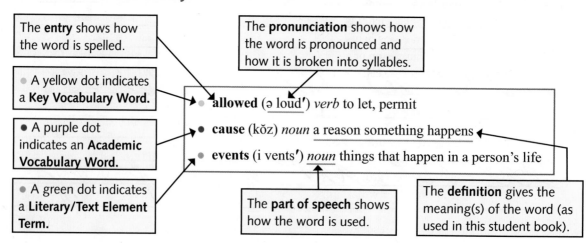

The **entry** shows how the word is spelled.

● A yellow dot indicates a **Key Vocabulary Word.**

● A purple dot indicates an **Academic Vocabulary Word.**

● A green dot indicates a **Literary/Text Element Term.**

The **pronunciation** shows how the word is pronounced and how it is broken into syllables.

● **allowed** (ə loud′) *verb* to let, permit

● **cause** (kŏz) *noun* a reason something happens

● **events** (i vents′) *noun* things that happen in a person's life

The **part of speech** shows how the word is used.

The **definition** gives the meaning(s) of the word (as used in this student book).

A

- **ability** (ə bil′ə tē) *noun* skill
- **accident** (ak′sə dənt) *noun* something harmful or unpleasant that happens by surprise
- **action** (ak′shən) *noun* thing that a person does
- **add** (ad) *verb* to put numbers together into a total
- **adopted** (ə dopt′) *verb* to make your own
- **allowed** (ə loud′) *verb* to let, permit
- **amendment** (ə mend′mənt) *noun* a change
- **angry** (ang′grē) *adjective* feeling anger
- **animal** (an′ə məl) *noun* any creature that is not a plant
- **approve** (ə prüv′) *verb* permission, consent
- **audience** (ŏ′dē əns) 1. *noun* a person or people who read something an author has written
- **audience** (ŏ′dē əns) 2. *noun* people who watch a play
- **aunt** (ant or änt) *noun* the sister of one's father or mother, or the wife of one's uncle
- **author** (ŏ′thər) *noun* someone who writes something, like a story or a poem

B

- **barn** (bärn) *noun* a place farmers keep their hay
- **beak** (bēk) *noun* a bird's mouth
- **behave** (bi hāv′) *verb* to act well
- **budget** (buj′it) *noun* a plan of income and expenses over time

C

- **caption** (kap′shən) *noun* word or words under a picture or illustration to explain what it is
- **cause** (kŏz) *noun* a reason something happens
- **character** (kar′ik tər) *noun* 1. a person or animal in a story 2. people in myths who can often do things that real people can't do
- **climate** (klī′mit) *noun* the type of weather that a place has
- **closing** (klōz′ing) *noun* to come or bring to an end, terminate, conclude
- **community** (kə myü′nə tē) *noun* a group of people, such as those in a town, or with similar interests
- **confirm** (kən fèrm′) *verb* prove that something is true
- **contest** (kon′test) *noun* a competition

- **context** (kon′tekst) *noun* the information around a word or phrase
- **court** (kôrt) *noun* a place where decisions are made about people who may have broken the law
- **cousin** (kuz′n) *noun* a child of an aunt or uncle

D

- **dates** (dāts) *noun* when things happen in a person's life
- **daughter** (dŏ′tər) *noun* a female child
- **details** (dē′tālz) *noun* more information about the main idea
- **diagram** (dī′ə gram) *noun* 1. a drawing with markings to show how something is put together or works 2. pictures and charts that can help you understand something
- **different** (dif′ər ənt) *adjective* unlike, not the same
- **discount** (dis′kount) *noun* an amount subtracted from a price
- **divide** (də vīd′) *verb* to separate (into parts), break up
- **document** (dok′yə mənt) *noun* a paper, such as a formal letter, contract, record, etc.

E

- **effect** (ə fekt′) *noun* the result of something else
- **elect** (i lekt′) *verb* choose someone for something by voting for him or her
- **energy** (en′ər jē) *noun* the power to do work
- **entertain** (en′tər tān′) *verb* to keep people happy
- **equation** (i kwā′zhən) *noun* a mathematical statement that two amounts are equal
- **events** (i vents′) *noun* things that happen in a person's life
- **examples** (eg zam′pəlz) *noun* show you how to do something and give you the answers
- **exercises** (ek′sər sīziz) *noun* math problems for you to solve
- **expense** (ek spens′) *noun* something that must be paid
- **expert** (ek′spért) *noun* a master at something, authority
- **explanation** (ek′splə nā′shən) *noun* 1. a reason why something is 2. tells you how to do something

F

- **fact** (fakt) *noun* true information
- **fall off** (fôl ŏf) *verb* to come off or not be on anymore
- **fare** (fâr) *noun* money you pay to ride a bus, train, or taxi
- **field** (fēld) *noun* a place where farmers grow things
- **fingerprints** (fing′gər prints′) *noun* prints from small lines on your fingers
- **fitness** (fit′nis) *noun* exercise
- **free verse** (frē vèrs) *noun* poems that don't rhyme
- **friendly** (frend′lē) *adjective* helpful, pleasant, agreeable

G

- **gate** (gāt) *noun* a metal or wooden door that closes an open space in a wall or fence
- **grain** (grān) *noun* a single seed of a plant
- **graphic organizer** (graf′ik ôr′gə nīz ər) *noun* a way to picture information
- **graphics** (graf′iks) *noun* pictures such as photographs and drawings
- **greetings** (grē′tingz) *noun* the first words or actions used on meeting someone, such as "Hello" or "Hi"

H

- **headings** (hed′ingz) *noun* what each section is about
- **healthy** (hel′thē) *adjective* in good health
- **heat** (hēt) *noun* feeling of warmth, or the quality of being hot
- **holiday** (hol′ə dā) *noun* a day of celebration or rest

I

- **identify** (ī den′tə fī) *verb* to recognize the identity of someone or something
- **illustrations** (il′ə strā′shənz) *noun* pictures, designs, or diagrams

- **index** (in′deks) *noun* a list at the end of a textbook that shows where to find specific words or topics
- **inform** (in fôrm′) *verb* to give information or facts to someone
- **information** (in′fər mā′shən) *noun* facts or things you can learn about someone or something
- **instructions** (in struk′shənz) *noun* statements that tell you what to do
- **interesting** (in′tər ə sting) *adjective* causing a wish to know more
- **invention** (in ven′shən) *noun* something useful created by someone

L

- **liberty** (lib′ər tē) *noun* freedom, right
- **lines** (līnz) *noun* what the actor says

M

- **main idea** (mān ī dē′ə) *noun* the most important idea
- **maps** (maps) *noun* illustrations that show where things happen
- **meaning** (mē′ning) *noun* a definition or an explanation
- **message** (mes′ij) *noun* piece of information someone is trying to give or communicate to someone else
- **miss** (mis) *verb* to feel a sense of loss
- **monument** (mon′yə mənt) *noun* built in memory of a person or historical event
- **moral** (môr′əl) *noun* a message or a lesson that you can learn from the story
- **motive** (mō′tiv) *noun* reason for doing something
- **multiply** (mul′tə plī) *verb* in arithmetic, to increase a number by a certain number of times

N

- **narrator** (nar′rā tor) *noun* a person who gives the scene and background information
- **national** (nash′ə nəl) *adjective* related to a nation
- **net** (net) *noun* something used to catch animals, like fish or birds

- A yellow dot indicates a **Key Vocabulary Word.**
- A purple dot indicates an **Academic Vocabulary Word.**
- A green dot indicates a **Literary/Text Element Term.**

- **nice** (nīs) *adjective* pretty, attractive
- **notes** (nōts) *noun* short written reminders of what you have read or heard

O

- **operation** (op′ə rā′shən) *noun* (in mathematics) a process, such as addition or subtraction, carried out on numerals, following certain rules
- **opinion** (ə pin′yən) *noun* a belief or idea
- **organism** (ôr′gə niz′əm) *noun* anything that is an animal or a plant

P

- **percent** (pər sent′) *noun* one part in each hundred
- **persuade** (pər swād′) *verb* to get someone to agree with you or to do what you want them to
- **physical** (fiz′ə kəl) *adjective* related to the body
- **plant** (plant) *noun* living thing that usually makes its own food from sunlight, soil, and water
- **polar** (pō′lər) *adjective* near the north and south poles
- **precipitation** (pri sip′ə tā′shən) *noun* rain, snow, sleet, or hail
- **prediction** (pri dik′shən) *noun* a guess about what will happen in the future
- **purpose** (pėr′pəs) *noun* a reason for doing something

R

- **represent** (rep′ri zent′) *verb* to show, give a picture or symbol of
- **rhyme** (rīm) *noun* words that sound alike
- **run** (run) *verb* to move legs and feet quickly across the ground

S

- **scan** (skan) *verb* look quickly to find something
- **scene** (sēn) *noun* part of a play that happens at one time
- **sequence** (sē′kwəns) *noun* the order that things happen
- **set** (set) *verb* to decide or plan

- **signature** (sig′nə chər) *noun* one's name written by oneself
- **solve** (solv) *verb* to find an answer or solution for something
- **son** (sun) *noun* a male child
- **spider** (spī′dər) *noun* a small, eight-legged animal that traps insects in silken webs
- **stage directions** (stāj də rek′shənz) *noun* notes in the play that tell the actors how to speak and move
- **stanza** (stan′zə) *noun* a group of lines in a poem
- **storm** (stôrm) *noun* heavy rain or snow with high winds
- **stream** (strēm) *noun* a small river
- **subject** (sub′jikt) *noun* what the text is about
- **subtract** (səb trakt′) *verb* to take away a number (amount) from another
- **subtropical** (sub trop′ə kəl) *adjective* places that have a climate that is warm and wet, and are often near tropical regions
- **summarize** (sum′ə rīz) *verb* give the main points of a story or article
- **symbol** (sim′ bəl) *noun* a sign, mark, picture, object, or event that represents something else

T

- **temperature** (tem′pər ə chər) *noun* the degree of heat or cold
- **time line** (tīm′līn) *noun* a graphic that shows when things happen
- **topic** (top′ik) *noun* a subject of attention, writing, conversation; a field
- **topic sentence** (top′ik sen′təns) *noun* a sentence that gives the main idea of a paragraph
- **trait** (trāt) *noun* characteristic or quality that someone has
- **transfer** (tran′sfėr) *verb* to move from one place to another
- **tribe** (trīb) *noun* a group of people who usually speak the same language, live in the same area, often in villages, and have many relatives within the group
- **tropical** (trop′ə kəl) *adjective* hot and damp weather that is typical of the tropics

U

- **uncle** (ung′kəl) *noun* one's mother's or father's brother

 V

- **value** (val′yü) *noun* to put a price on something
- **vote** (vōt) *verb* to cast a ballot or a vote for or against

 W

- **war** (wôr) *noun* fighting with guns and other weapons between groups, armies, nations, etc.
- **watch** (wäch) 1. *noun* a small clock worn on the wrist 2. *verb* to look at
- **weave** (wēv) *verb* to make fabric by crossing threads or other material over and under one another
- **weight** (wāt) *noun* the measure of how heavy something, or someone, is
- **when question** (wen kwes′chən) *noun* asks about time
- **where question** (wâr kwes′chən) *noun* asks about place
- **why question** (wī kwes′chən) *noun* asks about a reason

- A yellow dot indicates a **Key Vocabulary Word.**
- A purple dot indicates an **Academic Vocabulary Word.**
- A green dot indicates a **Literary/Text Element Term.**

Vocabulary List

The following is a list of vocabulary words found in *Milestones Introductory*. References are by Unit and Chapter numbers: WU, ChF = Welcome Unit, Chapter F; U1, Ch2A = Unit 1, Chapter 2A; U3, Ch1A = Unit 3, Chapter 1A, etc.

A

abilities U5, Ch2A
address WU, ChB; U1, Ch1A
aisle U7, Ch1A
apartment U1, Ch1A
apartment number WU, ChC
art WU, ChE
art show U1, Ch2A
auditorium WU, ChG

B

backpack WU, ChB; U3, Ch2A
bag WU, ChB
bald U2, Ch1A
banana U4, Ch2A
bank U6, Ch2A
bargain U7, Ch2A
baseball team WU, ChF
basketball game U1, Ch2A
basketball player WU, ChF
bathroom U4, Ch1A
beard U2, Ch1A
bed U4, Ch1A
bedroom U4, Ch1A
beef U4, Ch2A
belt U7, Ch1A
black hair U2, Ch1A
blond hair U2, Ch1A
blouse U7, Ch1A
blue eyes U2, Ch1A
board WU, ChD
book WU, ChB
bookcase U4, Ch1A
bookstore U6, Ch1A
broccoli U4, Ch2A
brown eyes U2, Ch1A
brown hair U2, Ch1A
butter U4, Ch2A

C

cabinet U1, Ch1A
cafeteria WU, ChG
calculator U1, Ch1A
carrot U4, Ch2A
cash U7, Ch2A
cash register U5, Ch1A
cashier U5, Ch1A
CD WU, ChF
cell U1, Ch1A
cell phone U3, Ch2A
chair WU, ChD; U4, Ch1A
change U7, Ch2A
check my e-mail U3, Ch1A
cheese U4, Ch2A
chef U5, Ch1A
chicken U4, Ch2A
city WU, ChC; U1, Ch1A
classroom WU, ChD
clean my room U3, Ch1A
clipboard U5, Ch1A
closet U4, Ch1A
clothing store U6, Ch1A
cloudy U3, Ch1A
coat U3, Ch2A
coffee table U4, Ch1A
coins U7, Ch2A
cold U3, Ch1A
community center U6, Ch1A
computer WU, ChD
computer and printer U1, Ch1A
construction worker U5, Ch1A
convenience store U6, Ch2A
cook U5, Ch2A
coupon U7, Ch2A
credit card U7, Ch2A
curly hair U2, Ch1A
curtain U4, Ch1A

D

dark brown hair U2, Ch1A
date U1, Ch1A
debit card U7, Ch2A
desk U4, Ch1A
dictionary WU, ChB
dime U7, Ch2A
dining room U4, Ch1A
do my homework U3, Ch1A
do your homework U2, Ch 2A

dollar bills U7, Ch2A
door WU, ChD
draw U5, Ch2A
dress U7, Ch1A
dresser U4, Ch1A
drinks U4, Ch2A

E

eat breakfast U2, Ch2A
egg U4, Ch2A
employer U1, Ch1A
end table U4, Ch1A
eraser WU, ChB
expensive U7, Ch2A

F

field trip U1, Ch2A
fire extinguisher U5, Ch1A
first name U1, Ch1A
fish U4, Ch2A
fix a bicycle U5, Ch2A
flag WU, ChA
flashlight U5, Ch1A
food WU, ChF
football game U1, Ch2A
forget U5, Ch2A
fork U4, Ch2A
fruit U4, Ch2A

G

game WU, ChF
garage U4, Ch1A
garlic U4, Ch2A
gas station U6, Ch2A
get dressed U2, Ch2A
get home U2, Ch2A
get ready for school U2, Ch2A
get up U2, Ch2A
gift card U7, Ch2A
glass U4, Ch2A
glasses U2, Ch1A
gloves U3, Ch2A

go to bed U2, Ch2A
grade U1, Ch1A
graduation U1, Ch2A
grains U4, Ch2A
grape U4, Ch2A
gray hair U2, Ch1A
green eyes U2, Ch1A
ground meat U4, Ch2A
guardian U1, Ch1A
gymnasium WU, ChG

H

hairstylist U5, Ch1A
half-off U7, Ch2A
hanger U7, Ch1A
hat U3, Ch2A
helmet U3, Ch2A
home U1, Ch1A
hot U3, Ch1A

J

jacket U3, Ch2A
jeans U7, Ch1A
juice U4, Ch2A

K

ketchup U4, Ch2A
keys U3, Ch2A
kitchen U4, Ch1A
knife U4, Ch2A

L

label U7, Ch1A
lamp U4, Ch1A
language arts WU, ChE
last name U1, Ch1A
laundromat U6, Ch2A
leave for school U2, Ch2A
lemonade U4, Ch2A
lettuce U4, Ch2A
library WU, ChG; U6, Ch2A
light brown hair U2, Ch1A
light switch WU, ChD
listen to music U3, Ch1A
living room U4, Ch1A
long hair U2, Ch1A
lose U5, Ch2A

M

mail carrier U5, Ch1A
map WU, ChA
math WU, ChE
meat U4, Ch2A
meet my friends U3, Ch1A
middle name U1, Ch1A
milk U4, Ch2A
mirror U4, Ch1
moustache U2, Ch1A
move WU, ChF
movie theater U6, Ch1A
mushroom U4, Ch2A
music WU, ChE
music room WU, ChG
music store U6, Ch1A
mustard U4, Ch2A

N

neighborhood places U6, Ch2A
nickel U7, Ch2A
notebook WU, ChB
nurse WU, ChA
nurse's office WU, ChG

O

occupations U5, Ch1A
oil U4, Ch2A
olive U4, Ch2A
orange U4, Ch2A
oven U4, Ch1A

P

pants U7, Ch1A
parent U1, Ch1A
park U6, Ch1A
pen WU, ChB
pencil WU, ChB
penny U7, Ch2A
pep rally U1, Ch2A
pepper U4, Ch2A
pharmacy U6, Ch2A
phone number WU, ChC; U1, Ch1A
physical education WU, ChE
picture WU, ChD
piece of paper WU, ChD
pillow U4, Ch1A

places in the community U6, Ch1A
plate U4, Ch2A
play U1, Ch2A
play basketball U3, Ch1A
play chess U5, Ch2A
play the piano U5, Ch2A
police U5, Ch1A
post office U6, Ch2A
practice your music U2, Ch2A
price tag U7, Ch2A
principle WU, ChA
program a computer U5, Ch2A
proteins U4, Ch2A

Q

quarter U7, Ch2A

R

rack U7, Ch1A
raincoat U3, Ch2A
raining U3, Ch1A
receipt U7, Ch2A
red hair U2, Ch1A
refrigerator U4, Ch1A
regular price U7, Ch2A
restaurant U6, Ch1A
restrooms WU, ChG
ride my bike U3, Ch1A
rug U4, Ch1A
ruler U1, Ch1A

S

salad U4, Ch2A
sale U7, Ch2A
sale price U7, Ch2A
salsa U4, Ch2A
salt U4, Ch2A
sandwich U4, Ch2A
scarf U3, Ch2A
schedule U1, Ch1A
school WU, ChA
school concert U1, Ch2A
school dance U1, Ch2A
science WU, ChE
scissors U5, Ch1A
shelf U7, Ch1A
shirt U7, Ch1A

shopping cart U7, Ch1A
shopping for clothing
    U7, Ch1A
shopping mall U6, Ch1A
short hair U2, Ch1A
shoulder-length hair U2, Ch1A
shower U4, Ch1A
sing U5, Ch2A
sink U4, Ch1A
size U7, Ch1A
skirt U7, Ch1A
snowing U3, Ch1A
social studies WU, ChE
sofa U4, Ch1A
soup U4, Ch2A
spoon U4, Ch2A
sports WU, ChF
stairs WU, ChG
state WU, ChC; U1, Ch1A
stethoscope U5, Ch1A
straight hair U2, Ch1A
street WU, ChC; U1, Ch1A
student WU, ChA
study for your test U2, Ch2A
sunglasses U3, Ch2A
sunny U3, Ch1A
sunscreen U3, Ch2A
sweater U7, Ch1A

T

table U4, Ch1A
teacher WU, ChA; U1, Ch1A
terrible U3, Ch1A

textbook U1, Ch1A
tie U7, Ch1A
toilet U4, Ch1A
tools U5, Ch1A
tub U4, Ch1A
TV show WU, ChF

U

umbrella U3, Ch2A
utensils U5, Ch1A

V

vegetable U4, Ch2A

W

wallet U3, Ch2A
wash the dishes U2, Ch2A
watch TV U3, Ch1A
water U4, Ch2A
window U4, Ch1A
work phone U1, Ch1A
workbook WU, ChD;
    U1, Ch1A
write your report U2, Ch2A

Z

zip code WU, ChC

Index of Skills

Literary Analysis

Comprehension and Analysis

analyze author's purpose, 115, 164, 165, 166, 167, 237, 398, 399, 400, 401, 402, 403

analyze characters, 219, 323, 326, 376, 377, 378, 379, 380, 381

ask questions, 115, 116, 133, 185, 188, 217, 220, 237, 240, 269, 272, 320, 343, 348, 377, 382, 399, 404, 433, 453, 458

author's purpose, 115, 164, 165, 166, 167, 237, 398, 399, 400, 401, 402, 403

build background, 112, 130, 162, 182, 214, 234, 266, 286, 318, 340, 374, 396, 430, 450

cause and effect, 268, 269, 270, 271

character, 219, 323, 326, 376, 377, 378, 379, 380, 381

compare and contrast, 168, 355, 382

compare media, 355, 411, 465

conclusion, draw, 292, 435, 458

detail, 236, 237, 239, 240, 433

distinguish fact from opinion, 404, 432

draw conclusions, 292

evaluate, 407

experiences, use own, 116, 135, 200

fact and opinion, 404, 432

identify main idea and details, 236, 237, 238, 239, 240, 433

inference, 116, 167, 237, 269, 291, 347, 403, 404, 453, 457

information questions, 320, 321, 322, 323, 324

instructions, follow, 294, 295

interpret
  charts, 137
  diagram, 134, 188

graphs, 137
  maps, 239, 240, 241
  pictures, 94, 165

main idea, 236, 237, 239, 240, 450

moral, 376, 383

multiple-step instructions, 294, 295

note-taking, 288, 290, 291

opinion, 272, 382, 404, 432

paraphrase, 187

persuasion, 432, 433, 434, 435

poetry, 164, 165, 166, 167, 198
  alliteration, 169
  rhyme, 164, 166, 198

predictions, make and confirm, 271, 321, 452, 453, 454, 455, 456, 457, 459

prior knowledge, 112, 130, 162, 182, 214, 234, 266, 286, 318, 340, 374, 396, 430, 450

problems and solutions, 273

purpose for reading, 132, 133, 134, 135, 138

questions, ask clarifying, 115, 116, 133, 185, 188, 217, 220, 237, 269, 272, 289, 292, 320, 321, 323, 324, 343, 348, 377, 382, 399, 404, 433, 453, 458

read and reread, 293

recall, 115, 116, 133, 135, 167, 168, 187, 188, 220, 237, 239, 240, 269, 272, 291, 292, 321, 323, 326, 343, 345, 377, 379, 381, 382, 399, 401, 403, 404, 433, 435, 436, 453, 455, 457, 458

recognize text features, 114, 132, 169, 189, 221, 241, 273, 293, 327, 349, 383, 405, 437, 459

relate to own experiences, 116, 135, 220

retell, 116, 220, 272, 348, 436

scan, 114, 115, 241

sequence, 216, 217, 218, 219, 220, 221

summarize, 167, 185, 342, 343, 344, 345, 346

supporting details, 236, 238, 239, 240

visualize, 94, 117, 292, 327

Text Genres

almanac, 496

atlas, 496

biography, 342

diary, 181

dictionary, 485

editorial, 432

encyclopedia, 496

expository text, 288

fable, 376, 383

folk tale, 376

"how-to" article, 88, 89, 334, 335

informational text, 452

Internet article, 40, 452

letter, 114, 118, 119, 144, 242, 245, 339, 466

magazine, 184

myth, 268

narrative, 216

newspaper, 432

online article, 40, 452

personal narrative, 373, 429, 441

play, 320

poetry, 164, 165, 166, 167

shape poem, 167, 198

textbook, 130, 132, 236, 288, 398

visual poem, 167

web article, 452

writing systems, 340, 345, 348

Literary/Text Elements and Features

alliteration, 169

author's message, 164, 165, 166, 167

author's purpose, 115, 237, 398, 399, 400, 401, 402, 403

bar graph, 137, 141

bibliography, 498

caption, 184, 292, 293

character motivation, 219, 323, 326, 376, 377, 378, 379, 380, 381

chart, 137

Reading

Reading Fluency

Reading Strategies

Independent Reading

Word Analysis

Concepts About Print

Phonemic Awareness

Decoding and Word Recognition

228, 232, 262, 263, 284,
314, 315, 338, 370, 394,
426, 427, 448

long vowels, 284, 314, 315,
338, 426

multisyllabic words, 110, 137,
231, 369

nonsense words, 250

onomatopoeia, 250

pattern recognition, 146

plurals
regular, 260, 261
irregular, 260

r-controlled vowels, 232

read aloud
adjust rate, 241
with expression, 189
with fluency, 189
with intonation, 189

root words (e.g., *look, looked,
looking*), 212, 264, 316,
372, 489

short vowels, 25, 50, 62, 63, 76,
77, 78, 79, 128

sight words, 117

silent *e*, 262

syllabication, 110, 137, 488

vowel digraphs, 263

word families (e.g., *-ite, -ate*),
146

Vocabulary and Concept Development

Academic Vocabulary

114, 132, 164, 184, 216, 236,
268, 320, 342, 376, 398,
432, 452

Key Vocabulary

113, 131, 163, 183, 215, 216,
235, 267, 319, 341, 375,
397, 431, 451

Vocabulary Development

academic vocabulary, 114, 132,
164, 184, 216, 236, 268,
320, 342, 376, 398, 432, 452

antonym, 162

assessing your skills, 17, 29, 55,
83, 97, 120, 140, 172, 192,
224, 244, 276, 296, 330,
352, 386, 408, 440, 462

categories of words
abilities, 332
after-school activities, 204
climate, 235
classroom objects, 18, 19,
44, 45, 102
clothing, 226
countries, 8
directions, 366
everyday activities, 174, 176
everyday objects, 228
family relationships, 162, 163
famous places, 390
favorite things, 70, 71, 72
first day of school, 4
foods and drinks, 278, 280
forms, vocabulary for, 105
furniture, 258
money, 442, 443
nationalities, 8
neighborhood places, 388
occupations, 308
places in community, 364
personal information, 31
problems and advice, 334
rooms, 84, 85, 256
school subjects, 56, 57
shopping for clothes,
420, 422
tools and equipment, 310
weather, 206, 207

compound words, 231, 474

context clues, 131, 180, 184,
185, 186, 187, 215, 235,
267, 287, 341, 397, 451

descriptive words, 154, 312

dictionary, 485, 497

figurative words, 327, 349

glossary, 189

homophone, 169, 447, 487

irregular verbs, 160

key vocabulary, 113, 131, 163,
183, 215, 235, 319, 341,
375, 397, 431, 451

metaphor, 349

multiple-meaning word,
131, 428

multisyllabic words, 110, 137,
212, 264, 316, 372

phrases for conversation
asking about sequence, 220
asking clarifying questions,
292
comparing and contrasting,
382
explaining a diagram, 188
give a weather report, 240
giving an opinion, 404, 436
organizing a production, 326
persuasive language, 458
presenting steps in a process,
136
reacting to poetry, 168
responding to people, 116
showing how characters feel,
272
using signpost words and
time expressions, 348

plurals, 260, 261

prefix, 212, 316, 489

root word, 212, 264, 316,
372, 489

rhyming words, 198

sentence context, 114, 132, 164,
184, 216, 236, 268, 320,
342, 376, 398, 432, 452

simile, 327

suffix, 264, 368, 371, 372, 489

symbol, 286, 290, 291, 292, 293

synonym, 130, 162

thesaurus, 485, 497

word families, 146, 198

Language Functions

asking about sequence, 220

asking clarifying questions, 292

comparing and contrasting, 382

explaining a diagram, 188

give a weather report, 240

giving an opinion, 404, 436

organizing a production, 326

persuasive language, 458

presenting steps in a process,
136

reacting to poetry, 168

responding to people, 116

showing how characters feel,
272

use signpost words and time
expressions, 348

INDEX OF SKILLS

Analysis and Evaluation of Oral and Media Communications

Viewing and Representing

Writing

Writing Applications

Writing Strategies

Text Credits

Unit 3 **Chapter 1** pp. 217–219, from RAIN, RAIN, RAIN! by Rob Waring and Maurice Jamall. Copyright © 2006 by Heinle, a part of Cengage Learning. Reprinted with permission, www.cengagerights.com. Fax 800-730-2215.

Illustrator Credits

Amy Cartwright/illustrationOnLine.com: pp. 6, 14 ("Gg" art and teacher), 16 (bottom), 25, 28, 42, 163–164, 205, 257, 319, 420, 422, 432, 443, 452
Jacqueline Decker/Storybook Arts, Inc.: 380–381
Viviana Diaz/Represented by Irmeli Holmberg: 374, 377–379
Patrick Gnan/illustrationOnLine.com: 185
InContext Publishing Partners: 154, 175, 329, 412, 444
Rob Kemp/illustrationOnLine.com: 238–241
Alan King/illustrationOnLine.com: pp. 16 (top), 54 (top), 72, 104, 113, 114 (top), 131 (7), 132, 148, 193, 200, 209, 215 (2, 4, 5, 6), 216 (top), 227, 229, 252, 258, 268, 280–281, 288 (top), 292, 376, 398

Gina Matarazzo/Represented by Kolea Baker: 167
Precision Graphics: pp. 14 (first three middle pieces of art), 36 (June and July calendars), 40, 66, 85 (floor plan in photo), 89, 90 (March), 95–97, 114 (bottom), 131 (8), 134–135, 137, 141, 187–188, 215 (3), 216 (bottom), 234 (bottom), 235–236, 245, 344: Permission to reproduce given by Sequoyah Birthplace Museum, illustration by Precision Graphics, 365–366, 368, 402
Racketshop Group: 214, 215 (1), 217–219
Jeffrey Thompson/Storybook Arts, Inc.: 269–271
Philip H. Williams/illustrationOnLine.com: 431, 433–434

Photo Credits

2 (top): ©image100/Alamy; 2 (bottom): ©Peter Arnold, Inc./Alamy; 3: ©Ian Shaw/Alamy; 4–5: Ed-Imaging; 5 (girl): ©JUPITERIMAGES/Comstock Premium/Alamy; 5 (map): Ed-Imaging; 6 (all except headshots): Ed-Imaging; 6 (left headshot): ©2008 Jupiterimages Corporation; 6 (right headshot): ©JUPITERIMAGES/Comstock Premium/Alamy; 7 (headshots): ©2008 Jupiterimages Corporation; 7: Ed-Imaging; 8 (top): Ed-Imaging; 8 (left headshot): ©2008 Jupiterimages Corporation; 8 (right headshot): ©Phil Date, 2007 Used under license from Shutterstock.com; 8 (flags of Afghanistan and Guatemala): ©2008 Dream Maker Software; 8 (all other flags): ©1994 Paul Wootton Associates; 9: Ed-Imaging; 10 (boy): ©Digital Vision/Alamy; 10 (book): ©Cre8tive Studios/Alamy; 10 (car): ©iStockphoto.com/skodonnell; 10 (cat): ©iStockphoto.com/Silberkorn; 10 (fan): ©iStockphoto.com/subjug; 10 (girl): ©IndexOpen; 10 (good-bye): ©iStockphoto.com/tBojan; 11 (cab): ©iStockphoto.com/DNY59; 11 (tub): ©iStockphoto.com/chiran; 11 (leaf): ©2008 Jupiterimages Corporation; 11 (shelf): ©Chuck Franklin/Alamy; 11 (dog): ©2008 Jupiterimages Corporation; 11 (bag): ©iStockphoto.com/subjug; 12 (man): ©2008 Jupiterimages Corporation; 12 (map): ©Map Resources/Alamy; 12 (pen): ©Christophe Testi/Alamy; 12 (pencil): ©iStockphoto.com/duckycards; 12 (sit): ©JUPITERIMAGES/Polka Dot/Alamy; 12 (teacher): Ed-Imaging; 13 (gym): ©iStockphoto.com/Rpsycho; 13 (arm, cup, dress, bat): ©2008 Jupiterimages Corporation; 13 (map): ©Steve Hamblin/Alamy; 13 (bus): ©ilian car/Alamy; 13 (cat): ©iStockphoto.com/Silberkorn; 14: ©2008 Jupiterimages Corporation; 18–21: Ed-Imaging; 22 (top two): Ed-Imaging; 22 (left headshot): ©Phil Date, 2007 Used under license from Shutterstock.com; 22 (right headshot and pens): ©2008 Jupiterimages Corporation; 23 (all top): Ed-Imaging; 23 (left headshot): ©Phil Date, 2007 Used under license from Shutterstock.com 23 (right headshot): ©2008 Jupiterimages Corporation; 24 (bag): ©iStockphoto.com/subjug; 24 (classroom): ©Masterfile Royalty Free; 24 (map): ©Steve Hamblin/Alamy; 24 (all other images): ©2008 Jupiterimages Corporation; 26 (left): ©JUPITERIMAGES/Comstock Images/Alamy; 26 (middle): ©Bubbles Photolibrary/Alamy; 26 (right): ©BOB DAEMMRICH/PHOTOEDIT; 28 (door): ©Mr Funkenstien, 2007 Used under license from Shutterstock.com; 28 (table): ©Masterfile Royalty Free; 28 (desk): ©7505811966, 2007 Used under license from Shutterstock.com; 28 (window): ©iStockphoto.com/pablohart; 28 (bulletin board): ©D. Hurst/Alamy; 28 (globe): ©2008 Jupiterimages Corporation; 30–32: Ed-Imaging; 33 (headshots, "Jack", and "May"): ©2008 Jupiterimages Corporation; 33 ("Tanya"): ©Masterfile Royalty Free; 33 ("Waseem"): ©iStockphoto.com/goodynewshoes; 33 (bottom): Ed-Imaging; 35 (top): Ed-Imaging; 35 (compass): ©Judith Collins/Alamy; 36 (desk): ©7505811966, 2007 Used under license from Shutterstock.com; 36 (door): ©Mr Funkenstien, 2007 Used under license from Shutterstock.com; 36 (leaf and leg): ©2008 Jupiterimages Corporation; 37 (head): ©iStockphoto.com/kickstand; 37 (board): ©Thomas Mounsey, 2007 Used under license from Shutterstock.

com; 37 (ball): ©2008 Jupiterimages Corporation; 37 (pencil): ©iStockphoto.com/duckycards; 38 (number): ©Phil Degginger/Alamy; 38 (all other images): ©2008 Jupiterimages Corporation; 39 (man): ©2008 Jupiterimages Corporation; 39 (pen): ©Christophe Testi/Alamy; 39 (car): ©iStockphoto.com/skodonnell; 39 (teacher): Ed-Imaging; 39 (box): ©Judith Collins/Alamy; 40: ©MERVYN REES/Alamy; 41 (top): ©MICHAEL NEWMAN/PHOTOEDIT; 41 (bottom): ©DAVID R. FRAZIER/PHOTOEDIT; 42 (top): ©GUILLEN PHOTOGRAPHY/Alamy; 42 (middle): ©DAVID R. FRAZIER/PHOTOEDIT; 42 (bottom): ©DENNIS MACDONALD/PHOTOEDIT; 44–45: Ed-Imaging; 46 (open): ©Petro Feketa, 2007 Used under license from Shutterstock.com; 46 (Stand up): ©Digital Vision/Alamy; 46 (all other images): Ed-Imaging; 47: Ed-Imaging, 48: ©2008 Jupiterimages Corporation; 49: Ed-Imaging; 50 (box): ©Judith Collins/Alamy; 50 (mop): ©Photodisc/Alamy; 50 (locker): ©iStockphoto.com/P_Wei; 50 (all other images): ©2008 Jupiterimages Corporation; 52 (top): ©Alex Kalmbach, 2007 Used under license from Shutterstock.com; 52 (bottom left): ©Art Resource, NY; 52 (bottom right): ©CNAC/MNAM/Dist. Réunion des Musées Nationaux/Art Resource, NY; 53: ©1994 Paul Wootton Associates; 54 (flags of Argentina and Britain): ©2008 Dream Maker Software; 54 (all other flags): ©1994 Paul Wootton Associates; 55 (paper): ©emily2k, 2007 Used under license from Shutterstock.com; 55 (backpack): ©iStockphoto.com/ronen; 55 (all other images): ©2008 Jupiterimages Corporation; 56–58: Ed-Imaging; 59 (top left headshot): ©Corbis Premium RF/Alamy; 59 (top right headshot): ©James Woodson/Getty Images; 59 (middle headshot): ©JUPITERIMAGES/Comstock Premium/Alamy; 59 (all other images): Ed-Imaging; 60 (top): Ed-Imaging; 60 (middle left headshot): ©2008 Jupiterimages Corporation; 60 (middle right headshot): ©James Woodson/Getty Images; 60 (bottom left headshot): ©2008 Jupiterimages Corporation; 60 (bottom right headshot): ©James Woodson/Getty Images; 61 (top left headshot): ©Phil Date, 2007 Used under license from Shutterstock.com; 61 (bottom left headshot): ©2008 Jupiterimages Corporation; 61 (bottom right headshot): ©Phil Date, 2007 Used under license from Shutterstock.com; 61 (all other images): Ed-Imaging; 62 (dinner and window): ©2008 Jupiterimages Corporation; 62 (inch): ©Pick and Mix Images/Alamy; 62 (kitchen): ©Patrick Eden/Alamy; 62 (milk): ©D. Hurst/Alamy; 62 (nickel): ©Sarah-Maria Vischer/The Image Works; 64 (hand): ©WoodyStock/Alamy; 64 (house, window, yogurt): ©2008 Jupiterimages Corporation; 64 (kitten): ©Ariusz Nawrocki, 2007 Used under license from Shutterstock.com; 64 (kitchen): ©Patrick Eden/Alamy; 64 (quarter): ©JUPITERIMAGES/Comstock Images/Alamy; 64 (water): ©D. Hurst/Alamy; 64 (yellow): ©Tetra Images/Alamy; 64 (zipper): ©Hugh Threlfall/Alamy; 68 (1): ©JUPITERIMAGES/Creatas/Alamy; 68 (2): ©2008 Jupiterimages Corporation; 68 (3): ©Glow Images/Alamy; 68 (4): ©1994 Paul Wootton Associates; 68 (5): ©Eyebyte/Alamy; 68 (6): ©INTERFOTO Pressebildagentur/Alamy; 68 (7): ©Pick

and Mix Images/Alamy; 68 (8): ©Michael Mahovlich/Masterfile; 68 (9, 10): ©Masterfile Royalty Free; 70–71: Ed-Imaging; 72 (Chinese food): ©D. Hurst/Alamy; 72 (pasta, chicken, baseball, and right headshot): ©2008 Jupiterimages Corporation; 72 (salad): ©Pablo/Alamy; 72 (pizza): ©D. Hurst/Alamy; 72 (fish): ©Elke Dennis, 2007 Used under license from Shutterstock.com; 72 (fruit): ©The Anthony Blake Photo Library/Alamy; 72 (soup): ©foodfolio/Alamy; 72 (soccer): ©M Stock/Alamy; 72 (basketball): ©DAVID YOUNG-WOLFF/PHOTOEDIT; 72 (football): ©iStockphoto.com/LUGO; 72 (left headshot): ©JUPITERIMAGES/Comstock Premium/Alamy; 73 (top left): ©Robert Fried/Alamy; 73 (all other images): ©2008 Jupiterimages Corporation; 74 (top): Ed-Imaging; 74 (middle left, bottom left): ©2008 Jupiterimages Corporation; 74 (middle and bottom right): ©Phil Date, 2007 Used under license from Shutterstock.com; 75 (top): Ed-Imaging; 75 (bottom left): ©James Woodson/Getty Images; 75 (bottom right): ©Corbis Premium RF/Alamy; 76 (bus): ©ilian car/Alamy; 76 (cup, umbrella, brush): ©2008 Jupiterimages Corporation; 76 (lunch): ©Corbis Premium RF/Alamy; 76 (number): ©Phil Degginger/Alamy; 76 (sun): ©Marc Vaughn/Masterfile; 77: ©Ilene MacDonald/Alamy; 78 (pen): ©Christophe Testi/Alamy; 78 (leg, exit, ketchup, neck): ©2008 Jupiterimages Corporation; 78 (desk): ©7505811966, 2007 Used under license from Shutterstock.com; 78 (address): Ed-Imaging; 78 (tennis): ©Rick Gomez/Masterfile; 80: ©Photodisc/SuperStock; 81–82: Ed-Imaging; 84–85: Ed-Imaging; 87 (top): Ed-Imaging; 87 (middle left): ©James Woodson/Getty Images; 87 (middle right and bottom left): ©2008 Jupiterimages Corporation; 87 (bottom right): ©JUPITERIMAGES/Comstock Premium/Alamy; 89 (top): Ed-Imaging; 89 (bottom left): ©2008 Jupiterimages Corporation; 89 (bottom right): ©Corbis Premium RF/Alamy; 90 (shoes, shirt): ©D. Hurst/Alamy; 90 (fish): ©Phil Degginger/Alamy; 90 (cash, chair): ©Judith Collins/Alamy; 90 (chin, ketchup, hedge): ©2008 Jupiterimages Corporation; 90 (sandwich): ©Iconotec/Alamy; 90 (catch): ©Stockbyte/Alamy; 90 (patch): ©iStockphoto.com/davincidig; 90 (watch, bridge): ©Hugh Threlfall/Alamy; 90 (judge): ©Corbis Premium RF/Alamy; 90 (badge): ©JUPITERIMAGES/Brand X/Alamy; 92 (thumb): ©Westend61/Alamy; 92 (math): ©Andrew Paterson/Alamy; 92 (tooth): ©delete/Alamy; 92 (ring, king): ©2008 Jupiterimages Corporation; 92 (wing): ©Christa Knijff/Alamy; 92 (sing): ©Digital Archive Japan/Alamy; 92 (bank): ©Garry Gay/Alamy; 92 (sink): ©Hugh Threlfall/Alamy; 92 (drink): ©JUPITERIMAGES/Creatas/Alamy; 92 (trunk): ©ilian car/Alamy; 94: M.C. Escher's "Relativity" ©2008 The M.C. Escher Company-Holland. All rights reserved. www.mcescher.com; 98 (2): ©2008 Jupiterimages Corporation; 98 (4): ©iStockphoto.com/duckycards; 98 (5): Ed-Imaging; 98 (7): ©Pablo/Alamy; 98 (8): ©iStockphoto.com/duncan1890; 99 (top): ©iStockphoto.com/aabejon; 99 (book): ©Cre8tive Studios/Alamy; 99 (chair): ©Judith Collins/Alamy; 99 (map): ©Steve Hamblin/Alamy; 99 (bus): ©ilian car/Alamy; 99 (pen): ©Map Resources/Alamy; 99 (leaf): ©2008

Jupiterimages Corporation; 99 (piggy bank): ©Garry Gay/Alamy; 99 (watch): ©Hugh Threlfall/Alamy; 99 (box): ©Judith Collins/Alamy; 100 (top): ©DAVID YOUNG-WOLFF/PHOTOEDIT; 100 (bottom): ©2008 Jupiterimages Corporation; 101: ©2008 Jupiterimages Corporation; 102 (student holding schedule): ©BOB DAEMMRICH/PHOTOEDIT; 102 (schedule): ©iStockphoto.com/Kameleon007; 102 (calculator, ruler): ©JUPITERIMAGES/Brand X/Alamy; 102 (computer and printer): ©Helene Rogers/Alamy; 102 (cabinet): ©iStockphoto.com/FrankyDeMeyer; 103: ©Blend Images/Alamy; 104 (top): ©iStockphoto.com/PhotoEuphoria; 104 (bottom left): ©Blend Images/Alamy; 104 (bottom right): ©2008 Jupiterimages Corporation; 106 (left): ©Corbis Premium RF/Alamy; 106 (right): ©James Woodson/Getty Images; 108 (hand): ©WoodyStock/Alamy; 108 (desk): ©7505811966, 2007 Used under license from Shutterstock.com; 108 (gift): ©D. Hurst/Alamy; 108 (all other images): ©2008 Jupiterimages Corporation; 109 (salt, help): ©2008 Jupiterimages Corporation; 109 (milk): ©Pick and Mix Images/Alamy; 109 (shelf): ©Chuck Franklin/Alamy; 109 (child): ©IndexOpen; 112: ©2008 Jupiterimages Corporation; 116: ©Don Smetzer/Alamy; 117: ©Corbis Premium RF/Alamy; 122 (field trip): ©Kim Karpeles/Alamy; 122 (concert): ©SPENCER GRANT/PHOTO EDIT; 122 (art show): ©Enigma/Alamy; 122 (graduation): ©Photodisc/Alamy; 122 (football game): Chuck Eckert/Alamy; 122 (basketball): ©JUPITERIMAGES/Brand X/Alamy; 122 (pep rally): ©Corbis Premium RF/Alamy; 122 (dance): ©Kevin Cooley/Getty Images; 122 (play): ©JUPITERIMAGES/Thinkstock/Alamy; 123 (top left and bottom two): ©2008 Jupiterimages Corporation; 123 (top right): ©JUPITERIMAGES/Comstock Premium/Alamy; 124 (middle left): ©Phil Date, 2007 Used under license from Shutterstock.com; 124 (middle right): ©James Woodson/Getty Images; 124 (bottom left): ©Corbis Premium RF/Alamy; 124 (bottom right): ©2008 Jupiterimages Corporation; 125–126: ©2008 Jupiterimages Corporation; 127 (two on left): ©2008 Jupiterimages Corporation; 127 (middle right): ©Phil Date, 2007 Used under license from Shutterstock.com; 127 (bottom right): ©Corbis Premium RF/Alamy; 128 (call): ©Larry Lilac/Alamy; 128 (ball): ©Judith Collins/Alamy; 128 (wall): ©ACE STOCK LIMITED/Alamy; 128 (walk): ©Stock Connection Distribution/Alamy; 128 (talk): ©JUPITERIMAGES/Creatas/Alamy; 128 (chalk): ©2008 Jupiterimages Corporation; 130: ©iStockphoto.com/lisapics; 136: ©UpperCut Images/Alamy; 150: ©ImageState/Alamy; 151: ©UpperCut Images/Alamy; 152: ©2008 Jupiterimages Corporation; 153 ("Karl"): ©JUPITERIMAGES/Brand X/Alamy; 153 ("Sue"): ©David Mendelsohn/Masterfile; 153 (all other images): ©2008 Jupiterimages Corporation; 154 (brown eyes): ©2008 Jupiterimages Corporation; 154 (blue eyes): ©Digital Vision/Alamy; 154 (green eyes): ©Steve Nudson/Alamy; 154 (moustache): ©2008 Jupiterimages Corporation; 154 (beard): ©Photodisc/Alamy; 154 (glasses): ©JUPITERIMAGES/Brand X/Alamy; 154 (top

headshot): ©James Woodson/Getty Images; 154 (bottom headshot): ©Corbis Premium RF/Alamy; 155: ©2008 Jupiterimages Corporation; 156: ©JUPITERIMAGES/Comstock Premium/Alamy; 157: ©Corbis Premium RF/Alamy; 158 (bread): ©PHOTOTAKE Inc./Alamy; 158 (fruit): ©Forrest Smyth/Alamy; 158 (gray): ©22DigiTal/Alamy; 158 (all other images): ©2008 Jupiterimages Corporation; 159 (sweater): ©D. Hurst/Alamy; 159 (swim): ©JUPITERIMAGES/Comstock Images/Alamy; 159 (twins): ©Big Cheese Photo/SuperStock; 160 (left headshot): ©Corbis Premium RF/Alamy; 160 (right headshot): ©2008 Jupiterimages Corporation; 162: ©JUPITERIMAGES/Creatas/Alamy; 163: ©2008 Jupiterimages Corporation; 165 (top): ©Front Porch Conversations, 2001 (acrylic on canvas) by Xavier Cortada (Contemporary Artist) Private Collection/The Bridgeman Art Library; 165 (bottom): ©Portrait of the Van Cortland Family, c.1830 (oil) by American School (19th century) American Museum, Bath, Avon, UK/The Bridgeman Art Library; 166: ©iStockphoto.com/RonTech2000; 170: ©Digital Vision/Alamy; 174 (get up): ©DAVID YOUNG-WOLFF/PHOTOEDIT; 174 (eat breakfast): ©rubberball/Getty Images; 174 (get dressed): ©Andersen Ross/Getty Images; 174 (get ready for school): ©TONY FREEMAN/PHOTOEDIT; 174 (leave for school): ©i love images/Alamy; 174 (get home): ©iStockphoto.com/squirmy1; 174 (homework): ©Tom Salyer/Alamy; 174 (go to bed): ©TONY FREEMAN/PHOTOEDIT; 175: ©2008 Jupiterimages Corporation; 176 (dishes): ©Andersen Ross/Getty Images; 176 (practice): ©iStockphoto.com/aabejon; 176 (study): ©2008 Jupiterimages Corporation; 176 (write): ©Masterfile Royalty Free; 176 (left headshot): ©Corbis Premium RF/Alamy; 176 (right headshot): ©James Woodson/Getty Images; 177: ©JUPITERIMAGES/Creatas/Alamy; 179 (left): ©2008 Jupiterimages Corporation; 179 (right): ©Phil Date, 2007 Used under license from Shutterstock.com; 180 (snow): ©iStockphoto.com/groveb; 180 (spoon, sled): ©2008 Jupiterimages Corporation; 180 (scarf): ©iStockphoto.com/toxawww; 180 (smile): ©simon battensby/Alamy; 180 (skin): ©AK PhotoLibrary/Alamy; 182 (eagle): ©Wesley Aston, 2007 Used under license from Shutterstock.com; 182 (flowers): ©iStockphoto.com/mschowe; 182 (ream of paper): ©iStockphoto.com/zoomstudio; 182 (frog): ©Storman, 2007 Used under license from Shutterstock.com; 182 (grasshopper): ©Eric Isselée, 2007 Used under license from Shutterstock.com; 182 (grass): ©Paul Maguire, 2007 Used under license from Shutterstock.com; 182 (all other images): ©2008 Jupiterimages Corporation; 185 (top): ©Manfred Danegger/Photo Researchers, Inc.; 186 (top): ©Leonard Lee Rue III/Photo Researchers, Inc.; 186 (middle): ©Joe McDonald/CORBIS; 186 (bottom): ©Peter Arnold, Inc./Alamy; 202 (top): ©2008 Jupiterimages Corporation; 202 (bottom): ©Tony Watson/Alamy; 203: ©Masterfile Royalty Free; 204 (friends): ©Adrian Sherratt/Alamy; 204 (e-mail, music): ©2008 Jupiterimages Corporation; 204 (bike): ©RHODA SIDNEY/PHOTOEDIT; 204 (watch TV): ©Corbis Premium RF/